SOCIAL WORK PRACTICE
WITH GROUPS

A Clinical Perspective

Social Work Practice
with Groups

A Clinical Perspective

Kenneth E. Reid

Western Michigan University

Brooks/Cole Publishing Company
Pacific Grove, California

Brooks/Cole Publishing Company A Division of Wadsworth, Inc.

Printed in the United States of America

10   9   8   7   6   5   4   3   2   1

Library of Congress Cataloging-in-Publication Data

Reid, Kenneth E.
Social work practice with groups: a clinical perspective / p. cm.
Includes bibliographical references and index.
ISBN 0-534-14820-4
1. Psychiatric social work.   2. Social group work.   I. Title.
[DNLM: 1. Group Processes.   2. Social Work.   W 322 R356s]
HV689.R38   1990
362.2″0425—dc20   90-2584
                                                                   CIP

Sponsoring Editor: *Claire Verduin*
Marketing Representative: *Thor McMillan*
Editorial Assistant: *Gay C. Bond*
Production Editor: *Timothy A. Phillips*
Manuscript Editor: *Dolores M. Crittenden*
Permissions Editor: *Marie DuBois*
Interior and Cover Design: *Lisa Thompson*
Typesetting: *The Font Works*
Cover Printing: *Phoenix Color Corporation*
Printing and Binding: *Arcata Graphics/Fairfield*

Some material in the following chapters has been previously published by the author, and is
reprinted by permission of the journals noted.
Chapter 6, material from Reid, K. (1988), "But I don't want to lead a group!" Some common
problems of social workers leading groups. *Groupwork, 1* (2), 124-134 (Whiting & Birch, Ltd,
P.O. Box 872, Forest Hill, London SE23 3HL, UK), and Reid, K. (1977), Nonrational dynamics
of the client–worker interaction. *Social Casework, 58* (10), 224–237. Copyright 1977 Family
Service America.
Chapter 8, material from Reid, K. (1986), The use of confrontation in group treatment: Attack or
challenge. *Clinical Social Work Journal, 14* (3), 224–237.

This book is dedicated to the students whose challenging questions helped me to appreciate the richness of group theory and to the group members whose growth demonstrated the value of small groups as an effective means for change.

PREFACE ....

This book is about individuals, groups, practitioners, and clinical settings. In particular, it is about how to work with people in small groups in a way that is therapeutic, growth producing, and life enhancing. It is about making sense out of behaviors and actions and finding solutions to complicated clinical issues. It's about the real world, in which some clients get better but some do not. It is about organizations that are supportive and others that are not so supportive. It's about theory and about practical techniques. It's about social work with groups, a viable means of influencing people's lives.

As is so often the case, this book was spawned out of frustration. Over the years, I have felt distressed that books written on social work with groups are not written with a focus on treatment. As a professor teaching graduate students, I had to look to other disciplines, such as psychiatry and psychology, in hopes of finding something that was congruent with the values and principles of social work. As a practitioner leading groups, I felt frustrated with the lack of honesty in textbooks, wanting a book that dealt with the real world of clinic and hospital life, rather than with ideal situations that lacked reality and relevancy to my clients. Finally, I wanted a book that would grow with the reader.

My primary purposes in writing this book are threefold: to teach social work practitioners how to do clinical social work with groups, to integrate small-groups theory and therapeutic principles in a way that is useful and meaningful, and to present techniques that increase the chance of each group's success and its members' growth.

My secondary purposes are a bit more ambitious. I want this book to be something that individuals read because they find it candid, truthful, and useful in their practice. I have aimed to make this book readable and to present its material in a manner that's practical for students and seasoned professionals. This book is written for a range of beginning and advanced students who are trying to understand what social work with groups is all about.

It is also written for social workers and other professionals employed in clinics, hospitals, social agencies, and residential settings. It is for practitioners struggling to bring about meaningful change in the lives of individuals and families, through the use of groups.

Throughout the book are techniques and strategies that work. This is a bold statement, but one based on fact. The body of information about the practice of social work with groups represents a distillation of information derived from practitioners working in diverse settings with multiproblem clients. These techniques and strategies make a significant difference and have a positive long-term impact on the individuals being served.

I hope my readers reach a point in which they are able to trust themselves and the curiosity, warmth, and caring that brought them into the helping professions; that increasingly they are willing to try out the ideas and take calculated risks; that they are willing to laugh with their clients and, more important, laugh at themselves; and that they are willing to establish and lead in a creative, spontaneous, and imaginative way, recognizing the wide range of choices and possibilities at their disposal.

The book is meant to be versatile and useful. At the same time, it is my conviction that skills and techniques alone are not enough. Therefore, to bridge the gap, there is a blend of theory and pragmatic material. The thrust of the book is to integrate theories and concepts of helping with strategies of interventions.

A distinctive feature of this applied text is its focus on the personhood of the group leader. This book explores how the practitioner's own personality, development, and life situation are brought into the therapeutic relationship and affect the treatment process. In this way, an effort is made to describe the therapist's participation in the relationship, as well as that of the client.

I have sprinkled the book liberally with clinical examples in an attempt to bring the material alive. But I have also done something unusual. Each chapter begins with a personal narrative, or what I have come to call a "note to myself," that conveys a piece of personal wisdom on the practice of social work. As with a worker and client, the writer and reader are fellow travelers on a similar journey. Each has something to teach, and something to learn from the other. Both travelers are enroute, far from where they begin and farther still from their destination.

As a matter of practicality, masculine and feminine pronouns are used alternatively, except in discussions of case material where the gender of a person is specified. I have also chosen to use the words *member, participant, client,* and *patient,* synonymously, as well as the words *worker, leader, therapist,* and *practitioner.*

The book is designed so the reader can read it straight through or else skip around. That is, I have arranged it in what seems to me the most logical order; you will find some cumulative benefits from reading it in the normal sequence. But I have also made each chapter fairly complete in itself so you can thread your own path and find the chapters relevant to your particular situation.

The book begins with the *what* of groups in social work and evolves to the *how* of leading groups in clinical settings. Chapter 1 provides an introduction to the use of groups and discusses the unifying assumptions of the book. Chapter 2 provides an historical perspective on the use of treatment-oriented groups in social work and describes some of the group-work models presently used. Chapter 3 examines the therapeutic factors that are unique to small groups.

In Chapter 4, the life-span metaphor, a fresh way of looking at group development, is introduced. Chapter 5 explores the group member as a biological/psychological/social entity. Chapter 6 looks at the reciprocity between leader and group member. Chapter 7 deals with the interpersonal skills a worker needs for success, and Chapter 8 considers worker interventions that promote interaction within the group. Chapter 9 addresses the elements that go into planning an effective group. Chapters 10, 12, and 13 address the initial, middle, and end phases of treatment. Chapter 11 considers the use of activities in groups.

I would like to thank a number of reviewers who have been helpful with their comments and suggestions. They include Professor David S. Derezotes, University of Utah; Professor Gerald E. Euster, University of South Carolina; Professor Carl Hartman, Wayne State University; Professor Betty Piccard, Florida State University; and Professor Susan Rice, California State University at Long Beach.

In preparing a book of this nature, the author invariably depends on the advice of clinicians and colleagues to provide balance and perspective to the project. I am especially indebted to the faculty of the School of Social Work at Western Michigan University for their sharp pencils and discerning eyes. Of special help were Judy Halseth, Ray Lish, Gary Matthews, Nathaniel McCaslin, Marion Wijnberg, Judith Morris, and Edward Pawlak.

Thanks also go to a number of excellent practitioners for their valuable comments, most of which have been incorporated into the book. I particularly appreciate the input of Robert Yesner of the Kalamazoo Regional Psychiatric Hospital in Kalamazoo, Michigan; John Mathieson of the Veterans Administration Center, Battle Creek, Michigan; and Helen DeFinta of the Harper Creek School District, Calhoun County, Michigan.

I want to thank Claire Verduin and the staff at Brooks/Cole who were a pleasure to work with from beginning to end. Finally, I want to thank my wife Eve and my daughter Heather for their constant support, encouragement, and patience.

Kenneth E. Reid

CONTENTS ....

11 PROGRAM ACTIVITIES 217

12 THE MIDDLE PHASE OF TREATMENT 241

13 THE ENDING STAGE OF TREATMENT 267

Contents

SOCIAL WORK PRACTICE WITH GROUPS

A Clinical Perspective

INTRODUCTION

1

hen I took my first group-work course, I learned the implicit but erroneous lesson that there was one correct way to work with groups. This proper way was, I assumed, based on what the professor championed and what the textbook advocated. When the groups I was working with failed to prosper or fell apart, I was quick to conclude that it was because of my failure to learn some obscure secret embedded within a missed lecture or a required reading.

My world became a bit more confusing when I took additional courses on group work from other professors whose approach was often different. Being somewhat naive, the burning question for me became "which one is right, and which one is wrong?" My groups were far from perfect, so I apparently hadn't found the secret.

Years later, in rereading some of these same books and reflecting on copious, yellowed, dog-eared classroom notes, I came to the conclusion that the problem of discerning a right way and a wrong way to lead groups was more my problem as an anxious neophyte than that of the professors or the authors. The differences had more to do with style than substance. Out of my insecurity, I hungered for someone to tell me what to do and how to do it.

Now, after the passage of several decades, the leading of countless groups, and the loss of some hair, the secret becomes clear. There is no right or single way to lead a group. Rather, the worker has a multitude of choices dependent upon the purpose of the group, the social/emotional capacity of its members, and the member's objective. The success or failure of the group will depend upon an integration of these factors—and lots of hard work.

• • •

This chapter addresses three primary questions. First, what is the overall goal of group treatment? More specifically, in our fantasy of fantasies, what will our clients look like once they successfully complete the group? Second, what are the general objectives of group treatment? Third, what are the implicit assumptions upon which group treatment in clinical settings is based?

THE IDEAL: A FULLY FUNCTIONING PERSON

3

• • • • • • • •

When we reflect on the individuals that seek help in clinics, agencies, group-living institutions and hospitals, the range and complexity of the clients' problems are staggering. Some of these individuals fit nicely into traditional diagnostic categories such as chemically dependent, borderline personality, neurotic, psychotic, and character disorders. Other clients wrestle with problems that seem to defy a simple clinical definition. Common to all is a combination of psychological and environmental factors, each influencing one another.

Some clients come because they choose to work on their problems; others come because they are told to do so by the court, their spouse, or their employer and because they will be "punished" in some way if they do not get help. Some are doctors, lawyers, professors, or fellow psychotherapists, while others are unemployed, on welfare, or without a place to sleep.

Some individuals are physically and mentally handicapped to the degree that they will require some form of institutionalized care for the remainder of their lives. Other individuals seek information or have issues that can be resolved in one or two sessions.

Some clients come through the door highly committed and motivated to get help. They are in pain and want relief. On the other hand, there are others who symbolically cross their arms and legs and through a combination of words and actions communicate "Treat me. I dare you."

Given such a vast array of lifestyles, motivation, and problems, a vexing question arises: exactly what is it that we hope to achieve through the therapeutic process, whether group treatment, family therapy, or one-to-one psychotherapy? At the most superficial level, we answer with terms such as *heal, cure, actualize,* and *strengthen.* These are complex words that beg closer scrutiny.

Social scientists, in defining the more integrated individual, have paid increasing attention to the positive aspects of human development. For example, Rogers (1961) writes of the "fully functioning person"; Combs and Avila (1985) of the "self-fulfilled person"; and Bonner (1965) of the "proactive person." These are statements of ideals and goals rather than descriptions of a static condition. In actuality, no one has reached this level. Each of us is on the road to "becoming" a more fully integrated person.

CHANGE THROUGH TREATMENT

Rogers (1963), observing how individuals grow through psychotherapy, describes the following changes.

First, there is greater **self-reliance,** with the improving person relying more than ever before on his or her own feelings and attitudes of right and wrong. The person is less dependent on what others expect and makes a basic commitment to live in a way that is meaningful and satisfying.

Second, the person demonstrates a **willingness to accept what he or she experiences.** Not only is the person more aware of his or her own feelings and attitudes but also the person does not try to run away from himself or herself or to disguise his or her real feelings. In addition, the person begins to look at the world in a more realistic manner, viewing it as it is rather than how he or she would like it to be.

Third, the person builds **trust in himself or herself** and increasingly comes to accept and trust the impulses and feelings that emerge. The person discovers that he or she fears himself or herself less and less and even develops an affection for his or her diverse feelings.

Fourth, a **willingness to continue to grow as a person.** The person tends to understand that being alive means continuing to grow and develop rather than reaching some predetermined level and remaining at that level.

The following passage from Rogers's (1963) description of the fully functioning person conveys this idea:

> He is able to experience all of his feelings, and is afraid of none of his feelings. He is his own sifter of evidence, but is open to evidence from all sources; he is completely engaged in the process of being and becoming himself and thus discovers that he is soundly and realistically social; he lives completely in this moment, but learns that this is the soundest living for all time. He is a fully functioning organism, and because of the awareness of himself which flows freely in and through his experiences, he is a fully functioning person [p. 19].

Another view of optimal functioning comes from the work of Maslow (1954), who, after studying the lives of famous leaders and historical figures plus 3 thousand college students, concluded that a self-actualized person is someone who is resilient and flexible and has the capacity to cope with adversity. Far from being a paragon of virtue, however, Maslow acknowledges that such a person is not free from guilt, hostility, conflict, or other emotions of less than noble status.

Leading Maslow's list of the attributes of self-actualized individuals are a more accurate perception of, and a greater degree of comfort with, reality. Such individuals do not have to fool themselves about the world and the people in it. Having an accurate and positive self-concept, they do not hide behind a mask through which they filter reality. They see the world as it really is and people as they really are. As a result, these individuals solve problems more efficiently, because they can make decisions in terms of how things really are and not how they wish they were. They like who they are, viewing themselves as acceptable and as making a meaningful contribution to the world around them.

Maslow's list divides naturally into two larger categories—attributes related to the quality of an individual's interpersonal relationships and attributes related to the individual's personality. Examples of the former include a deep involvement with a limited number of people and respect for the rights of others. Examples of the latter include autonomy, spontaneity, enjoyment of solitude, a freshness of appreciation of his or her world, and the ability to empathize with others.

The work of Jahoda (1958) represents one of the most comprehensive analyses of characteristics of optimal human functioning. After synthesizing the work of prominent and authoritative writers in the area of psychiatry and human development, she sets forth six basic concepts.

5
....

1. **Attitude toward the self.** The effective, or optimally integrated, person has a high level of self-acceptance and self-esteem, and a clear sense of identity.
2. **Growth, development, and self-actualization.** The person realizes his or her potential to develop and reflects evidence of growth.
3. **Integration.** The person acts in a congruent and consistent manner, reflecting the development of a harmonious relatedness between all aspects of his or her behavior.
4. **Autonomy.** The person develops and lives by a set of internal standards and values. His or her inner regulation provides an awareness of external data and the ability not to be controlled by the expectations of others.
5. **Perception of reality.** The person has the ability and commitment to perceive events for what they are rather than to distort reality out of fear. He or she has this ability and commitment in relation to social as well as physical reality.
6. **Environmental mastery.** Besides perceiving reality accurately, the person acts upon his or her perceptions. The person comes to terms with events and deals with them directly.

THE INTEGRATED SELF

So, you ask, "if we attempt to synthesize these ideas, what will the fully functioning person look like?" In essence, the answer is a person with increasing human effectiveness, depending on where the person is at his or her particular stage of life.

The person is self-sufficient, able to act decisively, and only minimally dependent on his or her social environment. The ideal is an individual who has:

- an openness to experience
- an inner directedness
- an accuracy of perception
- deep interpersonal relations
- sensory awareness and peak experiences
- spontaneity, autonomy, and creativity

Needless to say, the ideal of a fully functioning person is relative. What is fully functioning for one person is certainly not the same for some-

6

• • • • • • • •

one else. An individual who is paraplegic, brain damaged, or psychotic may realistically remain that way the rest of his or her life. Still, the goal is the same, that is to assist that person to live a fulfilled life in which he or she can fully love, work, and play to the extent that is possible.

Openness to experience.   A characteristic of someone who has achieved a high level of functioning is that of trust in himself or herself and the ability to look at all kinds of information. Although this information may be disturbing and painful, it can be processed without distortion—that is, without the person forcing it to be simply congruent with his or her fears or desires. The person deals with the world with a minimum of falsification, perceiving himself or herself accurately and realistically.

Openness implies facing the reality outside oneself, whatever that reality may be. It means a dedication to truth and to a life of continuous and stringent self-examination.

Inner directedness.   The individual has a cause and purpose not directed by others. He or she feels confident enough to overcome the pressure to do something simply because it is expected by others. Facades and masks that cause others to behave defensively or aggressively are analyzed and kept in check. The individual relies more on what he or she thinks than on what society expects or what friends and relatives demand. The person recognizes that he or she has options in life and chooses to live by the principle of living in a way that is deeply satisfying.

Accuracy of perception.   The individual accepts himself or herself and his or her limitations as well as accepting others. The person makes a serious effort to sort out the actual from the abstract and to distinguish the specific instance from what appears to be general and universal. When the individual makes an error by omitting or distorting data, he or she makes the appropriate changes without guilt or self-punishing defenses.

Deep interpersonal relations.   The person is able to love, and to allow himself or herself to be loved. The individual allows other people of the same and of the opposite sex to become close without retreating out of fear. As Maslow (1954) observes, although the individual may have relatively few personal friendships, those he or she does have are deep, confidential, and lasting. The person's circle of friends is small and is healthier, closer, and more productive than the friendship circle of someone who is not fully functioning.

Sensory awareness and peak experiences.   The fully functioning person has a heightened appreciation of himself or herself and of beauty, awe, and wonder. Emotional pain, rather than experienced less, is felt more acutely, and it is difficult to deny intense feelings of anger, rage, hurt, loss, and sadness. Joy, likewise, is magnified, and extreme feelings of pleasure and happiness are experienced in the form of ecstacy, elation, exultation, and jubilation. The person experiences no need to become high through the use of chemicals or alcohol because a better high can be achieved naturally.

The individual does not attempt to escape from these extremes and is willing to face and accept them as a normal part of being fully alive. He or she is able to experience a sense of outrage at the behavior of other people and institutions that are performing in a way that is inappropriate or unethical.

Spontaneity, autonomy, and creativity. The person can be spontaneous and feels free to be flexible in meeting change. The obverse is someone who is rigid and defensive. The integrated person can work and live with others; however, he or she is not dependent on others for approval, emotional well-being, or survival.

In summary, the integrated, or fully functioning, person is someone who can work, can love, and can play. The person is open to new experience, is inner directed, has an accurate perception of his or her world, has deep interpersonal relations, has sensory awareness and peak experiences, and demonstrates spontaneity, autonomy, and creativity.

OBJECTIVES OF GROUP WORK

Group work, by its very nature, offers unique opportunities for individuals to grow, to learn, and to heal. For example, a group may be used for corrective purposes when a group member already has a problem behavior. Or a group may be used for prevention when there is the potential danger of a member's dysfunction. A group may be used for the enhancement of a group member. Or a group may be used for the purpose of education and citizen participation.

Klein (1972, p. 31) observes eight specific objectives that are a part of group work and that fit social workers' historical mission of assisting individuals in their interpersonal relations and in their encounters with their environments.

1. **Rehabilitation.** The process of rehabilitation involves restoring someone or something to a previous capacity or level. The rehabilitation of a person can refer to emotional or mental difficulties or to behavior. It can also refer to a means of changing an attitude or a value.
2. **Habilitation.** The process of habilitation involves growth and development rather than treatment. The term *habilitation* suggests that some individuals who have difficulties may never have learned how to behave when they were younger; therefore, they cannot be restored as the term *rehabilitation* would imply.
3. **Correction.** The process of correction involves helping people who are having difficulties with social laws or mores and are offenders or violators.

4. **Socialization.** The process of socialization involves helping people learn how to do what is socially expected and how to get along with others. The related term *resocialization* suggests that an individual has regressed and needs to be trained again.

5. **Prevention.** The process of prevention involves anticipating difficulties before they occur and providing the necessary environmental nutrients people need. The preventive purpose of a group is manifest in situations in which a group member faces a danger of deterioration in personal or social functioning.

6. **Social action.** The process of encouraging social action involves helping people learn to change their environment in addition to coping and adapting. Through active involvement in the group, individuals learn to lead, follow, take part in decision making, assume responsibility for themselves, and assume responsibility for the larger community.

7. **Problem solving.** The process of problem solving involves helping people use groups to achieve tasks, to make decisions, and to solve social problems.

8. **Social values.** The process of encouraging the development of social values has to do with helping individuals develop viable social values that are relevant to living.

A group may be used for any one or all of these purposes simultaneously. A therapist's objectives for a group may change as the particular needs of its members change.

KINDS OF GROUPS

When we speak of groups that are established in clinical settings, it is natural to assume that we are speaking in terms of a counseling or therapy group for troubled individuals. But therapy groups are only one kind of group that occurs in clinical settings. The particular type of group established will depend upon a number of factors, including the purpose and objectives as defined by the worker, the needs of the potential group members, and the goals and resources of the sponsoring agency.

Corey and Corey (1987) identify six types of groups: therapy, counseling, personal growth, T group (short for training or laboratory training), structured, and self-help. Jacobs, Harvill, and Masson (1988) classify groups into seven categories: mutual sharing, educational, discussion, task, growth, therapy, and family. Toseland and Rivas (1984) list four categories of treatment groups: educational, growth, remedial, and socialization. They also include task-oriented groups such as committees, administrative groups, delegate councils, teams, treatment conferences, and social-action groups.

At the most basic level is the division between formed groups and natural groups. Formed groups are those that are established through some outside influence, such as an agency, and that are convened for a particular purpose. Most groups led by social workers are of this type. Some examples of formed groups are counseling groups, clubs, committees, and classes.

The participants of formed groups may or may not have the option of attending. Inmates in prisons, for example, are often required to attend a particular group. If they refuse, the consequences may be withholding of visitors or denial of a privilege. Patients in a drug-treatment center may be required to attend group therapy every day and may be forced to leave the program if they do not attend.

Natural groups, on the other hand, are those that develop in a spontaneous manner on the basis of friendship, location, or some naturally occurring event. Without external initiative, the members simply come together. Natural groups include peer groups, street gangs, and cliques. They also include friendship groups that occur in hospital wards and in units where patients live together on a daily basis. Whereas formed groups usually operate under the sponsorship of an outside organization, most natural groups are without sponsorship or affiliation.

Although the focus of this text is on formed groups, work with natural groups is a part of the social work tradition and should not be discounted. Skills and concepts used with formed groups can be applied to natural groups.

The following categories provide some idea of the rich possibilities and variety of groups. Each category is based on the primary purpose of the group. It is important to note that categories are not mutually exclusive and few groups sponsored by social agencies or by hospitals and clinics function with a single purpose. In reality, most groups are a combination of two or more categories and have a mixture of purposes.

EDUCATIONAL GROUPS

Helping professionals are frequently asked to provide information on topics such as divorce, schizophrenia, depression, human development, and child guidance. The request is not for treatment per se but for knowledge and information. Citizens look to the particular agency with its staff of professionals and collective expertise for direction in the form of lectures, seminars, and study groups.

Examples of educational groups include the following:

- a group of parents learning how to manage the behavior of their children
- a group of parents acquiring information on drugs
- a group of pregnant teenagers learning how to take care of their babies
- a group of adults learning how to deal with their aged parents
- a group of adults, separated from their spouses, learning about the divorce process and what they can anticipate

Is an educational group considered a therapy group? The answer is *no,* if we think of therapy as having to do with the treatment of emotional

10
• • • • • • • •

and behavioral problems. However, an educational group can be therapeutic in the sense that members share feelings and concerns and at the same time gain self-knowledge and skills.

GROWTH GROUPS

Growth-oriented groups have as their focus the facilitation of an individual's passage through the normal developmental stages. There is no assumption of pathology. Rather, the person is interested in becoming more aware of himself or herself as a struggling human being. Topics include interpersonal relations, values, problem solving, communication, and ways of thinking and feeling. Examples of growth groups include:

- a marathon encounter group for college students
- a consciousness-raising group for young women or young men
- a values-clarification group for children
- a socialization group made up of hearing, as well as hearing-impaired, students
- a T group (a training or laboratory-training group) addressing how groups work

Another category of growth-oriented groups are clubs and activities. These include interest groups, discussion groups, and performance groups such as drama, art, and other creative-arts groups. Experiences in such groups help participants develop social competence and provide enrichment.

MUTUAL-SHARING GROUPS

A mutual-sharing group (also called a support group) is generally made up of individuals who have a problem or an issue in common. The group enables participants to discover that other people share the same problem, feel similar emotions, and think similar thoughts. This sense of universality takes place as members share their feelings and personal experiences. Each individual finds that he or she rather than being alone is part of every other member and that everyone in the group faces the same basic problem. Some examples of mutual-sharing groups include:

- a group of recently widowed men and women
- a group of women or men who have a spouse in prison
- a group of Vietnam veterans who cannot find jobs
- children of divorced parents
- handicapped college students having difficulty with their studies

The role of the worker is to encourage sharing, risk taking, and mutual problem solving. He or she may ask members to speak directly to one another, may focus the discussion, and may limit story telling. Mutual-help groups stress a common identity based on a common life experience. The worker helps members explain their situations, offer suggestions to others, provide support, and learn from each other.

REMEDIAL GROUPS

The objectives of remedial groups, often referred to as psychotherapy groups, can be divided into three categories: supportive treatment, interpersonal growth, and intrapsychic growth (Levine, 1979). Objectives related to supportive treatment generally emphasize restoration, enhancement, or maintenance of each member's level and modes of function or of problem solving. Objectives related to interpersonal growth focus on helping members gain insight, growth, and change in their relationships. The intrapsychic-growth objective emphasizes insight development, which serves as the base for growth and change.

Some examples of remedial groups are:

- a group sponsored by a drug-rehabilitation center to help young men who are addicted to crack and cocaine
- a group of men or women who have difficulty with anger and who have beaten up their spouses
- a group of hospitalized patients suffering from depression
- an activity group of men and women in a daytime treatment center

TASK GROUPS

While not normally thought of as a form of therapy, task groups can have significant therapeutic value, particularly in residential settings such as psychiatric hospitals. Task groups include committees, social-action groups, and patient governments. Generally, their purpose is to accomplish a particular goal, or "charge," that has been delegated to the members from a higher source.

Harlow (1961) and Reid (1968) in discussing the use of task-centered groups at the Menninger Clinic observe the active role patients took in planning activities and addressing patient/staff problems. Patients, representative of the various living units, met with staff on a weekly basis in a patient-run government. Chaired by a patient, the group discussed issues such as food quantity and quality, weekend activities, and conflicts between staff and patients. Other groups of patients, with guidance from nursing and social work staff, planned and organized evening activities such as interest groups, clubs, dances, movies, and off-grounds trips. This patient-run government was seen by the hospital staff as a vehicle to help patients learn skills, enhance their self-esteem, gain prestige, and find legitimate new roles.

UNIFYING ASSUMPTIONS

The purpose of group treatment is to help group members cope and to help them reach a higher level of functioning. A group, which evolves into a social

12

• • • • • • • •

microcosm, provides a vehicle for its members to learn about their maladaptive interpersonal transactions, their distorted perceptions, and their dysfunctional communication. This learning occurs through self-observation and feedback from others. It also occurs as members test out new behaviors, both inside and outside the group.

The therapist's role is that of a real person. As therapists, we create a safe atmosphere, encourage group cohesiveness and appropriate norms, and challenge the members to view their world realistically. Focusing primarily in the here-and-now, we offer feedback, reinforce responsible behavior, and encourage risk taking.

The following are a series of assumptions that serve as the base for future chapters.

1. There are many different styles of leadership, different approaches to working with groups, and different formats of groups. The worker needs to be able to establish the group around the psychosocial needs of its members. So often, the exact opposite occurs. The practitioner has one basic style of working with groups and adjusts the clients to meet his or her needs rather than planning and adjusting the group to meet clients' needs. Within social work, there are a multitude of approaches to working with groups, based on how the therapist defines the purpose of social work, the goals of the group, the socioemotional state of its members, and the resources of the sponsoring agency.

2. Not all individuals do well in all groups. It is not unusual for a worker to take great pains to compose a group and then, during the first session, watch one of the members totally fall apart or act out in a way that negatively affects the other members. Sometimes, the worker has the intuitive sense that this might be the case prior to the first session, while at other times, it comes as a surprise.

Some individuals, because of their mental state, find groups too stimulating. If such a person has insufficient impulse control, for example, the safety of the other members and the worker may be in question. Other clients can so fear intimacy that they erect a thick wall around themselves to prevent others from getting close. Here lies a therapeutic paradox. The exact behavior that would seem to make the person an undesirable group member is so often the kind of behavior that can be effectively challenged and dealt with in a group. A treatment group is a place where members can practice and acquire new behaviors and learn to master themselves.

Every group has a different personality, and though group treatment, in general, may be the treatment of choice, a particular group may not be the correct vehicle. Pragmatically, for the worker, this may mean going outside the agency to find a group that meets the person's needs better than any in-house group can.

3. The worker in the group needs to be bi-focal, sensitive to each individual, as well as to the ongoing dynamics of the group-as-a-whole. For the beginning worker, inordinate energy is consumed by the problems of the individual member. What the person says and how it is said become the focus of our attention. As therapists, we listen intently to comprehend what is being communicated and not communicated. We listen to the member's story with the hopes of problem solving and reducing, if not resolving, their issues.

Sometimes, however, we listen so intently that we are unaware of what else is going on in the group. There may be covert discounting of our leadership ability. Or, there may be resistance in the form of a member's holding back meaningful thoughts or feelings for fear that he or she will be laughed at or punished. There may be the scapegoating of a member as a means of the group members avoiding looking at themselves and their behavior.

The worker needs to simultaneously keep track of what is occurring with each individual in the group and with the group-as-a-whole. This requires an awareness of each member and similarly an awareness of the themes and patterns of the group-as-a-whole. Accentuating one at the cost of the other diminishes the potential impact of the group.

4. The worker is in the position of influencing the outcome of the group by the way it is organized. To the uninitiated, it might seem that the worker has his or her primary influence on the group during the period between the initial session and the final session. This is untrue! Whether the group ever reaches its goal and fulfills its purpose will be determined to a large extent by the planning that goes on prior to the first session. The worker needs to seriously consider such issues as objectives, composition, location, support from colleagues and other staff, structure, format, and the worker's role within the group.

5. Everything that goes on in the group provides an opportunity for learning. There is an old joke in the helping professions: if clients come late, they are resistant; if they come early, they are anxious; and if they come on time, they are compulsive. Embedded within the joke is a kernel of truth.

So often we overlook seemingly insignificant patterns or even single actions that have meaning for the particular member. Some of our clients are late week after week because of their inability to find a baby-sitter. For others, lateness is related to the fear of sharing feelings and thoughts with the other members. Some members arrive 20 minutes early for group sessions each week because they want some time to become centered. For others, early arrival results from their desire to receive approval from the worker. By being first, they feel in a childlike way that the worker will like them best.

Some members arrive exactly on time because they plan their day so carefully that little time is wasted. For others, being precise as to time is typical of how they live their life. Everything is measured and in place. To be a few minutes late or to have objects out of place results in excruciating anxiety.

Because of the dynamic process within the group, there are hundreds of opportunities for members to learn about themselves and others. If some-

14

∙ ∙ ∙ ∙ ∙ ∙ ∙ ∙

one always comes early, arrives late, or is precisely on time, it may signal something the worker wants to address. Other behaviors or themes are:

- the reason for a member's absences
- a member's or group's feelings about shifting to another room
- a member's or group's silence during a session
- a group's difficulty in solving a problem
- a member's or group's anger toward the worker for missing a session
- a worker's dismissal of a member

The therapeutic possibilities for the worker are endless. The hard question becomes that of choosing what to deal with and what to ignore. There are situations in which it is valuable to address a particular situation the moment it occurs. There are other situations in which the practitioner is well advised to do no more than keep track of the pattern and address it at a later time. Themes and behaviors have a way of being repeated, and what is seemingly a missed opportunity reoccurs in a following meeting.

6. It is important for the leader to be creative in working with groups. No two groups are alike, and each group has its own personality. What will be successful in one group may fail miserably in another group. The "cookbooks" on group leadership that promise success by following a detailed formula are generally written by individuals who have spent very little time with groups.

The leader has to be willing to be spontaneous and to take risks. For example, talk-oriented groups, particularly those made up of adults, become so bogged down in words that the rhetoric stifles genuine communication. The worker needs to be free enough to shift gears and introduce activities that encourage members to move around and relate to each other in nonverbal ways. Inventiveness involves the ability to assess a situation and to create a meaningful solution.

7. The worker needs to have a defensible rationale for every intervention used in the group. It is not enough for us to lead a group freestyle, saying and doing things because "it feels good" or "it seems right." We need to be able to justify what we do. Justification requires us to articulate a reason and purpose for our actions.

Doing this becomes complicated for beginning workers who are trying merely to survive from session to session. They may find it difficult to explain why they said or did certain things and can only offer that it "felt right at the time." Still, we need to be cognizant of our actions—or lack of actions. Fortunately, through training, experience, and time, the worker's comprehension of the *whys* and *hows* of the treatment process become more evident.

Over the years, the term *conscious use of self* has suggested this ongoing awareness. Our strategies and interventions are deliberate and intentional. Three internal questions asked over and over again by the worker clarify his or her motivation and choice of actions: What is going on in the group right now? What do I hope to accomplish? Whose needs am

I meeting if I do what I'm about to do? The purpose of raising these questions is not to extinguish spontaneity or to reduce genuineness. Rather, the goal is to reduce worker self-indulgence and inappropriate interventions.

8. The basic core of the helping process centers around eight essential dimensions: empathy, warmth, respect, genuineness, concreteness, self-disclosure, confrontation, and immediacy. In many ways, these dimensions are terribly simple and at the same time so very complicated. When we, as workers, are deficient in any of them, our therapeutic effectiveness is reduced, and the potential impact of the group treatment on the client is lessened.

The effective worker communicates at a high level of empathic understanding. This means perceiving accurately and sensitively inner feelings of the client and then communicating this understanding in language synchronized to the client's experience of the moment. The worker is warm and respectful, demonstrating an unconditional positive regard for the client. When appropriate, the worker reflects who he or she is in an open authentic manner. The worker responds concretely to feelings and experiences and is able to press group members to attend specifically to problem areas and emotional conflicts. The worker confronts and challenges members to examine their feelings and behaviors. The worker can shift the focus from the there-and-then to the immediacy of the here-and-now.

In our attempt to be therapeutic, we sometimes play at being a therapist by falling back on some caricature, often an inaccurate one, of what a professional helper is supposed to be. Usually it is our clients who detect our mask or smoke screen. Perhaps if truly wise, they seek help somewhere else. Those who do return, come with greater resistance and defenses to keep us at bay. It is not that they do not want help; it is their recognition that in spite of the implicit message "trust me and I will help you," the worker is not trustworthy.

9. Each individual has the power to positively influence his or her family, community, and personal behavior. So often, group members have accepted the assumption that they are stuck in their life circumstances and do not have the internal or external resources to go beyond the sticking point. They experience a sense of deadness and feel they are nothing.

For some group members, this has become a lifestyle of maneuvering in and manipulating their environment. Perhaps they hide behind a mask of weakness, helplessness, and stupidness. Or perhaps they become depressed and passive/aggressive and cry, "Take care of me. I'm too helpless to take care of myself."

Convinced of their powerlessness to change, such group members actually prevent themselves from using their own resources. When such dysfunctional dependency occurs the client looks to the worker or other group members to make his or her decisions about what to do. The powerlessness the client feels is evident in the language he or she uses e.g., "I want to change my life, **but** I don't have the strength to do so." Or, the person may use disclaimers—that is, *maybe, perhaps, sort of, possibly,* and

I suppose. By using these words, the client shows his or her ambivalence and reinforces his or her sense of powerlessness.

Each of us has the power to change our lives. We also have the choice whether to use this power. Sometimes, for growth to occur, the worker and the group members have to challenge an individual into choosing between being proactive and using his or her potential, or remaining in a state of deadness and helplessness.

10. The effectiveness of group treatment is judged by positive client changes outside the group. If the client is an excellent group member but demonstrates no mental, emotional, or social change outside the group, the effects of counseling are negligible. The group needs to be action-oriented. The goal is for the individual to live a more productive, meaningful, and fulfilled life in his or her work, family, and community.

The therapeutic group is a kind of "relationship laboratory." Within the group setting, members experience everyday life situations related to problem solving, social influence, peer pressure, and the need to conform. When these experiences occur in a safe, supportive atmosphere, members are willing to examine their reactions, learn new ways of relating to others, and try out new behaviors. The members are constantly encouraged to transfer the learning occurring in the group to their life outside the group. They do this by setting objectives and establishing a plan of action. The supportive feedback from the group members encourages greater self-exploration and introspection and promotes the self-confidence necessary to attempt new and different ways of behaving.

What goes on inside the group is work. Genuine self-disclosure, confrontation, catharsis, and listening take a great deal of energy. For the members, it is not the physical energy required when carrying a heavy load. Rather, it is the emotional energy that leaves the individual psychologically drained. There is laughter and joy during a session, but these are balanced with expressions of sadness, pain, anger, and frustration.

11. Meaningful change occurs best within an atmosphere of trust and acceptance. An atmosphere of trust and acceptance permeates every aspect of the member/worker relationship. During periods of anger or conflict, the member has a sense of security. He or she feels unconditionally accepted and supported. This security is felt when the person reveals something personal that he or she previously regarded as unacceptable to share. The experience of being accepted reduces the feeling of threat, making it possible for the individual to take greater risks in examining the self and the environment.

Rubin (1970), referring to such a climate, writes that emotional output is appropriate and consistent and that it is **easy** to know what people feel. Feelings of all kinds are allowed, and how one feels is accepted openly and freely without threat of dire reprisal. This climate is not designed for the manufacture of saints or sinners. It is meant for human beings who have ordinary emotional responses and the need to express them freely. In effect, the atmosphere communicates: It's all right to feel love, and it is all right to feel anger. It's all right to express love, and it is all right to express anger. Your feelings are welcome here, and we would like to know what they are. You are loved and accepted and safe with all your feelings. You needn't stifle any of them to **please** us.

IN SUMMARY

This introductory chapter addresses the ideal of the *fully functioning person*. Although a relative term, it suggests an individual who is open, spontaneous, and creative, with an ability to form close personal relationships. The members as well as the worker are, each in their own way, in the process of working toward greater integration.

The group is a gathering in which members can learn new skills and behaviors in a supportive environment. Through interaction, members can receive feedback and caring and learn new ways of relating to others. There is no single way of working with groups. The worker's approach will be based on a multitude of factors such as the members' socioemotional level, the purpose and goals of the group.

2

AN HISTORICAL PERSPECTIVE

hen I was a little boy, my father often came into my bedroom at night just before I went to sleep. I don't remember him reading stories to me like I did with my children. We just talked.

We talked about me and the things that were going on in my life. He listened patiently as I shared my plans for Saturday, anticipated gifts from Santa, explained my problems with the neighborhood bullies and declared what I wanted to be when I grew up—I wanted to be a cowboy then.

He reminisced about important events in his life, such as his brief career as a boxer, his coming to this country from Ireland, and the hardships he had faced during the Great Depression.

He spoke of uncles, grandparents, family heroes, rogues, and eccentrics. He told stories that made me laugh—and others that gave me nightmares. He told me about the old country and tales of its troubled past.

I think back on those moments with feelings of warmth and joy. At the most basic level, he gave me the gift of his total attention. It was our time together. But something even more important came from the stories he told. He provided me a sense of personal continuity.

I was not just a little boy lying in a snug bed, I was someone special who had roots that extended back in history, and to another part of the world. By the force of circumstance, I was inextricably linked to a whole set of events and people, many of whom I didn't know but who shared a similar heritage.

It is this understanding of our roots and heritage that provides a sense of who we are and how we have reached this point in our journey. Unless we know where we came from, how can we know where we are going?

• • •

The use of groups in social work, as a method of helping, is relatively new. It has only been since the 1930s that group work has been accepted as a part of the social work profession. The use of groups as a means of treatment in hospitals, clinics, and other clinical settings is even more recent, having its beginnings during the Second World War. Still, the roots of group work are deep, and if we are to grasp the present and prepare for the future, we must understand the past. This chapter answers the question, what are the roots of group work, particularly as they relate to clinical practice?

21

• • • • • • • •

BRITISH ANTECEDENTS

The roots of group work lie in England in the 19th century, a period of immense change and social unrest resulting from developments brought about by the Industrial Revolution. The establishment of the factory system drew men and women from small villages and towns to manufacturing centers such as Bristol, Birmingham, Sheffield, and London. The sudden concentration of large numbers of people produced severe problems of housing, sanitation, and crime, and existing services were unprepared to manage these problems.

PROBLEMS OF THE FACTORY SYSTEM

With the growth of the factory system, the number of laborers who were completely dependent economically upon their employers increased. Workers no longer owned the means of production and had only their labor to sell. They were totally dependent upon their employers for wages. If wages were too low or employment ceased, they had very few other resources on which to fall back (Reid, 1981).

England gave an outward picture of national greatness and imperial power. Behind this facade, however, lay immense social problems affecting the lives of millions of families. The widespread poverty was in glaring contrast to the overall increases in the nation's wealth, most of which was possessed by a small minority of the population.

By the turn of the century, a number of movements had formed to address problems of housing, education, crime, and child labor. A multitude of charitable societies also came into existence to provide money and food for individuals and families in need. These organizations tended to have a religious orientation and were linked to an evangelistic fervor taking hold throughout England.

HUMANITARIAN IMPULSE

Individuals drawn to social-welfare activities were generally well-educated men and women, products of wealthy families, expensive schools, and religious upbringing. They viewed themselves as their brothers', and sisters', keepers and as having a moral responsibility for making the world a better place to live. They felt a sense of duty and shared the belief that a person's future reward or punishment was determined by his faith, but above all by his conduct.

One outlet for this desire to help was a growing array of clubs and organizations committed to working with individuals in groups. Some organizations—that is, social settlements and the Young Men's Christian Associations (YMCAs) and Young Women's Christian Associations (YWCAs)—were building-centered and offered programs and activities in the same location from week to week. Other organizations, such as the Boy Scouts, Girl Guides, and Ragged Schools, were not centered in a single location and so were more mobile. Without facilities, such organizations had to create activities that would draw members and keep their interest.

Most notable of the building-centered movements were the social settlements, closely tied to Cambridge and Oxford Universities. Settlement leaders such as Samuel Barnett, founder of Toynbee Hall, believed that educated university men living near and sharing with the poor could provide an example of high standards and that the students' leadership would inspire their poorer neighbors to achieve these standards.

It was expected that this encounter with the working class would provide the university students an opportunity to experience a level of existence hitherto unfamiliar to them and to enhance their knowledge of the human condition and life in general. On the more practical side, it was anticipated that many of these students would eventually move into positions in government and business and that the students' experience in the settlement would have prepared them to take a sympathetic approach to the poor and needy (Barnett, 1918).

Toynbee Hall, the first settlement founded in England, was like a university transplanted into a slum. It promoted picture exhibitions, extension classes, and special courses for the poor. Subsequent settlements, such as Oxford House, were to make extensive use of clubs for both children and adults, to establish savings banks for boys and girls, and to offer reading programs for the poor.

Whereas the settlements initially used small groups as a means of educating the poor and needy, the YMCA and the YWCA began using small groups as a means of saving souls. The YMCA was founded in 1844 as a prayer and missionary society committed to Bible reading. Many of its early leaders were suspicious of activities such as games and sports, which they considered simply amusements. Other YMCA leaders argued that if the YMCA was to be successful in attracting converted and unconverted young men, it would have to offer activities in the form of classes, recreation, and clubs. In 1888, the issue was put to rest when the group decided to build not only a reading room and a library in the London YMCA but also a gymnasium (Binfield, 1973).

The YWCA, a separate organization from the YMCA, was founded in 1876 by a group of London women committed to the religious development and welfare of young women. A major concern of the early YWCA was the large number of girls and women who after moving into the cities were unable to find safe housing, jobs that paid enough to support them, and wholesome leisure-time activities. Besides offering a safe place to live, the YWCAs held a wide range of classes—for example, cooking and sewing along with Bible study.

Although the Boy Scouts did not have a club room and gym, their uniforms, outdoor activities, camping, and badges had a special allure. In 1907, Robert Baden-Powell, a highly decorated military hero, founded the Boy Scouts as a means of building character in young men through camping, physical fitness, and woodcraft. A Social Darwinist, Baden-Powell believed that the British military's difficulty in winning the Boer War was a direct result of the physical and moral deterioration of English youth. If England were to survive and not decline like Rome, noted Baden-Powell, young men would have to be trained to be better fit—morally and physically.

The connection between the British military and the Boy Scouts was strong. Most of the early leaders of the movement were retired army officers. Boy Scouts were expected to wear uniforms that resembled those worn by British soldiers, meet in small groups called *patrols,* and participate in activities such as hiking, marching, signaling, and tracking (Reid, 1981).

THE AMERICAN EXPERIENCE

In America, the Industrial Revolution brought about far-reaching social and cultural changes. Cities grew at a phenomenal rate and were subjected to an unparalleled dislocation caused by the rapid economic expansion. To the cities came new ethnic groups. Uprooted from their long-time family surroundings, these groups confronted one another with deep mistrust.

As industries developed and factories were built, they were staffed by individuals willing to work for low wages under difficult and unsafe conditions. The average workweek was between 50 and 60 hours long. Skilled workers earned about 20 cents an hour, while an unskilled worker earned 10 cents an hour.

America was fertile ground for organizations, groups, movements, and clubs. In 1830, Alexis de Tocqueville observed that Americans had a propensity to form groups.

> Americans of all ages, all conditions and all dispositions, constantly form associations. . . . [They] make associations to give entertainments, to form establishments for education, to build inns, to construct churches, to diffuse books, to send missionaries to the Antipodes; and in this manner they found hospitals, prisons, and schools. If it be proposed to advance some truth or to foster some feeling by the encouragement of a great example, they form a society [Tocqueville, 1947, p. 319].

It was Tocqueville's opinion that the desire to form associations was tied to the principle of equality, a theme he viewed as fundamental to a democracy.

Group-oriented organizations that had formed in England several years earlier were copied and became a stylized American version of the original.

Toynbee Hall, for example, became the prototype for settlement houses founded first on the East Coast and then in large cities throughout the United States. Settlement pioneers such as Jane Addams, Ellen Gates Star, and Stanley Coit all made pilgrimages to England to meet with Samuel Barnett at Toynbee Hall. Upon visiting the London YMCA, Thomas V. Sullivan, a retired sea captain, established the first YMCA in Boston. William Boyce, after a trip to England, formulated a plan for an American version of the Boy Scouts. And after a visit with Baden-Powell and his family, Juliette Low founded the Girl Scouts of America in Savannah, Georgia.

Organizations interested in helping people collectively, such as scouting groups, YMCAs, YWCAs, Jewish Centers, and social settlements flourished in the larger cities. With their growth came articulation of ways in which a small group could be used. Some people viewed the small group as a viable means for the socialization of the individual. Others saw the small group as a force in maintaining a democratic society. Organizations and clubs varied to the weight they assigned to these two themes. Some accentuated one theme or the other, while organizers of social settlements attempted to combine both themes within the purpose and objectives of their organizations (Reid, 1981).

SOCIALIZATION OF THE INDIVIDUAL

The theme of socialization was based on the belief that the small group, whether a club or patrol, could be a positive means of character building and of enhancing the development of children. By coming together on a regular basis with caring and responsible leaders, boys and girls could learn both social skills and the values of the larger society. The leader was expected to serve as a model, give advice, and assist the group's members achieve the group's objectives.

The theme of socialization was influenced by the changing attitude toward play and recreation taking place in the 1900s. In previous decades, play was thought of as the activity that children and adults participated in to fill their leisure hours. This attitude began to change, with play increasingly considered a means for people to deal with reality, to adopt moral rules they could carry into their daily life, and to learn relationship skills.

Lee's book *Play in Education* (1915) became an important guide for settlement and recreation workers. It was Lee's thinking that leisure-time activities had the potential of preventing and curing physical and mental illness. Settlements and community centers began to develop playgrounds in order to provide safe areas for children's play. Hull House, for example, established one of the first playgrounds and sponsored organized games and activities supervised by a trained kindergarten teacher and a police officer. When the Playground and Recreation Association of America (later to be called the National Recreation Association) was formed in 1911, its officers included Theodore Roosevelt, Jane Addams, Luther Gulick, and Jacob Riis.

Large organizations dedicated to serving young people—including the Ys and scouting groups generally began as local endeavors started by a small number of citizens to deal with a particular group of children and subsequently evolved into a national or an international organization. Once interest in an activity such as camping was stimulated, the organization used that activity to encourage specific behavior patterns.

Some organizations stressed the development of loyalty, honor, physical fitness, social and racial consciousness, and love of country, class, party, or sect. Others had as a primary goal young people's intellectual development or increased appreciation of art, nature, and aesthetics. These aims were often expressed in such generalizations as *character building, development of personality, good citizenship,* and *control over nature*.

The Girl Scouts exemplified the socialization theme. Early in the organization's history, its leaders felt the Girl Scouts should provide a constructive group experience flexible enough to meet the needs and desires of its members and, at the same time, should foster in its members self-reliance, consideration of others, and a sense of social responsibility. Its programs included homemaking, outdoor activities, international friendship, arts and crafts, dramatics, music, and dancing.

MAINTENANCE OF A DEMOCRATIC SOCIETY

The theme of maintaining a democratic society was based on the belief that by becoming involved in group action and decision making within their neighborhood and larger community, individuals would become knowledgeable and skilled citizens. The settlements in England and America highlighted this theme in their commitment to the poor and those who were disenfranchised. For example, during the stock-market crash of 1929, the settlement Chicago Commons was deeply involved in encouraging social action to improve the conditions of unemployed workers. Italians, Poles, Greeks, and Mexicans who previously had come to the settlement for recreational activities began to study the causes of the emerging economic depression and its effects on their lives.

Discussions and debates took place covering many topics, including the need for work relief through public works and the need to develop security through old-age pensions and unemployment insurance. Taylor, reporting on the work of Chicago Commons in 1932, observed that the unemployed men initiated projects and developed a sense of control over their lives by serving on committees and delegate bodies. They organized self-help projects and sought direct contact with legislators interested in relief measures. One of the major accomplishments of the Chicago Commons residents was to organize a protest march on Chicago's city hall to make known their problems.

EDUCATION FOR PRACTICE

26

• • • • • • • •

In the years before group work became a course or a curriculum in a school of social work, group work was customarily viewed in terms of its setting rather than its methodology or its practice. Men and women working in settlement houses were "settlement workers"; those working in the YMCA and YWCA were "Y workers"; and those working on playgrounds were know as "recreation workers." As early as 1906, the New York School of Philanthropy offered a course of study that prepared students for positions in social settlements. And, by 1913, students could enroll in a full course of study for playground recreation work.

The first training course on group work was offered by Western Reserve University (later to be called Case Western Reserve University). This course was intended to provide training for positions of playground director. In 1923, a course in group service was developed for men and women interested in working with groups in the Cleveland area. The purpose of the course was to:

> train workers in the principles and methods of dealing with groups through club and class leadership; through promotion of activities and administrative work in social settlements, community centers, young men's and young women's organizations whose purposes are to give direction to the lives of their members through their group associations [Western Reserve University, 1923, p 2].

Schools that had begun to offer courses on group work drew on the writings of well-known social scientists such as John Dewey, William James, Robert McIver, Charles Horton Cooley, and George Herbert Mead. No longer was the group considered just an aggregate of individuals. Now, it was deemed a dynamic, vital organism that could be studied, influenced, and manipulated for both good and evil.

IN SEARCH OF A COMMON METHOD

By the 1930s, the settlement movement, the recreation movement, and the adult-education movement were well established in the United States. Similarly, the YMCAs, YWCAs, Young Women's Hebrew Associations (YWHAs), Young Men's Hebrew Associations (YMHAs), Campfire Girls, Boy Scouts, and Girl Scouts were all national organizations with trained and volunteer staff members. Through formal and informal discussions plus a convergence of training, workers in these organizations began to recognize that they had a great deal in common.

In spite of this recognition, the goal and purpose of group work were unclear. The term *group work* was used at times to designate a collection of social agencies otherwise called *the character-building, education/recreation agencies that worked with people in groups.* The term *group work* was also used to define a method of educational work, whether the method was applied in settlement houses, in agencies such as the Ys, and in schools, or in hospitals. Finally, the term *group work,* when preceded by the word *social,* designated a method in the broad field of social work.

27

Group work's linkage to social work was reinforced by the fact that a growing number of schools were offering courses on group work. And students interested in working in settlements, recreation centers, and youth-serving agencies were enrolling in these courses.

A number of distinctive characteristics differentiated group work in its early development from the more-dominant social casework (Pernell, 1986). These were the emphasis on **member** versus clients; **doing with** versus doing for; **doing** versus talking about doing; **activity and others as primary agents in the helping process** versus the worker alone as the primary agent; **personal and social development and social contribution as legitimate professional foci** versus a remedial and rehabilitative focus; **health and strength** versus sickness and breakdown.

Relations between group workers and caseworkers were uneasy. Some group workers felt that casework had already lost its commitment to social reform and that even though caseworkers spoke of changing communities and solving problems of poverty and unemployment, their real commitment was to working with individuals on a one-to-one basis. These group workers viewed the increasing interest in the professionalism of social work as leading to a further rejection of the reform tradition. Individuals working with groups criticized caseworkers for being so involved with the person's personal dynamics and ignoring the root causes of the problems (i.e., poverty, lack of adequate housing, etc.).

Caseworkers had many doubts as to whether group work should be a part of social work. In previous years, social casework had gone through a struggle similar to the one that group work was experiencing. Many caseworkers argued that anything lacking psychological grounding was inappropriate for the social work profession. Group workers were identified with recreation, and it was hard for caseworkers to think of activities such as play, arts and crafts, and dances as serious means of assisting people develop their personality or work on problems. Other caseworkers felt that there were similarities between the two methods of helping and that casework would be enriched by viewing clients from the perspective of "small group psychology" (Richmond, 1930).

An early attempt to examine the interrelatedness of casework and group work was Wilson's book *Group Work and Case Work: Their Relationship and Practice* (1941). Read by hundreds of caseworkers, it underscores the generic skills common to both group work and casework. Reading this book led caseworkers to experiment with groups, resulting in the introduction of group services into agencies that formerly had provided help only on a one-to-one basis. And reading this book served to remind group workers that a significant amount of their time was spent working with individuals—both inside and outside of groups and that it was important to understand the linkage of mind and body.

EARLY TREATMENT EFFORTS

While nearly all of the group work practiced before the Second World War occurred in leisure-time, recreational, and youth-serving agencies, a number of experiments occurred in which groups were used as a means of treatment. One of the first documented experiments took place in the early 1900s at Hull House and was briefly noted in Addams's book *The Spirit of Youth and the City Streets* (1909). The group consisted of young boys who were "drug addicts" who had been hospitalized. Addams wrote, "It is doubtful whether these boys could ever have pulled through unless they had been allowed to keep together through the hospital and convalescing period—unless we had been able to utilize the gang spirit and to turn its collective force toward overcoming the desires for the drug" (p. 66).

In 1918, an experimental recreation program was established at the Chicago State Hospital for the mentally ill. The wards selected for the experiment held close to 900 severely ill patients. In conjunction with the ward physician, the researchers assigned patients to various group activities, such as marching to piano music and doing other simple exercises in groups. Once the patients were able to handle this type of program, they were advanced into more complex patterns of activities, such as games and group dances. It was the researchers' hypothesis that severely ill patients who had the opportunity to watch more stable patients, as well as their therapist, would be influenced to participate (Boyd, 1935).

Another early experiment took place during the summer of 1929, this one at the Lincoln, Illinois, State School and Colony for the mentally retarded in conjunction with the Illinois Institute for Juvenile Research (Boyd, 1935). In groups with up to 20 members, children were taught dancing, sports, and games. At the end of the experiment, the researchers concluded that the small-group interaction had had a positive impact on the patients' behavior. The children quarreled less, played more happily and resourcefully together when undirected, worked more willingly, attempted to escape less, and were less destructive of the clothes and equipment than they had been before. In general, it was concluded by the researchers that recreation for the mentally retarded did more than merely occupy their time. By selecting activities that held the greatest possibility for growth, the researchers could help participants function at a much higher level than before.

In 1932, an experiment in group work was carried out at the Geneva Training School for Girls, an Illinois reform school for delinquents. The goal was to provide girls labeled *incorrigible* the opportunity to plan and make better use of their leisure time (Boyd, 1935). A result of the group work was the girls' growing ability to confront each other and handle for themselves behavioral problems in their living units. During one of the meetings, the girls reportedly asked the group worker to leave. Another staff member, curious about this, was told that "one of the girls had done something too bad for her [the worker] to know about, and they were taking it up in the club to see what ought to be done" (p. 130).

While these experiments were limited in scope, combined they raised the question of the purpose of group work. Some group workers in the more traditional fields of informal education and recreation contended that establishing groups in settings such as hospitals and training schools would detract from group work's purposes of encouraging citizen action and providing services to normal juveniles. For other group workers, these experiments raised the question of whether group work with emotionally ill individuals was group therapy—a form of treatment these workers were not trained to practice.

The sociologist Bogardus (1937), countered that group workers were engaged in activities that were more strategic than they had ever dreamed. By identifying personality difficulties early, he noted, group workers could help prevent disturbances from becoming deeper, chronic, and unmanageable. Group work, according to Bogardus, was a powerful force in augmenting casework and contributing to its success with disturbed clients. Later, he noted that organized group activities could lead to a more balanced personality. This could occur, he said, through such everyday activities as creative handicrafts and art, club participation and discussion, and being a functioning member of a democratically operating association (Bogardus, 1939).

INFLUENCE OF WORLD WAR II

The lessons of Nazi Germany accentuated the need for increased participation in community life and for the strength that grows in the individual and in the group from working together. These lessons also reminded that the group association has the potential of being dangerous and should be used with caution. The Nazi youth groups demonstrated that groups could be used to enslave youth, as well as to help them freely participate in society.

When World War II broke out, recreational and counseling services were set up for men and women in the armed forces and carried out through the American Red Cross. Recreation programs that heretofore had been used with healthy adults had to be adapted to the physical and emotional conditions of military patients in hospitals and service personnel stationed in posts and camps throughout the world. This change in focus proved frustrating for many of group workers, particularly those dealing with the injured. These workers recognized their lack of essential skills to deal with the social and emotional issues that interfered with the rehabilitation of injured military personnel (Reid, 1981).

The war also forced group workers to look at their assumptions, methods, and practices. Group workers had to deal with short-term transitory groups, a type unfamiliar to most of them. Soldiers who were part of an activity for several sessions were often transferred to another camp or hospital or shipped overseas. Congeniality, which had been considered essential to sound grouping, took a backseat to diversity, short acquaintances, and constant shifts of membership.

A psychiatrist, a psychologist, social workers, and recreation workers in military hospitals came together as part of the clinical team for each patient. These professionals were forced to devise new ways of cutting down on traditional detailed case histories, paperwork, and waiting lists. One of the ways this was accomplished was by turning to group psychotherapy, which had been used before the war by psychologists and psychiatrists to treat emotionally disturbed children and adults.

Group work was influenced by refugees from Central European countries. For example, Fritz Redl, Bruno Bettelheim, and Gisela Konopka brought to the United States a tradition of psychoanalytic thinking combined with group experience. Having grown up in an authoritarian family culture in Central Europe, they realized the significance of voluntary group participation to individual development.

Psychoanalysis, however, had neither the dramatic nor the exclusive impact on the people of Europe that it frequently had on people in the more highly individualistic and puritan culture of the United States. Many Americans viewed analytic therapy as a panacea for solving an individual's personal problems. To the professional trained in Europe, analytic therapy was only one of many treatments available. Konopka (1963), reflecting on her personal experience, writes:

> For myself, if I represent at all—at least in some ways—this group of immigrants, I must say that my first encounter with social group work in 1941 was a revelation. Having just come from a society that seemed to present an inescapable gulf between the individual and the group—which insisted that the individual be sacrificed to the interests of the group—I found the concept of individualization in and through the group exhilarating [p.9].

GROUPS IN CLINICAL SETTINGS

In the 1940s, a growing number of mental-health clinics and hospitals became interested in using groups as a part of their services. First, the Pittsburgh Child Guidance Center accepted a group-work student for a field placement. Later, Aspinwall Veterans Administration Hospital began using students for work with physically and mentally ill patients.

Not long afterwards, the New York School of Social Work developed fieldwork—in a project undertaken jointly with the Community Service Society of New York. A group-work student, in collaboration with caseworkers and a psychiatrist, began working with a group of children assessed as having serious adjustment problems. The group was carried for three years by group-work students and then transferred to a neighborhood center and again was led by group-work students (Coyle, 1960).

From these early experiments, group work with troubled children and adults spread throughout the country. In 1947, the University of Minnesota worked with the Amherst Wilder Clinic in St. Paul to establish a group-work program. In 1948, the Menninger Clinic in Topeka, Kansas, began an outpatient club upon the request of a group of hospital patients. At first, a caseworker served as staff person, but later a therapist trained in group work was employed to assume responsibility for the outpatient club.

The move into psychiatric settings, however, was far from easy. Few group workers knew much about mental illness and hospital settings. Most had to spend time becoming acclimated to these settings. Often, their previous experience with groups had been with character-building organizations or settlement houses. R. Fisher (1949), reflecting on his experiences at the state hospital for the mentally ill in Cleveland, notes:

> We had to have enough experience with patients so that we ourselves could be comfortable in our relationship with them before we could proceed further. We counted on the fact that our basic concepts in working with people would be sound and applicable in this setting too, and indeed before too long, found they were. We, of course, recognized that there would have to be adaptations in how to apply these concepts to this specialized settings to meet the particular needs of the emotionally disturbed individuals, but we were encouraged by the psychiatrist in our work and we learned as we went along (p. 3).

In 1942, Fritz Redl, a psychoanalyst on the faculty of the Wayne University School of Social Work (later to be called Wayne State University School of Social Work), initiated a project in Detroit to provide diagnostic services for disturbed children. The purpose of this Detroit Project was to provide firsthand knowledge as to the children's symptoms and behavior under stress. By observing these children in a group setting, the professionals were able to avoid the artificiality associated with gathering diagnostic data one-to-one.

Reluctant to call the work with the children *group therapy,* Redl used instead the term *clinical group experience* because, he reasoned, this term simultaneously kept the children's basic disturbances in perspective and emphasized that their group work was more than an educational experience. Redl explained, "I didn't want to call it therapy because there were many things that I just couldn't fix up in a summer. These kids had many problems, and I was not even pretending to resolve all of them" (Gottesfeld & Pharis, 1977, p. 80).

Four years later, Fritz Redl and David Wineman established Pioneer House, a residential treatment center for severely disturbed preadolescent boys. Besides the professional staff, casework and group-work students from Wayne University worked with the children and their families. Eventually reports of their work were published in the books *Children Who Hate* (1951) and *Controls From Within* (1952).

CAMPING AND GROUP WORK

A number of camps experimented with the group-work method as a means of helping disturbed children. In 1947, for example, the Toronto Big Brother Movement conducted a three-week camp for children whom the agency's psychiatrist and other staff members considered to be too disturbed to cope with regular camp programs (Aldridge, 1953). Once it was recognized that the camp experience could have therapeutic benefits, less emphasis was placed on activities, and greater emphasis was placed on individual needs and attitudes.

Camps also provided an entry point into group work for individuals interested in working with difficult youth. Young men and women working as counselors in camps such as Camp Wel-Met, Bronx House Camp, and the Educational Alliance Camps were recruited into group-work programs in schools of social work.

A PART OF SOCIAL WORK

Group work's identity crisis, which had begun early in its history, continued through the 1950s. The question remained: was group work a form of recreation, education, or social work? Some group workers viewed group work as a social movement that would strengthen democracy through citizen participation. Others perceived it as means to help people use their leisure time. Still others considered it a form of social work that could bring about permanent change in an individual's personality.

Increasingly, the term *social* was appended to the words *group work*, suggesting an identification with the profession of social work. By 1955, the problem became resolved with *social group work* officially becoming a designation within the National Association of Social Workers (NASW).

A MULTITUDE OF MODELS

By the mid-1960s, it was clear that rather than one model of group work there were several—including the preventive and rehabilitative model, the interactional model, and the social-goals model. Each has its roots deeply embedded within the history of social work and social group work.

Papell and Rothman (1966), reflecting on the various models, observed that over the years social group work has struggled with the question of its focus—the individual, the small group, or the larger society. When a formulation emerges that gives precedence to one of these, professional criticism is raised loudly from proponents of the other two.

Another question has to do with the societal function of social group work. Is its function provision and prevention, or is its function restoration and rehabilitation? Or, is the function of social group work a combination of these two?

THE PREVENTIVE AND REHABILITATIVE MODEL

This approach, often linked to the medical model, is based on social work's historical mission of service to those most in need. It is also based on the objective of ameliorating or preventing adverse conditions that negatively influence individuals and thus result in deviant behavior. While influenced by the early writings of Fritz Redl and Gisela Konopka, this model has, in recent years, been developed by Robert Vinter, Paul Glasser, and Charles Garvin.

33

· · · · · · · ·

The most appropriate clientele for groups based on this model include the physically or mentally handicapped, the legal offender, the emotionally disturbed, and the isolated or alienated person. Cultural and social norms provide general criteria for defining the nature of the problem behavior and the degree of change actually effected.

A key concept of this model is the use of a formed group, a group in which membership is predetermined and the individuals are selected by the worker. Viewed as both the means and context for treatment, the group is used to influence the client's participation and affords opportunities for direct worker/client interaction that contributes to change. With this model, the behavior of the individual is the focus of change.

The treatment process begins at intake and continues to its termination. First, the worker assesses each client's situation with reference to problems, causal conditions, and goals. Second, the worker plans activities in relation to this assessment. Third, the worker executes the treatment plan. Fourth, the worker evaluates the outcome. The worker also evaluates the barriers and the resources for change in the participant and in that individual's environment and considers these factors in helping the participant set goals.

The worker's goals and purposes for the group provide him or her with a general guide for establishing its composition. In composing the group, the worker seeks individuals who can have the maximum impact upon each other. The group must be capable of developing appropriate levels of cohesiveness, solidarity, mutuality, as well as viable internal structures, such as indigenous leadership and means of decision making.

The worker is viewed as a **change agent** who, by the very nature of his or her position, intervenes at the individual, group, and larger social-system levels to achieve individual treatment goals. The means of influence used by the worker are direct, indirect, and/or extra group. Using **direct means of influence,** the worker effects change through immediate interaction with a group member. As Vinter (1974) outlines, the worker may serve as:

- the central person—an object of identification and drives
- a symbol and spokesperson—an agent of legitimate norms and values
- a motivator/stimulator—a definer of individual tasks and goals
- an executive—a controller of members' roles within the group

Using **indirect means of influence,** the workers induce change by creating or modifying group conditions to help group members meet their goals. Indirect means of influence refer to those actions of the worker that influence the group in such a way as to have the desired effect on group members. Indirect means of influence include determining the group's purpose, selecting group members, and determining the group's size and operating and governing procedures.

Using **extra-group means of influence** refers to conducting activities outside the group on behalf of clients. Targets of these worker interventions include persons whose behaviors affect the client outside the group (for example, a spouse, or parent) and settings outside the group (for example, on the job, in the classroom, in the family).

Much of the knowledge that has contributed to the development of this model has been taken from individual psychological theories used in social casework. It also draws on role theory, small-group dynamics, and learning theory.

INTERACTIONAL MODEL

The interactional model (or reciprocal model) evolved from the early writings of Grace Coyle and was further developed by William Schwartz. In recent years, it has been expanded upon in the writings of Lawrence Shulman and Alex Gitterman. This approach suggests a helping process in which the ideal group state is one in which members help each other with problem-solving tasks related to a problem they have in common. With this model, such a state or system is not only desirable but also a necessary condition for problem solving to occur. And this state or system is not dependent upon the specific problem to be resolved by the group.

The interactional approach presupposes an organic, systemic, symbiotic relationship between the individual and society, which becomes the center of social work attention. This approach also presupposes a reciprocal relationship between the group and each client. The social worker, serving as the **mediator** or **enabler** between the two, has the responsibility of correcting and preventing imbalances in these relationships.

The worker both influences and is influenced by the worker/client system. The worker neither does **to** nor does **for** the client, but rather does **with** the client. The role of the worker is one in which the client reveals and makes available his or her aspirations, knowledge, and emotions within the boundaries of the "contract" between himself or herself, the group, and the agency.

Schwartz (1961) describes five major tasks that the worker addresses himself or herself to in the group situation:

- the task of searching out the common ground between the client's perception of his or her own needs and the aspects of environmental demands with which the client is faced
- the tasks of detecting and challenging the obstacles that obscure the common ground and frustrate the efforts of clients to identify their own needs and the needs of those "significant others" in their life

- the task of contributing data/ideas, facts, and value concepts that are not available to the client and that might prove useful to him or her in attempting to cope with that part of social reality that is involved in the problems on which the client is working
- the task of "lending a vision" to the client
- the task of defining the requirements and limits of the problem-solving situation in which the clients and the worker interact

An important aspect of the interactional approach is the theme of intimacy linked to the value of mutual aid. The worker strives to help group members talk to each other in a purposeful way and to invest in each other. This aspect requires the expression of feelings and the discussion of issues that are genuinely significant within participants' lives.

SOCIAL-GOALS MODEL

The social-goals model is not identified with a single formulation or a central theoretician. Still, its roots in the settlements and youth-serving organizations go back to the beginning of group work. Closely resembling the community-organization method of social work, this model attempts to deal with problems related to the social-order and social-value orientation in small groups.

Key concepts in this model are social consciousness and social responsibility and the idea that the group worker is helping broaden the base of a country's knowledgeable and skilled citizenry. This model envisages social change brought about by responsible members of groups within society. There is an assumption that a unity exists between social action and psychological health. Each individual is seen as potentially capable of some form of meaningful participation in the mainstream of society. And every group is thought to possess a potential for effecting social change.

The worker is viewed as an influential person with responsibility for the cultivation of social consciousness in groups. While the worker does not articulate a particular view, he or she does seek to inculcate a value system. The worker personifies the values of social responsibility and serves as a role model for group members, stimulating and reinforcing modes of conduct appropriate to their active citizenship.

MAINSTREAM MODEL

By the 1970s, there was a move toward an elaboration of the similarities rather than the differences between these models. Papell and Rothman (1980) observe that the convenience of the early separate classifications began to wane as a result of the mushrooming of knowledge and the proliferation of newer models within social work. As they point out, the emphasis that had been placed on differences, although necessary to model building, obscured the commonalities between the various models.

Konopka (1983), writes of her own frustration in trying to identify with a single model:

> I am asked by colleagues and students which model of group work I adhere to—the Social Goals Model, the Remedial Model or the Reciprocal Model. Aside from my revulsion against such atrocious terminology, my answer is clearly: Neither one, nor all of them together. I find it impossible to exclude the aims of any one of them [p. xiv].

Authors such as Hartford (1971), Lang (1972), Roberts and Northen (1976), Konopka (1978), as well as others, began to combine aspects of the earlier models in what has come to be called the mainstream model. The small group, according to this model, is characterized by common goals, worker and member authenticity, and mutual aid. The purpose of the mainstream group comes from an integration of the member's goals, as well as those of the worker. Members and worker engage in the process of determining objectives, setting boundaries, and problem solving.

A distinctive aspect of the mainstream group is the conception of group development (Papell and Rothman, 1980). This focus anticipates the creation of structures by the group through the emergence of indigenous leadership roles. These structures and leadership roles are nurtured by the worker to provide members with opportunities for fulfillment of both individual and group needs. Ideally, the group reaches a point where the leadership function, initially carried by the worker, is shared with the members.

Members are thought of as active recipients of help. They are expected to engage in the group process, assist each other, and take responsibility for the life of the group. The member is viewed as a social learner, expanding his or her skills in social functioning through the group situation regardless of the primary purpose of the group. The group is a testing ground where clients can try out new behaviors, roles, and ways of communicating. It is also a place where they can test out reality and receive feedback from the other members and the worker.

The role of the worker varies, depending on the needs of the group, the needs of each client, and the particular situation. The worker may be therapist, enabler, facilitator, or teacher. The style of the worker in the mainstream model is one of openness, respect, warmth, and genuineness. The worker makes a conscious attempt to reduce the social distance between himself or herself and group members. The leader may share his or her own feelings when such disclosures are useful and appropriate to the members and the group process.

EXPANSION OF CLINICAL SOCIAL WORK

In the 1960s and 1970s, a growing number of social workers were moving into clinical settings. With the move came the term *clinical social work.*

Although this term was relatively new, social workers were not new to clinical settings. For decades, there had been psychiatric social workers doing direct practice in psychiatric clinics, hospitals, and other institutions. There have also been medical social workers in hospitals and rehabilitation centers.

In 1984, the National Association of Social Workers defined the practice of *clinical social work* as "the professional application of social work theory and methods to the treatment and prevention of psychosocial dysfunction, disability, or impairment, including emotional and mental disorders" (p. 1).

As a part of social work, clinical social work shares the goal of enhancing and maintaining the psychosocial functioning of individuals, families, and small groups. The interventions offered by the practitioner include interpersonal interactions, intrapsychic dynamics, and life-support and life-management issues. The services offered by the worker consist of assessment; diagnosis; treatment, including psychotherapy and counseling; client-centered advocacy; consultation; and evaluation.

A distinguishing feature of clinical social work, and one that differentiates it from psychology and psychiatry, is the clinician's concern with the social context within which individual or family problems occur and are altered. There is the person, the situation, and the interaction between them. Within this **person-in-situation relationship,** the individual acts upon his or her environment and at the same time is acted upon by the environment.

Personal, interpersonal, and social functioning are viewed as propelled both by inner forces—that is, drives and defenses—and by outer forces—that is, the family, school, neighborhood, and community. Intervention, therefore, may be directed at either the person or the social situation or at some combination of the two. Viewed as "psychotherapy plus" (Strean, 1978, p. 36), the clinician seeks to modify each client's maladaptive defenses and increase the person's ego strengths. At the same time, the therapist never loses sight of the client's interactions and transactions within the clients social orbit. And the therapist seeks to modify those forces in the client's environment that hinder the client's personal and interpersonal functioning.

IN SUMMARY

The antecedents for the use of groups in social work lie in nineteen-century England. Organizations such as the social settlements, Boy Scouts and Girl Scouts, and the Ys developed as a means of strengthening a democratic society, building character, and socializing individuals. These same organizations were replicated in America, and with them came a greater appreciation and understanding of the power of a small group as a means of change. In the 1940s, small groups began to be used in clinical settings such as hospitals and clinics.

38
• • • • • • • •

The therapeutic process in the group comes, in part, from the decision making, the performance of tasks, the achievement of goals, and the sharing of feelings. While there is no single approach to working with groups, a number of models have evolved, each with roots embedded in group work's history. The goal of group work is to improve the social functioning of individuals by enhancing the meaningfulness of their life experiences and to expand the range of choices for individuals' behavior by providing a group environment capable of supporting different adaptive patterns.

SUGGESTED READINGS

COYLE, G. (1960). Group work in psychiatric settings: Its roots and branches. In *Use of groups in the psychiatric setting* (pp. 12–45). New York: National Association of Social Workers.

GLASSER, P., SARRI, R., & VINTER, R. (Eds.). (1974). *Individual change through small groups.* New York: Free Press.

REID, K. (1981). *From character building to social treatment: The history of the use of groups in social work.* Westport, Conn.: Greenwood Press.

ROBERTS, R., & NORTHEN, H. (Eds.). (1976). *Theories of social work with groups.* New York: Columbia University Press.

SCHWARTZ, W., & ZALBA, S. (Eds.). (1971). *The practice of group work.* New York: Columbia University Press.

WILSON, G. & RYLAND, G. (1949). *Social group work practice: The creative use of the social process.* Cambridge, Mass.: Riverside Press.

3

....

THERAPEUTIC
FACTORS
IN
GROUPS

efore my wife and I had children, counseling parents was a relatively easy task. Whatever the issue, be it toilet training, discipline, or sibling rivalry, I had the answer. Freud, Spock, and Erickson were quoted with authority in ways that would have made my old psychology professors proud.

This was up until the time our daughter was born. Heather entered the world complaining and did so for the ensuing six months. She was allergic to milk and experienced severe colic.

Night after night she cried, leaving her mother, a trained nurse, and me totally bewildered and exhausted. I can recall a night when I wept out of a sense of helplessness. We wanted to help her so much, but nothing seemed to work.

We looked to our pediatrician, but his guidance proved less than helpful. I turned to my highly trained colleagues, and their advice was inadequate. They never seemed to understand. We felt so isolated!

Being a trained professional made matters worse. I chided myself for not being able to help my own child. "If I can't help her," I asked myself, "how can I help someone else?"

When help came, it was not from physicians or colleagues. Instead, it came from other parents who had gone through similar struggles. They didn't give advice. Instead, they communicated understanding and support. They had paid their dues and clearly understood what we felt.

Thankfully, Heather, as well as her mother and I, survived those months. She is now an adult and has become a very special young woman. Still, memories of the pain and desperation linger.

Now, when parents come in with difficult children, I don't give advice. We talk about their circumstances and their feelings of frustration and helplessness. My responses, far from mechanical, come out of a sense of having been there. I, too, have paid my dues.

Why is it that so much of our helpful knowledge and wisdom occurs out of brokenness and pain? Genuine empathy is not just learned; it's earned. And, as clinicians, we are all wounded healers.

• • •

This chapter focuses on the therapeutic factors that are salient in group treatment and answers this question: what does group work offer that contributes to improvement in a person's condition and circumstances? More specifically, what are the advantages of group work over other methods of helping?

41

• • • • • • • •

ADVANTAGES OF GROUPS

A complex and fundamental issue for the therapist is deciding whether to use one particular means of helping rather than some other approach. The choices and the possibilities are endless. They include behavior modification, rational/emotive therapy, client-centered therapy, and supportive therapy, to name a few. At a broader level is the decision of method—individual, family, or group therapy. The natural inclination of most professionals is to work with the client on a one-to-one basis. This is not surprising, since most of us have cut our professional teeth in the two-person, or dyadic, context. Even if this were not the typical training experience, the two-person relationship serves as the expected setting for healing. This mind-set mediates the expectations and behavior of clients, as well as those of the therapist.

Too often, however, the decision as to approach or method is not based on the needs of the client or some carefully considered treatment plan as much as on the skill, knowledge, ability, or comfort level of the professional. It may be that the worker feels competent in one method and uses that method no matter what the problem. If the only tool is a hammer, everything becomes a nail.

The decision may also be based on the worker's fear related to a loss of control and a decrease in power. The very nature of family therapy or group work means giving up the relatively secure one-to-one or worker/client ratio for the less secure one-to-two ratio or an even less secure ratio such as the one-to-eight or so ratio commonly found in groups.

Once we go beyond the worker's cultural conditioning and personal fears, the therapeutic question needs to be: what is in the best interest of the client? To answer this question, we have to recognize that all three methods—individual, family, and group—are valuable. And each method, in its own way, has inherent properties that make it the treatment of choice in certain circumstances.

Individual, family, and group treatment have elements in common. Still, each is unique and offers therapeutic factors that the others do not provide, or do not provide to the degree needed. For instance, feedback—so much a part of group treatment—is also found in individual and family therapy. The difference is this: in a group, there are more people who can offer input and feedback to the client; whereas, in individual and/or family therapy, the potential is limited to one or two family members.

CHANGE WITHIN THE GROUP

42

• • • • • • • •

A group is not inherently therapeutic, and change does not happen automatically. It occurs in a sufficiently safe atmosphere, created and sustained by the worker. The development of this safe atmosphere requires the rudiments of basic human trust, as well as an environment in which individuals can be vulnerable. Herein lies a clinical paradox. For members to disclose their thoughts and feelings, take risks, and experience the therapeutic power of the group, there needs to be an atmosphere of trust. For this trust to develop, members need to take genuine risks and share who they are and what is going on behind their eyes.

One of the earliest systematic attempts to identify the therapeutic factors that go on in groups was made by Corsini and Rosenberg (1955). They posed this question: what within the therapeutic situation is of the essence? After examining 300 articles, Corsini and Rosenberg extracted nine factors. To be therapeutic, they conclude, a situation must allow the client to experience:

1. **acceptance**—a sense of belonging and of being emotionally supported and accepted by the group
2. **altruism**—a sense of being important in the lives of other group members by being helpful to them
3. **universalization**—a realization that the client is not unique and that other people share similar problems
4. **intellectualization**—the process of learning or acquiring knowledge
5. **reality testing**—the evaluation of issues such as personal values, family values, hostility, frustration, and personal defenses as events within the group unfold
6. **transference**—strong attachments to the therapist and/or other group members
7. **interaction**—the opportunity to relate to other people within the group
8. **spectator therapy**—gains made by observing other group members and, in part, by imitating their behavior
9. **ventilation**—the release of feelings and the expression of ideas previously repressed

To these factors Corsini and Rosenberg add a miscellaneous category that covers a range of mechanisms, including an opportunity for the client to experience suggestibility, sublimation, a sharing of common experiences, and spontaneity.

More than a decade later, Lieberman, Lakin, and Whitaker (1968) identified six "group properties," including the capacities to: develop cohesiveness or a sense of belonging among group members; control, reward, and punish group members' behavior; define reality for group members; induce and release group members' powerful feelings; distribute power and influence among group members; and provide a context for comparing oneself with other group members. In comparing group therapy with dyadic treatment, these authors feel that the group patient gets little practice in reflecting about himself or herself and his or her interactions with others, in examining his or her own feelings, in analyzing dreams, in linking present and past experiences, and in penetrating covert messages. On the other hand, they contend, the member of a group gets much practice in expressing his or her feelings to peers, in noting the consequences of such expressions, in attempting to understand and empathize with others, in learning from others about his or her impact on them, and in comparing himself or herself with others.

More recently, Yalom (1975), following in the interpersonal tradition of the psychiatrist Harry Stack Sullivan, developed the following list of 11 "curative factors": instillation of hope, universalization, imparting of information, corrective recapitalization of the primary family group, imitative behavior, altruism, group cohesiveness, interpersonal learning, development of socializing techniques, catharsis, and existential factors.

Incorporated into Yalom's classification are two interrelated factors having to do with interaction. The first is the interpersonal learning that occurs through feedback from, or the input of, the worker and the other members. The second is the concept of the group as a laboratory in which members can enhance their social skills, develop trust, learn to approach others, and learn to relate to others in the group.

Ohlsen (1970) identifies nine major therapeutic forces and suggests that for any client to benefit, both the counselor and the clients must recognize and use these forces:

1. **Commitment.** The client must recognize the need for assistance and be willing to talk about his or her problems, to solve them, and to change his or her behavior.
2. **Expectations.** The client must understand what is expected before he or she decides to join.
3. **Responsibility.** The client must take responsibility for himself or herself and for modifying his or her perceptions of the world.
4. **Acceptance.** Acceptance by the group enhances a client's self-esteem and encourages him or her to change behaviors.
5. **Attractiveness.** If the group meets the client's needs, has goals the client views as meaningful, and includes prestigious members, it will exert a greater influence on him or her than if it does not meet these criteria.
6. **Belonging.** All group members must sense a strong feeling of belonging.
7. **Security.** When the client feels reasonably safe in the group, it is easier for him or her to be open and to express genuine feelings.
8. **Tension.** The client's growth involves productive tension in the client and in the group.
9. **Group norms.** When the client accepts the necessary conditions

44
········

for a therapeutic group, he or she is then influenced by the group norms.

Over the years, certain elements have come to be recognized as more salient and influential than others, particularly in groups led by social workers. These include instillation of hope, self-understanding, imitation, learning from interaction, universalization of experience, reality testing, acceptance, self-disclosure, altruism, and guidance. All are inextricably interrelated. Although these factors cannot be easily separated, the importance or strength of one particular factor will vary depending upon the function of the sponsoring agency, the purpose of the group, the nature of the problem for which the members are seeking help, and the experience and training of the leader.

INSTILLATION OF HOPE

Without a sense of hope by the client, treatment wilts. It is hope that sustains the client through the early stage of therapy—when talking about feelings and experiences seems so awkward and frightening, when trusting total strangers with painful fears and secrets feels threatening and out of character, when the client's doubts about self-worth and the potential for genuine change are at their highest point, when the person is confused as to what therapy is and what is expected of him or her.

Hope nourishes clients during the middle stage of therapy during which hard decisions have to be made and taking a proactive stance becomes necessary—that is, when it is no longer appropriate to just talk about what they are going to do but time to commit to a plan of action that goes beyond their comfort zone, time to do something that is life-giving rather than self-defeating. Hope also helps in this stage during which saying what they truly feel begins to seem so much more authentic to members than "stuffing," or ignoring, their feelings or pretending to be something they are not.

Hope also sustains the client in the final stage of therapy as treatment comes to an end and it is time to go it alone without the therapist and caring others, whom the client has come to trust, when there is no longer an established time and place for the client to share his or her struggles and no therapist or group members, the special friends who listen and understand, to share the struggles with.

In individual and family therapy, hope comes from the therapist. Through our confidence, optimism, words, and actions, we convey the message that the individual's world truly can be better if he or she is willing to **work** in therapy. We ask the client to disclose their thoughts and feelings, to be open, to listen, to risk, and to try out new behaviors. Nonverbally, we nod our head, smile, and empathetically convey that we understand and the client is not alone. More important, we communicate that the client's particular problems can, in some way, be solved or at least modified. We may say, "Yes, I have worked with other people who have had the same kind of problem, and they have been successful" or "Treatment is very useful with a person such as yourself, struggling with this particular issue."

In group work, hope also comes from other group members. This is most clearly observed in the more classical self-help groups such as Tough Love, Alcoholics Anonymous (AA), Compassionate Friends, and Parents Anonymous, which generally do not employ professional leaders. In AA, for example, a new member who has been drunk earlier that day, feels he cannot make it through the next 24 hours without a drink. As others share their experiences, however, he finds meaningful support in hearing that 12 months ago the woman or man sitting next to him was at the same point and has not had a drink since.

Treatment groups that are at a mature stage in their development usually have members who demonstrate clinical progress and are able to reflect their successes. Sometimes, members who have been through previous groups with the worker are invited to participate both for their further personal treatment and also for their potential contribution to the group.

SELF-UNDERSTANDING

Group treatment has inherited from individual psychotherapy the belief that self-understanding is the heart of the therapeutic process. We use terms such as self-awareness, self-understanding, self-discovery, and insight to reflect this intellectual learning process. In short, the individual realizes something important about himself or herself.

This learning takes several forms. First, the member gains an understanding of his or her own personal dynamics through the discovery of previously unknown or unacceptable parts of himself or herself. Second, the member gains self-understanding through interpersonal learning, which occurs when he or she tries out new behaviors within the group and other group members share their impressions, feelings, and experiences.

Yalom (1975) observes that patients obtain insights on different levels. At one level, the member receives a more objective perspective on how his or her interpersonal behavior impacts other people. For the first time, for example, the client may learn that he or she is perceived by other people as cold, detached, or bitter. At a deeper level, the client reaches a more comprehensive understanding of the nature of the particular problem, for example, discovering that he or she avoids closeness out of a fear of being hurt. Perhaps the individual also learns how he or she got this way. In short, the client comes to understand the mechanisms that underlie his or her behavior and the origins of that behavior.

The impact of receiving feedback from six or seven people at the same time rather than feedback from just one person is hard to ignore. Feedback from one source can be easily shrugged off with a *What does he know?* It is nearly impossible, however, to ignore feedback when other

45
....

group members share the same perceptions or give the same feedback on more than one occasion.

IMITATION

A common characteristic of many individuals who seek help for personal problems is the lack of positive role models in their lives. Parents and other people significant to the client's development may have been violent, undependable, weak, seductive, or absent. These individuals may have had difficulty in expressing emotions—either overreacting or underreacting to events and circumstances. Rather than talking about their feelings, they acted on them without considering the consequences.

In individual counseling, the worker becomes a role model for the client to imitate. The client forms judgments about the worker from what he or she sees, feels, and hears the therapist do and say. The client observes how the worker dresses, what his or her office is like, the values implicit in what is being said and not said there. Consciously, as well as unconsciously, the client reads the therapist and internalizes the therapist's values, expectations, attitudes, and personal characteristics. The client's imitation of the therapist is both a result of observing that other clients have been successful after working with the therapist and a result of the client's discovering alternative ways of thinking, expressing, and behaving.

Group treatment, by virtue of its multiple interactions and relationships, expands the opportunities for a client to change through imitative learning. Individuals in groups have the opportunity to observe a multitude of interactions, methods of problem solving, and styles of relating. Instead of a single role model, there are numerous role models, the worker being only one of them. A member who has difficulty in expressing emotions, for example, is able to observe other members who are more assertive and who openly articulate their feelings. As it becomes evident that these other individuals are not harmed, the client becomes increasingly willing to make himself or herself vulnerable.

Referred to as *vicarious learning,* or *spectator therapy,* the observation of other group members or the worker allows the member to experience something of value for himself or herself. Such learning takes place when the member benefits by observing the therapy experiences of another person, when the client identifies with one or more other group members to the extent that he or she gains from their experiences, or when the member recognizes some positive aspect of the worker's behavior.

Clients constantly compare themselves with others in the group (Lieberman, Lakin, & Whitaker, 1968). They compare attitudes toward parents, husbands, wives, and children. They compare feelings about immediate events in the group. They compare the things that make them sad, happy, angry, and guilty. They also compare the ways that each member typically deals with and expresses feelings such as anger, affection, and joy. Comparisons of this nature force the member to reconsider what has been taken for granted by placing in bold relief new possibilities of feeling, perceiving, and behaving.

47

Modeling occurs in two separate stages: acquisition and performance (Rosenthal & Bandura, 1978). In the first stage, the member observes the activity that registers in his or her memory. In the performance stage, if given adequate motivation, the member initiates activity on his or her own. For instance, a client's behavior is inhibited by anxiety, until she observes another member engaging in the same anxiety-provoking behavior without being hurt. Increasingly the member's expectation of herself becoming more effective is enhanced. She becomes more resolved to change and is more willing to risk coping with the frightening situation. The actual performance of the previously fearful behavior serves to strengthen the member's sense of herself and to further boost her confidence.

Buchanan (1975), in discussing their group therapy with kidney transplant patents, describes the encouragement renal-failure patients experience from observing other group members gain their independence. After one young transplant patient enrolled in an educational program to prepare for employment, a 55-year-old small-business owner returned to manage his company although previously he had doubted his stamina and ability to do so.

Much of the early learning in groups is imitative (Rutan & Stone, 1984). Those clients who have difficulty tolerating and sharing strong emotions observe as other members interact intensely. These clients learn that other group members are not harmed and, instead, are drawn closer by such exchanges. When this realization occurs, the client's hope for change grows. Slowly and cautiously, the client begins to share feelings, imitating those who are more successful in that task. Each client's successes in using such imitative behavior make the group more attractive to its members, enhance group members' desire to belong, and increase group cohesiveness.

Group workers need to recognize the extent to which their own behavior influences the group (Corey & Corey, 1987). Through the worker's actions, and the attitudes they convey, norms related to openness, seriousness of purpose, acceptance of others, the importance of listening, and the desirability of taking risks are created within the group. The worker, according to Corey and Corey, teaches largely by example—by doing what he or she expects group members to do. Although the worker's role differs from that of the group member, the worker does not need to hide behind a professional facade. By engaging in honest, appropriate, and timely self-disclosure, group leaders can both participate in the group and fulfill the leadership function of modeling behavior for other participants' use.

LEARNING FROM INTERACTION

A member learns from his or her interaction with other group members. This occurs in two ways: (1) when the client tries out new, potentially positive

48
• • • • • • • •

ways of **initiating behaviors with** other group members; and (2) when the client tries out new, potentially positive ways of **responding to** other group members (Bloch & Crouch, 1985). For example, the client may share something to clarify the relationship between himself or herself and another member. The client may "check out," or try to determine, what another person has said so he or she can understand what is being communicated. The client may make an overt effort to develop a more honest, open relationship with one or more other group members. The client may express himself or herself in a more constructively assertive manner than usual. The client may challenge something the worker has said.

Joan, a very quiet group member, responded only when she was called on. Although silent, she was very much involved in the group. When asked if she preferred not to be called on directly, Joan offered that it was the only thing that seemed to get her to speak. It was agreed that the worker would continue to call on her, but Joan could choose not to respond. Later in the meeting, Joan volunteered that she wanted to work on being more actively involved in the group. At the worker's suggestion, Joan agreed to say one thing each session without being called on. In the following session, Joan asked a question of a member. She also volunteered to set up chairs before the next meeting.

A way that learning takes place is through the verbal and nonverbal responses of other members to something that a client says or does in the group. Group treatment provides a unique forum for feedback and the exchange of honest, explicit impressions. By contrast, feedback in dyadic counseling can only come from an authority figure—a significantly different source than one's peers.

We can distinguish three basic categories of member-to-member feedback. The first category is feedback from one or more members to a client **to characterize his or her behavior** in the group. For example, two group members tell a third member that she is rude, standoffish, controlling, quiet, seductive, or a clown. The second category is feedback from one or more members to a client **to characterize his or her appearance** at the moment. For example, the person is told that he smells, his pants are unzipped, his clothes do not match, or he has mucus on his face. The third category is feedback from one or more members **to describe their own personal reactions** to an aspect of another member's behavior. For example, other members might say to one member: "You make me angry when you . . ."; "I like it when you . . ."; or "I admire you when you . . . ."

As suggested in these examples, feedback can vary greatly in content. There is no limit to what a client will reveal about himself or herself. Similarly, there is no limit to the range of corresponding feedback. Feedback may be verbal or nonverbal. The previous examples were obviously verbal. Nonverbal feedback may take the form of a facial gesture, a tone of voice, or a nod of the head, for example.

Timing is an important factor in providing feedback (Bloch & Crouch, 1985). If feedback is given out of context, it will have little impact. If given too early, before an atmosphere of trust has formed, feedback may be perceived as a threat and rejected. Feedback is more valuable if it arrives close in time to the particular situation that has generated it.

Feedback is seldom consensual. Often, it is idiosyncratic, coming from the perception of a single member. On the other hand, sometimes feedback may come from the whole group. It is also worthy of note that feedback from a worker will have a greater impact on a client and will be perceived differently from feedback provided by peers.

UNIVERSALIZATION OF EXPERIENCE

Often when we are in pain, we feel totally alone and think no other person could have problems as bad. Women, for example, who have experienced sexual assault report feelings of separateness, isolation, and being different from other women. Instead of allowing rape victims to approach others and seek relief through sharing, these feelings lead rape victims to avoid others and to retreat into themselves.

Universalization is the realization by the client that "we are all in the same boat" and he or she is not alone. It is a recognition of the commonality of most problems, and a recognition that other people have morbid ideas, anxieties, or impulses similar to our own (Foulkes, 1964). Universalization has the potential of enabling the person to adopt a more detached view and to perceive himself or herself and his or her problems more objectively.

In recent years, with the advent of self-help or mutual-help groups, the relevance of universalization has come to be better understood. Self-help groups are organized around the purpose of maximizing the universality of experiences in order to provide individuals with support. Participants in these groups are undergoing **some** and perhaps **many** common experiences, whether it be the struggle to remain dry, to manage the behavior of an unruly teenager, or to grieve the loss of a dead infant. Mutually supportive, members of these groups share their pain and lessen their sense of isolation and of feeling "odd." Their sense of stigma also diminishes as the members change their self-perceptions by being with other people similar to themselves.

The following is taken from the notes of Lori, a 35-year-old professional woman participating in an actualization group.

> I continue to struggle with loneliness. We share how we came to choose our profession. I listen to stories of the members, as children, bringing home stray animals and being the one people seek out to talk out their troubles with. They are a wonderful group of rescuers and fixers. The leader has even been a lifeguard! My turn comes last and there is no way I can fit in with the stories preceding mine. I tell about my life painfully aware of my differences. I too am a rescuer and fixer but, alas, a more pragmatic one. Perhaps I favor more control and that is why the field of speech therapy appeals to me. Or maybe the problems encountered in social work are too all encom-

passing and I feel more adept at working with more specific problems. By the time I finish I am shaking inside at having shared so much of myself—what do they think? The response is favorable and accepting, although I have trouble perceiving it.

Referring to the following meeting, Lori notes:

there is a discussion of ways in which we all feel different about certain things. The attitude is one of nothing being swept under the rug; no, bring it out and examine it, feel it. We come closer to each other that day. The sense of "me too" is strong and we discover each others' [sic] differences. We still have a sense of being cautious but trust is building, nurtured by an atmosphere of safety and quiet acceptance.

In summary, universalization is occurring when a client perceives that other group members have similar problems and feelings. When this perception occurs, there is a reduction in the client's sense of uniqueness, and he or she feels less alone.

REALITY TESTING

Various writers have discussed groups as a *microcosm* or as a *reflection of society* (Dinkmeyer & Muro, 1971; Jacobs, Harvill, & Masson, 1988; Yalom, 1975). It is through the interaction with other group members that clients experience fears, anger, doubts, worry, and jealousy. It is in this same arena that clients reenact the ways they behave outside the group. Initially, the individual experiences the need to hold back or to be what others expect. As his or her comfort level deepens, "good behavior" lessens, and the **real self** is substituted for the **pseudo self.**

For example, individuals who have difficulty becoming close to others outside the group will have difficulty becoming close to group members. Individuals who struggle with being assertive with friends, family members, and employers will have difficulty being assertive in the group, particularly with the leader. Members who are verbose when they share experiences will be talkative in the group.

In the group, each member is placed in the position of having to negotiate situations—that is, to disclose their thoughts and feelings, solve problems, take risks, and reach out to other people. This provides the worker with two unique points of leverage. First, it gives on-the-spot assessment data. The information is fresh, firsthand, and uncontaminated by someone else's perceptions or reporting. It is information in the here-and-now rather than the there-and-then. Second, the worker is in the position to intervene immediately, and not after the fact.

For example, if a client reports that friends tell him he is a terrible listener, whether or not he is soon becomes evident as he interacts with other group members. If he interrupts other members, talks too much, or misinterprets what is said, the worker can point this out or, better still, can encourage other members to provide feedback based on their perceptions.

ACCEPTANCE

The feeling of belonging and being accepted is widely regarded as one of the most important factors in therapy groups (Lieberman, Lakin, & Whitaker, 1968; Ohlsen, 1970; Yalom, 1975). Clients referring to their experiences in a group speak of feeling "accepted by the group" and "able to be themselves." According to Bloch and Crouch (1985), acceptance operates when a member: (1) feels a sense of belonging, warmth, friendliness, and comfort in the group; (2) feels valued by other group members; (3) feels cared for, supported, understood, and accepted by other group members.

Eventually, the member feels unconditionally accepted and supported even when he or she reveals something about himself or herself which the member previously regarded as unacceptable. This feeling is documented in the following journal of a student in a group-dynamics seminar.

> It was significant to me when one or more other members could share genuine empathy or similar experiences. I was especially moved when Helen was so affected by Bill's disclosure of hurt, anger, and feelings of being worthless that she was compelled to share her own pain. That session was the most powerful for me. I have known Helen for three years and she has never volunteered a response in any class. I admired her courage and respect the risk she took to say what she did.

Another member wrote:

> A significant change seemed to be precipitated by Bill's revelation of an intense personal issue which was very immediate and painful for him. He was supported by the group. His sharing and the connection made by others increased the level of trust and the meaningfulness of the group which facilitated other sharing.

There are individuals who have had few opportunities for effective sharing and acceptance. This is especially true of psychiatric patients (Yalom, 1975). The individuals' limited opportunities stem from the fact that because of disturbed interpersonal skills, they have had few intimate relationships. This situation is complicated by fears and fantasies that make interpersonal sharing more difficult. For isolated patients, the group may have provided their only meaningful contact with other people. When the group is terminated and becomes a faded memory, however, participants can still remember the sense of acceptance and belonging they felt. They remember the group as a special place where they could be themselves without having to pretend.

SELF-DISCLOSURE

Self-disclosure is the sharing of personal material, by a client to other members in a group. The material shared concerns intimate aspects of the client that would not be discovered otherwise. The information is often about some previously hidden aspect, commonly described as "long-held secrets."

Sue, a 9-year-old who had been sexually abused by her father, was placed in an eight-week group for girls who had been molested. Her behavior in the group was described by the worker as erratic, impulsive, and unpredictable. When other girls spoke of their painful experiences, Sue's actions became clownish, or she did something to change the group's focus. She made it clear that she did not want to share her experiences or talk about her father.

When the group terminated, the worker felt that Sue had received little from the experience and recommended she be included in a similar group being formed. Approximately halfway through the second group, Sue began to speak of the incidents with her father. She spoke of being "bad" and responsible for her father's sexual advances. She said she was fearful that if she told anyone, she would make her mother angry and would be sent to live somewhere else. There were tears, anger, and frustration.

As Sue opened up, other members were supportive and accepting. Two girls also revealed the fear of reprisal by either their father or mother if they told anyone of their experience. Sue's ability to concentrate both inside and outside the group increased. In addition, she became less impulsive and more relaxed. The group successfully neutralized the excessive feelings of blame and guilt Sue had been feeling. The group also provided her with reassurance that the anguish she was experiencing was not the result of her behavior. Rather, it was related to her father's inability to control his impulses.

The worker who attempts to hurry a member's self-disclosure is usually frustrated. Clients such as Sue who have been severely traumatized need time to develop trust. Readiness to take risks develops slowly even under the best of conditions. The advantage of a group is that it lessens the person's isolation, pain, and guilt by encouraging the client to share his or her feelings with other group members who have had similar experiences.

There seems to be a curvilinear relationship between self-disclosure and psychological health. The person who does not disclose at all is probably unable to initiate relationships with other people and remains isolated (Jourard, 1971). On the other hand, the person who indiscriminately reveals highly personal information about himself or herself is likely to be maladjusted insomuch as he or she is self-centered and narcissistic. According to Cozby (1973), the individual enjoying positive mental health is characterized by high disclosure to a few significant others and medium disclosure to others in his or her social environment. The poorly adjusted person is characterized by either high or low disclosure to virtually everyone.

Self-disclosure is something that happens in a social context and involves risk taking. Once the information is revealed, the person doing the sharing cannot accurately anticipate the exact response of the recipient. The discloser may wonder: "Will I be laughed at?" "Will she understand my pain?" "Will he tell others?" "Now that they know my secret, will they hurt me?" Realistically, all or none of these may occur.

The particular information disclosed is less important than the sheer act of divulging personal information (Lieberman, 1981). It is the sense of well-being and the confidence in another human being and the feeling of acceptance that seem to be the active ingredients in making self-disclosure an important mechanism of change. The recipient of the discloser's personal revelation is not a passive receptacle. If the recipient responds with acceptance and unconditionality, the discloser's feeling of well-being is enhanced.

Not all self-disclosing in group treatment is helpful. Some clients divulge information that is deeply private and more appropriate for a confessional than it is for the group. Bloch and Crouch (1985), in delineating the distinction, write that the confessional involves both purgation and cleansing, on the one hand, and a judgmental response, on the other. While psychotherapeutic self-disclosure may involve revelations about some shameful act, it is not done for the purpose of being absolved or judged.

Another nontherapeutic form of self-disclosure is a stripping away of the clients defenses or privacy. Privacy and self-disclosure are not contradictory. The client does not have to "tell all" or "bare his or her soul" so that he or she is without defensive maneuvers. Nor does the client have to make some profound revelation that heretofore he or she has been unable to do.

Customarily, self-disclosure entails a shift in attitude that allows the person to share more than before of his or her private self with other people in a constructive fashion and to act more openly and honestly than before with himself and with others.

ALTRUISM

Members of a group feel better about themselves because of the assistance they provide to others. By trying to be helpful, they discover their value to. others which in turn enhances their self-image. According to Bloch and Crouch (1985), such altruism occurs when a client:

- offers support, reassurance, suggestions, or comments to help other group members
- shares similar problems with the purpose of helping other members
- feels a sense of being needed and helpful
- can forget about himself or herself in favor of another member
- recognizes he or she wants to do something for another group member

In treatment groups, individuals receive help through the process of helping other members. This occurs because of the reciprocity of the giving/

receiving experience. It happens through the social exchange of doing for other people, and, at the same time, receiving from them.

Often, an individual living in an institution becomes the perennial receiver. This person receives from family and friends who give and then leave. He or she receives from the nursing staff, doctors, social workers, and other paid professionals. During holidays, such as Christmas and Hanukkah, the person she receives from volunteer groups in the community that give gifts and sponsor parties. But, who does this person give to, and who receives from him or her?

Patients report a sense of being a burden and of having nothing to offer to other people. The receiver mentality causes the patients to experience feelings of helplessness and powerlessness. It also leads to their being self-absorbed and less sensitive to the needs of others. Helping other group members is refreshing and boosts such patients' self-esteem, particularly as they recognize that they, too, have something to offer.

GUIDANCE

Guidance, the imparting of information and the giving of direct advice, has long been a part of group therapy. In the early 1990s, Joseph Pratt gave instruction to groups of patients recovering from tuberculosis to help them learn how to better care for themselves. Maxwell Jones, in the 1940s, instructed his patients several hours a week on psychiatric symptoms and the structure and function of the nervous system.

The sharing of information is a key factor in self-help groups. The group becomes a forum for the exchange of information, and members are able to obtain a better understanding of the nature of their problem through the provision of specific information. One of the best examples of this information sharing is provided by Recovery Inc., a self-help group for people with debilitating psychological problems. At each of its meetings, the members follow a rigid format, beginning with a reading from *Mental Health Through Will-Training,* a book written by the group's founder, Abraham Low. Then, five or six members give examples of events that have upset them and how they dealt with these events in light of the group's teachings. Psychological illness is explained through the use of simple principles that are memorized by the group's members.

Psychiatric hospitals often use small groups to help new patients adjust to the hospital culture and to reduce any unnecessary pressure on them. From nursing staff and social workers, the new patients receive instruction on rules and expectations. In addition, the new patients receive information on activities and ward life from "alumni," patients who have been through similar meetings and are at a more advanced stage in their own treatment.

During the first new-patient meeting she attended, Miss Murphy, a newly admitted 23-year-old school teacher, complained about aggressive behavior by another patient on her ward: "I know I'm not as sick as Thelma is," she said, "but I'm afraid I might be if I am around her for long." The worker asked if other patients had experienced similar fears. After an uncomfortable silence, Mr. Brown, who had been in the hospital for some months and was soon to move into a family-care home, said that he had felt the same way when he first came to the hospital. But "I've come to understand that each patient is different, and that if I became more ill, it had nothing to do with anyone else but myself," he said. Several other patients admitted that they, too, were fearful and were relieved to find that others experienced similar problems and anxieties (Reid, 1968).

55
••••••••

At St. Vincent's Hospital in New York City, groups are used with relatives of patients in the burn unit. Topics discussed in these groups include: the role of nutrition in healing, the impact of burns on a patient's body image, and coping with pain. The workers found that the patients' relatives had many questions about pain and about the treatment that their family member was receiving. As the sessions progressed, participants spoke of experiencing guilt and anger at the hospital staff for not doing enough to help the patients. The exploration of these feelings, the education about the pain and treatments, and the concern demonstrated by the group workers helped these participants feel less guilty and less anxious and to strengthen their coping mechanisms (Lonergan, 1982).

In Summary

The various therapeutic factors—hope, self-understanding, imitation, learning from interaction, universalization of experience, reality testing, acceptance, self-disclosure, altruism, and guidance—have been separated for analytical reasons. In practice, overlap exists among them, and it is difficult to discern where one begins and another ends. Certain groups will highlight a particular factor; whereas, in other groups, the factor may be less important. For example, the use of guidance or didactic instruction found in educational-oriented groups may not be observable at all in groups that accentuate insight.

It is important that we are cognizant of the various factors and their effects upon the members. It is also important that we are aware of the potential that exists through full use of the factors. After all, these factors do not happen by accident. The worker is responsible for creating a climate and a type of interaction that promote growth and that encourage self-understanding and change. The worker's knowledge of these therapeutic forces and ability to use them are critical to the group's success.

Suggested Readings

Bloch, S., & Crouch, E. (1985). *Therapeutic factors in group psychotherapy.* Oxford: Oxford University Press.
Dinkmeyer, D., & Muro, J. (1971). *Group counseling: Theory and practice.* Itasca, Ill.: F. E. Peacock. See Chapter 4.
Yalom, I. (1975). *The theory and practice of group psychotherapy* (2nd ed.). New York: Basic Books. See Chapters 1–4.

4

THE GROUP CAULDRON

group's development is often thought of as a straight-line progression from beginning to end. This linear model suggests a positive trajectory upward with few dips and curves enroute. I wish groups actually worked this way. It would be so much easier for the group members and the worker.

It's my experience that group development is more like a ride on a roller coaster: First is the painstakingly slow and steady climb. Next comes a peak or two and then a sickening plummet as the honeymoon comes to an end. Then up go the cars again, and up further—and down. The highs can be breathtakingly high and the lows, frightfully low.

There is a set of unseen laws in action as the downward thrust provides positive momentum for the climb up to the next leg of the journey. Without the downs, I doubt if there would be the self-generated energy for the ups.

Some people don't like the ride, preferring greater constancy and predictability. There are some who become so unhelmed by the ride that they never go back, and there are others who grit their teeth and hang on grimly wishing it to be over.

Then there are those willing to relinquish control for a bit of adventure. They hang in there, swaying on the curves and clutching hard during the drops. Even though they are often scared half to death, they are drawn to the challenge. They have trust and faith that in spite of the heady ups and screaming downs there will be deliverance.

More important, once they catch their breath, they get right back in line for another ride. Energized from the experience, they recognize how exhilarating and incredibly life-giving the ride can be.

• • •

The term *group dynamics* describes the complex and interacting forces within groups as they operate to achieve certain objectives. This chapter examines group dynamics and answers two questions: First, how do groups develop and prosper over time? Second, how does the worker influence group dynamics in such a way that the group is cohesive and achieves its purpose and individuals change?

GROUP DEVELOPMENT

The process of development, whether we are referring to a human life or that of a group, suggests a patterned sequence of change. In contrast to random change, which is unpredictable, there is a certain degree of predictability in the process of development—with earlier behaviors or sequences serving as the building blocks for later behaviors. The organism, never static, advances and retreats in different ways and at different times.

59
• • • • • • • •

A basic knowledge of how groups develop over time is an essential tool for understanding the various obstacles a group must struggle with and in providing a framework to judge what action is needed in the group. Practitioners are often so overwhelmed by what is going on in the group that they fail to appreciate that the process is natural and to be expected. Knowledge of group dynamics serves as a means to understand and appreciate the particular needs and problems faced by group members. Knowledge of how groups develop also guides the worker in forecasting probable scenarios, setting objectives, and designing intervention strategies.

Social scientists have, for decades, grappled with the issue of sequence and order in a group's development. While theorists and clinicians agree that groups go through various stages, there is no agreement as to how many stages exist and what these stages actually look like. Unfortunately, most of the research on group development has been done in laboratories with task-oriented groups. Relatively few studies—other than those of an anecdotal nature—have focused on inpatient and outpatient groups.

Within the field of group dynamics there are different opinions as to the number of stages groups go through. Bales (1950), one of the earliest writers on small-group theory, describes three stages: orientation, evaluation, and decision making. Garland, Jones, and Kolodny (1973) list five different stages: preaffiliation, power and control, intimacy, differentiation, and separation. Sarri and Galinsky (1967) propose a seven-phase model: origin, formation, intermediate I, revision, intermediate II, maturation, and termination.

Two of the most expansive examinations of group development are the work of Hartford (1971) and Levine (1979). Hartford presents a five-phase scheme taking into account the normal cycle of the group and the activity of the worker. She suggests pregroup phases (private pregroup, planning in public, and convening); a group-formation phase; an integration, disintegration and conflict, reintegration or reorganization, and synthesis phase; a group-functioning and group-maintenance phase; and termination phases (pretermination, termination, and posttermination). Levine suggests four phases: parallel relations, inclusion, mutuality, and termination; plus three ongoing crises: authority, intimacy, and separation.

Given the fact that various theorists propose different numbers of stages, plus different sets of nomenclature, finding exact parallels is impossible. Table 4–1 is a comparison of eight different models of group development as described in the literature.

TABLE 4–1 Stages of Group Development: A Comparison

Life-Span Metaphor	Bales (1950)	Tuckman (1965)	Northen (1969)	Hartford (1971)	Sarri and Galinsky (1967)	Garland, Jones, and Kolodny (1973)	Levine (1979)
Conception			Planning and intake	Pre-group planning	Origin		
Birth *Approach vs. avoidance *Dependency vs. independence	Orientation	Forming	Orientation	Convening	Formation	Preaffiliation	Parallel relations *Authority crisis
Childhood				Group formulation	Intermediate I		Inclusion
Adolescence	Evaluation	Storming Norming	Exploring and testing	Integration, disintegration and conflict, reintegration or reorganization, and synthesis	Revision Intermediate II	Power and control Intimacy	*Intimacy crisis
Adulthood (Maturity) Advanced adulthood	Decision making	Performing	Problem solving	Group functioning and group maintenance	Maturation	Differentiation	Mutuality
Death			Termination	Pretermination Termination	Termination	Separation crisis	*Separation crisis Termination

*Ongoing

Why, you might ask, is it so difficult to agree on the stages that groups go through? One reason is that laboratory studies of developmental phenomena, particularly as these phenomena relate to treatment groups, are quite rare and seldom feature strict experimental controls or the manipulation of independent variables. Usually, the developmental data consists of the therapist's observations and those of professional observers who are present, most often as trainees. Such data are highly anecdotal in nature and reflect the clinical biases of the observers. Furthermore, such accounts are usually formulated after the fact and based on the observations of a single group (Tuckman, 1965).

Another problem is that most of the knowledge about group development comes from studies of time-limited, closed-membership groups. Generalizations of the findings to ongoing, open-ended treatment groups have often been made indiscriminately. There is certainly an overlap, but these two types of groups are not identical. For example, a treatment group has one specific beginning point. Yet, when new members are added, there are a multitude of new beginnings, each accompanied by the reemergence of themes and behaviors similar to those at the time of the initial sessions, as well as a predictable period of temporary regression.

While the stage concept cannot be taken too literally, experienced clinicians agree that groups do go through periods of life characterized by some underlying organization or emphasis. Each stage has characteristics that differentiate it from the stages before and the ones to follow. Each higher stage incorporates gains made during earlier stages.

Groups change at different rates, and progress is made unevenly, with steps forward and backward and then ahead to a new level of functioning. I have worked with some groups that seemed to move rapidly through several phases in a single session, while others appeared to get stuck and never became a group in any sense of the imagination. So, some groups seem to develop in an order that defies what is normally thought of as typical group behavior.

It would be easy to assume that what goes on in a group's development is inevitable and that nothing can be done to impact its direction. On the contrary! The worker, through the use of direct and indirect intervention, plays an active part in the group's development.

In summary, it can be said that the process of group dynamics is not as tidy as the theorizing about it; more specifically:

- Groups do not move along in an orderly sequence.
- Groups may revert to earlier stages.
- Stages cannot be thought of in any **pure** form but in various blends and combinations.
- A group's life span and development can and will be influenced by the worker and by the members.

Finally, there is a common misconception that in order to have a "good" and effective group, it is imperative that the group attain and maintain the most advanced developmental stage. If this were true, we would be asking the impossible of a large number of our clients, and many would drop out in frustration. Rather, there needs to be a reasonable fit between the level of group development and the members' social/emotional capacity and personality.

A word of caution is appropriate at this point. This book deals in large part with "average" groups, which begin after some planning, have a middle, and end after achieving their purpose. It describes "typical" behavior and discusses concepts, theories, and ideas about the growth of groups. **But there is no average group!** The concept of average is a convenient invention used to present a mosaic of different pieces in a way that makes sense. We need to bear in mind that each group is different, has its own personality, and differs from the "average."

Groups generally found in clinical settings are composed of a multitude of individuals who come from different backgrounds and who function at different levels. Some members have limited social/emotional capacity, and the group experience may be frightening and overwhelming to them. Because of the tremendous diversity in clients, some groups in clinical settings may never get beyond the early stages of group development and may end within three or four weeks because the members simply quit attending the sessions. Other groups may go on for years with the members totally bored, unable to communicate their discontent to the worker or other members.

THE LIFE-SPAN METAPHOR

The Life-Span Metaphor is an organizing principle that permits us to consider the various aspects of a group's development at a given period and to speculate about the interrelatedness of these various aspects. As a metaphor, it is a comparison with the stages in a human's life—conception, birth, childhood, adolescence, middle age, old age, and death. It emphasizes a belief that there are unique experiences at certain periods in the life of a group that deserve to be understood in their own right, as well as for how they contribute to the group's later development. Similar to the life of a human being, the life of a group may end at any stage in the group's development, sometimes even ending before the group reaches adulthood or maturity.

The concept of life stages is central to the organization of the Life-Span Metaphor model. For our purposes, a life stage suggests a phase or period of life that is characterized by some particular emphasis (see Table 4–1). Each stage has characteristics that differentiate it from the stages that precede it and the ones to follow. Stage theory proposes a specific direction to development, with each more advanced stage incorporating the gains made during earlier stages. However, development is more spiral or circular than linear. As a group struggles with the tasks unique to its particular stage, the group becomes better prepared for its future developmental stages.

The group circles through the various developmental stages and than does so again. Issues that were seemingly resolved resurface but this time at a different depth and breadth.

RECURRENT THEMES

There are two recurring themes in the life of treatment groups: **approach versus avoidance** and **dependence versus independence.** While both themes are apparent throughout the various stages, there are certain stages during which they are more observable.

Approach versus avoidance. The theme of approach versus avoidance has to do with intimacy, sharing, and self-disclosure. It occurs initially as an individual group member struggles with the question of whether or not to really be a part of the group. The individual must answer the question "Do I want to participate in this group or not?" Answering in the affirmative means the individual's disclosing who he or she is and being open to possible rejection and hurt. Answering in the negative means the individual's remaining in the status quo and missing out on a potential opportunity to grow and to resolve problems in his or her life.

The theme emerges for the individual as other members tell their story and the individual silently debates how much to share. "Should I say what I am thinking, or is it better to keep quiet?" There is a recognition that other group members seem at least somewhat comfortable in sharing and feel better after doing so. As other group members disclose their feelings, experiences, and thoughts, a basis is established for deeper intimacy among all group members, including the reluctant individual. Self-disclosure begets self-disclosure.

In many ways, the issue of approach versus avoidance parallels Erickson's (1959) initial psychosocial stage of trust versus mistrust. First, the individual needs to be secure enough within himself or herself to authentically share doubts, fears, and inadequacies. Second, the person needs to feel secure enough with the group per se to take risks and to disclose those very private pieces of the self that heretofore have been hidden.

There are times, however, when sharing significant information is not in an individual's best interest. Not all groups are trustworthy, and the private and meaningful details revealed may, in some way, be misused or misunderstood by other group members. Paradoxically, in such a group, the most functional response by the individual may be to **not** trust the other group members or even the worker.

Dependence versus independence. The theme of dependence versus independence refers to challenging the power and authority of the group leader. There is a desire on the group members' part to neutralize the worker, combined with a fear that they may be rejected or disliked by the worker. This ambivalence is illustrated by two separate and distinct feelings. The first, "I'm glad you are here, because you understand and can protect me. Please help me!" The second, "I wish you would leave me alone and not make me think or feel."

Less evident early in a group's development, the conflict becomes increasingly apparent as the group's members experience a sense of identity and recognize that it is acceptable to disagree with the worker, as well as with fellow members. The veneer of "nice behavior" is often replaced by heightened bickering, testing, defensiveness, and resistance.

The therapist may experience covert or overt pressure. Members may be emotionally or literally absent from a session. They may project onto the worker their feelings toward others in authority. They may push the worker to take more control or to do something they are fearful of doing themselves. They may even move to exclude the worker by not listening to comments or by not responding to interventions (Glassman & Kates, 1983).

CONCEPTION

Generally, the idea of having a group occurs long before the group's initial meeting. A group's conception occurs at the point when one or more people begin to think of a group as a plausible means of addressing some problem. There are a number of different names for this conception stage. Northen (1969) refers to it as the period of **planning and intake,** Sarri and Galinsky (1967) as the **origin** phase, and Hartford (1971) as the **pregroup consideration and planning** phases. The idea for the group may come from a worker, an agency administrator, another professional, someone in the community, or possibly a client. It may occur at a staff meeting as workers examine their agency's waiting list and recognize that a number of clients are struggling with similar issues and might work well together in a group.

The idea may occur as a worker reflects on similarities among the circumstances or problems of some clients. In examining my own caseload several years ago, I was struck by the number of recently divorced women with families who were coming in each week for individual counseling. While the women differed in age, education, and lifestyle, they had several important characteristics in common.

First, although mildly depressed, all were reasonably healthy. Second, each client found it extremely difficult to meet her financial responsibilities. Third, all of these clients were having problems dealing with the needs of their children. Finally, nearly all of these clients were experiencing a feeling of being abandoned by the men in their lives, which was affecting their relationships with other people. When these clients were asked individually whether they would be interested in being a part of a group, most of them expressed an interest in participating.

The idea for a group may come from clients requesting—or even demanding—that a group be formed to address a particular issue. For example, several mothers of teenagers, concerned with the amount of drug use in their neighborhood, contact the staff of a community mental-health clinic. They request help in becoming organized as a group and assistance in finding resource persons knowledgeable about drugs to serve as speakers.

Hartford (1971) refers to the initial pregroup phase as "private," in that no group—not even an aggregate—is formed. There is, instead, an idea or notion that may eventually lead to the formation of a group at some later date. The issues explored at this point—for example, who makes the decisions to have a group, what the suggested purpose of the projected group is, and how the group will be run—will have a great impact on what happens later.

For the worker, there may be the very practical issues of whether he or she can find the time to lead a group and whether he or she has the energy, skill, and resources to serve as the leader. There may be basic questions as to the kinds of support—for example, space, staff time, and supervision—the agency will be able to provide. There may be concerns about the group's composition and whether there are enough potential members to form a viable group.

Eventually, the idea of a group evolves into a plan for a group, and the decision is conveyed to others. This "public" pregroup phase involves a commitment to organizing a group for a particular purpose, with certain goals, for individuals whom the worker may or may not know. This is also the point in which individuals are invited to participate. A memo, for example, may be circulated stating the purpose of the group and the time and place for group meetings and requesting staff to refer clients who meet the criteria. Professionals in other agencies may also be contacted and asked to consider the group for their clients. Flyers may be put up in shopping malls, and articles describing the group and its objectives may be submitted to local newspapers.

Sometimes, the results of an advertising campaign are much greater than what was originally anticipated. For example, a somewhat enterprising graduate student, developed a self-help group for individuals suffering from neurofibrotis ("elephantman disease") and for their families. Assuming that there were relatively few individuals with the disease in the area, she was concerned that interest the group would be limited. To generate interest, she wrote an article for the local newspaper and was interviewed on a noon-hour television talk show. The night of the initial meeting, she was overwhelmed to find that the room, rather than almost empty, was filled with interested individuals.

The "public" group-planning phase may commence with the plans for the group already fairly well established in terms of location, composition, purpose, and activities. In other situations, however, this pregroup phase may be the time for determining exactly how much need there is for the group. Individuals who express curiosity or limited interest may be asked to share their ideas and state their preferences as to meeting time and location and to describe their previous experiences in groups.

An intake interview prior to the first session serves as a means of educating potential members about the group's purpose, as well as what will be expected of them. Such an interview is also a way to screen out any applicants unsuited to that group. Not everyone fits into a particular group, and by guiding the questionable group candidates to other services, the worker can prevent future complications.

No person joins a group without experiencing a mixture of apprehension and anticipation. Practical questions as to what the purpose for the group is, what expectations the leader has, and how the group will operate need to be answered. At a deeper level, group candidates feel anxiety about being accepted, understood, and respected. They are also curious about who will be in the group, and perhaps excited at the prospect of meeting new people.

A number of positive factors serve to motivate individuals to seek help. Most salient is the promise of respite from discomfort, dissatisfaction, or pain. Perhaps the individual himself or herself recognizes that something needs to be done; or perhaps family and friends are encouraging the person to seek help. Although the individual's problem may have existed for years, often the problem is viewed as serious only after a painful event puts the difficulty into bold relief. For example, acting-out behavior by a 14-year-old boy is ignored by the parents until he is given a two-week suspension from school for hitting a teacher. Or a middle-aged mother of three is suspected of having an alcohol problem. No one takes her drinking serious until she drives the family's station wagon into a ditch and one of her children is hurt.

Common to most people is the belief that personal problems can be solved without assistance from other people. It is not until we come to grips with the fact that the problem continues to exist and the solution or resolution is beyond us that we are willing to ask for help. Even then, seeking help is done with ambivalence: "I want help, but I don't want help." The negative side of the ambivalence may vary from mild reluctance to strong resentment and resistance.

During the conception stage, the worker is instrumental in determining the what, why, who, where, and when of the group. What is the purpose of the group, and what is it that he or she hopes the group can accomplish? Why is a group and not some other type of treatment the better choice? Who is it that can and should use the group? Are there individuals who might not do well in the group? Where will group meetings be held? When and for how long will the group meet? Is it enough to meet once a week for several months, or should the group meet more or less often, for more or fewer months?

BIRTH

The moment of birth for a group is the point when the members formally come together for the first time. This stage has been referred to by a number of names. Bales (1950) calls it the **orientation** stage; Tuckman (1965) the **forming** stage, and Levine (1979) the **parallel relations** phase.

The initial group session can be exciting, as well as frightening, for both leader and group members. It is that time when the ideas, thoughts, and plans formulated during the conception stage become a reality. In Ernest Hemingway's words, it is the "moment of truth."

A group is two or more individuals who influence one another through social interaction and who, to some degree, are interdependent. Seldom does a collection of individuals coming together for the first time meet this definition of a group. More accurately, a group at this stage is an aggregate, or a collection of individuals, with each person's center of attention focused on himself or herself and not on the other members of the group. Indeed, in the beginning, there is little or no internal organization, groupness, or dynamic interaction among the members. There is uncertainty, as well as relatively few norms to fall back on.

Group members generally experience anxiety as to the new situation and what will be expected of them. With this anxiety come a multitude of spoken and unspoken questions:

- What will I have to do?
- Am I going to like the other members?
- Will they like me?
- Will I be laughed at?
- Will I be forced to do things I don't want to do?
- Will I know anyone?

The members' anticipation and expectation of what will transpire in the group is strongly influenced by their previous experience in other groups. If a member has had a difficult time or has been traumatized in some other group, he or she will realistically be cautious entering this and future groups. In the 1960s when Synanon groups, which highlighted confrontational worker behaviors, were popular, workers continually found themselves having to explain to prospective members that "attack therapy" was not going to be used in the group. Some prospective members had experienced attack therapy firsthand, while others had heard about it from others.

The fears, fantasies, and general expectations of what will take place will also be influenced by movies and television. Movies such as *One Flew Over the Cuckoo's Nest* and *Bob and Carol, Ted and Alice,* popular during the 1960s, provide a frame of reference that will defy a group leader's protestations as to group-therapy fact and group-therapy fiction. Several years ago, an extremely popular television situation comedy, the *The Bob Newhart Show,* focused on the trials and tribulations of a psychologist and his therapy group. The "patients," hilarious caricatures of neurotic behaviors, came to represent to the public the types of individuals who attend therapy groups. Years later, when clients and students were asked to share their understanding of group therapy they still refer to this show.

67
• • • • • • • •

Common to most of us entering unfamiliar situations such as a class or a social gathering is the use of social rituals and pastimes as a means of dealing with anxiety. Individuals tell their name and ask questions of those nearby. Questions are asked of the person in charge as to plans and expectations. Innocuous questions may be asked as a means of locating and categorizing others by status or roles. Simple questions such as "What do you do for a living?" and "Where do you live?" serve as a means of placing others in perspective.

Individuals attending a group for the first time utilize similar behaviors as a means of containing their anxiety. This is most evident in the early minutes of the first session as participants enter the room. There is a "casing out" of other members to determine where they fit. Members try to locate some mutual interest with those around them by asking questions such as "Do you know" such and such a person?" and "Where did you go to school?"

Excessive dependency on the therapist is common in the initial session. The group members ask the leader questions about his or her expectations, about rules, roles, limits, and about how the sessions will run. They express concerns as to confidentiality and what can and cannot be brought up in the sessions. The members want to know the worker's role and how active or inactive he or she will be. At first, they may perceive the worker as the sole source of treatment and ignore the input of the other members.

The group leader needs to be mindful of the anxiety that members bring to the situation. While a group member may express a strong desire to join and work toward the group's objectives, the member may be fearful, and apprehensive as he or she approaches the unknown. The worker needs to address these feelings—both positive and negative—in an open and sensitive manner. The sharing of anxieties represents the first in-group experience of becoming involved and being less isolated.

CHILDHOOD

The childhood stage of a group refers to the period of becoming acquainted. Meeting other group members occurs in the first session and continues into later sessions. Hartford (1971) calls this acquaintance-making period the **group-formation** phase, while Sarri and Galinsky (1967) call it the **intermediate I** phase, and Levine (1979) refers to it as the **inclusion** phase. There is an uncertainty about the norms and the expectations the worker presents. There is anxiety about the ambiguity of the situation, and participants struggle to reduce the uncertainty by seeking direction, requesting advice, and suggesting activities.

The group members' affective ties to one another are limited. The group's interaction, which will be the hallmark of later stages, lacks depth and commitment. If someone drops out during the childhood stage of the group, there will be moderate concern. Likewise, if someone is added, the person is easily accepted. The members' lack of bonding to the group-as-a-whole and to the other members is primarily a result of their self-centered feelings of anxiety and apprehension.

The beginning stages of a group can trigger conflicts from a member's past. The following excerpt is taken from the group evaluation of Peggy, a graduate student in a self-actualization group.

69
• • • • • • • •

> For the first two or three sessions, someone new came into the group and this was unsettling for me. The feelings that I had are hard to explain but I remember feeling the same way when I was in foster-care and every so often a new kid would come into the family. With each new kid, I had to do some mental shifting of my position in the group. I felt replaced by people who were more extroverted, funnier, or somehow better than me. I felt the same way when Helen, Douglas, and Karen came into the group. All three of them have stronger personalities which can kind of overshadow mine.

The theme of approach versus avoidance is most apparent during the childhood stage. Participants do not know what they are to disclose and are afraid of sharing too much. Norms for ways of behaving have not been established, and there is fear of rejection and of appearing different. Until some preliminary sharing takes place, trust does not develop.

Pseudo interaction.   If one group member brings up a problem for discussion, other members experience a sense of relief that now the group is moving and has a focus. There may be unspoken collusion in which one participant raises an issue and other members provide seemingly useful suggestions and advice. A variation of this is the member who "sacrifices" himself for the group, presenting problems that seem to deny resolution. This may go on for several sessions until the members become fatigued or a more genuine issue surfaces.

Engaging in pseudo interaction provides payoffs to group members. By encouraging the "problem presenter" through the use of questions and requests for detail, other group members keep the spotlight off them, and the risk to them is minimal. Someone else is the center of attention, and they can maintain a low profile, reducing the probability of their having to share. The problem presenter assumes that he or she is fulfilling the contract by disclosing problems to the rest of the group and at the same time gains the attention of the other members.

Incidently, the worker may unwittingly participate in the collusion. Like the rest of the group, the worker may feel pleased that the group appears to be dealing with an issue and may feel relieved that the group's attention is on someone other than him or her. The members are talking, and the group has direction. Painful silences are limited, and a member appears to be receiving input and assistance. The worker sits back, takes a less active roll, and perhaps even contributes to the advice giving.

Levine (1979) speaks of a parallel-relations phase in groups analogous to the parallel play of young children. While these children play next to each other and to some degree interact, in essence they do not relate to each other. Likewise, group participants speak without listening, ask questions without hearing the answers, and ignore feedback even after requesting it.

REACTION TO AMBIGUITY

In groups where there is minimal structure, clues regarding how to act are few. Participants have to orient themselves through trial and error in order to figure out what will work. According to Rutan and Stone (1984), the ambiguity of the situation stimulates regression, with each member reverting to a personally important stage in his or her own development. How each member reacts to this ambiguous situation may represent a developmental stage that the individual passed through either successfully or unsuccessfully. This situation-induced regression by each member can sometimes be clinically useful to the therapist in gaining understanding of each member's manner of managing anxiety.

Each participant, in his or her own way, strives to reduce this ambiguity. Some members remain quiet, fearful of exposing themselves until they are sure of their ground. Some retreat into a world of their own. Some ask an excessive number of questions, pressing the worker to define the group situation. Some assert themselves, defining the group in their own terms.

Similarly, the group-as-a-whole has a need to reduce the ambiguity of the new situation. Its members may direct excessive energy toward deciding on how the group will operate. They may place inordinate pressure on the worker to take charge and may express resentment when the worker does not.

During this stage, it is useful for the worker to help the group members talk about their personal goals and articulate what it is they wish to work on or need from the group. The worker may encourage the members to take risks and to share meaningful aspects of themselves. The worker can also invite each member to become an active participant and to go beyond his or her public self and share aspects of his or her private self. By modeling behaviors of openness, authenticity, and honesty, the worker can establish important group norms.

ADOLESCENCE

About the time the group members appear to be settling in and addressing the group's purpose, there is a period of fluctuation in relationships, a period of increased tension and friction, and a period of conflict with the worker. Interaction is uneven and infighting common. A lack of unity becomes apparent, and the members challenge the structure created in the group's earlier stages. This change is illustrated by the practitioner proudly reporting one week how smooth his or her group is running and complaining the following week that the group is deteriorating, with members resistant and dissatisfied.

Authors use a variety of names to describe this stage. Sarri and Galinsky (1967) refer to it as the **revision** phase because there is a challenge to the existing group structure, accompanied by a modification of the group's purposes and operating procedures. Tuckman (1965) refers to this stage as a period of **storming and norming** because the members become hostile toward one another and toward the worker as a means of expressing their individuality and resisting the formation of a group structure.

Hartford (1971) refers to this as the phase of **integration, disintegration and conflict, reintegration or reorganization, and synthesis,** in which defenses are lowered. The "good" behaviors obvious in the group's earlier stages are exchanged for group members' disenchantment with each other, the group, its tasks, and the amount of autonomy they may have given up by becoming a part of the group. In short, the honeymoon is over.

Just as young people struggle with their personal identity and role confusion, during adolescence, a group in its stage of adolescence experiences a great deal of change and conflict. Although it is not uncommon for a group to experience its own peaks of optimism and valleys of pessimism **throughout** its life, during its adolescence, a group is especially likely to experience a sense of frustration and disenchantment. Whereas, to this point, the group has been the worker's group, the participants now begin to claim ownership of the group and are able to think about the group's meaning in new ways.

The group's adolescent stage is sometimes characterized by emotional outbursts and the expression of strong feelings by group members that serve as a means of their resisting self-exposure and maintaining control over what happens. Parker (1958) identifies this stage as a "crisis period," during which friction increases, anxiety mounts, rules are broken, arguments ensue, and a general structural collapse occurs.

As the members come to feel more secure with each other and their particular role as clients, they develop an increased sense of a group self. Their obedient and "good" behavior common to the childhood stage is replaced by withdrawal, anger, and hostility. Sarri and Galinsky (1967) observe that the extent of the challenge to leadership during the adolescent stage is based on how much the leader attempted to prevent engagement in leadership activities by other members during the previous stages. But, during this stage, the leader definitely can anticipate increased role differentiation within the group, with more members assuming leadership functions.

Not all members experience or express overt anger, rebelliousness, or assertiveness. For some, the emotional response is withdrawal, passivity, and compliance (Rutan & Stone, 1984). Many of our clients do not have easy access to more active forms of anger and use passive/aggressive behavior instead. As these individuals struggle to balance anger and withdrawal with assertiveness and compromise, there is the potential for insight and learning more functional behaviors.

It would be as inaccurate to suggest that every group has a volatile stormy period as it would be inaccurate to say that every young person between ages 12 and 18 has a crisis-ridden adolescence. Some groups are able to deal with their concerns and frustrations in a smooth, relaxed manner, accepting the group and leadership as caring, benign, and helpful. Other groups focus briefly on their own functioning, realign the structure, and go on about the business at hand.

In reporting on a counseling group of multiple-sclerosis patients in a Veterans Administration (VA) outpatient clinic, Power and Rogers (1979) write that by the sixth session the group members were moving at their own pace and generally choosing their own topics. Instead of directing comments to the leaders, the members began to talk to each other, and a communication pattern developed from their mutual understanding and the need to help each other through particular adjustment difficulties:

> after the sixth session the group members confronted the leaders as to "how do you think the group is going and what are your expectations now?" It appeared that not only did they want some validation for the group process, but also encouragement for their increased involvement in the group. Their own attitude toward the leaders changed from a more "authority-figure-you lead us" perspective to a "you are necessary for the group, yet we will call on you when we need your outlook" [p. 121].

This example underscores the reality that groups go about the tasks involved in their development according to the unique mix of their participants, and not according to an inexorable set of unvarying steps. The study of group dynamics is at best an inexact science. No two groups have the same personality.

Instead of a phase in the group's development, the adolescent stage may be a point of termination. In spite of the worker's best efforts, the group may get stuck and become unable to accomplish its purpose. This situation may result from a combination of many factors, including mistakes in group composition, a lack of promised resources, a misinterpretation of the member's abilities, or the worker's limited capabilities. No matter what the reason, the worker needs to engage the members in any decision whether to terminate the group and, if appropriate, help them examine their feelings and behaviors. The worker may also need to help the members find and link up with other services within the agency and/or the community.

Until this stage of development, the group has been the worker's group. The worker planned and established the group, set its goals and selected its participants. However, for the group to reach maturation, the leader needs to share power with the group members. The adolescent stage of the group, more than ever, is a time when it is important for the worker to nondefensively listen to what the members say and to be flexible whenever appropriate. By the worker letting go, the group is able to move toward a level of genuine "we-ness" and belonging.

ADULTHOOD (MATURITY)

73
. . . .

Adulthood for a group is that period marked by solidarity, cohesion, and more genuine involvement than the group has achieved before. The members experience a greater willingness to work on issues, disclose their feelings, and confront each other. The group has established customary operating procedures, traditions, and a style of doing tasks—that is, setting up chairs, serving coffee, etc., that persist from meeting to meeting.

Northen (1969) refers to this stage as the period of **problem solving,** Hartford (1971) as the **group-functioning** and **group-maintenance** phase, and Levine (1979) as the **mutuality** phase.

During this stage, patterns of communication within a group become predictable. Group members can anticipate what other members will say or how they will react to issues. They experience greater ease in challenging each other when something is said that seems inconsistent or inaccurate. There is also a greater range of communication, with most of the members sharing ideas, feelings, and problems each session.

As a group matures, it develops means of managing and resolving conflict. In its birth and childhood stages, conflict within the group is disturbing, because its members are unsure how to respond. In its later stages, its members recognize that the strong expression of difference need not result in the end of a relationship or cause the demise of the group.

Durkin (1981), utilizing general-systems theory, considers the mature group as having a balance between open and closed boundaries. If the boundaries are too open, they do not protect the individual sufficiently. Boundaries that are too closed stop the necessary exchanges of information and feelings. For the mature group, the boundaries are semipermeable, making it possible for new information to be appropriately processed. Because of these boundaries, the atmosphere of a mature group is potentially safe and allows for free interaction, for risk taking, and for authenticity.

DYNAMIC EQUILIBRIUM

A significant indication that a group has achieved the stage of adulthood is the amount of energy that goes into group members' fulfillment of the group's purpose. According to Braaten (1974/1975), when a group has reached this stage of development, its goals and purposes become clear. Communication within the group has improved for both senders and receivers, and the healing capacity has become unclouded. The group has become more truly therapeutic than before and the group members deal with increasingly deeper personal and interpersonal problems, such as autonomy, the fear of getting hurt, depression, hostility, intimacy, and closeness. Self-disclosure reaches a new peak and, with it, the members' giving up of their facades.

As the members spend time together, their sense of boundaries, cohesion, and "we-ness" deepens. The term *the group* is modified to *our group,* bringing with it a feeling of belonging. Some authors have likened this stage to the individual's experience of being a member of a family. They see the group as a family-like structure. Beukenkamp (1952) describes the adulthood stage as reliving the process of the family constellation. According to Beukenkamp, through the process of transference, group members react to one another as family members. This phenomenon is reinforced when members are in groups with a male and a female leader.

Whereas in the early stages of the group someone can drop out of the group without a great deal of attention, this is no longer the case during the adulthood stage. A member who now drops out of the group leaves a void and is missed by the other members—even if the person was not well liked. Group members may feel guilt that something was said that hurt the person, that they were not sensitive to the individual's particular needs, or that they did not do enough to convince him or her to stay in the group.

Someone joining the group for the first time during the group's adulthood stage experiences feelings of being an outsider, of entering an ongoing system with its own rules, norms, expectations, and history. Northen (1969) observes that the nucleus group already has a common frame of reference, although the group's values have become so much a part of its members that the members cannot readily verbalize them. The new member must discover these values and test them out before finding a place in the group.

During a group's mature stage, its members feel greater autonomy than before and, at the same time, appear more interdependent. They take a greater share of responsibility for what is happening in the group than they have done heretofore. They become more aware of one another, and pairing and subgrouping occur on the basis of mutual interest and concerns. And the members demonstrate greater empathy with genuine understanding of each other's struggles. The members look to each other—and not just to the leader—for help.

During this stage, the group members see the worker more realistically and attribute to him or her less godlike qualities. Worker/member conflict, which may have been disturbing in the earlier stages, is dealt with in a less anxious manner. Although the leader is still an active participant in the group, the group members are equally active in challenging and supporting each other.

The stage of adulthood is marked by increased cohesiveness and a heightened sense of group identity. The worker helps group members share, disclose their thoughts and feelings, and confront and support each other. The worker encourages the members to take responsibility for planning and carrying out activities and for focusing on realistic changes they wish to make in their lives outside the group.

Groups plateau in their development (Kadis, Krasner, Weiner, Winick, & Foulkes, 1974). Generally, this occurs because a group's members are still integrating material that has been ventilated and they are not yet ready to move on to new material. The plateau may occur after a period of relatively rapid therapeutic movement. It may occur after a vacation or around holidays like Christmas and Thanksgiving. It may occur after a member has left the group or when there has been another change in the group's composition.

ADVANCED ADULTHOOD

A group may reach a stage during which its members appear emotionally disengaged from the purpose and objectives previously established for the group. Although the group still meets regularly, its members participate without much enthusiasm or vigor. Confrontation differs in quantity and quality from that which took place in the previous stage. There is a flatness and lack of vitality.

Members dutifully attend meetings, all the while complaining to family and friends that they have little interest. "If I were to drop out, everyone would be hurt and angry at me." Even the very thought of suggesting that the group terminate generates in members a sense of being unfaithful to the worker and the rest of the group. The obvious ambivalence is the result of an urge to end and a desire to continue. Sometimes, group members express both sides of their ambivalence by verbally affirming their desire to continue with the group and, at the same time, missing sessions on a regular basis.

Levine (1979) speaks of a "separation crisis" and points out that an underlying fear of abandonment may keep a member from separating from the group. The fear of being rejected or punished by the others may prevent the member from asserting himself or herself. Extremely dependent members have an especially difficult time relinquishing the group as a source of gratification. Giving up the group means having to find another source of emotional support and experiencing the threat of developing new relationships.

When members seem to be attending group meetings out of a sense of responsibility and duty rather than out of desire, one of the most helpful things the worker can do is encourage the members to share their feelings and make the difficult decision as to the future of the group. Dealing with this matter may make it possible to reconstitute the group using some of the present members as the nucleus and adding new members. Often, however, considering the options for the group may involve allowing, and perhaps helping, the group to die a natural death.

DEATH

The end of a group occurs for various reasons. Sometimes, it is planned from the very beginning, with the members knowing in advance the date of the final session. For example, a time-limited group might be scheduled to end after 25 sessions. Or, in a setting such as a school, the final meeting might be set to coincide with the last week before a major holiday or with the end of a semester.

For other groups, the ending occurs as the result of drift and happenstance. Members no longer show up for sessions, and the numbers decrease to the point that it is no longer cost-effective to keep the group going. In still other situations, the members find the group different from what they expected and make clear their decision not to return.

The end of a group may trigger a whole range of approach/avoidance reactions in its members. On one hand is their sense of pleasure that the group is finally coming to an end. No longer will members have to travel to the agency, spending time and money talking about problems. Members may also feel relief that they will not have to subject themselves to painful self-disclosure and anxiety-producing confrontation.

On the other hand, members of the group may feel discomfort associated with separation and with breaking bonds that have developed. Each client has to say good-bye to friends who, weeks or months ago, were strangers. There is the relinquishing of a time and place in which the client received reassurance and acceptance. Termination means saying goodbye to a collection of individuals who were willing to listen and to provide support even though they did not always agree with the client.

Groups facing termination often respond through denial and avoidance. Bennis and Shepard (1956) explain that some groups circumvent evaluation and termination by agreeing to meet regularly after the official sessions are over. Garland, Jones, and Kolodny (1973) point out that members of some groups "forget" the worker's telling them when the group would end, and then profess to having been tricked when the final sessions are near. Members of other groups regress or appear to slide backward as if to say "How can you leave me now when I am no better than when we began?" In some cases, members fail to attend, and thus drop out, prior to the last session.

In groups where there has been significant bonding, the grieving process may be similar to that described by Kübler-Ross in her book *On Death and Dying* (1969):

- **Denial.** "There must be some mistake."
- **Rage and anger.** "Why me?" "This isn't fair."
- **Bargaining.** "Can we have another month?"
- **Depression.** "I feel terrible having to end."
- **Acceptance.** "All good things come to an end."

The possible variety of responses to termination was evident in a group of adolescent girls in foster care who met on a weekly basis. When the members were reminded that there were two weeks left before the group ended, two of the six members said that they were glad and could not wait for the group to be over. Three of the girls, who were active participants, announced that they were not going to attend the last two sessions. For these particular three members, leaving the group before the end was a way of reducing the pain of saying good-bye.

As a group comes to an end, each client deals with separation at more than one level. Most obvious is saying good-bye and separating from the group and the other group members. Less obvious is the resurrection of memories of other good-byes where there was pain and a sense of loss.

Because the ending of a group may trigger so many different responses—including flight, denial, repression, clinging together, and anger—the worker needs to help each member examine his or her responses. The worker also needs to help the members evaluate how the group has evolved and how they have grown since its beginning. And the worker needs to encourage the members to look to the future and apply what they have learned to the other systems in their lives, those outside the group.

77

. . . .

In Summary

Groups go through a number of developmental stages that are similar to the stages in a human's life. First is conception, the point when the worker begins to plan the group. After conception is birth, the moment when the group members come together for the first time. This is followed by the stage of childhood, when the members struggle to make sense of the group and its purpose. Adolescence is the stage characterized by a lack of unity, by a testing-out behavior, and by conflict. During the adulthood stage, there is greater sharing, cohesion, and openness. The stage of advanced adulthood suggests emotional disengagement from the purpose and objectives of the group. The final stage for the group is death or termination.

How the group develops will depend on the skill and style of the leader, the purpose for the group, the characteristics of the group members, the interaction between group members, and the length of the group's life. There is no such thing as an "average group" in that no two groups develop at the same rate.

Suggested Readings

COREY, M., & COREY, G. (1987). *Groups: Process and practice* (3rd. ed.). Pacific Grove, Calif.: Brooks/Cole. See Chapters 3–7.

DOUGLAS, T. (1976). *Groupwork practice.* New York: International Universities Press. See Part 2.

GARLAND, J., JONES, H., & KOLODNY, R. (1973). A model for stages of development in social work groups. In S. Bernstein (Ed.), *Explorations in group work* (pp. 17–71). Boston: Milford House.

GLASSMAN, U., & KATES, L. (1983). Authority themes and worker-group transactions: Additional dimensions to the stages of group development. *Social work with groups, 6*(2), 33–52.

HARTFORD, M. (1971). *Groups in social work.* New York: Columbia University Press. See Chapter 3.

NORTHEN, H. (1969). *Social work with groups.* New York: Columbia University Press. See Chapters 5–8.

SARRI, R., & GALINSKY, M. (1967). A conceptual framework for group development. In R. Vinter (Ed.), *Readings in group work* (pp. 72–94). Ann Arbor, Mich.: Campus Press.

5

THE
PERSON
AS
MEMBER

*I*t strikes me that in our use of externally imposed diagnosis, classification, and categories, clinicians become arbiters of what is right and wrong, healthy and unhealthy, functional and dysfunctional.

Whether we like it or not, we are one more agent of socialization and social control who influences the individual to conform to and comply with societal norms—even when these norms may mean a splitting of the person.

Unwittingly, we encourage people to remain in an unhappy marriage, continue in a line of work that lacks satisfaction, or behave in a way that is counterfeit and unauthentic. We persuade individuals to "accept" and to "adjust" to situations that require cutting off much of what is best in them, as well as extinguishing the sense to select whatever is most honest.

Having been a social worker in a psychiatric hospital, a community mental-health clinic, and a church setting, I understand this role of helping people to fit and adjust—but I don't like it.

I much prefer the role of liberator.

In the role of liberator, we guide people toward release from the clutches of the past, from the control of dominating impulses and emotions, from the overwhelming force of social pressure, from the power of excessive guilt, and from the sleep of repression.

As liberators, we help individuals recognize the depth of feelings, become less afraid of impulses, and look within for answers. Rather than helping clients become better adjusted, we guide them toward positive forms of rebellion. After all, anger and outrage, particularly toward indignities, unfairness, and injustice, are better than acceptance, adjustment, and a lifestyle of quiet desperation.

Liberation means self-definition, with individuals defining themselves in their own terms, and then living out that knowledge, boldly or quietly in a congruent self-styled way.

There is a paradox. Instead of the client being viewed as better adjusted, he or she may be considered a misfit and judged harshly by the significant others in the client's life, as well as by those who sanction our work.

I'm told by a friend who is looking for a job that there are not many social agencies or hospitals hiring liberators these days.

• • •

The group member, a biological/psychological/social entity, brings to the group a past, a present, and a future. Each group member embodies a unique set of dynamics influenced by his or her physical characteristics, family history, values, support system, defense mechanisms, and ways of coping with the stress and strain of the environment. This chapter addresses the question, what basic information does a therapist need in order to understand the person-in-situation, so as to plan, conduct, and individualize treatment within the group?

THE PERSON-IN-SITUATION

Fundamental to clinical social work is a recognition of the dynamic interplay between intrapersonal, interpersonal, and environmental systems. The relationship between all three systems is reciprocal, and when we influence one of these systems, we have an impact on the others. Similarly, problems are seldom confined to just one system. Dysfunction in one of these systems typically contributes to dysfunction in the others.

The term *person-in-situation* pertains to the interface between the individual and the human situation in which he or she is directly involved— for example, family, a job, group, neighborhood, classroom. The person affects the situation and at the same time, is affected by the situation. Hollis and Woods (1981), using the family as an example of a "situation," observe that an individual reacts to an external pressure and that the individual's reaction in turn becomes a pressure upon some other human being, who then responds with his or her own set of perceptions and needs. The situation never involves just one person but instead involves a multiplicity of persons having varying degrees of importance in the individual's life.

In assessing the client's situation, social workers as well as other helping professions have focused over the years primarily on identifying weakness and pathology. This focus has resulted in excessive labeling, the encouragement of individualistic rather than socioenvironmental explanations of human problems, and the false illusion that there is an identifiable solution or remedy for every problem (Weick, Rapp, Sullivan & Kisthardt, 1989). This focus has also resulted in a blame-the-victim mentality, in which the patient is viewed as the cause of his or her problem.

While this individual-problem or individual-deficit orientation has certain value, it needs to be counterbalanced by equal attention to the individual's capabilities and resources. Specifically, the worker needs to examine the client's personal gifts and acquired abilities and the client's strengths of character that have been of service, are admirable, and will remain important. It is the practitioner's obligation to also recognize such resources as the person's heroism in the face of obstacles, loyalty to loved ones, ability to put feelings into words, and courage to trust other people (Weinberg, 1984). We cannot takes these for granted but, instead, should accept the fact that the client possesses them and, that they are an integral part of that person's personality.

By going to either extreme—that is by accentuating primarily strengths or weaknesses—the worker misses the individual as a complete person. According to Maslow, doing this is similar to wearing rose-colored glasses and thus never seeing the client's existing pathology, weakness, and failure to grow or to wearing brown-colored glasses and thus not seeing clearly the healthward possibilities in the client. "One is like a theology of evil and sin exclusively; the other is like a theology without any evil at all, and is therefore equally incorrect and unrealistic" (p. 48).

A balanced perspective, one that addresses both strengths and weaknesses, emphasizes not so much the kind of life the person has had but what kind of life the person wants to have. Such a perspective brings to bear all the personal and social resources available to accomplish this goal.

IN QUEST OF COPING

Group work as part of social work is a process used to help individuals cope more effectively with their problems related to social functioning. These problems may be old or new. In either case, the intended outcomes of treatment are the same—mastery, problem solving, and the reduction of tension. As part of the therapeutic alliance, the group leader helps group members intentionally undertake some new or different forms of action to resolve their problems.

Coping is a term that is used loosely in everyday speech. In a clinical sense, **coping** refers to the various efforts an individual can make to deal with environmental pressures that the person cannot handle by natural reflexes or with acquired skills—pressures that precipitate a struggle, a trial, and persistent, focused energy directed toward a goal (Murphy, 1974; White, 1974; and Mechanic, 1974). Thus, coping is a set of responses a person can have to threats and dangers, frustrations, defeats, obstacles, losses, unfamiliar situations, and new or unknown demands from other people in his or her environment.

The concept of coping is based on the premise that the client has the capacity to identify his or her problem, to understand its underpinnings, and to use both emotional support and concrete community resources to solve the problem. Rather than emphasizing the defensive functioning of the ego, coping, focuses on the adaptive human capacities. These are the capacities that enable people to bring reason to bear on their problems, to survive outrageous assaults on their dignity, to cope with toxic interpersonal experiences, and to achieve some meaning and comfort in their lives. It is not until a person is unable to cope that he or she reaches out for, or is sent to get, help (Perlman, 1975).

INABILITY TO COPE

The inability to cope has many faces. It can be acute and time-limited, such as a crisis situation. Or, it can be chronically entrenched within the client's personality. The actual reasons for the problem—for example, deficits of resources within the person's environment, such as a lack of adequate housing or limited finances—may be quite clear. Or the reasons may be less obvious. For example, the problem may be a result of the person's endowments, such as deficits, disturbances, or distortions that negatively impact the person's way of perceiving and relating to those around him or her. Or the problem may be a result of the transaction between the person and his or her psychosocial realities of daily life.

Some authors (Bloch, 1978; Glasser, 1977; Brenner, 1982) suggest that atypical behavior—no matter how bizarre, disconcerting, or puzzling—can be viewed as a positive attempt to cope. What may be considered mental illness, for example, may be a "healthy" attempt to cope under stress. Cameron (1963) writes that even delusions and hallucinations, typically thought of as indications of a severe disorder, are better viewed as "signs that a patient is actively trying to cope . . . that he is actually trying to get well" (p. 618). For the worker, the task becomes that of helping the client identify what a disturbing behavior is intended to accomplish and finding more satisfactory ways of achieving that goal.

Coping is a person's effort to deal with some new, and often problematic, situation or encounter or an effort to deal in some new way with an old problem (Perlman, 1975). It is a process in which each person is engaged from birth onward at levels of the unconscious and the preconscious, and of full consciousness. The faculties and strategies involved in the coping process are those of the ego.

PSYCHOSOCIAL FUNCTIONING

A therapist's understanding of a group member is progressive, beginning with their initial contact and continuing throughout the client's treatment. The worker listens to the client's account of his or her concerns and history, and observes and experiences the client's style of communication. Direct observation of the client's affects and emotions often discloses valuable information as to his or her functioning. Direct observation also provides clues about the client's ability to experience and express a wide range of emotions that befit the diversity of a given situation (Hepworth & Larsen, 1986). The client's apparent orientation to time, place, and person, and his or her perceptions of external events provide clues about the client's reality testing and sense of self relations. The client's feelings about his or her roles, and how they are interpreted provide clues as to the functioning of the client's personality in interaction with his or her environment. The client's goals and objectives and degree of willingness to work toward them provide hints as to his or her motivation.

One of the first steps in understanding a potential group member is identifying the issues and concerns that have brought the person to the point of seeking help. Clients facilitate this task by volunteering an explanation of why it is they want counseling. Some clients begin with complaints of interpersonal difficulties (such as "I'm unhappy in my marriage"); other clients mention one or more specific symptoms that have prompted their seeking help (such as "I can't concentrate, and I seem to be nervous most of the time"); still other clients speak of discomfort in vague terms ("I'm just not happy"). To learn more, the worker must address with the prospective group member a number of specific questions:

- How long has the problem gone on?
- Is it chronic or of recent origin?
- Why is the person seeking help now (rather that last month or two weeks ago)?
- What does the person feel he or she can do about the problem?
- What resources does the client have available to solve or reduce the problem?
- What is the client's degree of motivation?

Answers to these questions provide an indication of the person's coping resources, the complexity of his or her problem, and the person's relative sense of confidence and/or helplessness in the situation.

PRECIPITATING EVENT

In spite of the fact that an individual may have lived with a problem for a period of time, a precipitating event or experience generally serves as the catalyst that induces the individual to seek or to be referred for help. Commonly referred to as the "breaking point" or the "straw that broke the camel's back," this precipitating event serves to intensify the concern and anxiety of the individual (or friends or family members) and to bring about a noticeable need for action. It is often at this point that the individual begins to mobilize his or her resources and solicit help from other people.

The precipitating event will vary. It may be a child's admission to the pediatric unit of a hospital (Cofer & Nir 1976), a patient's beginning dialysis (McClellan, 1972), a person's being severely burned (Abramson, 1975), a woman's being recently widowed (Crosby, 1978), or a man's suffering a stroke (Oradei & Waite, 1974).

EXPECTATIONS

Another inquiry that yields significant information relates to the client's expectations of the worker, as well as of the group. Questions such as

"How do you feel I can help you?" and "What is it that you hope to get out of being in the group?" elicit clues about the client's attitude toward seeking help, as well as reveal important personality traits of the client. Possible replies might range all the way from a mature response such as "I need help in making a decision" to an excessively dependent response such as, "I was hoping you would tell me what I should do."

Inquiring about the client's feelings and expectations about the group allows the client to voice the doubts and fears he or she is experiencing. It also provides the worker an opportunity to explore in greater depth the client's ambivalence about being in the group, his or her resistance to change, and personal concerns.

THE EMERGING SELF

The term *ego* refers to the organization of a number of basic functions governing a person's perceptions and interactions. These basic functions can be inner-directed or outer-directed, and they have adaptation and coping as their purpose. The ego is viewed as the structure of the personality responsible for a person's negotiating between his or her internal needs and those of the outside world.

According to Goldstein (1984), a person is born with an innate capacity to function adaptively. Throughout life, the person engages in a biological/psychological/social developmental process in which his or her ego is an active, dynamic force for coping with, adapting to, and shaping his or her external environment. The ego mediates between the individual and his or her environment and also mediates internal conflicts among various aspects of the person's personality. The ego can elicit defenses that protect the individual from anxiety and conflict, but these defenses can serve either adaptive or maladaptive purposes.

The ego is the part of the personality that performs the basic functions essential to the individual's successful adaptation to his or her environment. These functions are innate and develop as a result of maturation and the interaction among biological/psychological/social factors influencing the person. Most salient of these factors are the person's hereditary and constitutional endowment; his or her drives; the quality of the person's interpersonal relationships, particularly in early childhood; and the impact of the person's immediate environment (including sociocultural values and mores, socioeconomic conditions, social and cultural changes, and social institutions).

Being only one part of an individual's personality, the ego must be understood in relation to the individual's internal needs and drives and to his or her internalized characteristics, expectations, and values related interactions with other people in his or her environment. It is this same environment that has shaped and continues to shape the individual's personality and provides the conditions that foster or obstruct the person's successful coping.

EGO STRENGTH

Problems in a person's social functioning need to be viewed in relation not only to possible deficits in the person's coping capacity but also in relation to the fit between the person's needs, capacities, environmental conditions, and resources.

Tilley (1984), in discussing ego strength, lists the following elements:

1. to love oneself and others, to establish stability and constancy in relationships, and to engage in give-and-take in these relationships
2. to be aware of and express feelings of love, as well as anger, when appropriate
3. to be reasonably assertive and to feel confidence in behaving assertively
4. to work consistently and to feel satisfaction in productivity and accomplishment
5. to be able to concentrate, to learn, and to persist in order to complete tasks and achieve goals
6. to enjoy recreation and play, to relax, and to enter into social situations freely
7. to adapt to different environments with flexibility and to accept situations that cannot be changed and, conversely, take action to alter unacceptable situations when options are available
8. to establish self-control and discipline without excessive rigidity
9. to make independent decisions and assume responsibility for them
10. to make judgments of reality with a minimum of distortion

SOCIOCULTURAL FACTORS

Sociocultural factors can act as barriers in the psychotherapeutic process. Of particular significance are cultural, racial, and ethnic differences. Lum (1986), writes that in assessing any minority individual, a worker needs to start with the premise that the individual is competent, adequate, and different and is not automatically deficient or maladjusted.

The worker needs to achieve a balance between objective external factors of the community and his or her subjective internal reactions. Ethnic beliefs, family solidarity, community-support networks, and other cultural assets are all intervening variables.

The minority client interacts with and reacts to his or her social environment within an ethnic context. There are unique subcultural factors, (for example, values, beliefs, attitudes, etc.) that serve as intervening variables. The minority client draws upon familiar ethnic coping mechanisms when under stress. The worker needs to differentiate between external factors and subjective internal reactions of the client. Is the person's reaction typical of others in the community? To what degree is the problem a result of socioeconomic stress? What is the availability and accessibility of resources and supports?

For the ethnic-sensitive worker, a key element in understanding and evaluating clients from diverse cultural groups is their use of language. The worker has to be cognizant of each client's culture and to integrate this knowledge into his or her professional assessment of the client. Of special importance are the client's beliefs, affective expressions, and relationships with other people. The client's use of language opens a window onto the reality that is known and experienced by that client.

According to Green (1982), a worker needs to know in what way a client defines and understands an experience to be a problem. To determine this and to help the client solve the problem, the worker can rely on the client's use of language to label the problem; the availability and use of indigenous community resources; and the client's cultural criteria for determining when the problem no longer exists.

PROBLEMS IN LIVING

In evaluating a potential group member, a central question becomes this: What must the person do to improve his or her social functioning in a given situation? Or, put another way, what must the person do to cope more effectively within the world?

According to Gitterman and Shulman (1986), people are changed by their physical and social environments and in turn change their environments through the process of continuous reciprocal adaptation. In these complex interchanges, disturbances often emerge in the adaptive balance between an individual's needs and capacities and certain qualities of the individual's environment. These disturbances have the potential of disrupting the individual's customary coping mechanisms and of creating stress for him or her.

A client's problems arise in three interrelated facets of living. First are problems and needs associated with the client's life transitions, such as beginning school, getting married, getting a divorce, retiring, and dying. Second are problems and needs associated with the client's tasks of using and influencing elements of his or her social and physical environment such as schools, hospitals, social-service organizations, and communities. Third are problems and needs associated with overcoming any obstacles in the client's interpersonal relations that can generate maladaptive family and group tensions.

In assessing the individual, a number of specific factors need to be examined. These include the individual's adaptation to reality; judgment; control of drives, affects, and impulses; object relations; thought processes; ego defenses; adaptive mechanisms; frustration tolerance; and mastery and competence.

ADAPTATION TO REALITY

Coping effectively with the daily requirements of life requires an individual to achieve a fit between his or her perceptions of his or her internal and external worlds and the objective reality of those worlds. To determine whether an individual has achieved this fit, a worker must find the answers to these questions: How does the person perceive and negotiate with his or her environment? How does the person differentiate between ideas and perceptions? Does the person use feedback from other people appropriately to adjust his or her perceptions of reality? There needs to be congruence between the person's perception, evaluation, and judgment, on the one hand, and his or her life situation, on the other.

The basic skills a person needs for appraising reality are developed within the person's primary group, his or her family. As individuals travel through the life cycle, they are exposed to an ever-expanding array of experiences. How open or closed the person will be to these new situations is determined by the accommodating process cultivated wihtin his or her family (Mackey, 1985). If, as a child, the person internalized the outside world as a dangerous place, that perception will influence his or her readiness to risk involvement in secondary groups. Being able to perceive the objective world as a reasonably safe place facilitates a person's involvement in new social situations. A positive by-product of this involvement is expanded opportunities for the person to learn about the unfamiliar world beyond the safe frontiers of his or her primary group.

PERCEIVING STIMULI AND TESTING REALITY

There is a difference between the ability to perceive stimuli and the capacity to test reality. This is illustrated by a comparison of two group members. Carla, a 21-year-old divorced woman, is extremely sensitive to slights from friends and acquaintances. In her group, she frequently reports feeling emotionally bruised, particularly when other members confront her or become frustrated with her. In spite of her discomfort, she is able to identify her "hurt" response as being a life-long pattern and as being her problem rather than that of the person who has injured her. "Even when I know what they say is right, I want to cry. I've been like this since I was a little girl. It's automatic," she told the group.

Edna, an aggressive and verbose 48-year-old mother of two, is frequently in conflict with other members of her group. She is quick to judge them, using words such as *dumb, stupid,* and *jerk.* When other group members challenge her behavior, she overreacts in a defensive manner saying they misinterpreted her and are insensitive to her particular needs. She is unable to recognize the cause-and-effect relationship between her actions and the reactions of other group members. When Edna is challenged in the group, there is a strong likelihood that she will not attend the next following session.

For Carla, feeling discounted or being confronted is painful; however, at the same time, she is able to understand that her reactions have a lot to do with her personal background and extreme sensitivity and little to do with the intentions of the other members. On the other hand, Edna's walls prevent her from receiving fresh data and input from others. Her subjective world is so brittle that admitting she is in error is highly threatening. Her response is to defend rather than to listen to what is being communicated. This further limits her ability to accurately interpret reality.

An extreme manifestation of the inability to test reality and to adapt to it are seen in delusions—false beliefs that are adhered to but cannot be validated—and hallucinations—unfounded and mistaken perceptions or impressions that are adhered to but cannot be validated. Individuals with auditory hallucinations, for example, describe hearing voices that are very real to them even though other people may know that no voices exist outside the person's own mind. Reality for these individuals is limited to interior processes that are impaired and inaccurate. Their reality testing is inaccurate primarily because of the lack of fit between their subjective experiences and the objective facts.

PASSIVE DEPENDENCY

Some group members will present themselves as being helpless and powerless to effect any change in their lives, inside as well as outside the group. They communicate the inability to do the very things they must do to better their situation. A worker who falls into this trap deprives these group members of the right, as well as the opportunity, to take responsibility for themselves. The worker also prevents them from having the chance to develop the ability to manage their own affairs and deal with reality.

JUDGMENT

An individual's judgment is assessed on the basis of how the member handles everyday living and acts upon the outside world. Does the person have the capacity to take care of himself or herself? Is the person able to weigh the consequences of his or her actions? Are there some areas in the person's life where he or she makes good decisions and other areas where he or she makes poor decisions? In short, given choices, can the person make decisions that are life-giving rather than self-defeating?

The discriminating function of judgment is an important aspect of all thinking and involves the ability to anticipate the consequences of an action and, at the same time, to determine the appropriateness of the action. For example, a mother angry at her daughter for "sassing" her could conceivably go through the following imaginary internal dialogue:

> I'm so angry at my daughter for talking back that I could kill her. If I hit her with this stick, she'll stop being so nasty (and I'll feel better). But, what if I seriously injure her? Even though I'm angry at her, I love her and really don't want to hurt her. Not only that, if I did hurt her, I could be sent to jail. Maybe I should turn around and leave the room.

ANTICIPATING OUTCOMES

90

• • • • • • • •

Using good judgment implies anticipating sequences of events and acting in a way that is appropriate. This requires the ability to delay the initial impulse to make a decision in order to gain the time needed to scan various possible responses and to select an appropriate action. This means being able to weigh a number of choices, recognizing that for each there will be advantages and disadvantages.

According to Redl and Wineman (1957), some emotionally disturbed children ignore the cause-and-effect nature of their actions by lulling themselves into intensive delusions of the inviolability in dangerous situations. Others go even further and contend "I never can be caught."

> Not only are they [the second group] unaware of consequences . . . they go a step further than that: they make it an issue to believe that the laws of nature and social retribution have no effect on them. They run around like people with a magical charm around their neck and, as with those [the first group], actual evidence has no chance to sink in [p. 164].

As a means of protecting the reality of delinquent fun, these individuals resign themselves to accepting clearly mystical illusions as a basis for their lives.

CONTROL OF DRIVES, AFFECTS, AND IMPULSES

Closely linked with judgment is the ability to regulate, delay, modify, and express impulses and feelings. To evaluate a client's ability to exert this kind of self-control, a therapist can seek answers to these questions: Does the client overreact emotionally to ordinary events? Is his or her impulsive behavior antisocial or dangerous to the client or to other people? Can the client tolerate frustration or disappointment? Does his or her guilt reach a level where it is debilitating?

Ideally, a person is able to control his or her drives, affects, and impulses. He or she can tolerate unpleasant feelings such as anger, frustration, and anxiety without acting on them or becoming overwhelmed. The person may be angry and frustrated but has a reliable delay mechanism that allows him or her to tolerate the feelings.

It is important for a therapist to understand the relative strength of impulses, prohibitions, and stressors when evaluating an individual (Goldstein, 1984). While the maintenance, regulation, and control of impulses and affects are performed by person's ego, these functions are influenced by the amount and intensity of the impulses (the *id*) and the unpleasant emotions within the person. These functions are also influenced by the person's internalized constraints against expressing of his or her impulses (the *super ego*) and by the impact of frustrating, dangerous, or unpleasant circumstances in the person's life (*reality*).

Impulses and drives. Within the average person are ongoing internal civil wars around a multitude of issues. For example, a well-functioning 50-year-old housewife with three children, who is in love with a single man, decides to leave her abusive husband. In her thinking, her lover is more attuned to her needs and more sensitive to her feelings. The more she is with him, the more frustrated she becomes with her husband.

91
• • • • • • •

She contemplates taking an apartment and contacting a divorce attorney. But, increasingly, she feels excruciating guilt that she is not living up to her marriage vows. She worries how the children will react to a divorce and wonders how her lover will respond to her children. She struggles with how she will support herself and is fearful that the problems she is having in her present marriage will be repeated in a second marriage. She becomes depressed and has trouble sleeping. She overeats and gains 20 pounds. She finds herself less responsive to the needs of her children and becomes angry without provocation.

Given the circumstances, this patient's behavior is not indicative of someone suffering from a lack of impulse or drive control. In spite of her desire to flee the marriage, other powerful factors inside her are serving to counterbalance that desire.

On the other hand, there are individuals who cannot tolerate frustration and who chronically deal with their anxiety by assuming a flight response—for example, by drinking, using mind-altering drugs, or running away. A voice within such an individual screams out, "I want what I want when I want it, and to hell with the consequences!" A person like this has little tolerance for frustration and little ability to delay immediate gratification. Such a person has difficulty planning and finds it hard to stick with a situation—for example, a relationship, a job, or therapy—long enough to gain from it.

Internal critic. Often, when a group member shares personal experiences and feelings, his or her speech patterns are peppered with expressions such as "I ought to," "I should," and "I shouldn't." This happens because each person carries within, to some degree, an internal critic and censor. Referred to as the **super ego,** or **conscience,** this critic and censor consists of all the *thou shalls* and *thou shalt nots* the person has learned throughout life. The super ego is the composite of parental prohibitions, ideals, social standards, and values the person has derived from his or her environment through role models such as parents, special teachers, and selected peers. For many people, religious training and involvement in organizations such as the Boy Scouts or Girl Scouts or other youth groups were also particularly important in laying the foundation of their concepts of right and wrong.

Fundamental to a person's super ego is guilt. If a person does something that is contrary to his or her internalized *do's* and *don'ts,* the person feels discomfort. The practice of confession in certain religious faiths is one way of relieving this guilt and perhaps strengthening the conscience. Some people

92
• • • • • • •

derive similar benefits from talking to a counselor, confiding to a friend, or from "thinking it through."

A person's super ego has the potential of being punitive and destructive to that person or to other people. Some individuals suffer excessive guilt for their actions, thoughts, and feelings. Rather than a lack of regulation, they experience an overregulation that limits their activities and restricts their expression of affect. Their guilt becomes an overriding shadow they live with daily. It affects everything they do.

For practitioners, it is important to differentiate among the three forms of guilt—moral, pseudo, and existential—that their clients may experience.

Moral guilt.   Moral guilt refers to a violation of some moral, ethical, or contractual standard that a person holds either implicitly or explicitly. This is the kind of guilt that Walter, a 40-year-old certified public accountant and the treasurer of his church who admitted to embezzling several thousand dollars from his employer, was feeling. Unable to sleep or concentrate, Walter felt painful guilt for stealing the money. Long before he was apprehended, he knew that for his own peace of mind he would have to repay the money. And the other members in Walter's group, decided to focus on helping Walter determine what he was going to do. Walter's guilt, which had served as a catalyst, diminished as Walter admitted his actions and began to pay back the money.

Pseudo guilt.   Sometimes the quantity of guilt a person feels is inappropriate to the situation. For example, a person may experience excruciating guilt for a particular feeling—such as anger at a parent or happiness that a person has died—for a particular fantasy—such as killing a spouse or committing a sexual assault—or for a particular action—such as masturbation or shoplifting a toy. Although this guilt is very real to the person, it is excessive in proportion to the person's feeling, fantasy, or action.

An extreme example of pseudo or false guilt is seen in individuals who admit to having committed a crime, such as a murder, even when they have had no personal involvement. They are unable to separate their impulse to commit a comparable act from the actual event.

In comparing moral guilt and pseudo guilt, moral guilt is in proportion to the event and can be assuaged by realistic restitution or atonement. Pseudo guilt lacks proportion to the event and cannot be easily undone.

Existential guilt.   Existential guilt is the discomfort felt by a person who sells out on himself. He says *yes* when he means *no,* smiles when he is really angry, and is accepting when he is feeling outrage. Kavanaugh (1985) writes:

> We can try to talk them [feelings] away, drink or smoke them away, laugh or shout them away, or more often retreat from them through denial, but they will wait patiently to cripple us physically or emotionally as long as we reject our very identity as a person [p. 11].

If a person's self-image prevents him or her the luxury of experiencing such feelings as anger or hate, it will be these very feelings that destroy him or her.

Sometimes, the first step in helping someone is to assist the person to admit that his or her feelings—for example, guilt, outrage, anger—exist. The individual's psychic fire doors may have slammed so tightly shut that admitting the unacceptable is seemingly impossible. According to Greenspan (1983), this is especially true of women who deny their anger and, instead, turn it against themselves. Being able to talk about such feelings or expressing them toward the practitioner is often a client's first step in coming to grips with these feelings.

OBJECT RELATIONS

Object relations refers to an individual's capacity to form satisfying, mature, and permanent relationships and, at the same time, to maintain an internal sense of self. To determine whether a client has this capacity, a therapist must discover the answers to these questions: Can the individual develop meaningful friendships with other people and keep boundaries intact? Can the individual be close to another person without becoming so enmeshed with him or her that it is difficult to determine where one person begins and the other ends? Likewise, can the individual maintain space between himself or herself and other people without becoming disengaged to the point of emotional unavailability?

The quality of a person's object relations is most apparent by its absence. A person without this capacity has difficulty appreciating the feelings of other people or is unable to see the way he or she provokes and hurts them. Such an individual may have difficulty in being empathetic and in understanding another person's pain. He or she may experience only superficial closeness, not genuine caring or commitment.

Wilma, a 45-year-old graduate student, initially expressed pleasure at being in a self-actualization group. However, as the other group members began to speak of their pain, to express emotions, and to confront each other, she became frustrated. "Why can't we just be nice and supportive of each other," she pleaded. On several occasions when she was challenged by other group members, she withdrew to the bathroom. When other members disclosed painful events from their past, she was superficially sympathetic, which served as an irritant to the rest of the group. Her revelations about herself were descriptive but lacked depth.

Clients such as Wilma are very unlikely to be able to put to good use any treatment that requires much self-examination. They may engage in introspection, but it is likely to be a narcissistic or self-pitying type of introspection (Hollis & Woods, 1981). They often can be reached only to the extent that they believe that the group is safe, the worker is supportive, and they will be accepted as they are.

93
....

The worker can assist clients like Wilma by pointing out to them their self-defeating behaviors—for example, responding with pat statements, telling other members how to be or feel, or reacting judgmentally and critically.

THOUGHT PROCESSES

The ability to think logically and to communicate thoughts verbally is an important aspect of the fully integrated individual. To determine whether a client has this capacity, a therapist must find answers to these questions: To what degree does the client allow intrusions of magical or primary process thoughts? Can the individual focus on a subject and exclude distracting ideas or stimuli? Does the person have the ability to arrive at solutions to problems logically? How does the person handle symbolization and abstract concepts?

For the normal infant, primary process thinking, powered by the pleasure principle, dominates. Biologically as well as psychologically, the child seeks immediate instinctual gratification no matter what the consequences, as illustrated in the theme "I want what I want when I want it." Primary process thinking is further characterized by:

- wish-fulfilling fantasies
- disregard of logical connections between ideas
- no conception of time
- contradictory ideas existing side by side
- wishes represented as actual fulfillment
- self-centeredness

As an individual matures, his or her thinking becomes less of a primary process and more of a secondary process. Reality takes on greater significance, and the individual becomes better able to postpone instinctual gratification until a more appropriate time or place. Less reactive and more reflective, the more mature individual is more sensitive to the impact he or she has on other people as well as their impact on him or her. Increasingly more goal-oriented, the person is better able than before to solve problems in a meaningful manner. His or her "observing self" develops, making it possible to stand outside himself or herself and view the conflicts and struggles taking place within.

Developing a mature thought process is essential for a person's optimal adaptation and coping (Goldstein, 1984). The person who is controlled by his or her inner preoccupations without reference to reality cannot relate to the world outside. The person who cannot organize his or her thoughts in a logical, coherent way cannot communicate with other people. The person who is unable to use symbols agreed-upon by society cannot speak coherently or reason. The person who, when under stress, is unable to concentrate, remember, and anticipate will have difficulty solving problems. The person whose affects or emotions are disconnected from his or her thoughts and behaviors or whose impulses and feelings are expressed in a confused, unintelligible way cannot communicate to other people what he or she truly thinks and feels.

Other useful questions for a therapist to explore with a client are: Is any impairment in the client's thinking chronic or acute? How sophisticated is the client's ability to solve problems? Does the client have insight into his or her actions? Is there any carryover in the client's mind from one situation to another? Can the client postpone gratification?

EGO DEFENSES

Defense mechanisms are devices a person's ego uses to ward off anxiety aroused by the person's reaction to actual situations. It is important for a therapist to know what defenses a client uses and how much the client uses them to avoid responsibility. To find out, the therapist must seek answers to these questions: To what degree does the person deny external reality? In what ways are the person's perceptions of reality distorted by his or her defenses? Does the person attribute his or her own behavior or feelings to someone else? How much are the person's thoughts and feelings pushed out of, or repressed from, his or her conscious mind?

As it develops, an individual's ego is continually struggling with pressures exerted from within—that is, the person's drives and superego— and pressures exerted from without—the demands of the person's environment. To maintain a balance and protect the individual's emotional integrity, his or her ego employs a number of defense mechanisms. These defenses are a normal and necessary aspect of ego functioning. However, they become dysfunctional when they become so rigid or restricting that they cripple the person's freedom of expression.

According to Vaillant (1977), defense mechanisms can be divided into three categories: psychotic, immature, and neurotic.

Psychotic defenses. Psychotic mechanisms are used by severely regressed or fixated individuals who suffer from severe impairment of their reality-testing ability and thus lack the capacity to separate what is real from what is wished for, feared, or imagined. The same mechanisms are used by everyone during the ordinary process of dreaming, when the ego relaxes its guard over the unconscious. Psychotic defenses include denial of external reality, distortion of external reality, and delusional projection.

Immature defenses. Common in children and adolescents, immature defenses include fantasy, acting out, hypochondriasis (delusions that one has a physical disease), and passive/aggressive behavior. Similar to other defenses, immature defenses provide a means of defending against an uncomfortable thought, feeling, or urge.

Neurotic defenses.   Neurotic defenses are everyday mechanisms for dealing with stress by unconsciously avoiding responsibility for specific impulses and desires. Neurotic defenses include repression, intellectualization, isolation displacement, reaction formation, and dissociation.

ADAPTIVE MECHANISMS

Adaptive or coping mechanisms are dispositions or traits that influence the manner in which a person organizes and responds to his or her experience. To discover what coping mechanisms a client uses, a therapist must seek answers to questions like these: Is the person able to suffer short-term discomfort for a long-term gain? Is the person able to postpone gratification? Does the person have a sense of meaning in his or her life? Does the person have a sense of basic trust? Does the person have a sense of hope that something good will occur as the result of his or her actions?

Adaptive mechanisms differ from defensive mechanisms in two ways. First, an individual's preferences for defense mechanism's are determined primarily by his or her experiences in anxiety-provoking situations. Adaptive mechanisms, on the other hand, are influenced not only by the individual's experiences but also by aspects of his or her temperament that are constitutionally determined (Weiner, 1975).

Second, defense mechanisms are protective measures activated to ward off or bind anxiety that would otherwise be incapacitating. Coping styles constitute modes of dealing with experiences of all kinds. While they may at times be defensive or even maladaptive, they also include constructive and self-fulfilling ways of behaving and meeting various challenges.

Because coping styles consist of certain ways of organizing and responding to experience to the exclusion of other ways, a person's coping styles can narrow his or her behavioral repertoire sufficiently to produce resistance to treatment (Weiner, 1975). For example, some people are by nature relatively active in their approach to life, while others tend to be passive. A relatively active group member is likely to expect constant interchange, dynamic insights, and rapid changes within a group. The idea of sober reflection and a gradually expanding self-awareness may be difficult for him or her to tolerate.

A more passive group member frequently looks to the treatment process as something that occurs primarily through the actions of the worker. Whereas a relatively active group member may complain that not enough is happening fast enough, a more passive group member may grumble about the lack of direction he or she is receiving from the leader and proclaim how much more fulfilling the group would be if only it had more structure.

The most basic adaptive mechanism is deciding on a course of action, using free will to implement the action, and assuming responsibility for the decision by facing the consequences of the action taken (Weiner, 1986). Other adaptive mechanisms include stimulus seeking, mastery, sublimation, suppression, altruism, anticipation, and humor.

FRUSTRATION TOLERANCE

Clients vary as to their frustration threshold. As therapists, we must discover each client's tolerance for frustration. We can do this by seeking answers to questions like these: How does the client respond to various types of frustration? When something interferes with the client's pleasure-seeking wishes, how does he or she react? Does the client become angry, throw a tantrum, or give up? Does the client act out, take drugs, or get into difficulty with people in positions of authority?

Some individuals have an extraordinarily low frustration threshold. When exposed to a situation that confounds them, they are unable to contain their anxiety and instead give in to total indulgence of the full set of impulses waiting to be released. In short, the ego in such an individual does not do its job and becomes helpless in dealing with the onrush of intense impulses.

MASTERY AND COMPETENCE

The terms *competence* and *mastery* refer to a person's capacity and ability to interact successfully with his or her environment. A therapist must try to identify signs of competence and mastery in a client by considering questions like these: Can the client hold a permanent job or attend school? Does the client appear to have a sense of power to influence various aspects of his or her life. Is the client resilient to the normal stresses of daily life? Does the client experience a sense of pride in his or her accomplishments?

To attain a goal, a person must rely on a combination of his or her cognitive skills, intentional actions, and motor skills. In her studies of children's coping, Murphy (1962) concludes that **I do** is the precondition to the sense that **I am.** And, she says, this observation applies not only to children but also to adults who accomplish something they have been grappling with—for example, putting together a puzzle, building a piece of furniture, learning to play an instrument. If the doer judges the results to be "good," his or her thoughts and feelings about himself or herself as a doer are enhanced. If other people also express appreciation or in some way applaud his or her action, the doer is reinforced even further.

The implications for group members are significant. When the members of a group, as well as the group-as-a-whole, cope with problems in a direct and proactive manner, they assume an expanded sense of control. By taking action, they prove to themselves their potential to move from a sense of hopelessness and powerlessness to one of hope and powerfulness. As Mary Jane wrote in her evaluation of a group session:

> Today's group was helpful, I risked. . . . As an adult I continue to realize in relationships I must risk and be vulnerable. I learned I'm not the only one who struggles with the issue of intimacy . . . Most important I realize how much I want to continue to explore risk-taking in and out of the group.

In short, a person's feelings and thoughts affect his or her actions, and, conversely, a person's actions affect his or her feelings and thoughts.

MOTIVATION TO CHANGE

A practitioner must consider an individual's motivation, readiness, and capacity to use help before deciding what treatment plan or other services to recommend for the individual. To determine the person's readiness for help, the therapist must seek answers to questions like these: What is the nature of the person's motivation to change? Is the person's desire to change internal or external? Are the person's wants realistic and achievable? If challenged, will the person run away from or stick with the situation?

In addition to the capacity to perform a given action a client must show some signs of having tension that needs release and some signs of having motivation to reach an objective of importance to him or her. The tension and motivation can be expressed in different forms, such as anxiety, dissatisfaction with life, guilt, or even a hopeless dream or fanciful ambition. But the individual must show **some** signs of motivation, or the therapist will face a special challenge in trying to help the person.

In general, the more acutely distressed a person is with his or her life situation and the more the person would like things to be different from how they are now, the more willing he or she will be to bear the burden of being in treatment. Thus, the more a person wants to change and the more unhappy ther person is with his or her current life situation, the more inclined the person will be to attend sessions regularly, to talk about himself or herself, to consider interpretations that challenge previous views, and to persevere in the treatment process.

INVOLUNTARY CLIENTS

If a client comes to an agency or a group under duress from a parent, physician, judge, or principal or has made the appointment because someone else told them him or her to seek help, the client's motivation may be limited. This, however, does not preclude an individual's success in the group. Weiner (1975) writes that a self-referred, psychologically oriented patient may come with little appreciation for the effort and commitment psychotherapy will require and may quickly demur once he or she becomes accurately informed. Conversely, an involuntary, nonpsychologically oriented patient who needs treatment badly may become highly interested in treatment once he or she senses its potential for healing.

When group members are required to attend group treatment, they should be encouraged to ventilate their feelings about this requirement. For example, involuntary members may not trust the leader, expecting that what is disclosed will be reported to someone else or used against them. They may think that group treatment is a form of indoctrination. They may be concerned about other's gossiping. It is not unusual for an involuntary member to express his or her vehemence and frustration for having to attend the group, then participate actively within the group. Although a therapist in an institutional setting may not have the option of allowing members to drop out of a group, the therapist **is** in a position to help group members examine their fears and resistances. Members can be encouraged to talk about their feelings of anger and frustration and lack of control over their lives. They can also be given freedom to decide how to use their group time.

If a client appears hesitant and unsure about just what membership in a group may entail, it is common practice for the worker to see the client several times alone to discuss the client's reluctance rather than to ask for an immediate decision. When a worker puts heavy pressure on a prospective group member to join a group, the client may have a passive/aggressive reaction. For example, the client may agree to attend but not show up. The worker may find it more valuable to suggest that the client visit the group several times on a trial basis before making a commitment.

IN SUMMARY

This chapter focuses on the therapist's evaluation of the individual client's relative strength and coping capacity. The practitioner's assessment takes into account the client's adjustment to his or her environment. This assessment helps the worker appraise the quality of the client's relationships and the client's total emotional functioning.

In evaluating a potential group member, the therapist considers a number of areas: How does the person adapt to reality? How does the individual negotiate between his or her internal needs and the demands of the external environment in which he or she lives? How well does the person control his or her internal drives, affects, and impulses? Can the person form satisfying, mature, and permanent relationships with others? How firm is the person's sense of identity? How does the person respond to frustration or to interference with his or her pleasure-seeking wishes? The worker also needs to be clear as to the prospective group member's motivation and capacity to benefit from group work.

The role of the group worker is more than that of helping people adjust, but instead to free them from their past, from social pressures, from self-defeating behaviors, and from factors within the environment that prevent them from coping as fully functioning human beings.

SUGGESTED READINGS

COELHO, G., HAMBURG, D., & ADAMS, J. (1974). *Coping and adaptation*. New York: Basic Books.
PERLMAN, H. (1975). In quest of coping. *Social casework, 56*(4), pp. 213–225.
POLANSKY, N. (1982). *Integrated ego psychology*. New York: Aldine de Gruyter.
WEINER, M. (1986). *Practical psychotherapy*. New York: Brunner/Mazel. See pp. 35–41.

6

WORKER
IN
THE
GROUP

*T*ransference has always been a bit of a mystery to me. While it made sense intellectually, it was elusive when I applied the concept to my own life. This was up until the year my son David's teacher requested that his mother or I come in for a conference.

When I recall my own six years in elementary school, I have to admit they were some of the worst years in my life. So, in an attempt to be a good parent and help David, I went in to see his teacher.

Walking into the building was like returning to the hallowed halls of Longfellow Elementary. The lockers, pictures of Washington and Lincoln, and even the pungent cabbage odor from the cafeteria seemed the same.

The teacher—a tall, angular woman in her mid-50s—welcomed me into the room with a greeting reserved for children returning in September and for nervous parents. "Oh, Mr. Reid, I'm so glad you could come," she gushed. There was the sweet scent of flowery perfume, the kind that every teacher must receive by the quart at Christmas.

The wooden chair offered me was an exact miniature of the one she was sitting in. My 6-foot, 200-pound frame seemed to shrink as I sat, chin on knees, looking up into her eyes. The furniture began to look different.

David's teacher appeared concerned and disappointed. "David is not working up to his potential," she said," and "I'm worried about him."

My head began to swim. Other than these words, I can't remember anything else she said. Nor can I remember what I said. Probably I nodded a lot, affirming her concerns. I do recall feeling riveted to the seat, unable to move.

Here I was, a 35-year-old college professor with a Ph.D., regressing to a naughty little 6-year-old who was being a disappointment—again.

What seemed like hours ended abruptly with David's teacher saying, "I hope together we can help David. He is such a nice boy." With that, I struggled to my feet, mumbled something inane, shook her hand, and stumbled out the door, growing inches with each step. Once I sat down in my car, my mind and body returned to normal.

In a peculiar, irrational way, for 10 or 15 minutes, I was hooked to this woman. She was not just David's teacher, but a collection of friendly and not-so-friendly teachers out of my past, and I was sitting there projecting unresolved feelings onto her. It wasn't rational or logical, but it was very real.

It's hard to do psychotherapy and not believe in ghosts.

• • •

In this chapter, we begin to deal with the personhood of the worker and to examine the reciprocity between a group's leader and a group's members. Not only do we, as workers, influence the members of our groups, but we are also influenced by them. Two questions the chapter addresses are: First, how does a worker remain objective and, at the same time, enter into the often-confused world of another human being? And, second, how does the worker prevent his or her humanness from distracting the group's therapeutic purpose?

THE EFFECTIVE GROUP WORKER—AN IDEAL

Is there a generalized ideal of what the clinical social worker in a group should be like? The answer is probably *yes,* but it is difficult to agree on what that ideal is and more difficult to find workers who meet the criteria. As with any ideal, this one is something sought after but seldom achieved. Perhaps it is more valuable to think in terms of **essential professional and personal characteristics** rather than some standard of perfection.

There are seven characteristics that are found to a significant degree among effective social workers leading groups. These characteristics are courage, honesty, creativity, self-knowledge, empathy, an action orientation, and enthusiasm.

Courage. Effective practitioners have the capacity to act on their convictions and remain unswerved by immediate events. They are willing to take risks and, when appropriate, go "toe-to-toe" with group members, knowing that they will encounter opposition and anger from the members. They are willing to tell group members what the members do not want to hear. They are willing to become involved in difficult, emotional-charged situations that go beyond their own comfort zone. They are willing to confront individual group members and the group-as-a-whole about game playing, smoke screens, masks, and defenses. They are able to love and, at the same time, set limits.

Honesty. Effective therapists are truthful and respond to group members with honest feedback. They are willing to say what they think and feel, provided it is in the clients' best interests. They demonstrate a readiness to discuss everything introduced in the group. They convey who they really are, not appearing to be more or less than what they really are. They are concrete in their expressions, talking in terms of actual feelings and tangible behaviors instead of vague formulations, unclear generalizations, or obscure psychodynamics. They are willing to admit when they are wrong and not retreat into a defensive posture when they are challenged.

Creativity.   Effective leaders of groups can hold on to basic principles with tenacity but, if necessary, can modify their tactics without changing their goals. These social workers are not afraid to share themselves and their experiences if this will advance the helping process. They are able to laugh at themselves and with others. They are willing to try novel responses to old situations. These workers are spontaneous but not impulsive. They are inventive and not trapped in ritualized techniques or activities.

Empathy.   Effective practitioners respond from the client's frame of reference, because they are able to see the world through the member's eyes. They are able to experience the individual's emotions as if those feelings were their own and communicate this understanding accurately to the person, all the while remaining firmly rooted in reality. They do not judge other people but instead share in the pain, anger, and joy others feel. They give fully of themselves.

Self-knowledge.   Effective workers are neither paragons of virtue nor paragons of mental health. They are willing to look at themselves, openly acknowledging their strengths and weaknesses. They see themselves as living, growing, and struggling people who—like the client—are in the process of becoming. They view themselves as likable, desirable, and acceptable people who have dignity and integrity. They are unafraid of life, living their own lives with passion and zeal.

Action orientation.   Effective leaders of groups understand that insight and intellectual understanding are but a step in the change process. They encourage group members to set goals for themselves and work toward achieving those goals. They recognize that the true test of a group's success is the constructive changes in each member's life outside the group.

Enthusiasm.   Effective group workers bring enthusiasm to each group meeting—enthusiasm about the group's activities, the group's members, and the value of the group process. They believe in what they do and how they do it, which is reflected in their verbal and nonverbal behavior. This is not to suggest that group leaders need to be "cheerleaders." Rather, they must have faith in the process and communicate this clearly to group members.

     The ideal clinician, or in Shakespeare's words "the observed of all observers," blends the warmth of Carl Rogers, the tenacity of Fritz Perls, the logic of Albert Ellis, the social commitment of Jane Addams, and the values of Grace Coyle. Similar to the client, the worker is seeking wholeness and integration within his or her own life. The worker is willing to live the way he or she encourages group members to live. And the worker is committed to the never-ending goal of becoming a more fully functioning human being.

NONRATIONAL DYNAMICS OF TREATMENT

There are many misconceptions about group treatment. According to some people, group treatment consists of a helping professional plus a collection of troubled individuals who come together to receive advice regarding their problems. Because of a personal or family difficulty, each member needs assistance in managing his or her life. The process of change occurs when the group members share their problems and the worker, because of his or her infinite knowledge and wisdom, finds solutions and offers recommendations.

Healing, according to this belief, occurs once the member bares his or her soul and uncovers the root of the problem. And the relationship between the clients and the therapist is thought of as one-dimensional, with the social worker giving and the group members receiving.

The helping relationship—whether individual, family, or group—is not so simple or rational. In addition to its cognitive dimension, represented by memory, reasoning, judgment, and perception, the helping relationship involves significant noncognitive elements. And among these noncognitive elements are feelings, attitudes, and inherent patterns of behavior that are not really called for by the therapeutic situation. Such noncognitive elements are nonrational to the extent that they involve unconscious reactions and are inappropriate to what is occurring at the moment.

Second, and more important, the helping relationship is not one-dimensional, with a giver and receiver(s). Instead, it is reciprocal in nature, with all participants having an impact on each other. The professional participant—the therapist—influences and is influenced. Certainly, nothing is wrong with this as long as the professional remembers that the client's needs are paramount and are the focus of the therapeutic relationship. In essence, the professional relationship is for the client.

THE WOUNDED HEALER

As a social worker and group members join together to form a therapeutic alliance, each person brings into that situation his or her total life experiences. Each carries personal baggage such as values, prejudices, weaknesses, blind spots, and strengths. Each brings to the experience a history of relating to others, sometimes with success and at other times without. In this therapeutic alliance, group members may react to the therapist as if he or she were a significant figure out of their own original family. Similarly, the leader may react in exactly the same way, projecting onto the members his or her own unresolved feelings and conflicts.

It has been said that professional helpers are just like the clients they work with, but more so. We, too, have the need for social companionship, recognition, prestige, and security. We, too, have the need to be liked. We, too, are fearful and scared of the unknown. It is this very humanness that gives us the ability to enter the client's life, comprehend his or her pain, and assist in the client's growth process. Similarly, it is this same humanness that can lead us into a destructive relationship with the very individuals we are committed to help.

One of the "payoffs" of being a professional altruist, either employed by an organization or working privately, is the feeling of being needed. In addition, the practitioner may have been lured knowingly or unknowingly by the position of authority, by the dependence of others, by the image of benevolence, by the promise of adulation, or by a hope of vicariously helping himself or herself through helping others (Maeder, 1989).

Certainly, no worker likes to admit to any of these as a reason for his or her being in social work, but such motivations are a reality. In the role of helper, we are in the position of receiving symbolic gratification of our own needs through identification with the client or the patient to whom we are giving help. Fortunately, over time, a therapist can strike a fairly stable balance between giving care to others and receiving care (McCarley, 1975).

This theme of self-care and caring for others becomes indissolubly merged into the worker's professional attitude. Towle (1954) makes the following observation:

> To what extent . . . social workers have been misunderstood children who, out of their persistent need for understanding, now strive to understand others, is not known. To what extent they have been lonely individuals, who in this work vicariously seek intimate relationships, is not known. Nor is it known to what degree . . . social workers have been hurt children who, out of their persistent need for pity, now are sensitive rather than susceptible to the suffering of others [p. 80].

These feelings and motives, according to Towle, have the potential of allowing the social worker to be sensitive and aware of a client's deeper needs. At the same time, this precarious balance may be upset, with the worker **using** the client and the agency situation to an extent that is damaging and nontherapeutic.

An example of this type of using is manifested by a worker who puts in hours far in excess of those required by the organization. The worker's whole life becomes centered around clients and the agency, and the worker takes on the image of a "super worker." There is an excessiveness in the worker's commitment and dedication to the job, not unlike that of a workaholic. An unfortunate result of this pattern is the worker's eventual exhaustion and cynicism in both outlook and behavior. The pattern also leads to strain between the worker's role as a family member and role as an employee. A possible irony is that while the helper is frantically attempting to assist others, his or her own family may be on the threshold of deterioration.

107

INVOLVED IMPARTIALITY

As part of a therapist's education, professional values, attitudes, methods, and skills are superimposed upon the worker's humanness. The novice practitioner is taught to be nonjudgmental and not to force his or her own personal values upon a client. The budding therapist is encouraged to be objective and intentional, careful not to overidentify with or against the client. The worker trainee is taught that the therapeutic relationship is for the benefit of the client and that the worker's own personal needs are to be met elsewhere. The student learns that the acquisition of information is for the client's benefit and not to satisfy his or her own curiosity.

NARCISSISTIC PITFALLS

In spite of special training and personal commitment, clinicians are vulnerable to four narcissistic snares—the aspiration to heal all, know all, love all, and be loved by all.

To heal all.   During the professional socialization process, the beginning worker learns that the skills and knowledge he or she masters can have the direct effect of bringing about changes in clients' lives. Textbook examples describe situations in which the helper, using the correct intervention at the proper time, successfully helps group members resolve their problems. Just as in the 30-minute situation comedy on television, no matter what the odds against a successful outcome, by the end, all is well.

Unfortunately, because of the lack of pat answers and quick solutions, the treatment process is rarely that uncomplicated. Individuals seeking help at private and public agencies are often angry and frustrated with the helping process. By the time the worker meets a particular client, that client, may have dealt with a number of human-service agencies. The client may have struggled with the bureaucratic system and have become realistically cynical of those who profess a desire to help. The client may be frustrated that the change process requires time and extraordinary patience. In such instances, instead of finding someone highly motivated for treatment, the worker is faced with an individual who is defensive, angry, frustrated, and resistant.

If a mechanic finds his or her tools to be inadequate, the mechanic discards them and purchases new tools. If an accountant feels that a particular computer program is outdated, he or she can obtain another one. But professional helpers do not have this luxury. To a large part, it is the practitioner's **self** that is the therapeutic tool, and for this reason, the means of treatment is impossible to separate from the personality. Therefore, there is the potential for the worker to confuse the limitations of his or her professional capacity to heal with his or her sense of personal worth.

To know all.   Closely tied to the narcissistic snare of "healing all" is that of "knowing all." Group members often have the mistaken belief that the worker has the ability to mind-read and thus to know whatever is being thought and felt without its ever being articulated. Members unabashedly tell leaders, "You know what I'm thinking before I do." Such magical thinking would require both omniscience and clairvoyance, powers the professional does not have. The skilled worker consistently uses intuition and plays hunches but, in doing so, still bases his or her thinking on clinical data.

It is easy to fall into the trap of perpetuating this notion of magical thinking. Admittedly, there is something gratifying about being thought of as having special insights into the mind and motivation of someone else, and it provides a sense of power and strength in situations where we may have neither. However, such thinking can result in an unhealthy form of collusion between the worker and group members, with the members expecting the worker to know all and the worker being seduced into believing it, even when he or she knows better.

Such an unspoken arrangement generally ends on a less-than-positive note. When a member begins to suspect the worker really does not have the solutions to his or her problems, the member's reaction may be to question the worker's competence. Explicitly or implicitly comes the message, "If you were a good worker, you would have the solution and take away my pain." Even for the most skilled and competent worker, this is a forceful message and has the capability of triggering self-doubt in the worker.

The burden of this idolization falls directly on the worker, freeing the members from having to take responsibility for their own lives. According to Kopp (1972):

> Part of the reason that patients insist that I have already attained salvation is that if it were otherwise, how could I save them? Certainly at the beginning of treatment they do not imagine for a moment that each of us must save himself. How this experienced inequity between pilgrim and guru come about is as important as why it occurs. I get to seem so strong and wise as a function of the patient's disowning the responsibility of his own strength by projecting these assets onto my not-so-wide shoulders. . . . I often warn patients that my opium dreams of omniscience, omnipotence, and unbearable pleasures endlessly experienced will certainly tempt me to go along with his making me into Mr. Wonderful. I do not simply abandon myself to indulging in these pleasant fantasies. They always turn out so badly [p. 133–134].

As is usually the case when a group leader comes toppling off a pedestal on which group members have placed him or her, the members feel hoodwinked and betrayed. For a time, they are horrified to learn that enlightenment does not provide perfection, but rather offers the means of learning to live with an acceptance of imperfection.

To love all.   The third narcissistic snare has to do with the worker's belief that he or she should love all clients and respond lovingly to all aspects of each person seeking help. There is little doubt that social workers leading groups, as well as other helping professionals, have deep concern for their clients. The worker's knowledge, skills, and time are all part of the therapeutic process and are offered to help clients accomplish their goals. Sometimes, however, that which is offered in the name of caring is not interpreted in the same spirit in which it is given.

Group members may resist the worker's efforts to bring about change. There may be verbal and, in some instances, physical acting out, with the explicit command "I don't need your help. Leave me alone." Less assertive members and those who are more subtle in communicating their feelings may drop nonverbal hints that the worker is inadequate, does not understand, or in some way has failed to meet their expectations. And some individuals will attend one session and then fail to return to the agency without giving a reason.

Slivkin (1982), describing his work with a group of developmentally disabled adults, observes that a member's need to test the therapist's limits can be distracting as well as annoying. A member's acting out of rage, for example, is usually done in response to the member's internally generated needs and rarely in response to a given situation in a therapy group. However, a member may act out rage or use other defenses, such as massive denial of problems, projection, or emotional isolation, in order to maintain a reasonable distance between the worker and himself or herself. If the worker perceives these behaviors as personally directed, and reacts as if they were, the worker will lose the opportunity to become a significant person in that member's life, and the worker's therapy for that client cannot proceed.

To be loved by all.   The worker's need to love all may be complicated by the need to be loved by all. Bach and Goldberg (1974) write sardonically of the "nice" therapist who is loved by all of his or her patients but who has a limited impact on their lives. Because the therapist seems to be so sweet, kind, caring, and loving, patients find it impossible to become angry with him or her or even to express anger during a counseling session.

Because of his or her own needs, the "nice" worker tends to reward and reinforce the patients' dependencies, prolonging an unresolved therapeutic situation. As a way of accommodating the worker, the clients change little, though they always tell him or her that they have changed a lot. The worker's indirect aggression comes through as he or she duplicates the role of the overprotective parent by nurturing dependency and stifling aggressive and even assertive behavior.

COUNTERTRANSFERENCE

110

· · · · · · · ·

A practitioner's conscious and unconscious reactions, evoked by a client, have come to be labeled *countertransference*. Broadly defined as unwarranted or excessive attitudes toward or emotional reactions to a client, countertransference is a part of all treatment. Traditionally, inner reactions by the worker were viewed as something harmful and a hindrance to the therapeutic process. In recent years, however, countertransference has been thought of as a tool for the worker to use both in understanding and in assisting the individual and the group. The leader's inner reactions to clients can be a powerful instrument for discerning individual and group dynamics.

Some responses the worker experiences are a clear reaction to a particular individual. For example, a client's appearance, age, personality structure, socioeconomic class, race, and mannerisms have the potential of activating feelings and actions on the worker's part. Never static, these reactions vary with different clients.

Adolescents are extraordinarily adept at bringing a worker's nonrational feelings and actions to the surface (Reid, 1980; Marshak, 1982). A young person's volatility, narcissism, irreverence, and acting-out behavior may be as discomforting to the worker as it is for the adolescent's parents. The worker, unaware of his or her own sensitivity, may find the adolescent's challenges to traditional values frustrating and disturbing. This sense of discomfort and anxiety may block the worker from making a meaningful effort to treat the adolescent.

The worker's own unresolved conflicts, especially difficulties with parents or other authority figures, can cause the worker to covertly encourage acting-out behavior in adolescents. Some workers, responding to their unfulfilled desire to act out as adolescents, vicariously enjoy the descriptions of the sexual escapades of their clients' direct expression of anger to parents, teachers, and other people in positions of authority.

Some clients we like; others we dislike. Some we want to work with; others we secretly hope will choose to find assistance elsewhere. Some we feel very tender towards, while others generate anxiety, hostility, and fear in us. The responses we experience are usually more or less automatic, being nurtured by motives and needs operating outside our awareness (Reid, 1977a).

There are clients who have the ability to immobilize and overwhelm the helping professional. In an investigation of the countertransference of hospital staff toward difficult-to-treat psychiatric patients, researchers observed that different forms of psychopathology evoked different emotional reactions. Patients who scored high on character pathology triggered feelings of anger in staff members. Withdrawn, psychotic patients elicited feelings of helplessness and confusion in the staff.

Patients who were violent and agitated evoked marked variations in affect among professionals in the various hospital disciplines. Psychiatrists experienced helplessness and confusion; social workers and nurses reported fearfulness; activity therapists felt angry and provoked (Colson, Allen, Coyne, Dexter, Jehl, Mayer, & Spohn, 1986).

Other behaviors that often depict countertransference in groups include workers coming late to sessions (whereas they are generally punctual), ending a group session early (whereas they usually end meetings at a particular time), becoming quiet (whereas they are usually forthcoming), forgetting members' names, and failing to announce an upcoming vacation.

Indicators of a worker's countertransference can be subtle. For example, drowsiness, yawning, and cutting off a client in mid-sentence may signify that a worker is experiencing countertransference. Or the worker may notice a sudden sexual attraction to a group member or fantasies about the person during or after the meeting. The dreams that the worker has the night before or after a group session can also be a clue as to his or her feelings about group members.

According to Corey (1990), countertransference can have a number of other manifestations. For example, the worker may engage in seductive behavior, taking advantage of the leadership role as a way to win the special affection of certain group members. He or she may become overprotective by being a benign substitute parent. The leader may project onto clients some traits that he or she despises in herself, regarding those clients as not amenable to treatment or impossible to work with. The leader may see himself or herself in certain clients and overidentify with those clients to the point of being unable to work effectively with them.

Countertransference can be a diagnostic clue and also provide direction as to treatment. Leonard, a 12-year-old member in a group for emotionally impaired students, initially appeared depressed. In the group, he was excessively polite, nonassertive, and hesitant about expressing his thoughts. By the fourth month, he became more and more outspoken, using sarcasm and biting comments—often derogatory ones—toward women. According to his school's social worker, Leonard's mother was depressed, hostile, and dependent. His relationship with his mother was passive/aggressive and dependent.

The worker, a middle-aged female, was cognizant of her own growing anger toward Leonard's sarcasm and hostility. She did not want to react in kind, on principle and in recognition that she might replicate the same type of interaction with Leonard that he already had with his mother. So, the focus of the worker's interventions became that of intentionally helping Leonard express his feelings directly, without resorting to covert acting out.

There may be an excessive need on the professional's part to be liked, particularly by certain members. If so, instead of confronting those members, the worker may "pull her punches" and ignore comments or behaviors that he or she would normally challenge. The worker may fear that if he or she brings something to the member's attention, the reaction will be hostility and rage. So, the worker avoids material that is potentially dangerous and sticks to safe and predictable topics. In short, the worker's need to be liked inhibits him or her from confronting and raising pertinent issues.

A given member's impact on a worker and the worker's subsequent response will depend on a number of variables, including a mix of certain situational factors in the worker's life, the worker's unresolved neurotic problems, and whether and how the member communicates anger to the worker.

SITUATIONAL FACTORS

A group leader has a personal life that includes people, places, and events outside of his or her group work. No matter how hard we, as group leaders, try to separate our professional life from our personal life, it is difficult if not impossible to keep the two apart. Situations in our personal life will infringe on our role of helper and the counseling process. Conversely, the time we spend with clients will affect our personal life.

This merging of the worker's two worlds—private and professional—can be illustrated by the example of an unusually sensitive therapist who was leading a group while, at the same time, going through a bitter divorce. One of the members of his group, a middle-aged man, was also in the midst of a marital conflict. In evaluating this worker's comments and responses to this client, his supervisor noticed that the worker's own position was far from neutral.

Unconsciously, the leader was encouraging the group member to leave his wife and make a new life for himself, despite the client's protestations that he wanted to keep his marriage intact. When his supervisor explained his observation the worker was able to recognize his overidentification with this client because of his own personal circumstance. He realized he had been seeing himself in the client and using the client's situation to resolve some of the problems in his own life.

A worker's reaction to a client is sometimes based on cultural factors. For example, any implications that a White worker is insensitive to the needs of the Blacks in a group may activate a defensive reaction on the worker's part. Not wanting to appear racist, the worker may uncharacteristically avoid challenging the Black members and be overly and excessively empathetic with them. Any intimation of being a racist is painful for any worker. And it can be excruciating for a beginning worker, who is likely to be already experiencing considerable anxiety and self-doubt. To deal with this predicament, the beginner may be forced to fall back on the defense mechanisms at his or her disposal, but these may subsequently be challenged by the group.

A Black professional who is working with Black clients may experience a whole different set of problems (Sager, Braywood, & Waxenberg, 1970). A Black psychiatrist describes it as follows: "For the therapist who has fought his way out of the ghetto, the black patient may awaken memories and fears he would prefer to leave undisturbed." Kadushin (1972) writes that the Black worker finds himself anxious that the Black client is not living up to the standards of the dominant culture, and that such deviation reflects on the race as a whole.

The Black worker who is leading a group of White members often finds himself discounted, or perceived as less than competent (Davis, 1984). Group members may raise questions about the worker's professional ability and whether he or she is competent to lead the group. Members may even express doubts about his or her therapeutic training, knowledge, and skill.

113

PROBLEMS OF THE WORKER

The professional helper may bring to the group some of the same emotional struggles that the members bring. After all, no professional is immune to such feelings as hate, guilt, admiration, rage, envy, loneliness, and love. In fact, because of the close relationship between the worker's private and professional lives, there is a potential for problems to surface and become detrimental to the therapeutic experience.

A classical example is the worker who uses a client to meet his or her own sexual needs. A client who is seductive or sexually provocative may trigger some very strong sexual feelings in a worker. The worker may fantasize about the client during sessions. The worker may even recommend individual sessions for the client. Viewed from a transactional vantage point the client may be using seductive verbal and nonverbal communication to neutralize the worker and resist therapy.

Lawton (1958) referring to countertransference in a one-to-one relationship, observes that the immature and disturbed therapist may find a submissive and childlike patient "easy pickings," with seduction and "wooing" taking both verbal and nonverbal forms. Some of the verbal wooing devices of the therapist are calling the client by his or her first name too soon and without ascertaining the client's wishes; using affectionate or meaningful intonations of words; engaging in long, cozy telephone conversations; and asking for deep material too soon or too obviously.

At the nonverbal level, according to Lawton, the practitioner may visit the client's home at his or her request whenever the client undergoes an emotional emergency of a transference nature; may glance affectionately or meaningfully at the client; may put an affectionate hand on the client's shoulder or give the client a parental pat, and may regularly overrunning usual and conventional time limits for sessions. Instead of the worker dealing with the client's difficulties, the helping relationship becomes a vehicle to meet the worker's own personal unresolved needs and problems.

COMMUNICATION OF A MEMBER'S ANGER

Some members focus their anger on their group leader. A member who does this may express their anger toward the worker, by verbal and/or nonverbal means. Verbally, this anger may be expressed in the form of devaluation of the worker. In this case, the member conveys through language, his or her contempt for the worker as a person. Beginning workers who are

114
• • • • • • • •

leading children and adolescent groups are often shocked by the names they get called by some group members. A young worker observed.

> It took me a long time to get used to being called a mother-fucker and a son of a bitch. If some guy on the street called me a name like that I would clobber him. I have had to learn to ignore that kind of garbage and just let it pass without responding. Sometimes, I sense that the guys in the group are just waiting for me to blow up.

In launching a verbal attack, a group member may disparage "to the worker's face" his or her physical appearance (especially if the worker has some extraordinary feature), race *(nigger, honky),* or lifestyle *(hippie, queer),* for example.

The member may express anger in the form of hostile looks, physically pulling back, or increasing the pitch and volume of his or her voice. A suicidal client may intimate that he or she is overwhelmed with life and that "it's just not worth it." Such a member may hint at purchasing a gun or, in some way, doing something to hurt himself or someone else.

The worker is caught in a polemic. On one hand is the worker's professional commitment to helping the group member. On the other hand is the very human personal reactions of fear, anger, and rage that the practitioner experiences because of the client's behavior. The worker considers himself or herself as a compassionate, caring, and nonjudgmental person; however, instead of appreciating the worker's effort and dedication, the client makes the worker feel incompetent and impotent.

Reaction of rage. A natural human reaction to a client's angry actions would be that of rage and hate. However, the personality organization of the worker is usually such that these feelings, unlike other feelings, are unacceptable. Referring specifically to the feeling of hate, Maltsberger and Buie (1974) write that hate is inconsistent with self-esteem on the worker's part, and unconsciously a mobilization of defenses against it. A capable worker cannot permit himself or herself to behave according to such feelings, but neither can the worker afford the illusion that he or she differs from other human beings and that the feelings do not exist.

To the extent that these feelings exist at an unconscious level, the worker is generally unaware of their intensity. But these feelings surface during group sessions in subtle ways. For example, the worker may have difficulty paying attention. The worker may find himself or herself daydreaming, bored, anxious, or restless. The therapist may further act out this aversion to the client by yawning, glancing too often at his or her watch, and conveying in other nonverbal ways "I don't want to be with you, and I wish I were someplace else." When a worker begins to notice these signals, the worker may begin to distrust his or her capacity to be helpful and to question his or her ability to truly help other people. Unfortunately, the self-doubt triggered by one person can be generalized to the group or even a total caseload. The worker may actually develop doubts as to his or her capability to lead groups. For some, the painful question becomes further universalized with doubts as to his or her competence and capacity to be any kind of social worker or a member of any other helping profession.

Some workers use *reaction formation* as a means of dealing with emotions: instead of expressing their feelings, they express the opposite feelings. Thus, they repress their feelings of anger, hate, and rage and instead exhibit excessive and exaggerated love, caring, and understanding. The worker may also experience an anxious urgency to be of help and even intervene in circumstances on the client's behalf, beyond the purview of the group.

Cynicism.   Sadly, some professionals who have been in group work for several years are not merely shockproof to the pain and problems of their clients but hardened and cynical. Chekhov (1964), in his short story *"Ward Number Six,"* poignantly describes this state of mind:

> People such as judges, policemen, and doctors, whose attitude to human suffering is strictly official and professional, become so callous in the course of time and from force of habit that they cannot treat their clients in any but a formal way even if they want to; in this respect they are not at all different from the peasant who slaughters sheep and calves in his backyard and does not give a thought to the blood [p. 137].

A WORKER'S SEARCH FOR INCLUSION

Being the leader of a treatment group can be a way for a professional to experience acceptance and being included—something that he or she may not have experienced as a child or adolescent. Levine (1979) observes that leaders of therapy groups can be extremely empathetic with the interpersonal difficulties that their group members encounter, to the point of overidentifying with their clients. Such leaders bring to their groups hurt and hostility from previous experiences in which they were rejected, and they focus incessantly on issues of anger. However, the actual expression of anger in their groups is discouraged because these leaders have difficulty allowing their clients to express hostile and rejecting feelings toward each other or toward themselves. Generally, groups with this type of leader develop to a level of pseudo intimacy, as found in a normal adolescent group. As a result, the members of these groups come to group meetings with good feelings about each other but also experience a sense of **dis–ease** with any feelings of rejection or hostility they may harbor.

For practitioners who were very much the center of their peer groups during their adolescent years, there may be a search for the intimacy and power they experienced as leaders of these groups and now miss (Levine, 1979). Again, the issue is one of desiring acceptance and intimacy and, at the same time, being fearful of being rejected. To avoid the possibility of being rebuffed, these workers adopt more autocratic methods, structuring stiuations in their groups in ways that lessen the possibility of rejection. Viewed as benevolent despots, these leaders are often extremely sensitive to the overt and covert wishes of their group members and to give the members what they want so long as they themselves are feeling secure.

Sharing power.   Control can be an especially complicated issue for clinicians who come out of a background that placed a heavy emphasis on Dyadic counseling and individual psychodynamics. Williams (1966), discussing issues in training individual therapists to be group therapists, observes that even though these clinicians do not consider themselves controlling, they are fearful of losing control, especially in therapeutic situations involving a multitude of people.

While these individual-oriented workers may promote leader-to-member relationships in groups, they may be hesitant to encourage or allow relationships among group members. These leaders view the group-dynamic approach as diminishing their authority and threatening their self-esteem and personal control.

FEARS AND FANTASIES

Leading a group can be frightening. The group leader must cope with the problems that are a part of all psychotherapy, as well as with the problems that are unique to this aggregate of people who have come together to meet their personal needs and accomplish the group's goal (Reid, 1988). In addition, the worker must deal with the dynamics of the group and with the multiple relationships between himself or herself and members and among members. The relatively secure 1:1 or 1:2 worker/client ratio is exchanged for the less secure ratio of 1:many commonly found in groups.

In the more traditional practice of individual casework and psychotherapy, the clinician can close the office door and remain on his or her own "turf." In group treatment, this touchstone is usually missing. Seldom are group sessions held in the worker's office. They are more likely to be held in another room in the building or at another location in the community. In these settings, familiar touchstones—such as books, diplomas, and family pictures—are absent, and the worker is forced to find silent security in a pad of paper, a plastic coffee cup, or whatever happens to be close at hand.

In group work, the therapist also gives up power and control that is very much a part of dyadic counseling (Reid, 1988). In one-to-one counseling, the therapist is **the** helper. In group work, other individuals share in the therapeutic endeavor. The group leader, while still in a position of prominence, is but one part of the treatment process. If the worker's ego is fragile, if the worker desires excessive recognition, or if the worker needs to be the star, he or she will experience frustration, as suggested in the following observation reported by a newly graduated social worker:

> Whenever Flora speaks, the other members pay attention to her and take serious what she says. If I were to say the same thing, they wouldn't consider it as valuable. What really bothers me is that Flora just has a tenth-grade education and has held only menial jobs. Even though I'm the leader and have gone to graduate school, I'm embarrassed to say that her advice and interpretations are sometimes more on target than mine.

The novice worker in this example felt threatened by Flora and, at the same time, wanted very much to be accepted by the group. Such a situation can lead to a nontherapeutic, destructive, and competitive struggle with a group member (Reid, 1988).

PERFORMANCE ANXIETY

When leading groups for the first time, workers become emotionally distracted by a concern that they will be made to look foolish or incompetent. In the novice worker's mind, he or she is under close and constant scrutiny by the group members and needs to do the correct thing at all times. When there is premature attrition and members elect to drop out—or simply do not return—it raises fear in the inexperienced leader that this will reflect on his or her leadership and that the group members' confidence in him or her will diminish. During periods of silence, the novice worker feels a compulsion to change the subject or to fill the void so as not to give the impression of wasting time or appearing incompetent. By the end of the session such a worker may experience a secret sense of relief in having "fooled them again."

Threat to self-esteem.   All group workers feel vulnerable to annihilation through assaults to their self-esteem (Kottler, 1986). Even though a worker professes neutrality without a vested interest in the outcome, the worker cares about the outcome. However, when a client does not improve or a group is having difficulty, the beginning leader feels the pain and takes it personally. The novice therapist also worries about how others will view his or her competence based on the action of his or her clients. If the members get too loud or verbally aggressive, the worker fears, colleagues in nearby offices and clients sitting in the waiting room will view him or her as inadequate.

When group members express honest opinions and share painful feelings, there may be fear on the beginning therapist's part that the group is getting out of control and the result will be chaos (Reid, 1988). Aware of the powerful nature of the group influence, the novice leader may anticipate aggressive conflict that he or she will not be able to manage. Directly related is a fear that because of the group members' capacity to collaborate and to establish shared defenses, they will direct aggression toward their group leader. As a means of countering this threat, the inexperienced therapist may try to display his or her superiority by using technical language and interpretations or by becoming somewhat aloof and intellectually enigmatic.

Resistance.   Nearly every therapist has, at some time, harbored the fantasy of having to deal with unbridled resistance from a group. In discussions with their supervisors, novice leaders reveal these fantasies by asking *what if* questions in which they describe a potential action of a member or the group that might make them feel helpless (Reid, 1988): "What if no one shows up?" or "What if they don't talk and they just sit and stare at me?" or "What if they don't listen to me but take the bad advice of a more disturbed member?"

Fears, particularly those of a beginning group therapist, are often linked to the therapist's feeling socially impotent (Williams, 1966). The professional is so struck by and anxious over the massed psychopathology that he or she loses sight of the underlying community of human feeling and thought processes. "It becomes apparent that the therapist is resistant to the notion of being treated in a group and projects this resistance upon the patients" (p. 155).

Social workers, raised in a family situation that emphasized rationality, moderation of feelings, and the suppression of hostile communications are frequently preoccupied with the fantasy of excessive hostility breaking out in the group (Reid, 1988). This is evident in questions such as "What do I do if they begin to yell at me?" or "What do I do if they start fighting?" Instead of viewing conflict as a natural, normal, and desirable part of the group process, these therapists tend to think of conflict as something akin to violence, and thus something to be avoided and extinguished whenever it surfaces.

While violence within a group is always possible, it does not occur that often. Rappaport (1982), in describing work with prison inmates, notes that violent sessions were without physical abuse and that the prisoners verbalized feelings of relief during and after these episodes. Group pressure helped redirect the impulsive behavior of the inmates from physical expression to heated verbal outbursts, which the group members perceived as healing.

SOME PRACTICAL CONSIDERATIONS

The helping relationship is extremely complex. Both the group members and the worker are continually reacting to each other as they try to differentiate between reality and projections. They are also reacting to each other as they try to distinguish between accurate perceptions and misconceptions of each other. It is no wonder that workers, as well as clients, become frustrated and confused with the therapeutic experience.

As group workers, we must begin by studying our own behavior both to diagnose our countertransference and to bring it under control. For example, if we observe that we are talking too much during a session, we would do well to pass this resolution: none of that behavior for the next session. It may be excruciatingly frustrating to stick to the resolution. And we may even lapse back into excessive talking without being aware. But it is only when we are in control of our responses that we can begin to spot the client behaviors that are triggering our responses and to gain the perspective we need in order to help group members make changes.

It may be that the stimulus for our talking comes from silence in the group. Anxiety and pressure from a voice deep within screams out "fill in the void caused by the silence" or "provide the answer so the tension will be reduced." To the degree possible, we need to keep **at a conscious level** the impulses triggered by the situation. Without such conscious awareness, our chances for controlling our responses are limited. Key questions we need to ask ourselves include the following:

- What's going on in the group right now?
- What am I feeling right now in the group?
- If this particular member would drop out of the group, how would I feel?
- If I were to unleash my most impulsive response, what would it be?
- Am I playing a particular role in the group?

When a practitioner stays in touch with his or her personal reactions, the practioner's potential for learning about himself or herself and group members increases. Remaining in touch with his or her reactions creates a window through which the practitioner can view his or her own personality. Through this glass darkly, it becomes clear to the practitioner how he or she relates to certain kinds of individuals. This window also possibly allows the practitioner to get a glimpse of an unresolved area of personal conflict.

When a worker realizes that he or she is hooked into a nontherapeutic pattern, either with a particular member or with the group-as-a-whole, the question the worker must ask is: "*How* can I turn this situation into a learning situation and reduce the possibility of further damage to my clients and myself?" If the worker feels immobilized or in some way shut down by a group member or the group, it would be natural for him or her to want to strike out at the person(s). Instead, the worker's response needs to be thought out and proactive—and not reactive.

It may be that the clinician is too close to the situation and needs someone else—that is, a consultant or supervisor—to help examine the dynamics and to identify possible means of resolution. It may mean that the clinician

120
• • • • • • • •

must "unlearn" some old patterns appropriate to dyadic counseling but inappropriate to the multiperson orientation required in group treatment.

IN SUMMARY

This chapter explores the personhood of the worker in the group. Like the group member, the group leader brings to the helping situation a multitude of life experiences that impact on the therapeutic relationship. It is the worker's humanness that provides a basis for his or her relating to the members. However, this same humanness can be destructive and an impediment to change.

Groups create a unique social system with properties distinct from those found in dyadic counseling. The transactions between each group member and the group leader and the transactions between group members generate a whole series of actions and reactions. Of particular importance are the worker's fears and fantasies related to the group. The practitioner's self-awareness, especially a realistic awareness of his or her strengths and weaknesses, is an important asset. It helps ensure a balanced view of the members and thereby promotes a balanced treatment of their problems.

SUGGESTED READINGS

COREY, G. (1990). *Theory and practice of group counseling* (3rd ed.). Pacific Grove, Calif.: Brooks/Cole. See Chapter 3.

REID, K. (1977). Nonrational dynamics of the client-worker interaction. *Social casework, 58*(10), 600–606.

REID, K. (1988). "But I don't want to lead a group! Some common problems of social workers leading groups." *Groupwork, 1*(2), 124–134.

WEINER, M. (1986). *Practical psychotherapy.* New York: Brunner/Mazel. See Chapters 8 and 12.

WILLIAMS, M. (1966). Limitations, fantasies, and security operations of beginning group psychotherapists. *International journal of psychotherapy, 16*(2), 150–162.

7

FOUNDATION SKILLS

I recently received a phone call from a panic-stricken practitioner suffering the tortures of the damned. He pleaded for some quick advice on how to lead a group. The conversation went something like this.

"I'm really scared," he groaned. "I just found out that I have to lead a group tomorrow, and I've never led a group before."

Having said this, my anxious caller apologetically explained that a group therapist at his agency was going to be out of town and that he was to lead the group. "I wanted to take a course on group work but never had the time," he bewailed. To my advice that he get someone else to take the group, he said that there was no one else available.

Frankly, in the old days, I would have suggested a couple of books on groups or given him "how to" articles from a journal. Reports back from the foxholes, however, have been less than encouraging. Rather than helping, the books and articles have only confused the would-be leader and created even greater anxiety.

Now I share what I call my "quick-and-dirty" primer on leading a group. "Do the following, and you will be all right," I told him. "First, be warm, caring, and respectful. Second, listen hard to what the members are saying, and if you understand, let them know. Third, be yourself, and don't hide behind a professional facade. Fourth, keep the members on task and encourage everyone—including yourself—to say what they mean. Fifth, challenge the members to share what they are really thinking and feeling."

Having said all of this, I waited for an appreciative response. Instead, there was a bellowing silence. After a few moments, the caller retorted indignantly, "I know all that, but what should I do"?

I think Oscar Wilde was right when he said, it's silly to give advice, and to give good advice is absolutely fatal.

• • •

This chapter addresses the following question: what are the essential interpersonal skills and behaviors a practitioner needs in order to be successful with a therapy group? In summary, the answer is warmth and respect, empathy, concreteness, genuineness, self-disclosure, and the ability to listen. All are part of the therapeutic mosaic. Any one of these skills is—by itself—of limited value. These skills are inextricably connected, and when one is missing, the potential for meaningful changes in clients is greatly diminished. These skills and behaviors are the building blocks and serve as the base for the treatment relationship.

THERAPEUTIC INTERPERSONAL SKILLS

The essence of being a competent social worker is possessing interpersonal skills that promote positive outcomes in therapy and using these skills in the helping relationship. Having solid interpersonal skills is not the same as being able to use them in clinical practice. Many practitioners are sensitive and caring individuals in their private lives and yet are unable to utilize these same skills in treatment. For example, a group therapist with a gift for understanding personality theory may be unable to draw effectively on this sensitivity when confronted with a disturbed patient.

Other practitioners who are exceptionally sensitive to the needs of their clients are unable to relate to the needs of their own family, friends, and colleagues. I wonder what would be a worse epitaph, to be known as a splendid human being and a terrible social worker or a splendid social worker and a terrible human being. Neither epitaph has much appeal.

Research data on the effective therapist identify a number of core skills that serve as the foundation for the helping process (Carkhuff & Berenson, 1967; Egan, 1982; Truax & Carkhuff, 1967). These studies confirm that the most crucial element in the worker's contribution to a successful treatment is a genuine interest in people and a commitment to their growth. Essential interpersonal behaviors on the part of any practitioner are warmth and respect, empathy, genuineness, and concreteness.

Rogers (1962), in discussing the therapeutic alliance between therapist and client, writes that their personal relationship matters most. Some clients are touched only briefly by the therapist, while others become known intimately. In either case, the quality of their personal encounter is probably, in the long run, the element that determines the extent to which the group experience releases or promotes the client's development and growth.

WARMTH AND RESPECT

As noted in earlier chapters, the leader in a group tries to create an atmosphere in which the members feel safe, secure, and respected. But how is this atmosphere created? One way it occurs is through the worker's personal warmth and his or her acceptance of each individual in the group. Verbally and nonverbally, the leader can convey the messages "I prize you" and "I value you as a person."

The worker can also convey warmth nonverbally—through his or her facial expressions, posture, voice, and physical proximity. Group members report greater receptivity toward workers who use direct eye contact, who use facial expressions that are appropriately varied and animated, and who smile occasionally. Also, clients "approach," with greater frequency workers who convey attentiveness by listening, appearing relaxed, and being fully present rather than distracted.

Conversely, members—especially those sensitive to criticism and rejection—are quick to perceive the smallest of nonsupportive behavior cues, such as those that signal disapproval, shock, or condemnation. Facial expressions such as a frown, avoidance of eye contact, nodding the head excessively, or a rigid facial expression may be perceived by clients as signs that the worker is untrustworthy or evasive. Clients may interpret a leader's squirming, slouching, or pointing a finger for emphasis as a lack of caring or as insensitivity.

Egan (1982) observes that the group worker can express initial warmth through basic friendliness, which is different from "role warmth"—that is standard counselor warmth. Basic friendliness is also different from the warmth the worker would accord a close friend, in that the worker is not a close friend. If the practitioner becomes a "warmth machine," continually cranking out unconditional positive regard, the warmth will seem to clients to degenerate into an "oh-that's-all-right" kind of response that is spurious and unhelpful.

UNCONDITIONAL POSITIVE REGARD

The truly respectful group leader values each member as a person, independent of any evaluation the leader makes of that member's thoughts or behavior. As therapists, we must unconditionally accept whatever a member says or does as something that is part of that person and worthy of being understood. We must refrain from passing judgment on the individual's actions or assuming responsibility for his or her decisions.

This unconditional acceptance is easily misunderstood. It does **not** mean that we condone aberrant behavior and agree with the actions of the client. Taken to an extreme, that would mean the worker approves the criminal actions of those clients who are rapists, child molesters, and drug dealers, which is simply not the case. Rather, the acceptance means that the person is valued as a human being. A nonjudgmental reaction is synonymous with "nonblaming" and being "noncensorious."

A group worker's manner should indicate support **for** a client because the client is human (Egan, 1982). As therapists, we are available to each client and offer that person a personal commitment to be of help. We regard the client as unique, and we support the client in this uniqueness.

There are some things that a group worker's warmth is not. First, warmth does not mean sympathy. A group leader's response to a client's painful experience should not be "Oh, that's awful!" or "I'm so sorry to hear that." While such expressions of sympathy imply caring and warmth on the worker's part, they also suggest evaluation. Instead, the worker should give primary attention to the client's thoughts and feelings. For example, the worker might say, "That must have been very disturbing for you." This form of response emphasizes that the client's feelings and attitudes—rather than the worker's—take precedence.

Warmth does **not** mean that a group leader is a passive, benign, docile, and yielding figure who protects each group member and keeps the treatment situation free from anxiety. Our job as therapists is to help group members understand themselves better. This quest for greater self-awareness is not a painless pursuit. We do not back down from challenging the irrationality of a client's thoughts, feelings, and behaviors, when such a challenge is appropriate. And we do not shrink from telling a client how he or she appears at that moment, particularly if there is something about the person that is socially out of bounds—for example, having mucus on the face or unzipped pants.

The truly caring social worker makes a genuine effort to understand and confront members with the behaviors and underlying attitudes that are causing them social or psychological difficulty. In short, the professional conveys the message "I care about you to such a degree that I will take a risk and let you know what I am hearing, seeing, or feeling." The worker who rarely makes the effort to challenge and confront comes across to clients as distant, uncaring, and patronizing.

RESPECT FOR THE INDIVIDUAL

The respectful worker evaluates and challenges a member's statements and actions but does not judge or denigrate the person. There is a world of difference between a worker's saying "That was a crazy thing to do" (which, if properly expressed, can be a constructive observation) and saying "You are crazy" (which is a personal attack).

A lack of respect for a client is often communicated nonverbally and in subtle ways. A worker who keeps looking at the clock, stares out the window, yawns, or fidgets conveys inattention and lack of respect. Internal factors may prevent the worker from staying in psychological contact with a group member. These factors might include preoccupation with assessments of the individual or inner pressure to find immediate solutions to the client's problems (Hepworth & Larsen, 1986). Environmental factors such as extraneous noise, a ringing phone, an inadequate meeting room, or lack of privacy may also interfere with the social worker's being psychologically present.

Use of names. The use of names can also convey respect—or lack of it. In the United States, it is commonplace to call near-strangers by their first name. This "instant intimacy" occurs in banks, stores, and schools as well as hospitals, agencies, and clinics. Often, this intimacy is only one-way.

For example, an elderly female patient may call her male physician "Doctor," while he uses her first name. One wonders why the doctor does not offer the same respect to the patient that the patient offers to the doctor?

Calling individuals by their first name, without their permission can have disastrous results, especially in transcultural relationships. Various cultural groups view the use of the first name differently. Whereas first names symbolizing friendliness and equality are preferred by Whites in the United States, Blacks, on the other hand, prefer formality in professional address (McNeely and Badami, 1984). McNeely and Badam explain why this is the case:

> Today, blacks distrust whites who address them by their first names, sensing that this may be a method of forcing deference and the acceptance of inequality in status rather than a desire for the camaraderie found among equals. In addition, immediate use of first names by whites is likely to be perceived not only as ingenuine friendliness but as a conscious attempt by whites to deny blacks the proper respect accorded by the use of a title and surname [p. 24].

Historically, Whites in the United States have expected signs of deference from Blacks. Deference is an interaction style based on inequality of status in which those unequal in status address another using asymmetrical language (McNeely & Badami, 1984). The expectation of deference from Blacks developed along with their enslavement by Whites.

For example, Whites called slaves by their first name, but required the slaves to use *Mr., Mrs.,* and *Miss* as a sign of respect when referring to Whites.

In general, Blacks who live in the United States prefer the pattern of formality that calls for the use of titles such as *Mr., Mrs., and Dr.* when addressing another person. This formality certifies that the relationship is composed of equality and a mutually respectful distance. To call one by his or her first name is a privilege earned, not a right automatically granted through a casual meeting.

It is important to remember that norms of openness and honesty, so much a part of Western society, may be perceived differently by clients coming out of other cultures. In the Asian culture, for example, free exchange of opinions is contrary to the Asian values of humility and inconspicuousness (Ho, 1976). American Indian tradition dictates that Indians do not use their own name or the word "I" excessively. An Indian client, according to Edwards and Edwards (1980), may bring another person with them to an interview so that they will have someone there who can speak on their behalf.

When addressing a person of color, we must also keep in mind a "time-contextual framework" in referring to his or her racial or ethnic identity. For example, in addressing a Black client, we must consider whether this client wants to be referred to as *Negro, Colored, Black,* or *African-American.* The answer may center around the age of the person and the generation he or she identifies with at the same time. Older Black Americans may prefer *Colored* to *Black,* while younger individuals may prefer African-American to Black. The person's preference can be determined through direct questioning.

127

....

Eye contact. Eye contact can be another area of misunderstanding. Whereas Whites, particularly when they are listening, prefer maximum eye contact, Blacks tend to prefer minimal eye contact. In the White culture, it is a sign of respect to look the other person "straight in the eye." Black people tend to look away frequently (LaFrance & Mayo, 1976). A common result of this difference in cultural patterning is a misinterpretation of non-verbal cues. A white person who is using continuous eye contact as a sign of courtesy perceives a Black person who is frequently looking away as disrespectful. A Black person who is using intermittent eye contact as a sign of courtesy views a White person who is continually looking at him or her as intrusive and hostile.

● **Techniques: Practical considerations**
   1. Maintain direct, but gentle, eye contact with group members.
   2. Remain relatively relaxed in an "open" body position, a position that does not close yourself off to your clients. A classical example of a "closed" body position is sitting or standing with your arms crossed over your chest.
   3. Know the name of each group member, and be clear about what each individual prefers to be called.
   4. Do not assume that every group member likes to be addressed by his or her first name.
   5. Do not expect instant intimacy with group members.

EMPATHY

In referring to the complexity of defining pornography, United States Supreme Court justice Potter Stewart stated that he cannot define pornography, but knows it when he sees it. In some ways, defining *empathy* is like defining *pornography.* The term *empathy* is difficult to define, but we know empathy when we see—and experience—it. Empathy is the ability to understand people from **their** personal frame of reference rather than from our own. It is the ability to put ourselves "in another person's shoes" and to comprehend that person's needs and feelings. At the most sophisticated level, empathy is the ability to get inside another's world, see what that world looks like from the inside, and accurately communicate our understanding to the person. All of this is done without the worker losing himself or herself in the process.

In psychotherapy, empathetic understanding consists of the therapist's special sensitivity to the meaning of what the patient says and does (Weiner, 1975). The empathetic practitioner is able to perceive the patient's thoughts and feelings accurately and to recognize their significance, not only for what is being experienced at the moment but also for what may lie outside of the person's conscious awareness.

Although the ability to respond empathetically is considered a fundamental skill, many social workers fail to use it appropriately. Others dismiss the need for training in empathetic responding, describing themselves as already being empathetic in contacts with clients (Fisher, 1978). In his research on counselors, Carkhuff, Kratochvil, and Friel (1968) found that two thirds of the helping practitioners he studied demonstrated low levels of empathetic responding. He concluded that many of this group were either ineffective or were harmful to clients.

LEVELS OF EMPATHY

According to Egan (1982), there are two levels of empathy: primary and advanced.

Primary empathy. Using empathy at its primary level, a practitioner communicates a basic understanding of what a member is feeling and of the experiences and behaviors underlying these feelings. Empathy at the primary level helps the member explore and clarify problem situations from his or her frame of reference. Instead of digging deeply into what the individual is saying, implying, and feeling, the worker merely conveys that he or she understands what the client has been saying explicitly. In the early stages of group work, empathy is both a relationship-establishing skill and a data-gathering skill. Empathy enables a worker to establish rapport with a client; it helps the client develop openness and trust; and it helps the client explore himself or herself and the problem situations.

Advanced empathy. Using empathy at its advanced level, on the other hand, a practitioner conveys a deeper and more intense level of understanding. Advanced empathy not only gets at what the client clearly states but also gets at what the client implies or leaves only half-stated or half-expressed. Investigators Cartwright and Lerner (1963) have found that this second level of empathetic understanding is related to patient improvement in therapy.

To the casual observer, empathy may appear to be a relatively simple, easily learned skill. But seasoned therapists would vigorously disagree with such an observation. To them, empathy is probably the hardest helping skill to teach, as well as to learn. Empathy is so much more than a worker listening to a client, repeating back what has been said, and reflecting the surface feelings.

ENTERING THE CLIENT'S WORLD

To become aware of a client's circumstances and problems, a social worker must first enter into that client's sometimes chaotic world. This world may be upside down and turned around, as experienced by someone suffering from psychosis. This world may be gray and desolate, with no apparent light, as in the case of a man suffering severe depression after losing his wife, children, and home in a fire. This world may be frightening, as in the case of a 23-year-old, single, unemployed mother of three who has been diagnosed has having inoperable stomach cancer and a maximum of two months to live. This world may be totally hostile and uncaring, as experienced by an educated 55-year-old Black man who cannot find work because of his age and the color of his skin.

If we have never experienced these particular problems, is it possible to be truly empathetic? Some people would say *no*. To truly understand and honestly convey this understanding, these people say, we would have to experience similar circumstances. Johnson (1951), speaking of his work with handicapped children, writes that the reason workers do not understand these children better is because they themselves do not have handicaps.

> I wonder, however, whether it is possible for an individual who has never had a problem—if there are any individuals like that—to have any significant insights into the difficulties of individuals who do have serious problems. The point is that if you have not had a handicap, then all you can ever have, in the way of knowledge of the individual that you are attempting to help, is the kind of knowledge that is verbal [pp. 178–179].

Other people argue that even though the worker may not have experienced the client's exact circumstances, the worker has had other life experiences that allow him or her to understand feelings of pain, fear, despair, anger, and joy. And, if in touch with these feelings, the worker can effectively use them as a base for a beginning understanding.

COMMUNICATING UNDERSTANDING

Once we have entered into a group member's world in terms of the member's feelings, experiences, and behaviors, the issue becomes how to communicate our understanding. Obviously, it is not enough to merely understand what is going on in the client's world; this understanding has to be conveyed to him or her. The individual needs to believe and accept that the social worker is with him or her and that there is an expanding, connecting link between them. The onus of responsibility in communicating this understanding lies with the group leader. If the communication is done poorly, the member may not return to the group or may categorize the practitioner as just one more professional who verbalizes an understanding but has no real comprehension of the client's pain, frustration, or fear.

The group leader needs to engage the group member in the kind of dialogue that can lead to the development of a working relationship and to the clarification of the client's problem situations. Gradually, the group member needs to be guided to a point where his or her problems are broken

130

• • • • • • • •

down into manageable components that can be addressed and worked on. Arrival at this point allows the practitioner and client to concentrate their energies on problem solving and to not be overwhelmed by the complexity of the client's circumstances.

PROBLEMS IN EXPRESSING EMPATHY

Empathy can run aground on many shoals. A therapist may misinterpret a client's thoughts and feelings, may fail to listen attentively; or may pay excessive attention to the content rather than the meaning of a client's verbalizations.

Pretending to understand. It is sometimes difficult for a group leader to understand what a client is saying even though the worker is listening intently. A psychiatric patient, for example, may be confused, in a highly emotional state, or out of touch with reality. The leader may not have a clue about what the person is saying. When this occurs and we **do not** understand what a client is communicating, it can be detrimental to pretend that we do. A more honest response is to have the person repeat what he or she has just said. We might respond, "I think I have lost you. Tell me again what you said" or "I'm confused. Please start over again, because it's important for me to understand."

Admitting that we do not understand is preferable to letting the individual go on while we nod our head or pretend we understand. If we do not express our confusion, matters may get worse, and following sessions are unlikely to be helpful. And, more often than not, the individual benefits from the worker's verbal expression of bewilderment.

Some group members, for example, resist the clinician's every effort to understand them (Brenner, 1982). Even though they have voluntarily requested assistance, they seem determined to prevent progress at all costs. All of the therapist's comments or inquiries lead to the same dead end. The therapist's interpretations are, in one way or another, rejected, dismissed, or explained away by these clients. A group leader's attempts to empathize with such a client prove futile. The client may make a comment and then contradict himself or herself in the following session.

As therapists, we often react to this resistance with frustration and exasperation and yield to the temptation to label the person *passive-aggressive, resistant,* or *not motivated for treatment.* Such labels do little more than give us a "therapeutic rationalization" to blame the lack of progress on the client. We may feel a bit better and less guilty, but this reaction accomplishes little else.

Counterfeit response. Sometimes referred to as the "three-dollar-bill response," the worker uses words and expressions that, on paper, sound like empathy but are no more than hollow phrases devoid of genuine understanding. One example is the expression, "I hear you saying . . ." followed by a parroting of what the client has just expressed. Within two minutes, the worker again repeats, "I hear you saying . . ." The member need not be terribly alert to quickly recognize that the helper is playing with words by repeating them indiscriminately to every client.

So often, clients seeking counseling have already spoken to other professional helpers and have gained an advanced sensitivity as to who understands and who does not. Similarly, they are quick to perceive who is with them and who is against them. If they feel we do not care or are inept, they will (perhaps appropriately) pull back or in some way resist our efforts.

Inappropriate language. Social workers are most effective when their language is synchronized to and parallel with their clients' language. This means avoiding words that the individual client does not understand and not talking down to the person. Beginning workers often transfer to the therapeutic situation the language they have learned in the classroom. It is wise to remember that faculty members and classmates comprehend words and concepts such as *transference, ego, defense mechanisms,* and *repression,* but to most clients, this is "psychobabble."

A group worker may be tempted to use expressions that "fit" a particular age group or culture. For example, a White, middle-class graduate student working with a group of Black adolescent males wants desperately to be accepted. To achieve this, he uses excessive street slang—such as *cool, boogie,* or *man,* expressions not a part of his normal speech pattern. Rather than blending with and becoming closer to the young men, the worker finds himself mocked and discounted by them.

Although using informal language is acceptable, the expressions used need to be the group leader's own. The leader is not a street person or a teenager who regularly uses the client's langauge; and the worker gains no advantage by pretending that he or she **is** part of this milieu. Weinberg (1984) writes that it would be artificial and ridiculous of us, as therapists, to use a client's slang as if it were our own daily jargon.

> It makes much more sense for us to be who we are. If drug addicts want to consider me an outsider because I don't know the latest language for sticking a needle into my arm, they are free to do so. In many such cases, those people need their therapist to be an outsider, and would lose respect for the therapist who borrowed their language as if he wanted to belong to their crowd [p. 58].

It **is** useful, however, for us to make use of a client's language when referring to something the client has brought up. For example, the client tells us she has been "put down" or "messed over" by her teacher. Once we are aware of the meaning to the person, we, too, can use her term in discussing this and other situations with her.

● **Techniques: Practical considerations**
   1. Give yourself time to reflect on what a client is saying in order to identify the person's core message.

2. Keep your responses to a client short rather than long-winded.
3. Use words and language that you think the client can easily understand.
4. Avoid cliches such as "I hear you saying. . . ."
5. If you don't understand what a client is saying, tell the client.
6. Move toward the exploration of sensitive topics and feelings with a client gradually. Keep in mind that although you may be ready, the client may not be.

CONCRETENESS

Concreteness is related to responding in a clear, specific, and explicit, manner—as opposed to talking in vague generalities. By using concrete language, a worker ensures that his or her response to a client does not become too far removed emotionally from the client's feelings and experiences (Carkhuff & Berenson, 1967). Using clear and specific language encourages the therapist to be more precise and accurate in understanding the group member. Thus, misunderstandings can be clarified and the therapist's thinking corrected. Also, the worker's concrete use of language communicates to group members the importance of their attending **in specific ways** to their problem areas and emotional conflicts.

Specifying the contract. One of the first places concrete language needs to be used is in the contract that the worker has with each group member as well as the contract the worker has with the group-as-a-whole. Otherwise, there will be double agendas and discrepant client/worker expectations (Compton & Galaway, 1984). For example, a member might see one problem as the target of the worker's intervention, while the worker sees another. Or a member who is expecting some form of **tangible help** with a problem will become frustrated while the worker is pursuing a different agenda, such as trying to get the client to see what is **causing** the problem. To the traditional axiom of "starting where the client is" is the addendum "and let the client know where you are, and where you are going."

In contrasting low and high levels of concreteness, Truax and Carkhuff (1964) define **a low level of concreteness** as when there is a discussion of anonymous generalities or when a discussion—even a discussion of "real" feelings—is conducted on an abstract level. They define a **high level of concreteness,** on the other hand, as when specific feelings and experiences are expressed. For example, if a group member says, "I hated my mother!" or " . . . then he would blow up and start throwing things," the group member is talking about a real emotion or a specific event. Concrete expressions always deal with specific emotions, situations, or events.

Group members are prone to speak in generalities, to use imprecise language, and to send mixed messages. For this reason, a group worker gets plenty of opportunities to practice and encourage concreteness. As group leaders, we can do this by clarifying what we hear. For example, we might ask," Are you saying . . . ?" or "Do you mean . . . ?" as a way of understanding what the person is trying to communicate. It may be that we missed the point because we were simply not listening. Or it may be that the individual's thinking was scattered and he or she gave a confusing account.

Another way for us to check out what is being said is to repeat back to a member what we heard. "Let me be clear as to what you are saying. You're saying . . . ." We can repeat the exact words or can paraphrase what was said.

CLARIFYING TERMS

Clients use words and expressions that have a multiplicity of meanings. For example:

- "I'm going crazy!"
- "I'm having a nervous breakdown!"
- "I can't take it any more!"

It is natural to assume that a group's members and leader, are basically on the same wave length and that there is common agreement among them as to meaning of most expressions. More often than not, however, each person is using a different reference point and coming to a different conclusion. Whereas an overwhelmed mother of six may say she is having "a nervous breakdown" (inferring a temporary loss of control), the worker may interpret her words as a request for hospitalization. To the client, the expression "I can't take it any more" may signify her exhaustion, as well as a need for some time away from her children. For the worker, it might appear to be a suicide threat.

When we hear such expressions, we need to help clarify their precise meaning by pressing the individual to explain his or her meaning. If the speaker is referring to something abstract such as a principle, it is useful to have the person give a concrete example from his or her own experience to illustrate what he or she means. For example, we might say to a client, "You say you want to be happy. Share with us what you will be like when you are happy." Again, it is our task as group workers to unravel each client's distortions and to challenge the client's erroneous conclusions in a facilitative and caring manner.

I-STATEMENTS

Group members will often substitute terms such as *the group, we, you,* and *one* for the word *I*. For example, a group member might say:

- **the group** wants
- **we** all feel
- **you** always
- **one** wonders sometimes

A group member may feel safer using the plural *we* or *the group* than using *I* because the member assumes that everyone in the group feels the same as he or she does. However, allowing the *we* pattern to become a norm can become self-defeating for the group-as-a-whole. It encourages a pseudo consensus, or "groupiness," rather than individual thinking. It also inhibits individual members from challenging each other for fear of violating the group's spirit of good will and for fear of disrupting any feelings of unanimity within the group.

The group worker needs to model, teach, and remind group members to use personal pronouns such as *I*. To do this, the group leader might note, "You have said **we** several times. Now, try saying the same thing but using **I** terms." Or the therapist might ask, "Do you really mean **the group** feels anger, or is it that **you** feel angry?"

If a therapist is aware of dissenting positions among group members, it is valuable for the therapist to question whether others in the group actually feel the same as the speaker does. The group leader might ask, "Tom has said **the group** was not happy last week. How do the rest of you feel?" It should be no surprise that often what initially appears to be the feelings or sentiments of the total group is really the expressions of one or two of the group's more articulate members. Whatever the result, it is important to determine how each member feels.

INTELLECTUALIZING

Intellectualization is a tactic commonly used to avoid the work of the group. Intellectualization occurs when group members indulge in explaining away and theorizing about feelings and realities rather than dealing directly with them. Issues in the here-and-now that are painful, confusing, and threatening lose their viability as they are elevated to a higher level of abstraction in the there-and-then. The group member who is using intellectualization feels protected and insulated by talking about problems existing "out there" in abstraction rather than dealing with pain being experienced in the here-and-now. For example, a client may more easily discuss anger she once felt toward a far-way relative than the anger she feels toward the man sitting next to her.

Clients are not the only ones who intellectualize. Workers often find themselves lecturing and "professing" to a therapy group. This nonproductive behavior bogs the group down and places obstructions in the way of its growth. Usually, when a clinician begins to wax authoritatively, it is because of his or her anxiety and insecurity. Therefore, lecturing happens more frequently during periods when a leader is unsure of what is going on in the group or is doubting his or her own competency.

Group members often trigger worker intellectualization by asking what appears to be an innocuous question such as these. "How come some groups seem to work, and others don't?" or "You have led groups before. How do we compare?" or "How come so many marriages now end in divorce?"

Instead of keeping the group on task, the worker responds with a mini-lecture on group dynamics or the perils of marriage.

A group worker needs to constantly monitor his or her own communication and quickly move a group back on track. If the presentation of information is germane to the group's discussion, the leader should only present it in terms of its relevance to group members' specific situations.

135
· · · · · · · ·

● Techniques: Practical considerations

1. Help group members clarify the meaning of any of their words, expressions, or comments that seem vague or unfamiliar to you.
2. Help group members personalize their comments through the use of I statements.
3. Avoid vagueness and generalities in your own comments.
4. Keep the group's focus on the here-and-now rather than the there-and-then.
5. Avoid giving lengthy lectures and long-winded directions.

GENUINENESS

An open and honest group leader has a tremendous advantage. First, group members perceive their interactions with such a leader as uncomplicated, straightforward, and usually appropriate. Second, because the leader is not playing a role, the separation between group theory and the method used by the leader is almost nonexistent. Third, the authentic helper is more visible and tends to convey the impression of strength and assurance.

Workers who are "real" and transparent enter into their relationship with groups without presenting a front or a facade. This means that such a worker is aware of the feelings he or she is experiencing at the moment and can communicate these feelings to a group if it seems appropriate to do so. To us, as therapists, being "real" and transparent means being ourselves rather than denying who we are.

GIVING FEEDBACK

Congruence is the antithesis of presenting a facade or defensive front to clients. When we are functioning in a congruent manner, according to Rogers (1961), we can look at the world around us openly and without fear; we can see ourselves accurately and realistically; we can trust ourselves, and look at any and all data without defending ourselves or distorting reality; we can accept facts about the world and about ourselves; and we can trust all of our feelings rather than fearing them.

As therapists, we must provide group members with honest feedback. This is not to say that we always need to reveal what we are thinking. There are many situations in which it is prudent to keep information to ourselves. If, however, our clients are going to change their circumstances, they need accurate information as to the consequences of their behavior.

Jourard (1971), in referring to his own personal evolution as a therapist, writes that his self-disclosures to patients—checked by common sense—became increasingly less premeditated and more spontaneous. He notes that his trust that his therapeutic actions would not harm his patients grew and that his fear of situations with which he could not cope diminished. Anxiety on his part, he observed, usually resulted in his making technical, and hence impersonal, responses to patients.

> When I am lucky enough to recognize my anxiety, I will sometimes say. "You are making me anxious." If I am concerned or worried, I let this be known.
> If a patient asks me a question that I genuinely would rather not answer, I tell him [*sic*], "I'd rather not answer." I give him [*sic*] true reasons, too. The most succinct way I have of describing what I do is that I strive to give the patient an openness of my self in that moment. I believe that he is entitled to an honest expression of my self as a professional man, and this is what I give him [p. 147].

To be genuine with a group, a worker also needs to have courage and the capacity to act on his or her convictions (Shapiro, 1978). The worker needs faith to hold onto these convictions with tenacity, to follow with determination the focus he or she has chosen, and to meet, in an accepting manner, the opposition to his or her leadership, which at times may explode with some violence. Courage enables the worker to penetrate, sometimes blindly, into new areas or to meet crises with aplomb.

NEGATIVE MODELING

Besides modeling positive behaviors—respect, warmth, concreteness, empathy, and authenticity, a group worker sometimes models negative, or undesirable, behaviors. Egan (1970) writes, "If the leader-member is not congruent and not socially intelligent in other respects, then his presence in the group will be disturbing rather than growthful and the participants will have to spend a good deal of energy learning how to deal with him" (p. 126).

If we put on a polite or professional front that doesn't permit us to function in a congruent way, the probability of our bringing about positive change in a client diminishes. Workers who opt for the "psychiatric deadpan" or the "perpetual smile"—viewing it as professional—too often remain themselves untouched, unmoved, and unaware. Yet to have insight into and to be responsive to the needs of individual members, a therapist must be aware of his or her own personal needs. Reik (1956) observes that to recognize and understand what takes place in the minds of others, the worker has first to look into himself or herself. "No deep insight into human minds is possible without unconscious comparison with our own experiences. The decisive factor in understanding the meaning and motives of human emotions and thoughts is something in the person of the observer . . . himself"

(p. 263). Such a searching is only possible when a division of oneself has preceded the observation.

As therapists, we develop responsiveness to our clients as we clarify in our own mind therapeutic function, our goals, the things we believe in, and who we are. We need to know about our modes of adaption, our predispositions, and our feelings. In short, we must know ourselves and be honest with ourselves as social workers and as human beings. Or, as written long ago on the temple of Apollo at Delphi: "Know thy self."

DIRECT CHALLENGES TO THE WORKER

What does a worker do when directly confronted by a group member or the group-as-a-whole? Often, challenges and verbal attacks come after the worker has set limits, thwarted group members, or, in some way, assumed an opposing position to that of the group or of particular group members. The exposed position of leadership can make a group leader a tempting target.

Suppose, for example, that the leader of a growth-oriented group tells one of its female members that she needs to examine her reasons for not attending the past three sessions. Later in the meeting, the same member might angrily announce that the leader is insensitive, incompetent, rude, unprofessional, and basically inadequate. And several other members, supporting the first one, might say they have been feeling the same thing. A "normal" reaction on the worker's part would be that of defensiveness.

As human beings, we tend to strike back when we, or our position, is threatened. We may look for justification to prove that we are right and the attacker is wrong. We may seek other members to support us, hoping to win them over to our side, encouraging a "we" and "they" situation.

Fear of conflict. Some practitioners consciously suppress anger and hostility within their therapy groups in order to reduce the likelihood of an attack. These therapists perceive conflict as dangerous and something to be avoided. Such a group worker's style becomes that of an always gentle, friendly, caring father/mother who always says the correct thing in the least offensive manner. Unfortunately, this saintlike role is not only unnatural but nontherapeutic.

As professionals, we need to keep control of the part of us that seeks peace at any price. This does not mean we should be abused or become an emotional or physical punching bag for individual members or the group. On the contrary, we need to be strong and set reasonable limits, but not run. What we have to do is go beyond the "normal" reaction and keep control of the part of us that wants to protect, defend, and counterattack. The capacity to tolerate confrontation, challenge, and attack is crucial to our effectiveness.

Nondefensive response. In spite of a group worker's feelings of fear, hurt, and anger—which are certainly genuine—an appropriate response to an attack within the group setting is to ask for more information. The worker might say, for example, "You are angry at me. I need to know what it is I did that upset you." It is also helpful for the worker to elicit specific examples or descriptive information by responding. "Tell me exactly what I said." In addition, it is useful for the worker to encourage other members to provide their opinions. The worker can do this by asking, "How did the rest of you view the situation?"

Attacks on the worker in a group is more common than in individual treatment, because a group is basically a system that offers mutual support (Kadis, Krasner, Weiner, Winick, & Foulkes, (1974). An attack on the worker provides an opportunity for the entire group to examine the reasons behind the attack, as well as its significance. So often, the underlying symbolic function served by the attack is as important as its actual content.

As the group members share their feelings, it is essential that the worker listen carefully to their words and comprehend their feelings. The worker's body language should be relaxed and open rather than defensive or guarded. If the leader has made an error of commission or omission, it is appropriate for him or her to apologize. But, the leader need apologize only if he or she has done something wrong.

The way a group leader responds to confrontations will affect the willingness of group members to take risks and to trust in the future. As therapists, we can serve as reliable role models if we respond openly during confrontations and not become defensive. To do this, we must avoid running either from the group members or from the conflict itself.

● **Techniques: Practical considerations**
1. Be aware of how you respond to hostility—particularly to hostility directed at you.
2. Be nondefensive if group members express concern with the group or your leadership.
3. If you have made an error in a therapy group admit your error to the group members.
4. If you don't know the answer to a client's question, do not fake an answer.
5. It is not necessary for you to answer all the questions asked by group members. Turn as many questions as possible back to the members, and have them struggle with the answers.

SELF-DISCLOSURE

Closely tied to worker authenticity is worker self-disclosure. There are two types of self-disclosure by group workers. The first type consists of self-disclosing messages that express the worker's personal reaction to the client or to the group-as-a-whole during a session. The information shared is of a here-and-now nature. For example, the following messages disclose a group worker's thoughts and feelings:

- You have been working hard, and I'm pleased with your progress. This group has been through a lot since its beginning, but the work is starting to pay off."
- "You have had a great deal of pain in the past two years. You have lost your job, and you have gone through a divorce. I feel your sadness, as well as your anger. I often wonder if, under the same circumstances, I would manage as well."
- "I'm angry! You said you want a group, and then no one shows up. I need a straight message. Do you want the group to continue, or is it time to end?"

The second type of leader self-disclosure consists of messages that focus on struggles or difficulties the worker is experiencing or has experienced that are similar to the problems of a member or the group. This type of self-disclosure is illustrated by the two examples that follow.

- "I was in a group that had the same kind of difficulty at its termination. We were glad that it was ending, but we didn't want to say good-bye to our friends."
- "The kinds of problems you are having with your child are the same I'm having with my 9-year-old. She makes me so angry I could scream."

BALANCED PERSONAL SHARING

In practice, the amount of leader self-disclosure that occurs within therapy groups varies greatly. At one end of the spectrum are practitioners who are careful not to make themselves personally known to their groups (Corey & Corey, 1987). They keep themselves mysterious and keep their personal involvement to a minimum. Some of these practitioners prefer this approach because they view their therapeutic role as that of a "screen" onto which group members project their own feelings. These transferred feelings are those the members have experienced toward family members and other people in positions of authority. Through this re-creation of their earlier relationships, the group members can expose and work through their unresolved conflicts.

Other practitioners hesitate to reveal themselves personally because they do not want to lose their "expert" image or the "doctor/patient" relationship. They assume that if they are perceived by the members as "equally human," this will contaminate the therapeutic relationship. Such workers keep their personal life and their personal reactions to group members and to the group-as-a-whole hidden from the group. Instead of saying how they feel, they focus on identifying themes, clarifying, and encouraging members to participate. They play the role of moderator, coordinator, and enabler.

140
• • • • • • • •

The following poem, *We Meet Again,* by Tom Prideaux places the worker's lack of self-disclosure in bold relief.

With half a laugh of hearty zest
I strip me of my coat and vest.

Then heeding not the frigid air
I fling away my underwear.

So having nothing else to doff
I rip my epidermis off.

More secrets to acquaint you with
I pare my bones to strips of pith.

And when the exposé is done
I hang a cobweb skeleton. (ed. note expose has mark over e)

While you sit there aloof, remote,
And will not shed your overcoat.

At the other end of the spectrum are practitioners who say whatever is going on in their mind as they consider the thought or feeling genuine and honest. The number of individuals using this approach has increased since the 1960s due, in a large part, to the growth of laboratory-training groups and encounter groups. This approach is also common among inexperienced group leaders trying hard to prove they are just as human as their group members. They unabashedly disclose details of their personal life and share, without hesitation, problems with friends and family. More often than not, the worker using this "let it all hang out" therapy is as limited in flexibility and restrictive in actions as the overly controlled or "deadpan" worker.

The practitioner who strives only to create a mystique of egalitarianism between group members and himself or herself may provide no leadership at all. Maslow (1962), in reflecting on this problem, notes that there are situations in which the "good leader must keep feelings to himself, let them burn out in his own guts and not seek the relief of catharting them to followers who cannot be helped by an uncertain leader" (p. 6).

There is a middle ground, in which a group worker discloses—but not too much or too little. The worker's willingness to disclose his or her reactions or experiences is not the result of a compulsion, but a means to an end. That end is helping group members model the worker's behavior and thus learn for themselves how to disclose. An additional end is helping the members develop useful alternate frames of reference that they did not have before joining the group.

What follows are guidelines for determining the appropriateness of a worker's self-disclosure.

Timing.   Self-disclosure by a group leader will have different effects on group members at different stages in a group's development. In the early stages, when the members are more vulnerable and unsure of the worker, the worker's self-disclosure of highly personal or intense information can be easily misunderstood and misinterpreted (Simonson, 1976). Rather than encouraging reciprocal self-disclosure, it may be threatening and lead to defensiveness and emotional retreat by group members.

Practitioners are well advised to avoid sharing personal feelings and experiences until a basic level of rapport and a basic trust in both the worker and the group have developed. Once the members manifest such trust, the worker can respond with increased openness and spontaneity whenever appropriate.

Appropriateness. The information disclosed by a group worker should have relevance and meaning for the current situation. If the information presented changes the topic or mood without a reason that the group can understand, the self-disclosure is usually not appropriate. The "honest worker" according to Parloff (1969) attempts to provide only the information that the clients can assimilate, verify, and utilize. Thus, before disclosing something, the worker should ask himself or herself, "Where is the group now, and will what I say set it in a different direction or cloud the issue?"

Motivation. The reasons and needs that prompt a specific self-disclosure by a worker should be examined. As practitioners, we are not in the group primarily so we can be honest; rather, we are in the group to help the members grow as individuals. We are not there to meet our own personal needs at the expense of the group members. **The professional relationship is for the client.**

Over and over, we need to ask ourselves, "What of my own needs are being met by the disclosure or the intervention?" One therapist, thinking she would help a group of women who had been sexually molested, shared details about her own painful relationship with a sexually aggressive step-father. After, she had gone into some detail, accompanied by tears, one of the members suggested that the worker find a therapist to talk to about her pain. Already overburdened clients do not need to be further burdened by the leader's problems.

● **Techniques: Practical implications**
1. Tell each group who you are, but don't say too much too soon.
2. If there is something painful or intense that you are considering disclosing, be sure the group members have a basic sense of trust in you and in the group-as-a-whole.
3. Make sure you understand your motivation before you decide to share a piece of personal information with group members.
4. Be selective in what you disclose about yourself, and do not burden your clients with your personal pain and struggles.
5. If you find yourself using a therapy group to solve your own problems, realize that it is time for you to seek help.

ACTIVE LISTENING

Listening is hard work, and few people do it well! Characteristic of most of the clients entering a therapy group is a feeling that they have not been heard much by other people. They describe themselves as feeling alone, unimportant, invisible, and different. Often, they enter the group feeling this way because their subjective experiences were not validated or responded to in their family of origin. For example, as children, when they were fearful or in pain, other people responded to them by saying:

- "That's crazy."
- "You're silly to think that."
- "Why are you unhappy? You have so much to be thankful for!"
- "Stop crying, or I'll give you something to cry about!"
- "You're stupid to feel the way you do."
- "Act your age!"

The adults in the client's life may have paid attention to the client only when they approved of what the client was saying. The client may have repeatedly been cut off and interrupted. He or she may have been discounted and thus learned through painful experience that his or her feelings and thoughts were of little value. Or, the client may have received attention from adults only when he or she misbehaved.

At the end of the initial interview with a client, it is not unusual to be thanked profusely for the help provided. This can be a surprise to a practitioner, especially if the practitioner feels he or she did no more than gather information—no interpretations, no suggestions, no answers. He or she **merely** listened. Clients often volunteer that no one truly listens to them—not their spouse, their best friend, and sometimes not even the therapist they have been paying for counseling. Or they say that when they have shared their pain, fears, or experiences with such "significant others" in their lives, they have felt compelled to package the information or feelings in such as way as to not offend or frighten their listener.

Listening is a prerequisite to the therapeutic alliance. The competent social worker—whether working with an individual, family, or small group—needs to be able to listen. When we fail to listen, the individual may be discouraged from further self-exploration, we may tackle the wrong problem, we may devise the wrong strategy, or we may not validate and confirm the person's subjective experience.

Clinical social work requires active listening. It is our job as clinicians to make sure that we really **do** hear what a client says—and that we let the client know that we are listening. Therapeutic listening helps our clients talk about **all** aspects of their concerns, not just what is superficial, immediately apparent, or safe.

We can demonstrate in various ways that we are listening. First, we can use our body language, the way we sit and the way we look at the person. Second, we can remember from meeting to meeting important details disclosed by the members. Third, we can ask questions and make interpretations from the data provided. Fourth, we can remember the names of people whom the members have brought up weeks earlier. Fifth, we can sort through piles of information and uncover an integrating theme. Finally, we can go beyond the layers of content and reflect on the members' feelings.

RECURRENT THEMES

As therapists, we must listen for recurrent themes in what group members say. As each group member shares his or her experiences, the member repeats certain words, feelings, concerns, and ideas. Although it may take a while for us to identify the synthesizing themes, they are there. For example, one group member may communicate in a multitude of different ways that "I'm powerless to do things differently " or "It's all my fault." Although the disparate material that each group member presents may at first seem unrelated and disconnected, themes are usually present and become evident to the worker who keeps listening.

Similarly, as each group member shares experiences, a repeating pattern of emotions or affects will emerge. The underlying feelings of sorrow, bitterness, rage, guilt, or shame that pervade the person's life will become clear. If we can identify the repetitive theme or primary affect that links together the client's experiences, the client will feel we understand (Teyber, 1988).

Themes are not limited to what an **individual** expresses. There are also **group** themes that recur during the life of a group. One common group theme is that of the group's powerlessness. Through words or actions comes the message "This group has little or no power to make a difference. No matter what we do, things won't change." Or there may be the group theme of "If it weren't for you, . . ." In this case, *you* refers to some person or thing that serves as the group's announced reason for its lack of success. The group might communicate, "If it weren't for you, Leader [Teacher, Doctor, Parent, Police officer, or Judge] I would be a happy, healthy person."

INCONSISTENCIES

Sometimes when we listen closely to a person, we sense that his or her words and nonverbal cues are dissimilar. For instance, a woman talks about her feelings of anger toward another group member. She says the group member was insensitive to her the week before when he told her, "You are more comfortable complaining about your problems than doing something productive to make things better." After she laments how awful she has felt all week, a self-satisfied smile comes to her face, and she changes the subject. Why the smile? Does she really feel angry and hurt, or is her saying so just an excuse to hammer the other person? Which message do we believe? Maybe this client recognizes what she is doing—perhaps not. By raising these questions, the worker presses the group member to reflect on her actions so the member and the worker both can better understand her internal feelings and her external behaviors.

There may be an inconsistency between what a member says he or she wants to do and what the member actually does. Week after week, for example, a 17-year-old member of an adolescent treatment group says he is going to give up drinking: "I know I have to stop. It's killing me." He then reports a recent incident during which he became deathly ill after consuming a six-pack of beer and nearly wrecked his father's car. His words are clear, "I want to stop." However, his actions say something else, I choose not to (or cannot) stop. The leader has a variety of choices. He or she can deal with what the client says, can deal with the behavior the client has reported, or, can address the contradiction between the two.

NONVERBAL BEHAVIOR

We also "listen for" the nonverbal cues of individual group members and the nonverbal cues of the group-as-a-whole. We listen by scanning the group with our eyes as a way of picking up the various reactions of the members. We also use our ears to hear what is said and what is not said.

Individual members.   In terms of an individual group member's nonverbal cues, we look for changes in facial expressions, hand gestures, tears, the tone of voice, and shifts of the body. A client's nonverbal messages may contradict each other, and they may contradict the verbal portion of the client's communication. Such contradictions are important in group therapy because they usually signal some area of confusion or pain that the client may need to deal with. Again, a group worker may choose to respond directly to such a contradiction. For example, the worker might note, "You said you were angry when the cop grabbed you, but you're smiling as you tell us about it." Or, the worker may choose to respond to a portion of a client's contradictory message. For example, the worker might stay, "I'm not clear why you are smiling—what's going on?"

The exact meaning of nonverbal behavior will vary from person to person, and a group worker needs to be cautious neither to overgeneralize or to oversimplify. For example, in one client, teary eyes might signal sadness and frustration in another client, the tears might result from trouble with a contact lens. Twisting, rocking, or squirming in a chair might be a sign of guilt in one person, but of a distended bladder in another person. When we sense that something is occurring within a group member, it is advisable to check it out rather than to assume we know what is happening.

The group-as-a-whole.   A group-as-a-whole can also send out nonverbal cues. Sometimes, these clues are far from subtle. For example, no one may show up for a session if a group confrontation with the worker occurred the previous week. Or subgroups may meet in the parking lot after the session to rehash what has been discussed.

Sometimes, in a session, there is a hostile period of silence during which no one seems willing to offer ideas, feelings, or thoughts. Even though the members have not consciously set out to be silent, nothing is offered.

Simply observing what goes on in a meeting provides a practitioner with a rich supply of information. Who comes in with whom? Where do members sit? What members sit together? Who comes to the meeting early, on time, late? Are members sitting away from the group? Do some members look at the worker when they are talking with someone else? Who talks first? Who needs to be coaxed to speak? What is the tone of the group—friendly, angry, muted, depressed, excited?

THE WHY QUESTION

A misused form of inquiry employed by many clinicians is the *why* question. In our search for the etiology of a problem or for an explanation of a pattern of behavior, we may press a group member to share his or her opinions and ideas. For example, we might ask:

- "Why did you hit your sister?"
- "Why did your husband leave you?"
- "Why do you feel the way you do?"
- "Why are you quiet?"
- "Why are you acting the way you are acting?"

For a practitioner, the word *why* is employed in the search of information. For a group member, however, the word *why* may connote disapproval and judgment. It is linked to having done something wrong or behaving badly and triggers a need in the member to justify the action, feeling, or belief in question.

Predictably, the effect of *why* questions on the group members will be negative, particularly for a member who has grown up in an environment in which *why* almost always implied blame and condemnation (Benjamin, 1981). Naturally enough, such a member will react to the word the way he or she has learned to react to it over the years, even though the worker is using *why* simply to make a genuine inquiry. Thus, whenever this member hears the word *why,* that word will trigger a defensive reaction—a defense of himself or herself, a withdrawal and an avoidance of the situation, or an attack.

Children and adolescents are particularly adept at parrying *why* questions. They have learned that *why* means *change your way to the way adults want you to act.* Some have learned that there is no **meaningful** reply to the question that will satisfy adults. So children and adolescents typically use responses such as "because" and "I don't know." Rather than feeling safe to explore and examine what is going on, they feel threatened and adopt a fight-or-flight position.

● Techniques: Practical considerations

1. Listen for group members' feelings and emotions when the members speak of their experiences.
2. Check out what group members are saying, so that you can make sure you understand.
3. When you don't know what to say to group members, say nothing.
4. Pay attention to members' nonverbal cues.
5. Listen more than you speak in the group.
6. Avoid asking group members *why*.

IN SUMMARY

Interpersonal skills essential to leading therapy groups include: warmth and respect, empathy, concreteness, genuineness, self-disclosure and the ability to listen. In a therapy group, a group leader can convey warmth and respect through his or her acceptance of group members. The way the group's leader comes across to its members is of utmost importance in his or her ability to create a nonthreatening, accepting atmosphere for the group. Empathy involves comprehending the subjective world of a group member and communicating this understanding to the member. Concreteness refers to the group leader's ability to clarify the facts and feelings conveyed by group members and to couch his or her own responses in accurate, clear, and specific language.

A group leader is genuine when acting congruently and without pretense—when he or she does not hide behind defenses but rather honestly shares his or her honest thoughts and feelings with the group. A group leader can use two types of self-disclosure: the leader can disclose his or her personal reactions as something happens in a group or can disclose experiences from his own life, but the leader must make sure doing so will help the group members. Listening requires the group worker to tune in to the verbal and nonverbal communication of individual group members and of the group-as-a-whole to identify recurrent themes and to identify inconsistencies that might reveal group members' confusion or pain.

SUGGESTED READINGS

BENJAMIN, A. (1981). *The helping interview* (3rd. ed.). Boston: Houghton Mifflin.

COURNOYER, B. (1984). Basic communication skills for work with groups. In B. Compton & B. Galaway (Eds.), *Social work processes* (3rd ed., pp. 294–303). Pacific Grove, Calif.: Brooks/Cole.

EGAN, G. (1982). *The skilled helper: A model for systematic helping and interpersonal relating* (2nd. ed.). Pacific Grove, Calif.: Brooks/Cole.

GITTERMAN, A. & SCHAEFFER, A. (1972). The white professional and the black client. *Social casework, 53*(5), 280–291.

REID, K. (1977). Worker authenticity in group work. *Clinical social work journal, 5*(1), 5–16.

8

WORKER
INTERVENTIONS

musician friend, who works in a piano store, tells me that if a particular note, such as an F sharp, is played on a piano, the same note on other pianos in the room begin to vibrate sympathically.

I was reminded of this recently while leading the second session of a group. One of the members shared a particularly painful experience, and it stirred something deep within each of us. There was a nodding of heads and even some tears. The words and feelings resonated deep within each person. No one else had experienced the exact situation, but we all understood.

Emotional vibrations seemed to be transmitted throughout the group. The member's revelations prompted others in the group to share their feelings and experiences. Individuals who, a week earlier, had been strangers became, in a special way, sisters and brothers. In Martin Buber's words, the relationship between each person evolved from "I-It" to "I-thou."

The sense of isolation self-imposed by group members seemed to diminish. In its place emerged a growing affirmation of self and a bonding, which was to serve as a foundation for their further risk taking.

As this onion-skin film of separation was peeled back, a quintessential lesson about the human condition was revealed. No matter how much we deny it, each of is a part of every other human being.

● ● ●

This chapter examines the role of the group worker in greater detail. There is an assumption that the essential skills—warmth and respect, empathy, concreteness, genuineness, self-disclosure, and the ability to listen, discussed in Chapter 7—are already well developed in the worker. Unless the worker has incorporated these interpersonal skills and become able to use them effectively, his or her attempts at more advanced interventions will appear shallow and manipulative and will prove ineffective.

The question this chapter addresses is this: what are the worker interventions that promote interaction and that can result in meaningful changes in a group member's life? The focus of this chapter is on leadership functions and on co-therapy.

LEADERSHIP FUNCTIONS

A group leader's functions involve both the sharing of his or her technical expertise and the modeling of appropriate behavior. As a technical expert, a group worker provides group members with information, asks them questions, and gives them direction. As a model-setting participant (and thus not actually a group member), the worker uses his or her own internal processing and responding to help group members take risks and discover their own potential for growth.

Goulding (1975) talks of the three Ps that every effective therapist provides for group members: protection, permission, and potency. An effective group worker protects each group member from unhelpful confrontation and from oversupport by other members, as well as from excessively self-critical behaviors. An effective practitioner gives each group member explicit and implicit permission to try new patterns, explore feelings, respond honestly, and to have fun. An effective clinician offers potency because group members develop confidence in his or her skills, knowledge, and sensitivity—which make believable and trustworthy the protection and permission the clinician offers. This potency is a critical factor in a therapist's ability to help a group move **beyond** superficial interaction and **into** the real process of treatment.

To be therapeutically potent, a group worker must be genuine and transparent. The worker's humanness cannot be covered up with a facade of professionalism. The worker must be able to authentically acknowledge his or her feelings of frustration and satisfaction, excitement and concern, and joy and pain in a way that does not project responsibility for these feelings onto the group. Above all, this kind of honesty requires the worker to willingly accept and admit to fallibility and humanness.

The beginning group worker, as well as the seasoned practitioner, makes mistakes; this comes with the territory of being a group leader. It is not unprofessional to own up to these mistakes, along with whatever frustration or embarrassment they carry in their wake. Appearing infallible presents a confusing and perplexing example for group members. As therapists we are forced to weigh a client's every word and evaluate a client's every move—as well as our own—which can result in quasi-authenticity. Ironically, this is the very behavior that many group members initially exhibit and need to go beyond in order to get on with their growth.

A group leader's functions are those actions that the leader takes in order to reach an agreed-upon purpose and objectives. They in no way represent a bag of tricks. Rather, they are the requisite interventions based on his or her training, theoretical orientation, and personality. The following leadership functions, while not mutually exclusive, are comprehensive and relevant to the therapeutic process that occurs in group treatment.

GUIDING INTERACTION

A primary function of a group leader is guiding and promoting interactions occurring in groups. This function is especially important in the beginning stages of a group, or when new members join an established group. At times like these, group members are unclear as to their role and the situation is ambiguous. Clients who are new to group work, are unclear as to what to do in a group and are afraid to say things for fear of being misinterpreted. They also expect to ask questions of the therapist—as they would of their doctor, accountant, or lawyer—and to receive specific answers in return. In addition, they may want to share information about their circumstances but hesitate out of fear that they will be thought of as aggressive or pushy.

The group worker needs to be active in the early life of the group in order to keep the group goal-oriented and to assist with member-to-member interactions. The worker should lead a discussion of the group's purpose and goals and what it means to be a member of the group. The worker should explain his or her own role and what the members can expect from him or her. The worker should also discuss group guidelines and pertinent issues such as activities, attendance, risk taking, confidentiality, self-disclosure, and confrontation.

To lessen their sense of separateness, the therapist should help the group members identify common denominators. The therapist can do this by making a conscious effort to accentuate the similarities rather than the differences among group members. For example, the group leader can ask participants to say their names, to discuss their concerns, and to express their feelings about being in the group. Also, the worker should share leadership responsibility by encouraging participants to help each other.

The worker can also encourage group interaction by being sensitive to the group members' comfort and safety. The therapist can point out the location of bathrooms, drinking fountains, and phones and discuss the availability of coffee or snacks. And the worker can make sure the physical arrangement of the meeting room fosters communication. For example, he or she can set chairs in a circle, as opposed to a square or an ellipse, as a way of encouraging member-to-member interaction.

As a group moves beyond what Bach (1954) calls the **leader-dependence** phase, its members become increasingly willing to assume responsibility for their own actions and growth. When this happens, the worker's task becomes less one of promoting interaction and more that of facilitating interaction. The term *facilitation* implies that action is taken to **enhance** that which is already occurring. And this is what the group leader begins to do. The group itself provides the stimulus that propels it into action. The practitioner responds to the group's action by suggesting methods that make communication patterns used by the group more effective and meaningful.

The worker encourages group members to talk about their problems in such a way that the problems can be resolved. Instead of answering questions directly, the worker reflects the individual's feelings, identifying patterns that may not be obvious. The worker interprets for group members their communication patterns and addresses the members' self-defeating behaviors. The worker encourages members to provide honest feedback and to "hold up mirrors" to each other so that each member is provided a view of himself or herself through the eyes of others.

CONSOLIDATING

An especially useful function of a group leader is that of drawing together and consolidating diverse elements that may be beyond a group member's level of consciousness. The leader does this by linking connecting themes in a brief and coherent manner so that the members can deal with them.

151

·······

SYNTHESIZING

One aspect of consolidating is that of synthesizing each group member's verbal and nonverbal communication. This is done by making connections between what the person says and what he or she does; by making his or her implicit feelings and thoughts explicit; by pointing out recurrent themes in the member's behavior; and by bringing the member's hidden agendas to the surface.

Practitioners also synthesize by connecting comments, themes, and concerns from previous group meetings so that group members can see how material they have shared in the past relates to the present (Dyer & Vriend, 1975). A member may talk about four or five isolated incidents in his or her life and not recognize how these incidents are linked. By establishing the relationship between these separate fragments, the worker helps the member fit together interrelated parts of his or her personal puzzle.

Therapists can also link together specific issues—such as conflict with authority figures, fear of taking risks, or feelings of excessive guilt—that a group member is struggling with. Discovering such connections is no simple task for the worker. It means bringing together seemingly unrelated bits and pieces and relating them in a way that the group member can understand. After linking several comments made by a client, for example, someone who has difficulty with strong emotions, the group worker might say,

> Have you noticed how often the word *anger* comes up in your comments about yourself? Two weeks ago, you told how angry you were with the program. Last week, you said you were angry with your supervisor, and also with one of your professors. A couple of minutes ago, you said you were angry with me. What do you suspect this pattern means?

Making such a linkage requires a group worker to recall what has been said earlier and then to search for the thread that winds through the individual's transmissions. It is like playing Bach's *Brandenburg Concertos* the first time and hearing only harmonious, unrelated segments but then, after listening to the same music played several more times, suddenly recognizing a basic motif, or pattern. The pattern was there all the time; however, the listener was not attuned to its subtle nuances.

SUMMARIZING

In group work, summarizing refers to a group leader's concise review of the core points discussed by group membes. Generally, a summary is done at the end of a meeting as a means of pulling together divergent threads. During their interactions, members are often so intent on listening to the details and sharing their own thoughts and feelings that they lose sight of the larger picture. The group leader can help the members gain perspective on what has transpired during the meeting by summarizing, as shown in the following example:

> We have covered a lot of ground in the past 90 minutes. We have talked about confidentiality, the support group members receive from their spouse, finding time for ourselves, trying to make others happy, and feeling confident in what we are doing on the job. Of these, are there any issues you would like to discuss in greater depth next week?

Often, a summary can also be helpful in the middle of a meeting by providing members with an opportunity to reflect on what has taken place. At mid-meeting, a group worker might say:

> So far, we have discussed the anger individuals feel toward the hospital, particularly about the insensitivity of the staff and the limited visiting hours. We have 45 minutes left. Is there anything else you would care to say about these topics before we move on to something else?

Often, members cannot remember what occurred during the previous meeting. In addition, the members who were absent may feel lost and unable to follow what is going on. So, some group workers begin each session with a synopsis of the previous session. Here is an example:

> If you recall, last week we talked about the group's ending in a couple of weeks. Some of you said you felt a sense of relief that Wednesday nights will no longer be tied up. Others spoke of feeling sad about the group's ending. Does anyone want to add to this list or share something that was especially meaningful to you last week?

A summary at the beginning of a session will sometimes provide the group worker with clues to unfinished business. For example, group members may talk about the feelings and thoughts they experienced on the ride home or tell about a dream they had related to a particular group topic. They may also tell of their frustration regarding what was, or was not, said.

Bridging.   Because of the span of time between sessions, groups that meet once a week often have difficulty in getting started. Beginning the group with a brief summary of the high points of the previous session serves as a way of bridging between meetings. Likewise, a summary at the end can be used as a means of bringing to the surface ideas and concerns for the following session. With either timing, the reason for summarizing is not to rehash what has been previously discussed but to enhance continuity between sessions.

PARTIALIZING

In group work, *partializing* refers to a group leader's breaking of a group member's problems or concerns into manageable units. It is the process of separating out from the universe of problems brought to a group by a member those issues that are to become the focus of treatment. The leader's objective is to assist each group member problem solve in such a way that the complexity of the task or issue does not seem overwhelming to the member.

Partializing, as a sorting-out activity, conveys a number of important messages to group members. First, partializing shows that the tasks and the problems faced by each group member and the group-as-a-whole are manageable. Second, partializing shows clients that they can best deal with any problem when it is broken down into smaller segments. Third, partializing assists the group in concentrating its energies on the purposes that brought its members together. Finally, the act of specification sets the stage for evaluating each member's and the group's productivity (Balgopal & Vassil, 1983).

REFRAMING

Often, a client has a rigid view or definition of his or her problems. From the client's particular perspective, the problems have only very limited solutions. From other people's perspectives, however, there may be a multiplicity of possibilities.

In some cases, a client may expect to succeed against all odds and thus may misdefine his or her problem to match those expectations. Sarah's limited and mistaken definition of her problem is a case in point. Sarah, a tired-looking 32-year-old mother of five who was attending a women's group for the first time, complained of being physically exhausted and depressed. She said she could not understand the reason for her tiredness, since typically she was robust and full of energy. When encouraged to talk about her circumstances, she related that she was responsible for taking care of her invalid mother. She and her husband were having financial problems because her husband had lost his job. In addition, two months earlier, she had had her third miscarriage in two years.

For Sarah, there was little or no recognition of the relationship between the circumstances in her life and her physical condition. She was just doing the things she expected herself to do as a wife, daughter, and mother. The group members, on the other hand. expressed their astonishment that Sarah was able to function at all. One group member asked her, "How come you are not more depressed?" A member the same age as Sarah admitted, "If it were me," "I would take to my bed and not get up."

The worker, with help from the group, began to reflect back what Sarah had said, underscoring the point that any one of the issues Sarah was trying to deal with was enough to exhaust a person. Sarah soon recognized that the feelings she was experiencing were a "normal reaction" to a set of complicated and painful problems. She also began to identify life-enhancing activities—such as exercising and taking time for herself—that she could reasonably include in her daily routine.

In other cases, a client may expect to be a failure and thus may misdefine his or her problem to match those expectations. Such a client distorts reality to fit his or her expectations of inadequacy. For example, Franklin, a 41-year-old man unhappy in his marriage, was afraid to seek a divorce. He had considered leaving his wife as a way of finding peace but was fearful that their children would be abused by his wife. Franklin's perception of himself for staying in the marriage was that of a coward. This perception fed into his sense of being weak and incompetent.

The group leader helped Franklin rethink his weaknesses and strengths by suggesting that it took courage for Franklin to stay in the marriage and to protect the children from physical harm. Rather than resulting from weakness, Franklin's actions—reframed by the leader—required great strength.

Here again, the group member had a certain mind-set based on unrealistic expectations and a faulty perception of his problem. By reframing the problem and thus providing the client with a fresh perspective, the leader freed the client to problem solve in a more creative manner. In short, the client began to view as normal circumstances that, heretofore, he had viewed as abnormal.

SUPPORTING

There are times when individual group members and the group-as-a-whole need the support of the therapist. At those times, the worker can provide support in a number of ways. First, he or she can encourage the expression of **thoughts** on subjects relevant to the group. The worker can solicit group members' opinions and feelings and then respond in such a way that the members know they have been heard. Second, the worker can assist a group member during periods of crisis when the member is confused as to what is happening internally as well as externally. The worker can also provide support whenever the member ventures into new and frightening territory where the outcome is uncertain.

Third, the worker can encourage a group member to ventilate **feelings,** especially those—such as fear, anger, hurt, rage, grief, or hate—that are frightening to the member. For many clients, feelings and thoughts are the same. Such clients have an inability to differentiate between them.

Worker as rescuer. A common mistake is a group worker's offering support before a group member or a group has had an opportunity to fully experience a conflict, or some intense feelings (Corey & Corey, 1987). Although the worker's intervention is done with the best of intentions, it may abort or block feelings the member or group needs to experience. For example, a group member who is in tears because the worker has confronted her for being absent may need to experience the hurt and anger she feels toward the worker before she can think about her own actions.

155

Holding back and not rescuing when an individual or a group is floundering can be agonizing to a group worker. His or her helping impulse is triggered, and the worker wants to help. The therapist's knee-jerk reaction is to step in and make things right. But, difficult as it may be, not rescuing is often the most productive strategy. On average, in a group setting, it is more valuable for the members to work things out and solve their own problems. It may take longer for them to do it themselves, but their gains in learning and their added feelings of competency are worth the discomfort (Posthuma, 1989).

Whenever a group member begins to critically examine his or her own behavior, the member will experience some internal resistance to being truly honest. Resistance of this nature is natural, in that no one easily gives up something that has been a part of his or her life-support system. Giving up a behavior means taking a risk, even when that behavior is self-defeating. Whenever we ask someone to be honest with himself or herself about the causes of his or her behavior, the person must either defend against such an onslaught or admit to alternative ways of thinking and behaving.

For a client, admitting to new possibilities of thinking and behaving means having to rework what, up until now, the client has taken for granted. The client may experience this as rejection of a part of himself or herself (Dyer & Vriend, 1980). The client may think, "If I become something different, then the old me was no-good, and I must admit this." As group leaders, we will be constantly asking clients to examine large chunks of what they have become, as well as behaviors that no longer work for them. It is at this point that our encouragement, reassurance, and support are vital in helping the person give up self-fortifying and self-defeating behavior.

CONFRONTING

Professional helpers tend to be uncomfortable with conflict and reluctant to confront their clients. While the reasons for this reluctance are unclear, it may be related in part to the type of individuals drawn to the helping professions. It may also be related to the overriding need of many professional helpers to be liked. Most of us like to be thought of as a warm, benign, loving, surrogate parent who is supportive and caring no matter what. However, it has been observed by some writers that such a lack of willingness to confront clients has produced an anemic form of therapy that purports to seduce illness away (Douds, Berenson, Carkhuff, and Pierce, 1967).

156
....

Confrontation is a part of psychoanalytic as well as nondirective therapies. Various psychoanalysts (Greenson, 1967; Lang, 1973; and Schafer, 1983) have underscored the value of confrontation as a critical strategy in bringing to the surface a patient's unconscious information. Before there can be helpful interpretation and subsequent "working through," the patient must deal with that which he or she has been avoiding. Gendlin (1970), writing from a client-centered perspective, encourages clinicians to go beyond the client's "experiential field" and to confront the person's behavior from the therapist's personal frame of reference. Rogers (1970b), in reflecting on his own professional evolution, admits that he is willing to express himself and his feelings openly as data for the person to use but not as a guide or an imposition. "If I am angry I will express that anger as something within myself and not as a judgment on the other person" (p. 519).

The word *confrontation* conjures up images of antagonism and attack. Within a treatment context, it may bring to mind stories of groups in which "attack therapy" and the "hot seat" were not only the therapeutic norm but also the major form of intervention. The term *confrontation* connotes anger, hostility, discomfort, and aggressiveness. It suggests being punitive and insensitive to someone.

For our purposes, *confrontation* is defined as a conscious act initiated by a group worker to bring a client and a group-as-a-whole into direct contact with their strengths, weaknesses, blind spots, and resources (Reid, 1986). Confrontation can be a humane and sensitive way of conveying understanding and, at the same time, a means of challenging group members to deal constructively with their verbal and nonverbal actions. For this to occur, the clinician first has to be aware of his or her reasons for wanting to confront. Ideally, confrontation is an invitation for group members to engage in self-examination so that they can see themselves as others see them. During the life of a group, this self-examination and self-challenge are expected to occur both in the group and in clients' activities outside the group.

GROUP OR INDIVIDUAL FOCUS

A group leader can direct confrontation at either the actions of a group or the actions of one or more of its members.

Challenging a group. Challenges directed toward a group are usually centered on themes and process, particularly on the group's communication patterns, roles, resistance, and decision making. The leader's objective is to enhance group interaction so that the group develops ways of functioning that facilitate communication between members while providing a setting for their reality testing. As therapists, we must help the members keep their focus on the problems and issues central to the group's purpose.

The following are examples of themes frequently addressed in groups.

- reluctance to make decisions
- challenges to the worker's authority
- scapegoating of a member
- inability to make a decision or solve a problem
- frustration with prescribed limits
- apathy
- separation and loss

In challenging the group-as-a-whole, the worker's emphasis is on the process. The leader uses confrontation, as well as other techniques, to isolate certain types of interactions between group members and to enable the group members to establish greater intimacy. Focusing on the group-as-a whole is seen by many therapists as a unique situation within which interactions between members can be influenced. The worker can challenge the barriers that prevent full interpersonal interaction within the group. Attention is on the **here-and-now** rather than the historical **there-and-then** and, in general, **between** members as opposed to **within** members.

Challenging an individual.   Confronting the actions of an individual in the group is similar to what we do in the more traditional dyadic encounter. The worker helps the group member examine his or her behaviors, communications, and assumptions with the goal of bringing about cognitive, emotive, and behavioral changes. The primary difference lies in the fact that a group, in time, develops into a social microcosm in which members are more their genuine selves than they are pseudo selves. Their interactions with other group members becomes increasingly similar to the way the individual interacts with the significant people in his or her environment.

This social microcosm offers two important clinical advantages for the practitioner. First, it provides direct opportunities to view the person in action, rather than having situations described after the fact by the client or someone else. Second, it provides an immediate, avenue for intervention. Thus, the relationship patterns that are replicated can be observed and directly addressed in the group. Initially, it may be the worker who challenges the member's action; however, as the group becomes more comfortable, other members begin to challenge as well. As an atmosphere of trust increases, the individual becomes more willing to take risks, express painful feelings, and test out new and more productive behaviors (Yalom, 1985).

A worker needs to be judicious in confronting individual group members. The worker must be sensitive to each individual's ability to hear and adequately process the worker's challenge (Reid, 1986). If a member is disorganized or confused at the moment, it does little to add to the disorganization by further challenging him or her. A well-developed sense of timing on the worker's part allows the group member to mobilize his or her resources and go beyond his or her present limits and perceptions.

Behaviors and actions the worker may wish to confront, either with the group-as-a-whole or an individual member, include discrepancies, distortions, resistance, games, and smoke screens.

CONFRONTING DISCREPANCIES

In dealing with discrepancies, we confront the differences between what is said and what is done; what is wished for and what actually is; how something is perceived by others and what is being experienced; the values expressed and the behaviors exhibited (Reid, 1986). Sometimes, the individual or the group is fully aware of the inconsistencies in actions, thoughts, and values; while in other instances, there seems to be little awareness of the inconsistencies. Some examples of discrepancies between what a client or group says and does are as follows:

- A client says, "I want counseling and know I need it," **but** the person does not attend sessions.
- A client says, "I am going to stop smoking" **but** five minutes later lights up a cigar.
- Several group members say, "The group is very important to us," **but** no one talks or shares feelings.

CONFRONTING DISTORTIONS

Clients often distort reality to fit their needs. They may identify or define themselves in a certain way and never challenge the assumptions. Group treatment is especially valuable in confronting a client's distortions, specifically the illusion of helplessness and powerlessness.

Illusion of helplessness.   A sense of helplessness is a recurring example of an unchallenged feeling often experienced by clients. Seligman (1975) has postulated that learned helplessness is linked to reactive depression and is acquired when a person comes to believe that his or her actions will have no impact on the outcome of a situation. Clients experiencing this sense of helplessness have three beliefs in common. First, they believe that their sense of helplessness reflects a personal inability to control outcomes. Second, they believe that their sense of helplessness is proof that they are basically inadequate in every aspect of their life. Third, they believe that their sense of helplessness will go on indefinitely rather than be situational and time-limited.

Mrs. Miller, a 38-year-old member of a group the author led, reported a pattern of episodes in which she rescued her son, Kevin, when he was in trouble with neighbors, the school, and the police. She was fearful of Kevin and especially concerned with his lying and stealing. His stealing had reached the point that she had begun to take her purse with her to the bathroom to keep Kevin from taking her money. Several weeks earlier, she had been forced to forfeit several thousand dollars in bail money when he did not show up for a court hearing. "Every time I try to help him, it is like he spits in my face," she reported.

As the patterns of her unsuccessful rescue attempts became evident, the worker and then other group members confronted Mrs. Miller with her protective behavior. Initially, she denied rescuing Kevin and became angry with the group. After several sessions, she role-played a situation in which she stood up to Kevin. In subsequent sessions, she still spoke of her temptation to assist her son but also of her more positive efforts to help him face the consequences of his actions. More attuned to her own excessive need to protect, Mrs. Miller evolved from feeling helpless to having a sense of greater control over her own actions. This was no easy task for Mrs. Miller. With the group's support and encouragement, she was able to assume a more assertive posture with Kevin. A major accomplishment for Mrs. Miller was refusing to let Kevin stay in her apartment, and not accepting his collect phone calls.

Theme of powerlessness. Like the theme of helplessness, the theme of powerlessness runs through groups, and the lives of individual group members. Powerlessness is a person's inability to manage skills, knowledge, and/or material resources in a way that enables the person to effectively perform the social roles he or she values and thus receive personal gratification (Solomon, 1976). The sense of powerlessness is especially prevalent within the Black clients, Hispanic clients, and other members of minority communities. It is also characteristic of the mentally ill, the aged, and students.

A major task of a group leader is to empower group members to take responsibility for their own lives inside and outside the group. To empower group members the leader must share his or her leadership with them and accept them as fellow human beings with their own innate dignity and intrinsic value. As therapists, we are committed to helping each group actualize and use its own creative potential. To this end, we strive to create conditions conducive to the group's growth and maturity.

CONFRONTING RESISTANCE

In group work, the term *resistance* refers to an attitude on a group member's part that seems to make the member fight treatment and try to preserve ways of acting that are psychologically crippling and self-defeating. Ordinarily, such resistance can be seen in the member's communication style, including his or her nonverbal messages. For example, a group member may actually place his or her chair apart from the rest of the group or may assume a posture that creates distance between himself or herself and the other members. The person's refusal to speak or share feelings and ideas impacts on the other members and defeats the group's purpose. So, the resistance of one group member can influence the treatment of other group members, as well as his or her own.

How the group worker handles the withdrawn member will depend on the leader's knowledge of the member's circumstances and previous experiences in the group and on the specific effect the member's behavior is having on other members. For example, it may be appropriate for the worker to coax the withdrawn person into speaking. Or, perhaps, the leader will decide to wait the person out. Another possibility is for the worker to remind the member of a previously agreed-on rule of the group (Reid, 1986). The worker might say:

- "Dennis, you have been distant from the group for the past three sessions. It was the group's decision to share and be open with each other. You are going against what you and the hers agreed on."
- "You didn't agree to be a part of the group just when it felt good. Share with us what's going on behind your eyes."

The worker might also urge the other members of the group to give the withdrawn member feedback as a means of drawing him or her into the group. To do this, the worker might say, "Obviously, the way Dennis is sitting is making some of you uncomfortable. Tell him what you are feeling about his actions."

Monopolizers present similar problems for both the worker and the group. During moments of silence, these individuals fill the gaps with personal experiences or information that may or may not be pertinent. In the early stages of the group, this behavior is viewed by other members with relief, because it redirects attention away from them. Although the monopolist frustrates them, the other group members do not always articulate these feelings. Instead, they experience silent rage, pull back emotionally, and use nonverbal cues to suggest their contempt and disgust.

A useful intervention is for the leader to confront the group members about what is going on inside them at that very moment. More specifically, the leader can encourage each person to say what he or she has been experiencing—but has not shared. The group-as-a-whole may also profit by examining its exploitation of the monopolist. The group leader might comment, "What would the group do without Susan? When there is silence, you can always depend on her to reduce the tension."

Other possible areas of focus are the group's reasons for inactivity, fear of assertiveness, fear of hurting the monopolist, or anticipation of retaliation. The leader might say to the group, "Susan has been telling about her fight with her boyfriend for the past five minutes. When I look around the group, I see people yawning, giggling, and looking out the window. Tell Susan what you are thinking."

Once a monopolist is established in a group, the only way to change his or her behavior is through confrontation, which may reverberate with negative repercussions throughout the group process. Therefore, it is necessary to identify monopolistic behavior early and act to create a more balanced pattern of communication characterized by participation by the entire group (Trotzer, 1977).

CONFRONTING GAMES AND SMOKE SCREENS

The term *game* has come to mean an ongoing series of complementary transactions that progress to a well-defined predictable outcome (Reid, 1986). Games and smoke screens, like distortions and resistance, are used by group members to avoid intimacy and evade involvement. Clearly, these diversions have obvious negative outcomes, such as preventing a client from developing deep and meaningful interpersonal relationships. Unfortunately, they also provide "payoffs" and secondary gains for a client, including control over other people, a way to avoid anxiety, and a way to avert psychological risk. For some clients, games are a way of life. These clients express feelings that are deliberately chosen to fit the occasion, see only what they wish to see, and hear only what they wish to hear. They also use people to their own ends, caring little about the impact they have on the other individuals.

A pattern that frequently becomes apparent in groups is the classical *yes, but* situation, in which a group member seeks advice from the worker and other members and then rejects the helpful assistance they offer. Here's how a group member playing *yes, but* might sound:

Member A: "I can't decide whether or not to . . . ."
Member B: "Why don't you . . . ?"
Member A: "Yes, but . . ."
Worker: "Why don't you . . . ?"
Member A: "Yes, but . . . ."

This series of transactions can go on indefinitely, or until the participants tire and give up in frustration. Usually, the worker and members soon feel frustrated, stymied, and defeated. If the pattern persists from meeting to meeting, the members experience over and over the sense of being victimized and "hooked" into a loop that has no end. Once the pattern is identified, the leader needs to address it in a caring and responsible manner. If a *yes, but* player is not confronted, his or her pattern is reinforced, and the individual will continue to manipulate other people both inside and outside the group. A possible confrontation for the worker to make to Member A's *yes, but* is "I'm uncomfortable with what's taking place. First, you ask for help. Then, when other people give you ideas, you discount them." An even more powerful challenge by the worker might be "Are you sure you want advice? I see you asking for assistance then rejecting it. You did the same thing two weeks ago." In both examples, the worker provides feedback as something of his or her own: "I'm uncomfortable with . . . ." and "I see that . . . ."—with the worker specifying something he or she has noticed about the member's behavior. The leader's comments must relate to a concrete action by the client, and not to the client as a person. In fact, it is important that the group member be provided with as much concrete detail as possible touching on what the experience meant for the worker and for other group members.

A smoke screen has some of the same characteristics as a game and also serves as a way of hiding a client from the intimacy of strong emotions and close personal relationships. It is common, for example, for a client to use pseudo intimacy disguised as self-disclosure and authenticity. Rather than revealing his or her emotions, the client uses socially desirable behaviors to mask what is really going on inside. On the surface, the person appears genuine, transparent, open, and in touch with his or feelings. Under the surface, however, the individual experiences acute distrust of what is gong on within himself or herself and within other people. The client perceives that relationships involve only two alternatives: to control or to be controlled.

A caveat. Sometimes, it is a group leader in conjunction with group members who pressure a client into being something he or she is not. An illustration of this is Stanford's (1972) reflection on his experience in an encounter group. After some effort on his part to be open and honest with the other group members, he was told that he was being defensive and dishonest.

> Their continued attacks on me soon made me aware that openness was not getting anywhere with this group. Perhaps it wasn't openness that they valued (despite their continual admonishing me to "open up") . . . . I decided to give each member, not openness, but whatever it was I sensed he wanted from me [p. 3].

Once Stanford assumed this counterfeit facade of openness, he became accepted by the other group members as a valued member of the group. Ironically, he was being reinforced for his dishonesty and phony behavior—something antithetical to the group experience. If, by omission or by commission, we allow a member's pseudo openness to go on without being challenged, we tacitly reward the use of games and smoke screens. If, on the other hand, we expose the pseudo openness to the group and confront specific members with their behavior, the false behavior frequently stops altogether.

POTENCY OF LANGUAGE

There are times when confrontation by a group worker is not heard, or has minimal impact on a group's or a member's behavior. The group or member may simply ignore or discount the kinds of verbal responses that workers judge to be the essence of empathetic understanding, unconditional positive regard, and good taste. It is at such a moment that a seemingly "rude" and abrasive challenge from the worker is useful for its shock value.

Depending on the kind of language normally used in the group, a practitioner's forceful challenge—"I don't buy what you are saying!" or "I think you are conning yourself!"—can have a remarkable impact. In a more cryptic way, the worker might respond confrontationally with an acrimonious comment such as "Garbage!" "Crap!" or "Bull Shit!" However, the leader must be prudent in using expletives and emotional-laden words. If over-used, they quickly lose their magical power. They can also be offensive and alienate certain clients, who become so blocked by the medium that they fail to hear the message.

• Techniques: Practical considerations

1. Confrontation with group members needs to be gradual so that they can assimilate what is being said.
2. You can make sure confrontation is legitimatized if you make it a part of your contract with group members.
3. Group members will perceive too much confrontation too soon as an attack.
4. You should use confrontation only after a foundation of trust and acceptance has been laid within the group.
5. A group member who is being challenged will be less resistant and defensive if the member is told what effect his or her behavior is having on other group members—and does not simply have his or her behavior labeled as being a certain way.
6. The strength of your confrontation with a group member must be proportioned to the degree of fragility and the degree of disorganization within the person you are confronting.

PROCESSING

In group work, *processing* refers to a leader's verbal response to something that is happening in a group at a particular moment. This particular focus is, according to Yalom (1985), the truly unique feature of experiential groups such as therapy groups and encounter groups.

There are many socially sanctioned activities in which an individual can express emotions, help others, give and receive advice, confess, and discover similarities between himself or herself and other people. But where is it permissible for a person to comment in depth, on here-and-now behavior, and on the nature of immediately occurring relationships between people?

Yalom writes that, process commentary among adults is taboo social behavior. It is considered rude, impertinent, shocking, intrusive, or flirtatious. It is observed generally in the context of extreme conflict, and when it surfaces, when individuals comment about each others' manners, gestures, speech, physical appearance, one can be certain that the battle is bitter and the possibilities of conciliation chancy.

Often referred to as *immediacy,* the focus of a group worker's processing may be a single here-and-now transaction in a group or the sum of an individual's or a group's transactions. Nevertheless, processing by a leader always invites group members to explore relationships that are in the here-and-now.

Processing has two purposes. First, a leader can use processing to bring out into the open something the leader feels about himself or herself, a member, or the group-as-a-whole. One rationale for doing this is the assumption that holding feelings inside, particularly negative ones, will inhibit effective communication between people and prevent them from forming closer relationships. Second, a leader can use processing to provide feedback about some aspect of a specific interaction as it occurs. The worker might share his or her feelings about the interaction or might describe something that he or she observes as going on in the interactive process.

Any decision on the worker's part to focus on an individual rather on the group, or vice versa, must take into consideration the framework of the particular group—its purpose, structure, goals, duration, and membership (Levine, 1979). For example, it is seldom useful to engage a short-term crisis group in exclusive exploration of here-and-now experiences, when the group's concern is the crisis at hand. Likewise, expecting members of an education-oriented group, to focus on in-depth feelings toward each other when their reason for attending is to gain information, is folly. At the other extreme, if a long-term, open-ended group of outpatient drug abusers does not deal with the here-and-now of their process, the group's members will miss major opportunities for emotional growth.

Bi-focal perspective. A group leader is in a unique position to observe sequences, cyclical patterns of behavior, and events that have happened in the past, juxtaposed with what is occurring in the present. Because the worker is neither **in** the group nor a **group member,** he or she has a broader perspective than the members. The leader can store information that to the participants is irrelevant but to the trained practitioner is grist for the therapeutic mill. This expanded diagnostic perspective provides the leader with an opportunity to see the total group and individual dynamics both in the moment and over time.

According to Egan (1970), processing is a way of keeping a group honest. A group worker does this by stopping what is going on and examining what is occurring. For example, the leader might interrupt the discussion and ask, "All right, what have we been doing here? What's going on? What's been happening?" The leader thus encourages the group to stand outside itself and become its own critic.

THINKING IN THE HERE-AND-NOW

As social workers, we are trained to think historically, and much of the diagnostic work we do is a form of psyche archeology. To gather needed information, we ascertain in a hundred different ways what has happened in the past and what its impact is on the present. To move into a here-and-now mind-set requires a shift from the past to the present tense. Rather than "What was?" we ask, "What is?" To focus on the present, we might ask ourselves, "What is going on right now?" and "What am I feeling?" and "I'm feeling discomfort; where is it coming from?"

Yalom (1983), in discussing the importance of the here-and-now, writes that the group worker's task is to channel outside to inside, abstract to specific, and impersonal to personal. Thus, if a group member starts with an abstract complaint, such as "I am too easily intimidated," the worker must find a way to transform that abstract comment into something specific related to the group. The therapist might say, "Look around the room today. Who here intimidates you?" The worker, according to Yalom, is like a shepherd who is continually rounding up strays—strays into "outside" material, strays into discussions of past events of their lives, and strays into abstract intellectual discussions. The here-and-now focus requires the worker first to think in the here-and-now by listening to himself and herself and his or her inner experiences, which over time can serve as a finely tuned guide. As therapists, we are sometimes immediately aware of our emotional response—we feel, angry, hurt, afraid, sad, anxious, or disappointed. At other times, we are less attuned to our specific feelings, but our intuition tells us something is not congruent. Some inner red flag within our psyche recognizes the significance of our own before our conscious mind has had time to process the data.

At these moments, we are faced with what would appear to be a therapeutic impossibility. That is, the worker focusing on his or her own sensations and feelings and, at the same time, being aware of all that is going on within each member and also with the group-as-a-whole. There is a kind of shuttling-back-and-forth movement of attention from self, to individual members, to the group-as-a-whole, and back again. We hear what a member says and observe the member's facial expressions and other nonverbal cues. We see the reactions of the other group members to what is being said. At the same time, we notice our own reaction to the person and his or her reaction to us and to the other group members.

Internal clues. A worker's ability to enter into another person's world though genuine empathy makes it possible for the worker to merge with the experience of the member, to consider what is being said (sometimes tolerating his or her own discomfort), and then to communicate this understanding. As therapists, we tune into our own internal process and find our inner rcd flags alerting us to what is occurring. There may be a shift in our body posture—for example, a leaning forward, a sitting back, or a crossing of our arms and/or legs. Another clue to us that something is wrong might be a feeling of boredom, frustration, or anger. Or we might find our mind wandering or discover that we have not been listening for the past few minutes.

Responses of this nature are generally not accidental or random. Rather, they are clues that something is going on for us that we need to address. Something a member has said or done has touched our inner self. It is at this point that we must reflect on what the member was saying or doing before our reaction and use that as a bridge to our own internal state. If we discover something relevant to the interaction, it may be useful to share it with the group. If, on the other hand, it is directly related to our personhood and external to the group, it is better to set it aside, after acknowledging it as a concern to be dealt with later.

● **Techniques: Practical considerations**
1. Think in the here-and-now.
2. Listen to yourself; trust your own instinct.

3. Ask group members what they see as going on in the group.
4. Process frequently what is going on between group members, as well as between the members and yourself.
5. Wherever possible, shift a there-and-then focus to a here-and-now-focus.

SOME ADDITIONAL FACTORS

A group worker's character, personal qualities, and philosophy of life all play a part in the therapeutic process. For this reason, it is important for the worker to trust himself or herself enough to be spontaneous, creative, and open. In addition, we must respect group members, prizing them because they are human. We must care about them enough to challenge and confront them. We must be careful to reveal ourselves to group members only if and when it is appropriate. We must be ethical and do nothing to hurt any group member. We must help group members find their own solutions to their problems. And we must empower the members to take responsibility for their own lives.

Our role as group worker makes two additional therapeutic factors useful to us. These are humor and the use of metaphors.

HUMOR

Therapy is serious business. Individuals come because of their fear, anger, frustration, grief, and sorrow. They speak of helplessness, hopelessness, death, suicide, rage, and violence. But, not everything that goes on in a therapy group has to be heavy and grim. With pathos, there can also be joy, happiness, and laughter. Frankl (1962), in his observations of life in the German concentration camps during World War II, writes that under the most wretched conditions, humor made it possible for prisoners to get through each day in spite of their torment.

Benjamin (1981), in reflecting on humor as a part of the therapeutic process, observes that when appropriately used it can be as helpful as many other leads or responses, if not more so. Different from sarcasm, ridicule, or cynicism, it is the light touch of humor which stems from empathic listening and which reflects a positive outlook on life. It is a very individual and personal response for which there is no detailed recipe.

Sometimes, the humor in a group causes us to laugh spontaneously with the group members; at other times, we unwittingly provoke the laughter of the group. But we can also use humor—in the form of an amusing anecdote that fits the situation—to ease tension and lighten the atmosphere.

Humor should be neither artificial nor contrived but spontaneous and natural. It may even consist of no more than a raised eyebrow, a smile, a gesture. When humor breaks through, it brings the group members closer together and to the leader by establishing an additional bond and a sense of confidence in the helping nature of human rapport.

Humor is a powerful tool within the therapeutic process. Exaggeration, paradoxes, absurd situations, puns, and jokes can help the members over a rough spot, minimize their anxiety, and promote their cohesion. It serves as a social lubricant that can elicit a shared response to something.

Humor has another side. It can also be hostile, angry, and aggressive, and can be used by one person as a defense for dealing with anxiety at the expense of another person. It can wound those seeking help, resulting in higher walls and stronger defenses. Humor should be good-natured, not hostile; democratic, not patronizing; and genuine, not forced (Wubbolding, 1988).

Groups create their own special jesting style over time. There may be focus on the characteristics of a group member or of the leader, with that person becoming the "butt" of jokes. There may be put-downs and quick one-liners about which the member outwardly laughs, but inwardly cringes. In other groups, there is gentle teasing with no offense given or perceived. The laughter is **with** someone and his or her particular circumstances, and not **at** the person.

The worker, by what he or she says and does, will set the tone. If, as social workers, we are self-deprecating, able to laugh at ourselves and take ourselves (but not the treatment process) lightly, our clients will take risks and make themselves vulnerable, If, on the other hand, they expect to be laughed at and ridiculed, they will closely monitor their thoughts, experiences, and ideas before sharing them in our groups.

USE OF METAPHORS

Group members frequently use figures of speech to describe their perceptions of themselves, of other people, or of their situations: "Sometimes, I feel like a doormat." "My life is like a jail, and I want to break out." "I feel like I was in a cocoon, and I'm now a butterfly."

There are a number of reasons for a therapist to use metaphors (McClure, 1987). First, metaphors enable the group worker to verify the stages of a group's development. Second, they provide information about members' identities. Third, metaphors provide a method for directing the group's attention from a past-centered to a present-centered focus. Fourth, they offer a method of creatively generating feedback about the group's processes. Symbolic and metaphoric images can also enhance the range and power of the leader's therapeutic interpretations and can increase the openness of group members to these interpretations.

Metaphors can come spontaneously from group members, or they can be suggested by the therapist. In one group a member described herself as being like a pinball bouncing off people and never developing any real connections. Several other group members picked up on her pinball image, humorously observing that when they tried to develop a friendship with her, she "bounced" away. The term *pinball* came to be a label used by the members to describe someone who could not develop or sustain relationships.

In another group, Ruth, a 45-year-old graduate student, complained in a vague manner that she was being pulled in different directions by the people in her life. She reported, "My professors, my children, my husband, and my mother are all taking from me, and I have nothing left to give." The worker picked up on this image and requested various group members to stand up and simultaneously pull on Ruth's arms and legs and to say loudly, "I need you." After a minute of amused pulling and pushing by group members, Ruth announced that this was exactly what it felt like. The situation was repeated, but this time Ruth was coached to disengage from the hands that were pulling on her and assertively tell each person that she was tired of being pulled and to stop. Ruth did this twice. The first time, she giggled, especially when she was referring to family members. The second time there were tears in her eyes and anger in her voice.

Metaphoric and symbolic imagery can also be used in the context of the group-as-a-whole as it struggles with group themes, conflicts, or normal developmental issues. For example, a group of graduate students, three weeks before the final session and four weeks prior to graduation, began to talk about their feelings regarding death. This opened up a number of issues, including ending the group, saying good-bye to people they cared for, leaving the university, giving up the student role, finding a job, and moving out of the community. It became evident to the members that there were multiple deaths taking place in their lives, all at the same time.

Group treatment provides unlimited metaphors for group members in the form of stories, analogies, and actual events. Effective metaphors are appropriate to the situation and tailored to the group. They are designed to heighten certain aspects of a message in a manner that will be accepted by the listener.

● Techniques: Practical considerations

1. Listen for metaphors.
2. Whenever possible, use a group member's own metaphors.
3. Keep your metaphors simple, and use as few words as possible.
4. If group members seem unable to relate to a particular metaphor, do not force it.

CO-THERAPY

The operational definition of *co-therapy* varies greatly. For some it refers to a two-leader situation in which one leader—the therapist—is dominant, and the other leader—the co-therapist—is less active. A version of this has been referred to as the apprentice model. In that model, the leader who is more experienced than the other assumes leadership, and the second leader learns by watching and trying his or her hand at leading during the sessions.

A more common design, particulary in social work, is one in which both practitioners share the leadership of a group (Corey & Corey, 1987; Levine, 1980). The leaders "flow" with each other and lead jointly. Yalom (1985) states categorically that a co-leadership arrangement involving "anything other than two therapists of completely equal status is in my experience inadvisable (p. 422).

Mullan and Rosenbaum (1978) underscore the need for equality and for "compatibility in temperament" between co-therapists. These authors point out that co-therapists must accept each other emotionally, understand each other's methods, and have the same treatment goals. According to Mullan and Rosenbaum, the prime requisites for co-therapists are emotional acceptance and mutual respect. Neither therapist should feel the need to mold the other, to become defensive, or to use the group as a forum for rivalry.

According to Napier and Gershenfeld (1989), few co-leader relationships are in fact **co,** or equal. Even when co-leaders themselves demonstrate equality, group members tend to pay more attention to one leader than to the other. Differences between co-leaders—in their levels of experience, backgrounds, and leadership styles—make it almost impossible for group members to perceive the co-leaders as equal. These differences, according to Napier and Gershenfeld, will also influence the individual leaders in terms of their sense of importance, their level of activity, their sense of responsibility, and their visibility in the group.

ADVANTAGES

In individual therapy, the client receives the full attention of the worker. In a small group, with six to ten members, it is difficult for the worker to keep track of each individual. By having two leaders, there is less likelihood of an individual's becoming lost in the shuffle. Also, not every clinician works well with every client. Biases, prejudices, and weaknesses can be minimized with the strength of one worker complementing the weakness of the other.

With co-therapy, the group members get two leaders for the price of one. If one worker is sick or on vacation, the other can fill in. If one leader is tired, feeling lethargic, or has had a bad day, the other is there. With certain populations, such as psychotic adults, aggressively acting-out children, and impulsive adolescents, the wear and tear on professional staff members is extraordinary. In such groups, one worker can attend to a particular problem, such as a member who walks out or one who is out of control, while the other maintains the ongoing work of the group.

Co-leadership has a number of other advantages, particularly for a beginning group worker. It provides a second set of eyes and ears and allows for a more complete and accurate view of a group. It reduces the potential for undetected blind spots in either leader. It also allows each worker the opportunity to slide back and forth between the active and passive mode, and in so doing, to take turns with the other leader at being more actively responsive and more observational.

169
• • • • • • • •

In some ways, the presence of two therapists offers a replication of a two-parent family (Shilkoff, 1983). Effective interaction, problem solving, and conflict management between leaders can provide a model that members can imitate and identify with. For example, if a group's members have an opportunity to see two workers in conflict without hurting each other, they come to understand that it is possible to disagree without being rejected or harmed. This is especially meaningful when co-workers are of the opposite sex. It may be the first time some members have seen a man and a woman working together without one giving up his or her individuality when a conflict develops between them.

When one worker is focusing on a single individual, particularly when there are strong emotions, the second worker can keep track of the other group members, as well as objectively following the dyadic transaction. It is not unusual for a lone leader to become so engrossed in a one-to-one transaction that he or she fails to recognize what is occurring with the group-as-a-whole. During such a transaction, other group members may become bored, angry, or frustrated or perhaps may go unnoticed in spite of being ready to offer fresh insights.

Another advantage of co-leading is apparent when one leader is affected by a member to the degree that countertransference is obvious (Corey & Corey, 1987). The leader's objectivity may be distorted to the degree that he or she is unable to work effectively. Then, the other leader can assume greater responsibility for working with the member. This second leader can help both individuals—that is, his or her co-leader **and** the group member—explore their feelings and address the issue more openly. The second leader can function as a sounding board, can check for objectivity, and can offer useful feedback.

In an organization such as a hospital, sharing group leadership with other professionals—for example, psychologists, physicians, nurses, recreation therapists—has the potential for reducing interdisciplinary problems. Colleagues can be exposed to each other's direct work with patients. Through this exposure, they can gain a greater awareness of the full scope of the clinical role. Lonergan (1982), in discussing a stroke group at St. Vincent's Hospital in New York City reports the appreciation that social workers gained for the physical therapists and speech therapists after co-leading groups with them. The special expertise of these professionals made it possible for aphasic and partially paralyzed patients to participate more fully in the group process. The interactions between the social workers, physical therapists, and speech therapists also cleared up some misunderstandings these professional colleagues had had about each other's therapeutic functions.

DISADVANTAGES

There are also disadvantages to having a co-leader. One major disadvantage is that each leader must find a compatible co-leader—someone with whom he or she can work comfortably in a relationship based on basic trust, respect, and liking. For example, some workers are warm, supportive, and benign. If such a worker is paired with someone who is demanding and confrontational, both workers may become too frustrated to be effective. And, since no two counselors do therapy the same way, even compatible colleagues will have some natural conflicts, disagreements, misunderstandings, and miscommunication.

Some co-leaders become competitive and develop a rivalry. One or both workers may seek to be dominant and the center of a group's attention (Corey & Corey, 1987). In an attempt to be the star, such a leader might actively put down his or her co-leader during a session. The co-leaders might act out their differences in and through the group. For example, one worker might become angry and covertly, as well as overtly, subvert the other's efforts with the group. Such a relationship between co-leaders is bound to have a negative effect on the group.

Another disadvantage is the fact that having two workers leading a group is expensive. Some agency administrators take this point one step further, arguing that it is economically wasteful. They say that because there is a shortage of trained workers, it is more efficient to split up group workers and have each one lead separate groups. In short, co-leadership may be a luxury that many agencies cannot afford.

Coordination.   Part of the expense of co-leadership is the time required for co-leaders to coordinate their actions in planning for a group. Their coordination activities must include making a concerted effort to discuss their work together both before and after sessions. The postgroup debriefing is especially important. It is at this time that the leaders can discuss the themes of the session, what they did and did not feel good about, their perceptions of each other's performance, as well as their critiques of their own roles and performance within in the group.

Two leaders provide a unique opportunity for an impact on individual group members. For the impact to occur, however, the co-leaders need to have a working relationship based on trust and openness. At the most basic level, each leader must support the ideas verbalizations, and challenges the other leader expresses in the group. In the following example, one leader follows up on a challenge made by the other leader pressing the group member to reflect on his or her actions. The supportive co-leader said, "When my partner said you were bull-shitting the group, you ignored what she said and kept right on talking. What did you hear?" In such a situation, the workers have to be careful that the group member does not perceive the workers as double-teaming—pitting two against one.

● **Techniques: Practical implications**
   1. Co-leaders need to have equal responsibility in planning their group, selecting its members, and getting it started.
   2. Before the initial session of their group, co-leaders should discuss with each other their expectations, reservations, strengths and weak-

nesses, past experiences in groups, and theoretical approaches.
3. Co-leaders need to reach an agreement as to exactly what the term *co* will mean in their leadership of a specific group.
4. Co-leaders need to allot time for pregroup and postgroup discussions.

IN SUMMARY

This chapter examines a number of worker interventions that result in desirable changes in group members and groups. The therapist guides and promotes group interactions; consolidates by synthesizing, summarizing, and partializing; reframes; supports; confronts; and processes. The group worker actively provides feedback to group members, challenges them, and relates to the members in the here-and-now. The worker also uses humor and metaphors as means of facilitating group interactions.

There are advantages and disadvantage to using two therapists. When the workers are compatible and allies, they can be supportive of one another and share leadership responsibilities. For this to occur, they need to exchange their thoughts and ideas before, during, and after each group session.

SUGGESTED READINGS

ETTIN, M. (1986). Within the group's view: Clarifying dynamics through metaphoric and symbolic imagery. *Small group behavior, 17*(4), 407–426.

POSTHUMA, B. (1989). *Small groups in therapy settings: Process and leadership.* Boston: College-Hill Press. See Chapter 9 on co-leadership.

YALOM, I. (1983). *Inpatient group psychotherapy.* New York: Basic Books. See Chapter 4 on leading in the here-and-now.

9

....

ESTABLISHING THE GROUP

I

• • • • • • • •

love kaleidoscopes. Look through the cylinder and you see an exquisite arrangement of shapes and colors. Then, give it a turn, and the tiny bits of colored glass form a new and even more extraordinary design.

Groups are very similar. There is an initial pattern of interaction, structure, and leadership. Then a change occurs, such as a shift in location or the addition or loss of a member, and a new set of patterns become apparent.

I once worked with a group that seemed to go nowhere for the first four sessions. What little self-disclosure there was sounded flat and artificial. Communication was primarily leader-oriented, with hardly any interaction between members.

The group was stuck, and I felt hard-pressed to influence the situation. First, I tried different activities to increase interaction. Then, I directly challenged group members about their lack of involvement, hoping to get some sort of an energized reaction. The only things the members could agree on were that they didn't feel safe in the group and that they felt distant from each other.

Clearly, part of the problem was the room. We were meeting in the lounge of a church that had heavy, thickly cushioned, high-sided chairs—the kind that once you sit down in them, you have difficulty getting up. The room offered very little privacy. It couldn't be closed off. And at least once or twice a session, someone's walking through would bring a halt to the group's discussion.

The group decided to move to a more private and intimate room in the basement. The chairs would be harder. And the room would be colder, but it would be ours. The room was carpeted, so those who wished could sit on the floor. Large windows, overlooking a woods, established a tone of airiness and light.

Much to my pleasure, there was a dramatic change in the group's inter-actions. Members who had directed most of their remarks to me began to talk directly to each other. Self-disclosure and sharing were noticeably more gen-uine and less forced. There was physical touching and even some hugging.

While moving to another room was a relatively minor change, it had special significance for the members. The new room provided greater privacy and a place the group could call its own. The barriers created by the heavy chairs no longer existed, and individuals were actually, as well as symbolically, shoulder to shoulder around the circle.

The change in the room was like a turn in a kaleidoscope. The various pieces, fundamentally the same, were now rearranged in a unique and distinct mosaic.

• • •

This chapter discusses the elements that go into the planning of effective groups. During the conception or pregroup stage, the practitioner is faced with a vast array of choices that can positively or negatively affect group conditions. It is important to understand these choices and their implications in order to minimize problems and enhance the chances of achieving the group's purpose.

The chapter answers this question: what are the factors that need to be considered in establishing a group? Issues discussed include: determining the group's purpose, composition, size, and duration and acquiring administrative sanctions.

THE PLANNING PROCESS

Many groups do not prosper because of a lack of careful thought and planning during the conception stage. Their leaders, while well intentioned, fail to consider in detail their clients' needs, the meeting environment, the sponsoring organization's expectations, and the leaders' own objectives. Similarly, they fail to address some of the more practical implications of the group's structure—for example, who will be in the group, and where and when the group will meet. Planning cannot be left to chance; it needs to be done in a mindful, rational, and logical manner.

GROUP PROPOSAL

A detailed proposal is especially useful in planning a group. Such a proposal serves as a means of clarifying the rationale for the group, taking into consideration its potential members, the group-as-a-whole, the sponsoring organization, worker activities, and the meeting environment. It is a preliminary plan that sorts out the direction the group will take and a rational format for reaching the leader's goals for the group. The more specific the proposal the better.

The following questions are commonly addressed in a proposal:

1. What is the primary focus of the group? Is it education, growth, mutual sharing, or behavioral change?
2. What is the purpose of the group? What does the group worker hope to achieve?
3. What population is to be served by the group? What are the unmet needs of that population?
4. Will the group be lead by one or two workers? Who will lead the group?
5. Who will be in the group? How will members be selected?
6. What number of group members is best in order for the group to achieve its purpose?
7. How will the members be prepared for the group?
8. What issues/topics will be addressed in the group?
9. Where will group meetings be held?
10. What people need to be checked with in advance of the first meeting—that is, supervisor, chairman of the board, director, janitor?
11. What ground rules need to be established for the group at the onset?
12. What will be the group worker's role?

These questions need to be given serious thought and answered as honestly and specifically as possible.

PURPOSE

A group's purpose is its ultimate aim and reason for existing. This desire for the group is derived from a number of sources, including the sponsoring agency, the therapist(s) assigned to lead the group, and the needs of the agency's clients. Generally, the group's purpose is determined by these therapist(s) and by other agency staff as individual clients' needs become apparent. The group's purpose is established within the framework of an organization that has its own sanctions, purpose, and mission. The needs of individual clients of the organization are translated into a group's purpose when the agency decides to create a group to respond to the needs of some of its clients.

When the purpose for establishing a group is based on **real** client needs, there is some assurance that the goals individuals have in joining the group will be similar and in harmony with the agency's and the worker's goals. Such similarity of intentions becomes the foundation for the development of a dynamic group commitment to the group-treatment process. This interface of the three major kinds of goals—the organization's, the worker's, and those of the group members—becomes a major source not only of the focus but also of the energy of the group's effort.

A purpose that is clear and reflects compatible expectations provides a basis on which group members can develop a bond and a means for achieving their goals (Levine, 1980). If a group's purpose is unclear or if the agency, the worker, and the clients have different expectations, there is danger that the group will be weakened by interpersonal conflict. Over time, such conflict depletes vital energy from a group and reduces the potential for its members and the group-as-a-whole to achieve goals. A group with a clear and unified purpose tends to be more self-dependent, self-initiating, cooperative, and cohesive than a group whose purpose is unclear or splintered.

Statement of purpose. A brief statement of a group's purpose consists of information on why the group is meeting, how it is going to conduct its work, and what will be expected of its participants. Such statements are, by design, broad in nature yet specific enough to provide information so that potential members can decide whether the group might be of benefit to them. The following are some examples of purpose statements:

• "The group will focus on the problems of being a single parent. Information will be presented on child-rearing principles. Participants will be invited to share concerns they are having with their children and to receive feedback from other members."

• "The group is for children of divorced parents. Through the use of peer support, members will be encouraged to discuss their concerns and to develop appropriate coping skills that will enable them to grieve their loss and to heal."

• "The group is for new patients living on the psychiatric ward. Discussions will focus on their orientation to life in the hospital and on the reduction of unnecessary stress. Members can bring up specific problems and receive advice from staff and other patients."

• "The group is for newly admitted patients with a spinal-cord injury. There will be a videotape of an individual with a spinal-cord injury who is relating her experiences in adjusting to her handicap and in completing a rehabilitation program. The videotape will be followed by a group discussion led by a trained leader with the assistance of former patients."

• "The group will provide a support system for terminally ill patients suffering with metastatic cancer. Group members will be encouraged to explore their feelings regarding their illness, their relationships with family members, and their medical treatment. Training will be offered in meditation and in autohypnosis for pain control."

• "The group will provide a forum for dialysis patients, their families, and the treatment team to discuss patient problems and engage in joint problem solving."

ASSESSING THE NEED

Once a group's general purpose is determined, the next step is to identify which clients might need the help to be offered. Such a beginning assessment does not involve extensive procedures such as establishing goals for members or agreeing on individual contracts (Toseland & Rivas, 1984). Instead, this initial assessment assists the group worker in refining the purpose of the group and the possible membership that might be recruited.

Practitioners are well advised not to establish a group simply because doing so is a part of their professional role. A group should be proposed only after the worker has done preliminary background investigation to determine what clients' problems are and whether some of the clients can be effectively treated through the group approach.

In planning a particular group, practitioners have numerous sources of information—such as their caseload, their colleagues, and professionals from other agencies—to help them determine whether there is adequate interest in such a group. Needless to say, it is important to make use of all such sources of information to obtain as comprehensive a picture of clients' needs and problems as possible.

REACHING OUT

Probably the most obvious source of information about clients' needs is the organization's present and past caseload. For example, the clients of some organizations tend to face certain problems because of the nature of their illness. Patients in psychiatric facilities, for instance, frequently have difficulty adjusting to community life after extended hospitalization. Many of their difficulties—such as problems handling money, finding housing, or taking medications— are predictable. To make the transition easier for its clients and to reduce their potential for readmittance, such organizations have developed predischarge groups.

There may be clients having problems with life changes—positive as well as negative—can be the focus of a group. Marriage, parenthood, beginning school, graduating from school, changing jobs, retiring, and moving are generally a blend of joy and pain, happiness and sorrow, anticipation and regret. Crisis events also represent a difficult a time when people need support. Such crises might occur before or after major surgery, might be the result of a serious accident, an assault (including rape or incest), a death, or a divorce.

A shared source of environmental stress might be the basis for a group (Gitterman, 1986). Parents of mentally retarded children, for example, can be of support to each other around issues of child rearing. They may also benefit by working together to establish community resources and to challenge the unresponsiveness of organizational representatives. In addition, groups may be organized with a social-action focus to help consumers of services deal effectively with the organizations providing those services. A by-product of such a group is improvement in the group members' ability to gain control and mastery over their environment.

The need for a group may result from problems people living together experience related to their relationships and communication. Individuals living in natural units—for example, students in classrooms, patients on wards, and participants in rehabilitation programs—can develop maladaptive and dysfunctional patterns that diminish their potential to meet their personal goals. For example, patients in a psychiatric unit may be struggling with so much interpersonal stress from living together on restricted units that they have difficulty working on the particular issues that brought them to the hospital.

179

An important aspect of assessing individuals' potential for membership in a group is determining whether or not the candidates share the worker's perception of their unmet needs and of the tasks facing the group (Toseland & Rivas, 1984). Do the candidates feel the need for the group, or is the interest coming primarily from the professional(s)? Shared perceptions and expectations will lead to group cohesion and increase group members' satisfaction with the group's functioning. This will mean, in turn, that the group worker will spend less time dealing with obstacles and resistance than he or she would in a more fragmented group.

PRELIMINARY RELUCTANCE

The potential members of a group may feel no need for the group. In this case, the group worker will find himself or herself in the position of having to convince them of the group's potential and value. This is often the situation in hospital settings where patients are weary of dealing with their problems and would prefer to be left alone. It is also typical of involuntary situations—such as life in a prison or on probation—in which people are required to attend a group. They do so with the attitude of "Treat me, I dare you." In such a case, the worker needs to be prepared for resistance and to plan interventions that will overcome it, whatever form it takes.

Potential members of a group may have misperceptions about groups. They may feel that group treatment is second-rate therapy. They may feel their actual experience will be diluted because it is shared time rather than individual time. There may be the fear of being contaminated by other people in the group. Potential candidates sometimes respond to an invitation to join a group by saying, "If I listen to then, I'll just get sicker" or "What will I gain from hearing others complain? I have enough of my own problems."

One of the group worker's most effective tools is the willingness to **listen** and **understand** the thoughts and feelings of a potential group member is communicating. In reaching out to potential members, the worker's primary goal is to establish an emotional connection and begin a working alliance. This means hearing the person's anger, frustration, fears, and expectations. It also means recognizing what is important to the person, expressing genuine concern about his or distress, and communicating that the person is someone of worth that will be treated with respect and dignity.

In a paper on reaching people who generally do not take advantage of small-group services, Breton (1985) writes that it is a misinterpretation of behavior to categorize clients as either motivated or unmotivated.

There are no such persons as unmotivated persons. There may be persons who are motivated to do nothing, or motivated to take no risks, or motivated to keep away from meaningful relationships, but their behavior is purposeful, and guided by their perception of a specific outcome or goal: and goal-oriented behavior is motivated behavior [p. 9].

All actual users and potential users of services are decision makers who may seek workers' services or not, who may accept or reject workers' offers of services, and who may respond or may not respond to attempts to engage them in a change process if they formally start using the services.

GROUP COMPOSITION

Who is to be included in, and who is to be excluded from the group? Not every candidate is appropriate for a particular group and it is important to determine in advance whether a candidate's needs can be best met by the proposed group, some other group, or another method of treatment, such as individual or family therapy. Although many theorists offer specific inclusion and exclusion criteria, our understanding of group composition is far from complete.

PERSONAL INTERVIEW

A personal interview, while time-consuming, is the best method for determining a candidate's appropriateness for a specific group and preparing the person for the group. First, such individual contact provides an opportunity for the clinician to glean information relevant to the fit between the candidate and the type of group being formed. Does the person want to be in the group? How is this person similar to and different from other prospective members? What may hinder this person from attending the group? Examples might include need of a baby-sitter, lack of transportation, limited time, or conflicting activities.

Second, a personal interview permits the worker and member a chance to meet each other before the first session, and to discuss the group's purpose and the member's expectations. It is a time to talk about important issues such as the worker's role, confidentiality, the member's fears, and what will occur during the sessions. Already having a sense of the worker as a person will make the initial group session easier for the member. And, this way, although the participants do not know each other, they do know the worker. The personal interview also makes the worker's job easier; it ensures that the group members are not strangers to the worker but, instead, are individuals whom he or she has come to know personally.

For some groups, screening is unnecessary. An education-oriented group, for example, may be open to anyone interested. Its composition may not be a significant factor. In groups with a treatment orientation, on the other hand, an assessment of the individual's appropriateness is essential;

it helps the worker make sure that each member can be helped and, more important, that no member will be harmed. Each group member will influence the group and likewise be influenced by the group.

181

SOCIOEMOTIONAL CAPACITY

In determining how well a prospective member will fit into a particular group, a group worker will need to consider the client's socioemotional level. The better a client's reality testing, the more likely he or she will be able to benefit from a group. Many of the clients who receive counseling in clinical settings neither have a positive sense of self nor are able to assess social situations or deal with reality. It may be these very limitations that serve as the reason they are being referred to a group.

In verbally oriented treatment groups, a client's ability to communicate is essential. During a screening interview, the worker must try to answer these questions: Can the client share feelings? Is the client able to discuss his or her problems without being defensive or blaming others? Can the client tolerate frustration? It is not unusual for a few withdrawn patients to be placed in a group of very active talkers in the hope that such a placement will encourage them to talk (Levine, 1965). However, the problem for the withdrawn patient generally is intensified rather than lessened in such a group. Thus, it may be more advisable to place withdrawn clients in a group in which the other members have a similar capacity to communicate.

According to Levine (1979), it is usually better for group members to be in the same socioemotional range for direct therapeutic purposes. Group members in the chronic schizophrenic range generally do better in groups of other chronic schizophrenics or with a mixture of chronic and acute schizophrenics. People in the neurotic range of social emotional functioning are often too uneasy and too frightened by chronic schizophrenics and have a difficult time identifying with them.

The treatment setting will also be a consideration. Certain members' behavior will almost certainly force the group to want to eject them (Kadis, Krasner, Weiner, Winick, & Foulkes, 1974). This is true, for example, of a client who is undergoing rapid psychological decompensation. In an inpatient setting such a person may be better tolerated because of the group's awareness of the availability of institutional support. Although such a member would bring an outpatient group to a standstill, in an inpatient setting, the group need not bog down in directing its energy toward helping the person relate on a day-to-day basis.

SEX COMPOSITION

A group worker must also take into consideration the sex composition of any group he or she is planning. The sex composition of a group can have dramatic implications for the group's functioning and outcomes (Aries, 1973; Carlock & Martin, 1977; Martin & Shanahan, 1983). Aries, in a study of all-male, all-female, and male/female groups, found that men and women revealed different aspects of themselves in a group, depending upon the group's sex composition. Men in all-male groups tended to concentrate on competition and status topics. Women in the all-female groups tended to express great interpersonal concern for each other and to discuss themselves, their families, and their relationships outside the group.

In male/female groups, Aries found, interaction between the sexes was emphasized more than interaction between members of the same sex. The atmosphere was more intense and excitement-filled than in groups having members of only one sex. Women in male/female groups were more passive than those in all-female groups and allowed the men to initiate and take part in interactions with greater frequency than they did themselves.

In their study, Carlock and Martin found that women in an all-female group expressed considerable dissatisfaction with the climate of their group and with its particular intensity level and lack of closeness and excitement. Yet, these groups experienced the greatest positive gains of all group participants.

Carlock and Martin recommend that if the group experience is to focus on sex roles and the relationship between the sexes, then members of both sexes should be included. However, they warn that leaders of mixed groups should be prepared for the high level of tension that will likely develop and should themselves be wary of falling into traditional sex-role patterns. If, on the other hand, a leader wishes to help women concentrate on intrapersonal issues such as self-acceptance, realization of their personal power and choice, and identification of fears and avoidances, Carlock and Martin recommend an all-female group composition is more desirable.

RACIAL COMPOSITION

How many Black and how many White members should be in a group? There is no clear answer to this question. And there is not much empirical evidence to support specific guidelines for a worker planning a group. According to Davis (1979), Blacks and Whites are sensitive to the dynamics of race as it pertains to groups, and this factor needs to be considered in composing a group. White members (as well as White workers) may experience more anxiety in racially mixed groups than will the Black members in these groups (Davis, 1984).

A group worker may encounter resistance to having a significantly greater percentage of either Blacks or Whites in a group. Members of each race tend to offer more valid reports of their true feelings to someone of their own race. Davis (1980) posits that the reluctance of whites to have a greater number of Black members may result from a fear of being psychologically in the minority or outnumbered.

Differences in race may be less of an issue when group members are attempting to complete a task rather than examining their relationships with each other. As a group's potential for intimacy increases, more of the group leader's time and effort may be required to address the race-related feelings of its members. The salience of a group member's race appears to increase as the intimacy of the group increases.

183

● **Techniques: Practical considerations**
   1. Personally interview each candidate before the first group session.
   2. Select group members who are different—but not too different.
   3. Trust your intuition as to who will and who will not do well in a particular group.
   4. A group's composition should depend on the group's type and purpose.

HOMOGENEOUS OR HETEROGENEOUS

Homogeneous . . . . Heterogeneous

Conventional wisdom suggests that for a group to be viable, it should be both homogeneous and heterogeneous. While this is easy to say, it presents some logistical problems for a group worker. First, what are the criteria for judging how homogeneous a group is? Second, what are the criteria for deciding how heterogeneous a group is? The following characteristics are the ones group workers usually consider in determining a group's homogeneity/heterogenity (Flapan & Fenchel, 1987):

   1. Sex—one sex or both?
   2. Age—similar ages or a wide range of ages?
   3. Marital status—married, single, or mixed?
   4. Intellectual ability—a narrow or wide range of intellectual ability?
   5. Education—one level of education—for example, only college graduates—or a mix?
   6. Socioeconomic status—same social class or a sprinkling from various social classes?
   7. Ego strength—same vulnerability and similar capacity to deal with problems or a range of competence and coping ability?
   8. Problems—similar real-life problems for members to deal with or quite different problems?

HOMOGENEOUS GROUPS

There are instances in which a particular kind of homogeneity is a basic element in the plans for a group. However, the homogeneity is usually of a limited nature. For example, a group worker might plan a group for battered spouses, alcoholics, sexually abused children, single parents, or patients with a terminal illness. But, within each group, the worker would probably permit differences among the participants based on other factors.

Homogeneity in age is usually a factor in groups for children. Likewise, gender homogeneity is often a factor in self-help groups that address issues of identity. But, again, a great deal of heterogeneity is likely in each of these types of groups.

Highly homogeneous groups have definite advantages over highly heterogeneous groups. Members of highly homogeneous groups identify with one another more quickly, and they feel more comfortable, especially in the early stages of the group. Their commonalities increase their identification with each other and enhance the cohesive development of the group. Consequently, members of these groups get down to work much faster.

On the other hand, there are distinct disadvantages to having a highly homogeneous group. Since the members of such a group assume they understand each other, they may not press or challenge one another in the same way as members of a highly heterogeneous group would. The level of therapy may thus be more superficial than in a highly heterogeneous group (Flapan & Fenchel, 1987). Because there is less diversity in a highly homogeneous group, the subject matter under discussion may not appear as interesting to its members. They may also have fewer opportunities for reality testing. For example, a group of drug addicts or child molesters may encounter more inappropriate support in a highly homogeneous group and less confrontation than they would in a more heterogeneous group.

HETEROGENEOUS GROUPS

Individuals who come into a group with different life experiences, levels of expertise, and coping patterns add spice to the group and facilitate the therapeutic process. This diversity provides group members with an expanded set of perspectives and opinions. Different points of view and critical input stimulate and challenge the members to examine their problems from diverse perspectives and to do something proactive about their problems. Bach (1954) writes that heterogeneity gives members the experience of learning to relate to different kinds of people. Glatzer (1956) notes that in a group with a broad diversity of personalities, there is more rapid therapeutic movement, as well as a greater sense of support and greater compassion.

There are definite disadvantages to a highly heterogeneous group. Most obvious is the reality that its members may not be able to relate to each other. It may take longer for individuals to disclose their problems and to form a bond. There may be more defensiveness and more resistance in the beginning, and members may drop out because of these early frustrations. There may be more subgrouping among members who identify with one another on the basis of race, education, socioeconomic status, or gender.

Bertcher and Maple (1974) suggest that a group is more effective when its members have highly homogeneous descriptive attributes—for example, age, occupation, or marital status—and highly heterogeneous behavioral attributes—for example, aggression, depression, or child-abusive behavior. Common descriptive attributes help foster interaction and compatibility.

Heterogeneous behavioral attributes, on the other hand, increase the chances that members will be constructively responsive to each other.

Clinicians must find a balance between diversity and commonality. Groups should have enough differences to generate interest within their members and enough similarities to make their members feel comfortable and identify with one another. Two useful rules of thumb are the **porcupine principle** and the **Noah's ark principle.**

Porcupine principle.   This principle of group composition suggests that there is a delicate balance between members' being similar and members' being different. Like porcupines in the woods during a blizzard, they have to be able to get close enough to keep warm, yet not so close that they prick each other to death.

Group members should have similarities. If, however, they have too many, the similarities will prevent the group from becoming viable. If group members are too different, on the other hand, the group may not function.

Noah's ark principle.   It is written that when Noah selected animals for the ark, he chose at least two of everything. This principle suggests that in composing a group, a worker should be careful not to have just one person of any particular race, gender, or lifestyle. If, for example, a group is going to be composed of men and women, there should be at least two men and two women. If the group is going to have Blacks and Whites, there should be at least two Blacks and two Whites.

In short, homogeneity or heterogeneity is not an ideal in itself. For certain problems and objectives, homogeneity may be of value. However, too much compatibility can enable group members to resist efforts to modify their behavior. Too much or too little stress can result in a surplus of anxiety or a surplus of apathy.

In composing a group, a leader needs also to consider how each person will interact with other members and affect the group-as-a-whole. Will the client monopolize? Is the client extremely aggressive? Will the client invite scapegoat behavior from others? Sometimes, answers to these questions will be apparent, while at other times, the leader will need to trust his or her intuition.

Luchins (1964), in referring to his personal experience as a group therapist, writes that there is value in having a mixed group and not worrying about homogeneity or heterogeneity. An exception is when in the actual conduct of the group, it is found that certain members do not fit in spite of all efforts to integrate them.

> the problem is not one merely of heterogeneity or homogeneity but also of developing a group which can function. Uniformity of symptoms, or interests, or opinions, or of social or personality characteristics does not necessarily make for the most organized or best functioning groups [p. 96].

Any criterion of suitability for therapy holds—in relation to a certain kind of therapy and therapist, and in relation to a given time and place. What may work for one clinician may be disastrous for another. The successful use of a criterion also depends on what changes the leader wants to encourage in the behavior of a client or in his or her personality, as well as on what rate of change the leader hopes to see.

OPEN OR CLOSED MEMBERSHIP

Open Membership . . . . Closed Membership

The group leader needs to decide whether a particular group will be open or closed to new members. An open group maintains a consistent size, the leader replaces members as they leave. In a closed group, the same members stay together from the beginning to the group's termination.

CLOSED GROUPS

Because a closed group has a restricted membership, there is a greater likelihood of cohesion, bonding, and identification among its members. The issue of trust becomes less of a problem because participants, over time, come to know each other. By contrast, in an open group, each new member changes the interpersonal relations in which the original members are involved and establishes a new situation to which the new, as well as the original, members must adapt.

Dinkmeyer and Muro (1971) recommend closed counseling groups for adolescents and adults. They feel that because a group must move or pass through certain phases for optimal effectiveness, the addition of new members limits the group's continuity and retards its cohesiveness. The introduction of a new member forces the group to cover old ground. If the new individuals are inexperienced in groups, they tend to move the group away from here-and-now work to topics that hinder group growth. For the worker, it means spending additional time assisting the new individual to work into the mainstream of group life.

There are disadvantages to using a closed group format. Closed groups can die because of attrition. If, for example, a group loses members, it has no way of replacing them and so may not be able to continue. Another issue is that not all individuals do well in cohesive intimate groups. The intimacy required can be frightening, and some members overtly or covertly resist the closeness.

OPEN GROUPS

The term open group in itself suggests the possibility of different models (Henry, 1988). First is the **drop-in** (or **drop-out**) model characterized by a flexible approach to who is and who is not a group member. Members are self-selecting, and entry criteria are very broad. Members attend as and when they wish for an indefinite period.

Second is the **replacement** model, which typically has a fixed upper limit of members so the group's size remains compatible with its purpose. The group worker selects all members so he or she can regulate the entry and exit process. When a group member leaves, the worker will identify someone to fill the vacancy.

The **re-formed** model is the third permutation. According to this model, a group members contract for a set period of time, during which no new members are added but original members may drop out. At the end of the contract period, a new group is formed. The re-formed group consists of some old and some new members.

The prime advantage of an open-ended over a closed-ended group is its constant flow of members through the group. If someone decides to drop out, a new member soon fills the vacancy. From an economic perspective, an open-ended group makes sense in that clients can be put in the group whenever there is an opening rather than having to wait until the group is re-formed. Open-ended groups are often found in hospitals. Predischarge groups, for example, experience a constant flow of patients from the hospital back into the community.

Another advantage of an open-ended group is that clients can join the group when they need it and can stay as long as they choose. This is especially valuable for someone who is in need of urgent and temporary help, such as someone going through a crisis (Aguilera & Messick, 1982; Klein, 1972). Such clients do not have the luxury of waiting for a new group to form. An open-ended group offers timely and immediate help.

GROUP SIZE

Small Group . . . . Large Group

Like the terms *heterogeneity* and *homogeneity, small* and *large* are relative terms. At what point does a collection of individuals move from being a small group to a large group? A more useful question is this: compared to what is a particular group small or large? There is no optimal size for a group. The size a practitioner establishes for a group will be based on the group's purpose, as well as the practitioner's own level of comfort. If a group is to be assembled for the dissemination of information, with little personal discussion and limited interpersonal relationships, its members can conceivably number in the hundreds. If, however, everyone is expected to take part and there is an emphasis on close relationships, a smaller group—5 to 12 members—is desirable.

The smaller a group, the more demands it places on its members for involvement and intimacy. Also the easier access to each client it provides for the worker.

The lower limit of a group is determined by the fact that a critical mass of individuals is required to become an interacting group (Yalom, 1985). When a group is reduced to a size of four or fewer members, it often ceases to operate as a group. Interaction between members diminishes, and the practitioner finds himself or herself engaged in individual therapy within a group situation.

The larger a group, the less time there is for working through individual problems. Larger groups allow greater anonymity, making it possible for a person to hide, withdraw, or become lost. The larger a group, the more formal its structure becomes, the more the group fragments into subgroups, and the greater the need for formal leadership patterns (Klein, 1972). The larger a group, the less individualized attention members receive and the fewer interactions they have. There is less pressure to attend a large group because members' absences are not as conspicuous as in smaller groups (Toseland & Rivas, 1984).

Gitterman and Shulman (1986) observe that smaller groups make a greater demand for participation, involvement, and intimacy than do larger groups. Shy, anxious, or less-than-adequate-feeling members may find the pressures in a very small group too great. The level of the group's demand on them may exceed their level of tolerance. "A moderate size group (approximately seven to nine) can provide regressed schizophrenics, for example, the necessary interpersonal space that may be unavailable to them in a smaller group" (p. 66). Groups that are quite small may also have insufficient resources for diversity and vitality or for linking up with a "buddy."

Few theorists agree on the ideal size of a group. Klein (1972) writes that five to seven members is often cited as an ideal based on an assumption of their regular attendance. Yalom (1985) recommends seven members but says that five to ten members is an acceptable range. Gouwens (1964) suggests that a group should have no more than 12 and no fewer than 8 members. "If the patients are regressed and withdrawn, the group should be larger in order to lessen the amount of responsibility each member has to assume for what takes place during the session" (p. 54).

It can be anticipated that members will sometimes be absent and that some members may drop out during the course of a group. These realities need to be kept in mind in determining a group's size and in choosing its members. Having at least eight members provides a cushion if one or two cannot attend. It is also to the worker's advantage to have additional candidates "in the wings" in case the optimum number of members no longer attends, because some members have dropped out.

If a therapeutically oriented group is to function effectively, each member must be able to feel safe discussing feelings, to interact meaningfully with others, and to obtain feedback. In establishing a group's size, a group worker needs to consider each client's maturity, ability to invest in others, and attention span.

DURATION

Time-Limited . . . . Ongoing

189

. . . .

Exactly how long should a group run? Again, there is no right or wrong answer that is appropriate to all groups. A group worker has several options, each with its own advantages and disadvantages. At one extreme is the time-limited group that has a definite number of sessions—for example, 15 or 20 sessions with a defined beginning date and ending date. In school settings, time-limited groups often run from the beginning term to the end of the term or to a holiday.

The advantage of a time-limited group is that the specification of a time span encourages productive work. Group members recognize that the group is not going to go on forever and feel increasing pressure to achieve their objectives. Pragmatically, if the worker has made an error in developing a time-limited group, there is an end point in which the group can be reformulated as opposed to it going on indefinitely.

The primary disadvantage of a time-limited group is that the time allotted for the group may not be enough for the group to reach its goals. In some groups, the members experience early resistance and just reach the point where they begin to share significant thoughts and ideas when it is time to end. In other groups, the members develop so much anxiety over the time limit that they strive too hard to succeed within the specified time period and accomplish nothing at all.

An ongoing group's major advantage is that it allows each member adequate time to work through issues in depth and the group leader enough time to offer each member the support and challenges he or she needs in order to make significant life changes. Not everyone makes changes in their life in 12 or 16 sessions. Many group members need a greater amount of time in the relatively predictable group setting before spreading their wings outside the group. The disadvantage of an ongoing group is that it fosters dependency and is often less productive than a time-limited group.

I personally prefer time-limited groups of approximately 20 sessions. While a 20-session group is generally not considered a long-term group, it does provide enough time for a sense of trust and for cohesiveness to develop. At approximately the 16th session, I ask members to decide whether or not they wish to continue beyond the final date. Those who want to join a second 20-week group are encouraged to articulate what it is they hope to achieve by being part of a re-formed group for 20 more weeks.

To help each member decide what to do, I invite the input of other members. Interestingly, it is often this feedback that encourages a person to continue in the group. Ben, a 30-year-old minister, for example, at first made it clear that he had had enough treatment and was not planning to sign up for another 20 weeks. However, comments from other group members such as those that follow surprised Ben and convinced him to rethink his decision. One member caustically observed, "You're the last person who should quit. You have finally begun to work." Another told him, "That's the dumbest thing you have said since we began. You really need this group." Because of these remarks and additional feedback from us. Ben decided to continue into the next group.

If most of the members choose to continue, there is a two-week break, and then the group begins again. If a significant number of members drop out at the 20th session, a reconstituted group is formed with "alumni" of the former group plus new members. A strength of such an arrangement is that it encourages individual members and the group-as-a- whole to examine their progress and to make whatever changes are needed to achieve their goals.

Another time-limited option is the **minimarathon,** in which members attend a session that lasts six to eight hours. Frey (1987), in a discussion of minimarathons with incest offenders, writes that a minimarathon permits greater flexibility than groups that meet on a weekly basis, both in directing the group and in observing the process. Because the members are together over an extended period of time, their defenses are lowered, and they are more willing than before to admit to their actions.

> As the day progresses, each man holds the group focus for an extended period, during which he details his incestuous behavior. This alone often results in an intensity of affect not previously seen in the offender. The men begin to recognize their own defensive verbalizations and support each other's honesty. Group cohesiveness begins to develop as each man moves beyond previous abilities and discloses his behavior and feelings [p. 534].

Minimarathons can be used as a single treatment unit or in conjunction with other modalities. Frey (1987), in discussing her work with incest offenders, indicates that she requires 8 to 12 weeks of weekly group sessions.

LENGTH AND FREQUENCY OF MEETINGS

How long should a group session last? Should a group meet more than once a week? The optimal frequency of group meetings and the optimal length of each session have not been established. Often, the criteria a group worker uses, particularly with children and limited-functioning adults, is their frust-ration tolerance and attention span. For these clients, a group session that lasts an hour or more may generate so much anxiety that most of the worker's time is focused on behavior management and limit setting. Therefore, rather than an hour-long session, it may be better to hold two 30-minute meetings per week.

In some settings, such as psychiatric hospitals and day-treatment centers, group membership changes from week to week, and there is very little continuity between sessions. Nearly every session has one or more new members. According to Yalom (1983), the only logical clinical solution is for a group worker to hold meetings as frequently as possible. This may mean meeting seven days a week if staff scheduling permits. By increasing the frequency, the group worker can ensure a stable core of members who may help to provide a consistent, safe, and trusting atmosphere.

For relatively high-functioning adults, meetings of one and one half to two hours is the norm. This provides enough time for each member to share and not so long that fatigue sets in. Dinkmeyer and Muro (1971) note that a group of such members once established, will initiate action for more frequent meetings on their own. This is because of their increasing recognition of the benefits of the group and their desire to move and grow.

The question often arises as to whether extra time should be allowed for the continuation of a discussion once a group's formal time is up. Sometimes, the problem has to do with the fact that the members do not get into significant issues until the last 15 minutes. In other instances, the group may have been working most of the session and simply needs more time. Luchins (1964) suggests that in the former instance, the pattern should be pointed out to the group, and the meeting should end at the designated time. In the latter instance, Luchins says, the group should be allowed to remain a few minutes longer or to come back later when time is available. Usually, as members become more organized, they are more efficient in dealing with each other and with their own problems and finish on time.

● Techniques: Practical considerations

1. Seek a balance by selecting group members who have similar personal characteristics but different coping skills, life experiences, and expertise.
2. Sitting still in the same chair, for some people, can be excruciating. Provide the opportunity for group members to get up and move around.
3. The duration of group sessions should be influenced by the members' attention span.
4. If a group has a limited number of members, keep in mind individuals to add to the group in case someone drops out.

PHYSICAL ARRANGEMENTS

The physical setting where a group meets will have a powerful influence on the behavior of its members. Sadly, most social agencies are built for one-to-one counseling, and the worker has to be resourceful in finding space that contributes to rather than detracts from a group's development. While physical arrangements may seem of little importance to the worker who must work with whatever location and furniture the organization provides, he or she should strive to establish the best possible conditions within the framework of what is available.

192

● ● ● ● ● ● ● ●

Flapan and Fenchel (1987) suggest that at least four factors related to a group's physical setting will affect the interaction between its group members: privacy, intimacy, comfort, and concentration. It is important that members have a sense of privacy and that people outside the group will not hear what is happening there, will not suddenly enter the room, and will not use it as a passageway. A group's concentration is enhanced if there are no distracting noises or views. The temperature should be maintained at a comfortable level since a room that is too cold or too warm will negatively influence the group's interactions. A group member sharing his experiences in a group wrote, "I felt very comfortable with the room setting, although I remember being freezing cold. This compounded my sense of anxiety, and several times I found myself unsure whether I was shivering from cold, or from nervousness."

Too large a room will distract from a group's feeling of intimacy and may present problems in behavior management. Foulkes and Anthony (1957) suggest a small room for group work with latency-age children.

> The disadvantages of working with children of this age in a large room gradually became clearer over the years. The large room allowed the children to scatter, to get away from the therapist, to become inaccessible to interpretations, and to become caught up in fragmented group activities and subgroup formation. The idea of a small room evolved from the need to keep the members in close therapeutic contact with the therapist [p. 209].

Likewise, too small a room may be troublesome. For example, in some members, a small room generates a sense of panic and anxiety. It is as if their personal space is being violated and they are forced into intimate contact with people whom they do not know.

A table may provide a place for each participant to rest a cup or glass and, at the same time, serve as a barrier for group members and the worker to hide behind. For certain clients, for example, those who are very fearful, they may at first need a place to hide. Muro and Freeman (1968) write that the lack of a table in one of the groups they led was a definite hindrance, because several female members who were wearing dresses indicated they could not sit comfortably and concentrate on what was going on.

Soft overstuffed chairs and couches, while comfortable, may be perceived by young children as trampolines to be jumped on. Likewise, objects such as blackboards, a television set, folding chairs, and windows may send out the subliminal message "Play with me." This message may not be apparent to a worker until the worker finds himself or herself in direct competition with these objects.

In general chairs for a group session should be arranged so that the worker and each member can see all of the others members. And, if a table is used, a round one is generally preferable to a square one.

Use of Food

One of the least examined aspects of treatment has to do with the use of food during group sessions. The social custom of offering refreshments as a means of creating a relaxed and intimate atmosphere is very much a part of our culture. From a psychoanalytic perspective, many of our clients are "orally fixated" and associate food with love and caring.

193

Is it appropriate to have refreshments in a group session? Some therapists, out of a concern that group treatment may turn into a coffee klatsch, allow no refreshments at all. Or, if they do, the therapists distinguish sharply between the refreshment time and the therapy time. Other therapists argue that providing refreshments such as tea, coffee, and/or cookies, conveys the message that the setting is safe and the comfort of the individual members is important. Such therapists place the food within easy reach of group members and encourage individuals to take it whenever they want it.

Food has particular value in working with children. Often, sessions are held after school, a time when the group members are tired and experiencing reduced energy. Food can increase their energy level and can be used as a positive reinforcer. The worker, however, needs to be cautious in serving a food or beverage heavy with sugar, because of sugar's potential for stimulating excessive activity levels.

O'Brian (1977), discussing his work with groups of schizophrenic patients observes that food is often an excellent way of stimulating interaction among members who are withdrawn.

> One of our groups, which was composed of very withdrawn members who could not interact verbally, was prompted to begin sharing a communal meal at the clinic. Each was given the responsibility for a different part of the meal. At first, the therapist had to organize the patients, but later the members did this themselves [p. 152].

According to O'Brian, the members rotated the responsibilities, took pride in their own contribution of food, and began to show feelings for one another. Eventually, they were able to contribute verbally and discuss topics other than food.

Agency Sanction

Sanctions from the sponsoring agency are essential in developing and leading therapy groups, particularly in schools, clinics, and hospitals. Unless these sanctions are in place, a group is doomed to fail. And these sanctions need to be vertical as well as horizontal. Vertical sanctions refers to approval and support from the director or from some other administrator who has legitimate power and who is in a position to give both approval and support.

In a court system, this person may be a judge; in a school, the principal; in a hospital, the medical director.

To understand and acquire institutional sanctions, the worker needs to analyze which organizational and interpersonal forces are apt to encourage or to restrain the development of the group (Gitterman, 1986). Since these environmental forces and others affect all organizational processes, the worker must evaluate any feature in the environment that might affect the development of the group.

Lonergan (1982), in discussing the failure of two treatment groups in a general hospital, concludes that it occurred because she did not properly analyze the hospital's medical hierarchy. In each instance, she received approval for the group from the medical directors and assumed that their approval would filter down to the attending staff. Soon, it became obvious that the medical directors were not the true leaders of their departments and that an attending physician was the real source of power and leadership. And the attending physician insisted on terminating the group.

Horizontal sanctions refers to the approval and support of peers and members of other disciplines. Without these sanctions, a group may be undermined or sabotaged. For example, a worker might plan a group for clients of an agency and then receive no referrals from his or her colleagues on the staff. Or a therapist might receive a paper referral of a client and then find that the client has not been informed of the referral and so does not show up for the group.

Sometimes, the members of other disciplines, instead of being very supportive, can "become the enemy." Often, this results from a battle over "turf," and the client can be caught in the middle. In other instances, such problems result from a lack of communication between staff members in different disciplines. In a large Veterans Administration medical complex, for example, group leaders complained that every time they held group sessions, nurses came in and took patients out of the meeting for medication, for physical therapy, or for appointments with doctors. After analysis of the situation, it was found that the nurses' actions were not meant as hostile acts but resulted from the nurses' misunderstanding of the group's purpose. The nurses had their responsibilities and were following orders in an efficient manner. More important, they had not been told they were not to take patients out of the group.

Power is not always limited to administrators, other group workers, and members of other disciplines. Someone without therapeutic training— such as a secretary who assigns rooms or a janitor who sets up chairs and cleans the building—may also have some impact on a group. Often, the most powerful individual in an agency after 5:00 P.M. is the maintenance person who locks and unlocks the door. Many groups have stood on the steps of an agency while a worker frantically searched for someone to unlock the door because the worker forgot to inform the maintenance staff there would be an evening meeting.

IN SUMMARY

The importance of planning a group cannot be overemphasized. The worker can begin by examining the needs of his or her agency's clients and determining whether or not these needs can be met through group treatment. In addition, the agency and the practitioner's personal objectives for the group must be clearly stated and assessed. It is valuable for the group worker to conduct a personal screening interview with each prospective member to determine the appropriateness of the candidate for the group and to provide him or her with information about matters such as the group's purpose, content, and guidelines.

The worker influences the group by establishing and modifying group conditions, which in turn affect the members. These conditions include the group's purpose, composition, size, session length, type of membership, and duration, and the setting where the group sessions are to be held. It is essential that the group worker keep other staff members and the agency's administration informed of the plans for the group.

SUGGESTED READINGS

BERTCHER, H., & MAPLE, F. (1974). Elements and issues in group composition. In P. Glasser, R. Sarri, & R. Vinter (Eds.), *Individual change through small groups* (pp. 186–208). New York: Free Press.

DOUGLAS, T. (1976). *Groupwork practice*. New York: International Universities Press. See Part 2.

KLEIN, A. (1972). *Effective groupwork: An introduction to principle and method*. New York: Association Press. See Chapter 2.

MULLAN, H., & ROSENBAUM, M. (1978). *Group psychotherapy: Theory and practice*. New York: Free Press. See Part 3.

THE
BEGINNING
PHASE
OF
TREATMENT

I would love to say to inexperienced group workers that once they have led five or six groups, the initial meeting of a group will be a piece of cake, and they will feel little or no anxiety.

They will have to go to someone else for that advice. Frankly, I am always apprehensive during the first session, just as I'm a bit nervous during the first meeting of a class that I have to teach.

The hour before the members arrive, I have a difficult time settling down. I drink more coffee than usual, and I experience free-floating anxiety. Doubts and questions as to the group's composition begin to haunt me. Are the individuals going to show up? Will they relate to the rest of the group? How are particular members going to react to each other? What have I forgotten? Can I be myself without wearing some therapeutic safety mask that hides my authenticity and hinders my own genuineness within the group?

When I am thinking clearly, I tell myself to relax and not to worry. This is not just a glib flight into positive thinking on my part. It's based on reality. I have had my share of Murphy's Law–ridden groups with people not showing up and individuals having difficulty in relating—although these groups have been the exception.

Once everyone says who he or she is and we go through guidelines for the group, my anxiety diminishes. Although I usually share my feelings of discomfort with the members, I doubt if they really believe me. Wrapped up in their own anxiety, they have difficulty comprehending that the worker— who appears so secure—is feeling some of the same emotions they are experiencing.

Maybe I'll never be able to exorcise the pregroup demons buried in my psyche. I can live with the symptoms. There is bittersweet solace in the knowledge that no group worker has ever died from the anxiety of the initial session.

• • •

This chapter addresses the beginning phase of group treatment and explores the elements that enhance as well as hinder a group's success during its initial meeting. The chapter answers this question: what can a group worker do to increase the effectiveness of a group's first session?

A COMING TOGETHER

The first 15 minutes of a group's initial session is significant for two reasons. First, it is the beginning point of the particular session. For the next hour or so, a set of strangers, meeting together for the first time, will begin to share their thoughts, ideas, experiences, and feelings. They will be asked to take risks and to move beyond their comfort zone. Second, the first 15 minutes is the beginning point of an ongoing group that will continue for weeks and possibly months. The strangers sharing the meeting room are taking the first step in establishing a cohesive group predicated on meaningful self-exploration and honest and appropriate feedback.

For anyone who has never been in a clinically oriented group, many group rules, expectations, and activities may seem new and strange. In the beginning, group members experience awkwardness, uncertainty, anxiety, and a sense of anticipation. Their first meeting is alive with the feel of beginning. The members are filled with hope of what this experience can mean for them. They experience fear and apprehension of the unknown. This aggregate of individuals is not yet really a group, but it **is** already started on the fascinating discovery of whether it can become one (Smalley, 1967).

Throughout a group, its members continually appraise both the worker and the other group members. The worker represents power and authority and is viewed as the arbiter of acceptable and unacceptable behavior within the group. Behind the client's eyes are many questions about the therapist:

- What is the group worker really like?
- Will the group worker like me?
- Will the group worker laugh at me if I say the wrong thing?
- Will the group worker protect me if I'm attacked?
- Will the group worker respect me and my feelings?

Until group members have a sense of how the practitioner operates and have decoded the meaning of his or her verbal and nonverbal behavior they will continue to test the practitioner. And they will maintain their defense mechanisms until they are reasonably certain that their safety in the group is ensured.

Group members also continually size each other up as to strengths and weaknesses. Each client asks himself or herself questions like these:

- Will the other group members hurt me?
- Are the other group members sicker than I am?
- Can I trust the other group members?
- Are the other group members supportive and sympathetic, or are they attacking and threatening?

Group members may wonder if others in the group who struggle with the same problems they do, will be able to help them? There may be competitiveness if some of the group members have already been in individual counseling with the worker. Now, they must share this person, who has become special to them, with other group members.

GETTING STARTED

No matter how well prospective members have been prepared, the first session produces not only excitement but also anxiety. Once the door is closed and the meeting begins, group members look to the therapist for direction. In their search for structure within this novel situation, they laugh nervously and engage in polite small talk. The beginning of the first session is marked by hesitant statements, and awkward pauses, and a recurrence of previously answered questions. In the initial stage of the group, clients are preoccupied with themselves rather than with group concerns, and they experience only a limited sense of connection with other group members.

It is our sensitivity, as workers, to the meaning of this particular beginning that will be a vital factor in lessening the anxiety and enhancing the individual's commitment to the group. One way we do this is by making the unknown known. We start by repeating information previously discussed in pregroup interviews. We go over the purpose of the group, our objectives and expectations for the group, what it means to be a group member, and what we, as therapists, will be doing in the group sessions.

We encourage the involvement of members by having them express their hopes, intentions, fears, and concerns. The more quickly each member gets into the action of the group, the more readily the member can direct his or her life force and energy toward dealing with the situation, rather than protecting himself or herself against its impact. Our responsibility is to help the individuals find a place to take hold and to emotionally join the group as active participants.

Smalley (1967) writes that the need for a group worker to appreciate the promise and problems of beginnings cannot be overemphasized. It is essential that the group worker allow group members to stay involved with the group's beginning and to let it be a beginning in all its inevitable awkwardness and tentativeness, rather than rush them to try to solve all the problems in the first group session. The goal in any beginning group is to facilitate the discovery of a common base so the worker and members can begin to work together toward a common purpose. To help the members see themselves as a group, the group leader can explain the rules of the group and break down the elements of each rule into manageable guidelines that the members can put to use immediately.

The group worker, according to Shulman (1984), should design the structure of the first meetings to meet these specific objectives:

1. introducing group members to each other
2. making a brief, simple opening statement to clarify the agency's or institution's stake in sponsoring the group, as well as having members raise issues and concerns they feel are urgent
3. obtaining feedback from group members on their sense of the match between their ideas of their needs and the agency's view of the treatment it can provide them
4. clarifying the role of the group worker and the worker's method of attempting to help group members work
5. dealing directly with any specific obstacles that hinder this particular group's effort to function effectively
6. encouraging intermember interaction instead of discussions between only the group leader and each group member
7. developing a supportive culture in which group members can feel safe
8. helping group members develop a tentative agenda for their own and the group's future work
9. clarifying the mutual expectations of the agency and group members
10. gaining some consensus on the part of group members about the specific next steps by, for example, determining what themes or issues they want to begin with in the next session
11. encouraging honest evaluation of feedback about the effectiveness from group members.

Many of these objectives can be dealt with quickly, while others are interdependent and can be addressed simultaneously. Objectives such as encouraging honest feedback about the effectiveness of the group will require a number of sessions.

ACCENTUATING SIMILARITIES

The ambiguity of the group's beginning can be reduced by the group worker's helping the members discover their common denominators. These common denominators are any similarities in their life experiences, difficulties, concerns, feelings, and ways of responding to situations. The worker can do this by having each group member give his or her name and describe what he or she hopes to gain from the group. It is also useful for the worker to ask each member to share his or her feelings, particularly how the member is feeling at the moment—for example, scared, excited, frightened, happy.

Learning that others have the same feelings about being in the group is itself supportive to group members. During the initial session of one group, a scared and anxious client found courage when he heard that other group members were also feeling frightened. They too, he learned, felt unsure of themselves and were unclear as to the therapist's expectations.

Regardless of differences in race, sex, occupation, or any other distinguishing personal attributes, group members begin to learn that what they are experiencing is similar to what other group members are experiencing. There is a sense of universality and with it the beginning of cohesion in the group. Paradoxically, by talking about their anxiety and lack of trust, a group's members can begin to create a preliminary foundation of genuine trust.

In sharing **her** early experiences in a group, a client named Margaret, writes:

> I think the one thing that had meaning for me in the first session was when all of us were able to get some of our anxiety and fears out by asking questions of the leader and each other. I started to feel more comfortable when we went over the expectations, rules, and confidentiality issues that I had been concerned about prior to the group. I guess the sharing of the other members meant a lot for me also. Even though I did not say very much the first session, I gained from Robert and Linda sharing their feelings about being in the group.

A group worker can use any of several means of asking members to share. Most common is the round-robin in which everyone—including the worker tells his or her name and something about himself or herself. Because each person is expected to take a turn, individuals are forced to speak, even when they may prefer to remain silent. Often, however, members are so anxiously preparing in advance what **they** are going to say that they do not listen to what others are saying. In fact, the round robin contradicts the ideal of speaking freely and spontaneously, listening to others as sensitively as possible, and working in a warm flexible climate suited to the members' needs (Benjamin, 1978).

A group leader can address questions to the group-as-a-whole, instead of focusing on one person. The worker might ask the whole group, "Would each of you give your name, and something about you that makes you different from everyone else in the group?" Long silences in the first few sessions may discourage or frighten some members, who may then decide not to return. But, by using open-ended and indirect questions, the group worker can encourage anyone to respond and can keep pressure from being placed on any particular individual.

Planned dyads are another useful introduction activity a group worker can use. The worker can pair up members and ask them to tell each other certain things about themselves, based on suggestions from the worker. After five or ten minutes, the worker can invite the pairs to return to the larger group and can ask each member to introduce his or her partner to the rest of the group.

Group members often begin interacting with each other without prompting from the leader. Some will talk about why they are in the group and what they are hoping to achieve. Others will talk about their feelings at the moment—for example, their nervousness, anger, anxiety, fear, or self-consciousness. In this case, instead of taking over and officially beginning the session, it is sometimes useful for the group worker to unobtrusively listen and then to gradually invite other members to join in the discussion. By sitting back and observing, the worker is in a unique position to gain understanding of each member, to observe the group process as it develops, and to formulate general statements about the ongoing interaction.

It is an axiom that once a group member has said something, no matter how general or simple, the easier it will be for the person to speak a second or third time. A corollary is that the longer it takes for an individual to speak, the more difficult it will be when he or she finally does speak. If a group has difficulty sharing, the group worker can raise questions to elicit reactions to what one of the members has said or done. During the first sessions, it is important that the clinician be flexible—neither sitting in rigid silence nor "taking over" as the director of the interaction (Flapan & Fenchel, 1987).

RITES OF ENTRY

It may be valuable for the worker to establish a point of entry or initiation for candidates prior to their full membership in an already functioning group. Nowinski (1990), in describing the use of group treatment with adolescent drug abusers, explains that each candidate has to prepare and share his or her personal history of using mood-altering chemicals. The candidate is assisted in the preparation of the history by sponsors—adolescent members further along in their own treatment, prior to the candidates' first meeting. The candidate is told exactly what is expected and what will happen. Afterward, the person asks the group to determine whether or not the history is acceptable. If it is acceptable, the candidate requests group membership.

New members who have passed this rite of entry are formally welcomed into the group. Those who are rejected—usually because of denial behavior—may ask to repeat the rite or to be referred to alternative treatment. Such a rite of initiation has the potential of building group cohesiveness and enhancing group members' motivation to work in the group. It also, according to Nowinski, balances the power between members and the worker.

● **Techniques: Practical considerations**
1. Encourage group members to share their thoughts, feelings, and expectations about being in the group.
2. Do not hurry the group's beginning, even though group members may appear ready to move on.
3. During the initial session, encourage everyone to share something about himself or herself.
4. When in doubt, focus group members' attention on their feelings.

ESTABLISHING RAPPORT

Kellerman (1979) observes that in order for a group to have stabilized level of tension, the group must have unambiguous leadership, clearly defined rules, open communication channels, a well-established dominance hierarchy, effective reality testing, and low narcissism. None of this can be readily accomplished without a structured approach to group leadership. The leader must be active enough to be viewed as consistent; must be a reinforcer of members' attempts to assume new roles in the group; must be a facilitator of communication; must be a facilitator of members' reality testing by encouraging members to share information; and must be a reinforcer of interpersonal sensitivity.

Some authors (Jacobs, Harvill, & Masson, 1988) caution a therapist not to open a group's first session with a minilecture on issues such as ground rules, meeting time, and frequency of meetings, because doing this sets a "leader-dominant" tone. The members may hear very little of the presentation because of their anxiety. Another common mistake is to begin by asking members about their expectations when they are uneasy about being in the group and have not yet met one another.

Monologues by a group worker should be limited to a very few minutes. If they are not, the group members will feel as if they are in a classroom with a teacher talking "at them." The worker also needs to pause and invite participants to share their reactions and ask their questions. Although, from the leader's vantage point, everything he or she says may be perfectly clear, it may not be so to all members. In addition, the group members may raise questions and concerns about matters totally unrelated to what has just been said (Benjamin, 1980). In this case, the worker will have to determine how to reply and in what way to react. But the worker's goal should be to convince the group members that they have been heard, even if, for the moment, they do not receive definite answers to all of their questions.

Excessive group structure and leader activity can encourage a group's dependency. This is particularly significant in early sessions before the norms of the group have been firmly established. Early in each group's development, its members will search for clues to the workings of the group and the worker's style. If it is evident, for example, that the worker will call on individuals when there is a lull in the discussion, there will be little or no volunteering of information. The members will also look to the worker to provide topics, resolve conflicts, offer advice, and be the one to confront any objectionable behavior. By asking a lot of questions, the worker may lead the members to expect and depend on his or her questions to reveal information. As the worker runs out of questions, the members are left hoping the practitioner will figure out what to ask. In short, the members will expect the group leader to do the work of the group.

THE GROUP CONTRACT

No matter how explicit a therapist is in explaining the purpose of a group during his or her preliminary interviews with clients, the group members will still have some questions as to the group's purpose, the leader's role, and their own role. As these issues are clarified during group sessions, it becomes easier for the members to select and make appropriate responses. If, on the other hand, the group's purpose remains ambiguous, the individuals will need to expend extra energy just to determine how they are to act, and what the boundaries are.

In group work, the term **contracting** has come to refer to clarifying the purpose for the group, clarifying the leader's and members' roles, and soliciting client feedback on these matters (Schwartz, 1976). At a general level, contracting has to do with explaining the agency's purpose in offering the group, as well as determining the common ground between this purpose, the group members' needs, and their sense of immediate urgency. At a more specific level, contracting makes explicit the worker's role, the mutual need that members have for each other, and the mutual expectations and obligations of the group leader and the group members.

Contracts can be between a group member and the group worker, as well as between the members and between a member and the group (Garvin, 1981). For example, with the group worker, a group member might contract to be more assertive in the group or to attend every session. The same member might also contract with another member to refrain from calling each other names or from bullying a third member. In addition, the same member might contract with the group-as-a-whole to be more self-disclosing during sessions or to be more active in looking for a job.

During a group's initial session, it is essential that the worker repeat basic information regarding the group's purpose, how the group will be conducted, and its ground rules. None of this information should surprise the individual members. It would already have been discussed during the individual interviews—unless there were no screening interviews. In that case, it is particularly important for the worker to go over this information in the first session and also to reiterate it during the second session. In the beginning, members are often so preoccupied that they do not comprehend the group's purpose, their particular role, the worker's role, and what will be expected of them. If these issues are not made clear early in the group's development, they will come up over and over again and hinder the group's progress.

EXPLAINING THE WORKER'S ROLE

Group members should have explicit information as to the leader's role, rather than having to guess. Again, this information is presented in the pregroup interviews and in the initial session. Making the worker's role clear benefits goup members whether the worker's role is that of facilitator, therapist, or teacher. The following examples show how the worker might clarify his or her role in each case.

1. Before we go any further, let me explain to you my role as **facilitator.** My task is to assist you in achieving the group's purpose of helping you better adapt to being divorced. I will be encouraging each of you to share your thoughts, feelings, and concerns. I will be challenging you to look more closely and in greater detail at your actions inside and outside the group.

Now, I have to tell you up front that I have not been divorced. I have worked with lots of people who have been divorced. I will not give you advice but will depend on others to share what has worked for them.

2. As the **therapist** in the group, I will be asking you to discuss the sexual abuse you experienced as a child. I recognize that this will not be easy. I also know that if you are to resolve what happened in the past, you will need to address it openly. We will be talking about the past, as it relates to the present and the future. It is my expectation of myself that I will be honest and open. Likewise, I hope you will feel free to be open. If at some point you feel I'm not being honest, please tell me.

There may be times when I may have to draw the group back to the task at hand, especially if we get off target. I will also be stopping the group at certain points and asking you to process what is going on within the group.

3. My role in this group will be primarily that of **teacher.** For the first half hour of each group, we will talk about problems in child rearing, and I will show movies as well as discuss human developmental stages. After that, I will invite your questions and try to respond to some of the problems you are facing. I will also draw some of you into sharing what has worked for you as you raised your children.

The initial group session is an appropriate time for co-leaders to explain their roles. It is also the time to discuss a particular technique or model—for example, transactional analysis or behavior modification—that the worker will be using.

The reality that the group worker is not a **member** of the group should be emphasized. Our role as therapists is to assist the group members to work on themselves within the helping environment. Group leaders who do not state their responsibilities and demonstrate their credibility by behaving as leaders invite challenges to their leadership (Dyer & Vriend, 1975).

CLARIFYING THE CLIENT'S ROLE

Most group members a worker deals with will have had no previous experiences with a therapy group, and they will be unclear as to what is expected of them. They will have concerns and questions such as:

- Are we to self-disclose? If so, how much?
- Is it all right to disagree with the worker?
- What if I don't feel like talking?
- What will the sessions be like?
- Can I really say what I feel?

Egan (1970), in discussing contracts in encounter groups, suggests the use of a detailed statement in which the major variables are spelled out in writing. Members are asked to read the contract and then decide whether they want to participate in the experience. Elements of Egan's written contract address these matters: group goals, group leadership, the nature of the group experience, and rules related to immediacy, expression of emotion, and the core interactions—such as self-disclosure, listening, support, and confrontation. According to Egan, the contract is both a stimulus and a safeguard that moves the participants toward intensive interaction.

● **Techniques: Practical considerations**
1. Do not overwhelm group members with information.
2. Make clear the member's role, the worker's role, and the group's purpose.
3. Be prepared to repeat information you have already presented to group members during their pre-group interviews.
4. Be attuned to your own anxiety and discomfort.

GOAL-ORIENTED PRACTICE

A group leader should help each group member establish realistic and attainable personal goals that provide the member with direction. These goals state what the person should be doing differently by the end of the group. According to Locke and Latham (1984), establishing problem-managing goals for each group member is useful for a number of reasons. First, setting goals focuses the member's attention and action and provides a vision toward which the member can direct his or her energies. Second, setting goals mobilizes the member's energy and effort. Third, setting goals increases the member's persistence, resulting in his or her working harder and longer. Finally, setting goals motivates the member toward action and makes him or her less inclined to engage in aimless behavior.

Clear and realistic goals are easily established for some clients during their pregroup interview. This is the case for an individual who is relatively clear as to the problem, can articulate his or her expectations, and can identify strategies to achieve his or her goals. For example, during her interview, Wilma, a 22-year-old extremely obese college student, being considered for group treatment, was very specific about her reasons for joining the group.

> I'm overweight and unhappy—and I know why. Being fat is my way of keeping men away. I'm tired of being fat. I'm lonely and figure it's time to get my life together. I want to lose weight and begin to have some men friends. When I lost weight before, I got scared and went on an eating binge. This time I need lots of support.

Wilma is, however, an exception. Clients who have never been in counseling, who are unfamiliar with group treatment, or who are in nonvoluntary settings may have difficulty in selecting appropriate goals. When this occurs, the group worker is well advised not to force the issue. Instead, it is more realistic for the worker to encourage the group member to attend several sessions and **only** then to decide in what ways the group can be most useful.

Allowing a client's goals to emerge in a natural way can be an advantage. Group members who have been helped to clarify a problem through a combination of probing, empathy, and challenge can begin to see more clearly what they want to do with their problems. As the members learn about themselves through honest feedback, they are in a better position to realistically articulate what they want from the group.

Typically, in the beginning stages of a group, clients have vague ideas about what they hope to accomplish. They say they want to "feel better," "enjoy life more", and "be happier." These statements, according to Egan (1990), are a "declaration of intent," and not goals. They are an indication by a client that the client intends to do something about a problem situation. To become goals, however, these statements must be made specific and concrete in regard to the changes desired.

DEVELOPING WORKABLE GOALS

For goals to be effective, they must be explicit, realistic, and attainable; clear; and measurable and verifiable.

Defined in explicit terms. Goals need to be stated as specific outcomes—for example, "In two months I will lose 8 pounds" or "By Friday of next week, I will have put in five job applications." These goals define the desired end results in such a way that everyone involved is clear about the changes to be accomplished (Nelsen, 1981).

Realistic and attainable. Goals must be realistic, and they must be attainable during the life of the group. Too often, group members formulate goals that are unrealistic or overly ambitious, sabotaging their own efforts. For example, a man decides he is going to enter law school but does not have the financial or academic resources to do so. When it becomes evident that he cannot attain this goal, he feels frustrated and becomes depressed. Before setting a goal, it is vital for a group member to consider his or her capacity to achieve the goal, the resources he or she has available, and the environmental constraints that mitigate against his or her accomplishment of the goal.

Measurable and verifiable. Goals must be stated in such a way that a group member can measure his or her own progress. The group worker can encourage the client to answer this fundamental question: "How will I know whether I have achieved my goal?"

As each member's goals are formulated, they are shared openly in the group. This provides opportunities for the member to examine, in more depth, the goal's negative as well as positive consequences. Examples of negative consequences might include losing friends when a member chooses not to drink or use drugs, being rejected by someone of the opposite sex when a member asks someone for a date, and being fired when a member acts in an assertive way on the job.

209

A NOTE OF CAUTION

To this emphasis on the value of setting goals, it is important to add this warning: the worker needs to be careful that the group does not become so goal-governed (different from goal-oriented) that the richness and freedom of the group experience is lost. Ongoing tension over making goals and objectives technically correct can work to the detriment of the individual member and the group-as-a-whole (Langer, 1989). Neither life nor group work is ever neat or linear. Eisner (1979) writes, "Many of our most productive activities take the form of exploration or play. In such activities, the task is not one of arriving at a preformed objective but rather to act, often with a sense of abandon, wonder, curiosity" [p. 100].

GROUND RULES

The limits imposed on a group may be specific to the group, and/or general rules of the sponsoring agency or institution. These limits are presented in the pregroup interview and the first session as a means of orienting group members. They are repeated again as the rules are tested and experienced by the members. Ground rules include expectations about attendance, absences, smoking and eating during the meeting, and members' rights and responsibilities. Many groups also set forth rules prohibiting physical attacks on other people and physical acting out.

The most universal rule in group work is that of confidentiality. While most clients entering treatment trust the clinician, they are not sure of the other group members. It is reassuring, therefore, for group members to hear that they do not have to risk sharing personal information until they are ready and until they trust the group to respect their privacy.

Most groups work from the expectation of "whatever goes on in the groups stays in the group." Some therapists feel that a group member should not share any information discussed in the group with anyone outside of the group, including the member's spouse (Pierrakos, 1978). Other group leaders do not mention confidentiality because they are convinced that if a member is going to break the rule, he or she will do so regardless of warnings from the worker or other group members (Luchins, 1964).

Confidentiality has its limitations, particularly with children and adolescents, groups of parolees, and groups of involuntary patients in a psychiatric hospital or clinic. If, for example, information from a therapy group is going onto a member's record or chart, the member should be informed of this even before the initial group session. It is essential that we, as group workers, clearly state how much confidentiality we can promise to our

210

• • • • • • •

clients. Then, our clients can decide for themselves what and how much they will disclose (Corey & Corey, 1987).

The sponsoring organization's expectations regarding confidentiality may differ from the therapist's expectations. A student working in a county jail established a group for incarcerated men. After the third session, it became evident that information shared in the group was being passed on to jail administrators. Group members complained that they were being disciplined for what they said in the group. Enraged, the men blamed each other and the worker for the "leak." Several weeks later, it was discovered that there was a listening device in the group room and that the sessions were being monitored by jail administrators.

MINORITY CLIENTS

Racial and cultural differences are a salient interpersonal factor and have significance for group members and leaders (Davis, 1984). Therapists who have minority members in their groups often have little or no knowledge of the person's culture (Davis, 1984; Edwards & Edwards, 1980; Ho, 1976). The result is insensitivity to the minority clients that negatively affects the group's composition, communication, and process.

In the past three decades, there has been a growing interest in race, ethnicity, and the importance of cultural differences. While this new awareness is often reflected more in political than rhetoric in actual understanding, one result has been more attention paid to the psychological impact such differences can have on client/worker interactions. In short, more therapists than ever before realize that class, color, age, nationality, and gender differences have the potential for increasing the social distance and limiting the empathy and understanding in a therapy group.

ABSENCE OF TRUST

The development of trust is critical in working with minority clients. Edwards and Edwards (1980), in referring to work with Native-American groups, suggest that group workers can expect that it will take three to six months before they are accepted by people in traditional Indian communities. One reason for the wariness is the rapid turnover of social workers. Another reason is linked to the difficulty a minority client has trusting someone identified as the oppressor. Edwards (1982) raises the question "How can we expect self-disclosure by the oppressed to the oppressor?"

In reference to group work with a Chicano population, Brown and Arevalo (1979) suggest the identification and use of informal resources within the community—for example, an intermediary person whom the clients respect. They say it is also valuable for a group worker to take a personal interest in their clients' culture and language in order to develop the helping relationship. By showing concern and interest in a client's family and sharing information about himself or herself, a group worker can break down some barriers. Brown and Arevalo also point out that it is beneficial to involve family members, particularly the father, in obtaining permission for other family members' involvement in a group.

211

It is incumbent upon a group worker to recognize that trust, in the early phases of any group, may be limited. But trust will increase if the group's members come to believe that the worker has their best interest at heart. As therapists, we need to be careful not to overestimate a relationship in its initial stages. Even though the therapeutic alliance is developing and client goals are being worked on, a minority client may still desire distance in the relationship.

VALUE DIFFERENCES

A group worker needs to be cautious not to let stereotypes or generalizations serve as his or her knowledge base for understanding a client's needs and reactions. What may be a norm in clinical practice may be contrary to the cultural norm for a client. For example, group members in therapeutic settings are expected to confront one another whenever they think it is appropriate. Asian Americans, however, view aggressive, confrontational behavior as rude and unacceptable (Ho, 1976). Similarly, group members are expected to talk about themselves and their experiences. Native Americans reared in the traditional ways of their tribes, however, find introspection and talking about themselves difficult. Indian people are expected to know their strengths and not to exaggerate them. They are taught to exhibit confidence and not to flaunt their skills. According to Edwards and Edwards (1980):

> American Indians believe that people should be able to understand one another, it is not necessary to explain one's feelings or problems in detail. The Indian client therefore often expects the professional person to be able to understand without the client having to voice concerns in detail [p. 501].

● **Techniques: Practical considerations**
   1. Have a sociopolitical understanding of the minority group you are working with. Be open to further developing that understanding.
   2. Do not avoid talking about cultural or racial differences when they are apparent.
   3. Have more than one minority member in a group at a time.
   4. Keep in mind that clinical knowledge based on the White culture is inadequate when applied to minority groups.
   5. Do not overburden minority members with the label of *expert,* or overuse them as resources.

WORKER'S ATTITUDE

A group leader's own attitude toward a group is often subtly expressed when the leader invites someone to join the group. If, as group leaders, we are ambivalent about our groups, we will communicate that nonverbally. There may be trepidation in our voice or a general lack of enthusiasm. The message "we want you to come" may be expressed so meekly the potential member feels no desire to join.

If we, as group workers, are not enthusiastic about our groups, the group members are not likely to be enthusiastic either. The result will probably be dull, listless, and boring groups. Enthusiasm means to have a zest and excitement for living, or in this context, for the group experience. Posthuma (1989) describes what happens when a group leader feels such enthusiasm.

> Many . . . group members, by virtue of their illness or life situations will have lost their zest, drive, and vitality for life. The enthusiasm [workers] display can be contagious, stirring members to engage in more energetic behaviors and interactions. Leader-therapists are also more likely to get personal satisfaction from the group if they embrace their role enthusiastically rather than just go though the motions [p. 95].

COMFORT LEVEL

Anxiety about the initial session of a group is as common for the worker as it is for the members. This anxiety manifests itself in behaviors such as overtalking, excessive use of structured activities, or a tendency to be quiet. During the initial session, some group workers ramble, think out loud, intellectualize, make premature interpretations, indulge in jargon, complicate that which is simple, and accentuate the obvious.

While there is no simple solution for avoiding these anxiety-provoked reactions, the worker **is** advised to think through the session in detail, including his or her objectives for the session and the specific activities he or she plans to use. If there is a co-leader involved, it is valuable to identify who will do what—for example, who will begin the session, introduce guidelines, and discuss roles. It is also beneficial to have a "Plan B" in mind in case, for some reason, what was originally planned does not work.

EXPECTATION OF ATTENDANCE

In institutional settings, the expectation that group attendance is required needs to be made clear to clients: "The staff believes that the group is important, and we want you to attend." The group worker's responsibility for ensuring his or her clients' attendance may not end there, however. The worker may need to check on them to see that they have not returned to bed. The worker may even need to walk with the clients to the meeting room and help each of them find a chair. For a worker in such a setting, expecting a moderate to high level of motivation, enthusiasm, and capacity for decision making by clients who are in an institution may be unrealistic, depending on the severity of their problems.

On the other hand, some therapists believe that when medical and psychiatric patients enter a hospital for help, the patients agree to cooperate with the treatment plan the hospital provides. According to Lonergan (1982), for example, staff should not have to go through a series of discussions about a patient's willingness to attend group any more than they would discuss a patient's getting a blood test or an X ray. Lonergan contends that the patient has already declared his or her intentions by coming to the hospital for help. The professional should develop the treatment plan and only enter into a debate if the patient objects to the plan.

An expected response from a reluctant patient is, "I'll go to the meeting but I don't want to talk." One way the leader can respond is by telling the reluctant person, "You don't have to talk. Just listen for a while." Such a response often avoids a conflictual situation in which a patient attends but then totally resists involvement—purely to spite the worker.

In the beginning session of a group, as in subsequent group sessions, the attention of the worker must constantly be divided between the group-as-a-whole and the group's individual members. This bi-focal perspective means that the worker has to relate to each group member, yet stay attuned to the group process. For someone without experience in work with groups, maintaining this dual focus appears to be an impossible task. It means relating to eight or so members, plus keeping track of themes, roles, issues, and dynamics.

The difficulty of this challenge is compounded if the practitioner has not initiated individual interviews with the group members during the group's conception stage. As a result, the worker finds himself or herself spending inordinate energy establishing worker/member relationships at the cost of facilitating member-to-member relationships.

CREATION OF TRUST

The need to establish trust during the initial stages of a group cannot be over-emphasized. Whether or not a climate of trust develops will be determined, to a large extent, by the attitude and activities of the group worker. If the worker has given careful thought to the purpose, goals, and structure of the group, he or she can inspire trust in the members. Likewise, by spending adequate time in the conception phase of the group's development and then informing the members of guidelines, responsibilities, and expectations, the worker can convince the members he or she takes the group seriously.

Initial trust can also come from the group members' perception that the group has a structure (Anderson, 1984). As if they are entering an unlit room for the first time and are fumbling around to find a lightswitch, the members search for clues about how they can and should act in a group. They grope for any structure that is familiar to them—a role, a norm, an assertion of status or power, a sign of approval, respect, or domination—anything that will shed light on the subject of how the group is structured and how they might function in it.

The group members expect the leader to provide answers to their questions and to reduce their sense of ambiguity. In particular, they look to the leader to validate them (Anderson, 1984). The members direct much of the initial communication in a group toward the group leader. At the same time, they carefully scrutinize the group leader's reactions for expectations and rewards. And the members tend to manifest behavior that has gained them approval from authorities in the past.

Clients new to a treatment-group situation will attribute to it many characteristics of the classroom. Implicit is their notion that they will be told things, that knowledge will be presented to them. In addition, the term *treatment group* has for clients connotations about the authority of the worker and the subordinate role of the group members. Real appreciation of the differences between a therapy group and a classroom comes after members are in the group for several meetings and begin to recognize that—instead of being passive observers with little power—they are active participants who have a great deal of power.

Corey and Corey (1987) write that the worker teaches most effectively through example. Experiencing the worker as a caring person, the members adopt behaviors and attitudes similar to those of the worker, including these behaviors:

- trusting in the group process
- having faith in the ability of group members to make changes in their lives
- listening nondefensively and respectfully
- accepting other group members without imposing one's own values on them
- being willing to engage in appropriate self-disclosure

Unless we therapists reveal ourselves, group members will develop expectations about us based on the mythology of the leader or charismatic parent figure—expectations that are unrealistic and unduplicatable in the world outside the group. However, we have the opportunity to show how we deal with the kind of personal crisis that regularly arises for us within the group: a group member's attack on us. Our own honesty and strength in dealing with such confrontations reveals a good deal about us. By watching us and thereby learning what to expect, the members can become freer to take risks themselves (Stoller, 1969).

The development and maintenance of trust within a group is not only the worker's responsibility. It is also related to the level of investment the group's members make in the group process. Some individuals will be unwilling to take risks and will resist the idea of sharing anything other than superficial material. Other members will wait passively for the worker to magically bring about change without any work on their part.

CLOSING THE INITIAL SESSION

The closing of the first session is a significant point in the development of a group. It is a time to summarize and to integrate what has occurred and to make plans for future meetings. It is a time for members to reflect on their experience and to share their thoughts and feelings. And it is a time to raise issues that are still unclear. The group is no longer something in the abstract; it is now a reality.

Too often group members appear to have a positive reaction to the initial session and then choose not to return for subsequent sessions. The possible reasons for a client's failure to come back are legion. Some individuals decide the group does not meet their needs, while other individuals feel the worker or other group members are insensitive and uncaring. One client might feel that more will be expected than he or she can possibly give. Another might simply feel bored and decide that counseling is a waste of time. Whatever the reasons, it is important that the worker be sensitive to each member's concerns and address them openly and honestly during the initial session.

There needs to be ample time for the closing of the first session. And the worker is well advised to let the members know 10 to 15 minutes in advance how much time remains. A summary is an effective way to begin the closure process. The worker can follow up by encouraging the members to reflect on what they liked or did not like about the session, to raise questions, and to identify any unfinished business. During the closing, the worker can also assign homework and encourage members to share their hopes and expectations about future meetings.

IN SUMMARY

The initial phase of group treatment is an important period in the life of a group. The group's members come together for the first time, share feelings, discuss the contract, establish goals, learn the guidelines, and begin working on relevant personal issues. The worker's major tasks are to facilitate open and honest communication and to establish an atmosphere of trust.

Its initial phase sets the tone for a group's future development. Group workers who are able to help group members set goals and develop a meaningful working contract are well-positioned to assist the group as it moves into the middle and final phases of treatment.

The creation of trust in a group will be determined primarily by the group worker's attitude and activities. The worker has to be especially sensitive to the needs of minority clients in the group. There are often value differences that can result in cautiousness, distrust, and resistance on the part of group members. Such differences need to be discussed openly in the group. Finally, the closing of the initial session is a time for the members and the worker to evaluate what has occurred so far and to reflect on how they can effectively use their future time together.

SUGGESTED READINGS

FRIEDMAN, W. (1989). *Practical group therapy: A guide for clinicians.* San Francisco: Jossey-Bass. See Chapters 4 and 5.

HENRY, S. (1981). *Group skills in social work: A four-dimensional approach.* Itasca, Ill.: F. E. Peacock. See Chapters 3 and 4.

NORTHEN, H. (1988). *Social work with groups.* 2nd ed. New York: Columbia University Press. See Chapter 5.

SHULMAN, L. (1984). *The skills of helping individuals and groups.* Itasca, Ill.: F. E. Peacock. See Chapters 8 and 9.

11

PROGRAM ACTIVITIES

T

• • • • • • • •

he group worker's attitude is an important ingredient in any group activity. When I worked as a swimming instructor at a camp in Maine during my sophomore year in college, I dreaded the early morning swimming classes, as did the children. The water was icy and the air frigid.

One brisk morning, the camp director, a self-glorifying combination of Sigmund Freud and Captain Queeg, spotted me wrapped warmly in a sweat suit and a towel, attempting to convince the campers to get wet. For every threat and promise I made, the boys found an excuse to stay out of the water. After watching my ineffectual teaching style for five minutes, the director took me aside and gave a memorable lesson on group psychology.

"First, they need a model," he commanded, "so take off your sweat suit and get into the water." "Second, your language is all wrong. The water is not cold; it's stimulating. The air is not freezing; it's bracing and invigorating." Then, he put his arm around my shoulders and whispered, "And, third, if you truly like what you are doing, tell your face, or I'll fire you." I climbed into the water.

In retrospect, I don't recall the air and the water ever getting much warmer. I do remember more children learning how to swim.

• • •

The chapter deals with the activities used in clinical settings and answers this question: what are some of the things a therapist can do with groups to enhance their cohesion and facilitate their members' growth? There is also a discussion of activities that are appropriate in residential settings such as psychiatric hospitals.

TALKING VERSUS DOING

To the general public and inexperienced clinicians, group treatment consists of children or adults sitting in a circle talking about their life experiences, sharing their feelings, and problem solving. The leader, perceived as a benign parent figure, guides the group members by making interpretations and offering wisdom, insight, and sage advice. While this pattern is not totally inaccurate, it is but one of many forms of group treatment available to the worker.

219

In reality, this template fits only a small segment of the clients that practitioners deal with in clinical social work. It does not fit children with limited verbal development, whose most significant life experiences, heretofore, have centered around play. It does not fit all of the aged, many of whom have difficulty communicating in words what they are thinking, feeling, and experiencing. It does not fit the aggressive, "acting out" adolescent, who chooses not to disclose himself or herself, and who is particularly resistant to opening up to adults. And this model does not fit the hyperactive child, who cannot sit still for more than three or four minutes at a time and feels a compulsion to run around the room.

Anyone who has worked with nonverbal children or adults has come to grips with the painful reality that "talk therapy" in the traditional sense has the potential of increasing the individual's sense of frustration, isolation, and inadequacy. The person may want to please the worker but is incapable of communicating ideas, feelings, and experiences verbally. The result is a frustrated client, as well as a frustrated worker (Reid, 1988).

The number and variety of activities that can be used in group work is infinite. They range from active to passive, from verbal to nonverbal, from observing to touching, and from simple children's games to high-level cognitive transactions. An activity may require only a few minutes or may consume one entire group session. The following is a sample of the activities commonly used in clinical settings:

- games
- arts and crafts
- drama, puppets, stories
- role-playing
- dancing
- cooking
- trips
- music, singing, song games
- sports
- structured exercises

With some imagination and resourcefulness, the practitioner can adapt any of these activities to fit a particular need.

It is worth nothing that the dichotomy of talking versus doing is actually a false dichotomy. Activities affect what happens at the intrapsychic and interpersonal levels. And the intrapsychic and interpersonal dynamics affect activities. Activities are the vehicle through which relationships are made and the needs and interests of the group members are fulfilled (Middleman, 1980).

PURPOSE OF THE ACTIVITIES

Appropriately chosen activities may either be the primary or secondary focus of a therapy group (Heap, 1977). A therapist who uses activities as a group's primary focus is making the assumption that learning takes place through doing. Middleman (1968, 1980), for example, views some activities as nearly complete learning vehicles within themselves for several reasons. First, the activities provide individuals with the opportunity to learn and experience a sense of themselves as creative and expressive people. The activities present challenges that encourage individuals to grow and verify their identity by learning to cope with their environment. Second, individuals learn better through action and behavior than through inactivity. Third, cognitive learning by individuals follows the awakening of all their senses through stimulating experiences. Fourth, nonverbal communication is more effective than verbal communication with some people.

A therapist who uses activities as a group's secondary focus of interaction is providing an arena for people to share. For example, a group of insecure or inarticulate individuals may find talking about common problems overwhelming and threatening. By using activities, such as crafts, drama, or games, the therapist provides for these individuals a transitory point where they can come together yet, at the same time, maintain some space and distance. The importance of these activities may gradually diminish as a result of the increase in interpersonal familarity and security the activities have promoted (Heap, 1977).

In analyzing ways in which shared activities might be used by group members for mutual aid, Shulman (1984) lists the following possibilities:

1. human contact —a meeting of a basic human need for social interaction.
2. data gathering—activities designed to help members obtain more information central to their tasks (for example, teenagers preparing to enter the work world by arranging a series of trips to business or industrial complexes)
3. rehearsal—a means of developing and practicing skills related to specific life tasks
4. deviational allowance—activities designed to create a flow of affects between group members in order to help the members build positive relationships with each other.
5. entry—activities can serve as a point of entrance into an area of difficult discussion (for example, playacting by young children as they create roles and situations that reveal their concerns of being abandoned by their parents).

Activities serve as diagnostic tools for assessing individuals, group dynamics, and decision-making processes. In discussing the use of program activities in a therapeutic milieu, Whittaker (1974) observes that while there is a surplus of intrapsychic data on children, there is a dearth of information on how children function in group situations. Without such background information, a clinician may be aware of a child's learning deficiencies and, at the same time, may be unaware that the child does not know how to have fun, compete, or compromise.

Whether we, as therapists, view activities as having a primary or a secondary focus in a group, our aim must always be to use the activities to promote interaction within the group and growth of the members. Therefore, we must select activities that relate specifically to the needs, abilities, and interests of the group's members.

STARTING WHERE THE CLIENT IS

A basic premise of clinical practice is that the treatment process for each client is built around the needs and goals of that client. In other words, the worker should gather facts about the person and evaluate the information in order to frame a plan of action to meet the client's needs. As part of the process, the worker should involve the client in establishing an action plan. Together, the worker and the client should form a therapeutic alliance. Too often, however, a therapy group is established to meet certain purposes without serious consideration of the individual's needs of each group member.

SELECTING ACTIVITIES

To make sure a group treatment program is on target for each group member, it is essential for the leader of the group to select specific activities that will allow each client to meet suitable treatment objectives. Over the years, a number of models have been developed for evaluating the suitability of program activities to meet specific needs of each group member and the group-as-a-whole. Gump and Sutton-Smith (1955) recommend that a group worker pay attention to such variables as the degree of skill an activity requires; the degree of competitiveness the activity stimulates; the amount of bodily contact required or permitted by the activity; the degree of interdependence the activity stimulates among players; the degree of leeway the activity permits for group members to respond on impulse; and the kinds of rewards and penalties available to participants in the activity, as well as how long the activity delays such feedback.

Expanding on this list, Vinter (1967) developed a framework for conducting an activity analysis that takes into consideration the physical space required, the behaviors required, and the types of responses generated by the activity. It is Vinter's rationale that each activity requires a specific set of behavior patterns from participants and therefore different activities evoke different behavior patterns within participants. He suggests these behavior patterns are conditioned or determined by the nature of the activity, relatively independently of the personality characteristics of the individual participants. Vinter contends that it is these very behavior patterns that can have important consequences for the individual members and the group. Through the informed selection and use of group activities, he feels, the therapist can help each client and the group-as-a-whole achieve or modify their behavior patterns.

222
• • • • • • •

According to Vinter, there are six dimensions relevant to each activity.

1. How prescriptive is a particular activity—that is, to what degree does it depend on a set of rules or other guides for conduct? Games such as chess, for example, are highly prescriptive in that they have numerous rules. In contrast, activities such as swimming have fewer rules and thus are less prescriptive. Some children, as well as some adults, have difficulty with activities that are highly structured and rule-oriented. Whereas such clients might have difficulty with the rigid rule structure of chess, they might have no difficulty with swimming.

2. Who or what controls the participants' behavior and interaction within a particular the activity? Controls may be exercised by another person—for example, by a group worker, another group member, a referee, or a team captain. Such an individual may determine how the activity is to be conducted and who shall participate at any given moment. Some controls for an activity may be external to the actual activity and unchangeable, while other controls may be internal, based on the attitude and goodwill of the participants.

Utilizing a leader's record of the behavior a group of teenage girls attending a Halloween party, Middleman (1968), illustrates how the controls—external and internal—for an activity helped a group of clients manage their impulsive behavior. The leader noted:

> The next game we were to play was called "Witch Hunt," and because of my hoarse voice and the excitement of the girls at this point in the evening, no one heard the rules but began to play anyway. The game consisted of the girls walking around in a circle to music; when the music stopped they were to dash around the room and hunt for witches, pumpkins, and owls. As it happened, several of the girls found some of the hidden things while I was giving directions. I told them that they were spoiling the fun of the game by finding them now, and they responded by saying that they would like to play it correctly. They all went out of the room then, and I hid the articles again. When the girls returned, they followed the rules and played the game well [pp. 196–197].

3. What kinds of physical movement does a particular activity require or permit? The movement may be of the whole body, as in football, or of only specific parts of the body, as in bridge or a group discussion. What are the freedoms and the limits inherent in the activity? What are the boundaries and physical barriers imposed by the activity? Can the members move around freely during the activity, or is their movement restricted?

In discussing their work with emotionally disturbed boys, Redl and Wineman (1957) observe that after the boys experienced long stretches of passive activities at school that frustrated them, their feelings of anxiety and irritation grew, and there was a piling up of aggressive impulsiveness in the boys that could hardly be kept in check.

If, at this time, we had exposed them to a program activity which again would have made similar demands, a disorganized blow-up of their aggressive energies with all of the subsequent problems around it would have been unavoidable. . . . Thus [we organized] a number of exciting seeking and running games or tumbling activities in the protective framework of our own home [to] drain off some of the impulse accumulation which would have invariably led to disaster if the youngsters had been exposed at that moment to a passive program like watching a football game [p. 330].

223

• • • • • • • •

4. How much skill and competence is required for performance of a particular activity? In this case, performance is not equated with excelling, but rather with participating. Some activities, such as playing tag or singing, require no particular skill. Other activities, such as playing most musical instruments or mountain climbing, require special skills or abilities.

In planning activities, a group leader needs to determine exactly what performance an activity will require of group members and whether the members will be likely to experience success with the activity. For example, the worker must consider whether a group of children with poor hand/eye coordination will be able to enjoy cutting out paper figures or coloring within a set of lines? If only a few group members will find success, the worker needs to redesign the activity so that all the group members are likely to experience some success.

Activities involving pencils and crayons tend to demand of participants tightly controlled movement. These activities are inflexible and demanding because the lines that participants can make with pencils and crayons are relatively fine. Watercolors painted with a broad brush, however, encourage broad strokes and wide movement. But watercolors are also harder to control, because they run and splash. Such a free-flowing medium may frighten anxious and insecure participants. It may also offer too few limits for undisciplined participants (Klein, 1972).

5. How much interaction does a particular activity require or allow among participants? Activities vary widely as to the quantity and the quality of participation they require or allow. For example, five children sitting around a table cutting out pictures do not necessarily have to interact as long as each child has paper and scissors. On the other hand, if there are only three pairs of scissors, each child will have to interact at some level to accomplish his or her tasks. If the worker's objective is to encourage communication, problem solving, and interaction, the worker can limit the number of scissors or perhaps influence the seating pattern.

6. What are the rewards inherent in a particular activity, and how abundant are they? All activities are capable of producing some level of gratification. This gratification may be intrinsic to participation in the activity, such as the satisfaction of being able to do something or to make something, or they may be extrinsic rewards, such as a useful or attractive object created by participants. Group members with little or no motivation to participate in an activity for these rewards may be lured into participation by additional extrinsic rewards provided by the worker both immediately and abundantly. Such additional rewards might include praise from the worker, recognition by other group members, ribbons, or other symbols of success.

Thinking the unthinkable. Activities and exercises have a diabolical way of going awry at the worst possible moment. For example, the bulb in the movie projector burns out, the guest speaker cancels at the last moment, the meeting room suddenly becomes unavailable, the agency's van filled with children runs out of gas, or the videocassette recorder fails to function, and so on. Obviously, there is no way to plan for each and every contingency. Still, a group worker is well advised to anticipate potential problems and have a Plan B to take the place of his or her original plan if the need arises.

● **Techniques: Practical considerations**
1. Remember that your own enthusiasm is an important asset in any group activity.
2. If you are using equipment, such as a projector, a videocassette recorder, or a tape recorder, test it in advance, and have a backup on hand.
3. End an activity when it is going well and the group members are enjoying themselves.
4. Try out an activity before using it with a therapy group.
5. Be prepared to switch activities in midstream if the need arises. Have an alternative activity prepared.

MISUSE OF ACTIVITIES AND TECHNIQUES

Ambiguity or a seeming lack of structure in a group can cause discomfort in its members. This same ambiguity or lack of structure can be equally distressing for an inexperienced group. Periods of conflict that seem interminable and moments of resistance during which a group appears likely to collapse can generate a sense of urgency in the worker. It is during these times that the group leader craves techniques, exercises, or gimmicks that will resolve the particular issue.

While the possession of such a set of tools can reassure a group leader, the maladaptive use can be destructive, masking certain situations and hindering a group's development. A leader can become so dependent on techniques that the leader feels lost without them. Rather than serving as a means to an end for such a group worker, the techniques become the end. Such a technique orientation results in a technical, packaged, deindividualized approach that is contrary to the basic values of social work.

The finished product of an activity may also take on a life of its own and disrupt a treatment program. According to Shapiro (1978), it is far less important to complete an activity than to deal with whatever behaviors and feelings are generated by the exercise. It is easy for workers to become so technique-centered—as opposed to process-oriented—that they seek to complete an activity at all costs or to follow certain rules in violation of certain group-leadership objectives. This is especially pertinent for ego-damaged clients whose skill level is painfully low. Too much emphasis placed by a worker on such a client's "finished product" results in unnecessary internal stress on the group member.

Before using an activity, a group worker should consider the following elements:

1. **Timeliness.** The group worker needs to be aware of current group processes and introduce an activity naturally, rather than superimpose it upon the group.
2. **Appropriateness.** Introducing a new activity may require new behaviors of group members; however, these behaviors should not be so new to the members as to surprise or overwhelm them and should not be contrary to the group norms. For example, immediately presenting an activity requiring excessive physical movement to a group of elderly women in a nursing home who are accustomed to sedentary activities.
3. **Consent.** Activities should be entered into voluntarily. If a group member chooses not to participate in a particular activity, his or her decision needs to be respected.
4. **Safety.** Group members need to be protected from harm. Activities can easily get out of control and thereby cause participants to get physically or emotionally hurt.

ADAPTATION OF ACTIVITIES

The quantity and quality of group worker's involvement in a group's activities will depend on the socioemotional level of the members of a group and on the group's purpose. For many groups, the members can be counted on to take full responsibility for planning and carrying out its activities. The role of the leader is that of enabler, participant-observer, or advisor. In groups where members are interested, but lack knowledge and experience of group life, are withdrawn or very aggressive, or out of touch with reality, the worker's role is more active. For example, individuals who are emotionally, physically, or intellectually limited may need ongoing assistance throughout the life of the group so they can carry out the group's activities. In groups of young children or of developmentally disabled, psychotic, severely handicapped, withdrawn, or aggressive clients, for instance, the worker may—out of necessity—remain primary and central to the group's activities. The long-term goal of the leader of such a group is to help the group become less worker-centered and more group-centered, with its members taking on more and more responsibility for planning, problem solving, and actually carrying out the group's activities.

In such situations, the worker can plan a progression of activities designed to establish the group's purpose, can take the initiative in introducing these activities, and can monitor the activities' effects on the members and the group's progress. When the interest of members wanes or members lose interest, the leader can introduce a new activity (Henry, 1981).

In discussing their work with a group of alienated, chronically ill, elderly Black clients in an inner-city primary-care center, Hirayama and Vaugh (1986) report:

> Prior to the meetings, all program ideas and materials were prepared by the worker. The worker presented the plans to the group for approval, modification, and solicitation of new ideas, but the response from the members was minimal; they suggested no new ideas. However, for these essentially less verbally inclined members, engaging in and sharing activities together made the meetings more meaningful. For example, the sheer joy of accomplishing a simple drawing, "Draw someone you love most," was expressed by a seventy-eight-year-old illiterate woman who had enormous difficulty in the use of hands because of paralysis. She drew a barely recognizable human figure whom she called her grandchild who lived in California, and she expressed her hope that someday he would come to visit her [p. 196].

Similarly, Sussman (1974), in discussing the treatment of a group of patients suffering from numerous physical disabilities —including retinitis pigmentosa, deafness, cerebral palsy, epilepsy, and borderline mental retardation—writes that the group got off to an inauspicious start.

> There were so many idiosyncratic personalities; petulant and truculent behavior had to be contended with; explosive outbursts had to be handled carefully; stark apathy called for patient and gentle prodding; irrelevant and incoherent chatter impeded movement; diverse esoteric, arcanic and culturally-based communication styles did not make for meaningful group communication, not to mention a host of other difficulties [p. 77].

But Sussman also reports that as the group progressed, its members requested greater time for each session. By their 17th session, they became more active, and the therapist less active. The members required less prodding; their spontaneity increased by leaps and bounds. "They would take the initiative by opening discussion rather than waiting for the therapist to do so. They would stage role-playing entirely on their own, assigning roles, switching roles, and directing "scenes" (p. 81).

In other groups—groups in which members have the ability to plan, to problem solve, to postpone gratification, to discuss their feelings appropriately, and to deal effectively with reality—the worker's role will be less central. In these groups, the participants may be eager to participate and may be capable of taking responsibility for initiating and carrying out the group's activities. If so, the worker's role becomes that of an **enabler,** someone to facilitate communication, interaction, and mutual aid.

SKILL TRAINING

Skill training in groups merges didactic and experiential learning. In addition to other treatment goals, the aim of the group is to cultivate behaviors that are viewed as desirable by either the participant or society. In higher-functioning groups, the kinds of life skills addressed include decision-making, communication, and assertiveness skills.

227
∙∙∙∙∙∙∙∙

For severely disturbed individuals, the skills taught may be rudimentary such as ensuring their own personal hygiene, riding a bus, eating in a restaurant, or doing their own laundry. Group work is an effective way of helping such a client establish himself or herself as a human being, rather than as a "misfit" without social rights and responsibilities.

Whatever their level of functioning, clients in group treatment can learn new behaviors that enhance their ability to initiate, develop, and maintain relationships. They can also modify any of their behaviors that intensify their social alienation.

Certain activities can be made a part of each client's daily routine. Dickerson (1981), working with a "club" of mentally retarded adults used activities as a way of teaching and a way of structuring each member's life. For example, she used crafts to provide each client with the opportunity to create an age-appropriate object that would require four stages to be completed. Dickerson's intent was to teach each client to be patient, especially in waiting for a reward. Dickerson used meal preparation activities to give the clients an opportunity to plan, prepare, and serve lunches for their friends, and thereby improve their ability to take care of themselves and also to interact socially with other people.

Dickerson had the clients make decorations to provide them with a way to personalize their meeting rooms and to enhance their sense of belonging. She initiated shopping activities to help the clients learn to use a variety of stores in the community and practice using money. She introduced table games to show the clients simple games that they could play alone or with one or two other people. Introducing these games enabled the worker to teach the clients to accept simple rules and to take turns. Dickerson also introduced conversations to teach social behaviors such as initiating a conversation, accepting a compliment, giving a compliment, and accepting or refusing a date.

Because skill training in groups is highly structured and the attainment of specific goals is most salient, there is usually a time limit for accomplishing goals and an incremental building of skills from session to session. The group worker structures the content of each session and actively leads the group's activities to facilitate the group's attainment of the agreed-on goals.

ROLE-PLAYING

Role-playing is a frequently used intervention strategy in groups that have skill training as their goal. The term *role-playing* covers a wide range of specific techniques used for the purpose of: (1) problem solving and conflict resolution, and (2) learning, in the sense of acquiring new behavior patterns.

Uses of role-playing. Role-playing has a number of uses in group work (Etcheverry, Siporin, & Toseland, 1986). These uses include the following possibilities:

Assessment. Role-playing can be used by a group worker to get a client to demonstrate or illustrate something and, in doing so, to provide objective, descriptive data. In a role-playing situation, such data are provided in concrete, personal, and emotionally meaningful terms. This would be the case, for example, if a group member reenacts a child's death for which he or she feels responsible.

Stimulation. By participating in the physical activity of role-playing, a group member can focus on his or her personal concerns, problems, and behaviors. Doing so will have a sensory impact on the participant and stimulate him or her to respond.

Understanding. By acting out a role in an unaccustomed way, a group member can gain self-understanding and insight.

Decision making. Role-playing can be used to encourage group members to formulate options and reach conclusions about facts or plans of actions.

Behavior change. Role-playing can provide a means for group members to extinguish undesirable behaviors, and to acquire and practice new behaviors.

Ways to role-play. Generally, role-playing in a therapy group is done in an open-ended, unstructured manner that allows for spontaneity and learning. The procedures for role-playing can be flexible.

Behavioral rehearsal. A group member can play himself or herself. This technique is helpful for assessment purposes and for the rehearsal of new behaviors. In addition, it facilitates insight into a group member's feelings, thought processes, and behaviors. This procedure involves group member's practicing newly acquired behavior within the relatively safe atmosphere of the group. Through the use of simulation, the group member can practice new behavior and receive input from the other members and from the worker. To intiate such a behavior rehearsal by a group member, the therapist might say, "Tommy, you are angry with your teacher. Let's see if we can figure out some ways for you to let her know how you feel. Whom do you want to role-play the teacher?"

Role reversal. A group member can take on the role of someone significant in his or her life space, such as a spouse, a parent, an employer, or a teacher. Doing this enables the member to experience a special situation from someone else's point of view. This technique is particularly useful for teaching empathy (Etcheverry, Siporin, & Toseland, 1986). It can also be used when two members of a group are in conflict or have a difficult time listening to each other and communicating openly. In such a case, the therapist might say, "Dee, I would like to try something. You be Jim and present his point of view. Jim, you be Dee and present her point of view. Each of you, use the other person's words and his or her gestures."

Sculpting. The group member is directed to "sculpt," or place himself or herself and his or her family or other special group as if the member is creating a painting.

Potential difficulties of role-playing. Done poorly, role-playing in a therapy group can be destructive (Etcheverry, Siporin, & Toseland, 1986). Potential problems include the following:

1. Encouraging a group member to role-play before he or she is ready or able to self-disclose or participate.
2. Too little or too much direction by the group leader in casting, planning, implementing, and closing the role-play.
3. Failure to protect and support the protagonist or other player.
4. Failure to use the procedures appropriately to achieve indicated objectives [p. 121].

ASSERTIVENESS TRAINING

Assertiveness is an important skill frequently taught in skill-oriented groups. In a series of graduated steps, group members are taught to speak up or to do things for themselves, at the risk of disapproval from other people. Assertive behavior involves the honest and direct expression of both positive and negative feelings in interpersonal transactions. Examples of nonassertiveness include denying one's own rights, not accepting compliments, being afraid to speak up, maintaining poor eye contact, using inappropriate facial expressions (such as smiling when angry or upset), and assuming nonassertive body postures (such as turning away and maintaining too much distance) (Galinsky, Schopler, Safier, & Gambrill, 1978).

A social work group is an ideal medium for learning assertion skills. Galinsky, Schopler, Safier, and Gambrill (1978), in reporting on successfully teaching such skills to welfare clients note that it is particularly beneficial for clients who need to learn effective ways of obtaining their rights and gaining resources, services, and information, as well as ways of coping with interpersonal transactions.

The basic elements of assertiveness training are as follows:

Education. First, the group worker explores the differences between aggression and assertion and asks group members to define realis-

realistic assertiveness goals that are relevant to their lives. Before a group member can become assertive, the person must accept that it is all right to act assertively. Before a group member can become assertive, the person must come to grips with the emotional cost of not being assertive. He or she must also accept that it is all right to act assertively.

Modeling. The group leader serves as a model for the group, demonstrating assertive behavior in his or her own transactions with the group as well as in simulated situations during role-playing. As members observe the worker's assertive behavior, they vicariously learn the skills. Eventually, the members serve as models for each other.

Role-playing. Behavior rehearsal serves as the primary vehicle for assertiveness training. The technique consists of a group member's role-playing a situation that has created, or can be anticipated to create, some difficulties for the member. Other group members and the group leader contribute by coaching and playing the roles of significant others in the situation. Initially, only situations that constitute low-level threats for group members are rehearsed. As the group progresses, however, the members rehearse more challenging situations.

Homework. Between group sessions, the group worker encourages group members to practice the assertion skills they are learning in the group. Then, at the beginning of each session, the worker asks each member to present an example of an actual situation in which the member was assertive.

FACILITATING THE GROUP PROCESS

A group leader needs effective ways of facilitating the group members' sharing of genuine thoughts and feelings. Rounds and dyads have come to be viewed as a way of helping members become focused, building comfort, and deepening the intensity of the group.

ROUNDS

A round—an activity in which every member is asked to respond, in turn, to a particular stimulus—is especially useful for gathering information and involving group members. It can be used for gathering information from members; getting members focused; deepening a group's intensity; building comfort, trust, and cohesion within a group; and drawing out quiet members in a group (Jacobs, Harvill, & Masson, 1988).

Finish-the-sentence round. To start a fill-in-the-sentence round, a group worker suggests an unfinished sentence and asks group members to fill in the missing words or phrase. For example, the worker might introduce such a round by asking each group member to use a word or phrase to complete one of the sentences that follow:

- At this very moment, I am feeling. . . .
- The worst thing that happened to me today was. . . .
- The best thing that happened to me today was. . . .
- The thing that worries me most in my life is. . . .
- The one thing I would change about myself is. . . .
- The one thing do I like best about myself is. . . .

Limiting each member to a word or phrase, encourages the member to be brief.

Degree-of-involvement round.   There are times during group work when it is obvious to the therapist that the group members have limited energy and are not focused on the particular issue or topic at hand. At times like these, the group worker can use a degree-of-involvement round to bring to the surface the splitting that has occurred and to press the members to think specifically about what they are experiencing. To introduce such a round, the worker might say to each member, "On a scale of 0 to 100, what percent of you is **here** in this room at this moment? If there is a part of you somewhere else, share that with us, and tell us the amount of you that is **there**."

In working with a group of women in a support group, I found that one of the participants was unusually quiet and pensive during the first 30 minutes of the session. When I asked how much of her was in the meeting at that moment, she embarrassedly answered that she was 20 percent in the group and 80 percent at home with her 10-year-old son who was sick and in the house by himself. I asked her if she would be able to concentrate during the session, and she answered that she would be able to if she could call home and check on her son. After making the telephone call, this group member appeared noticeably relaxed, and she fully participated in the group.

Member's role-in-the-meeting round.   At the end of a meeting, a group worker can introduce a member's-role-in-the-meeting-round to help members to evaluate clearly their role in the session. To introduce such a round, the group worker might say, "Would each of you describe your role in the meeting today?" or "Summarize your involvement in today's session."

In a variation on this round, the group worker might ask each member to describe the role of a person sitting next to him or her. In this case, the group worker might ask, "Would each of you describe the involvement and contribution during the meeting today of the person who is sitting on your left?"

This activity can be a real eye-opener if any of the members learn that the way they appear to other people is vastly different from what they anticipated. It is prudent for the leader to preface this exercise with a warning that each description will reflect only one person's perspective on what has actually occurred during the meeting.

DYADS

A dyad is an activity in which two group members are paired to discuss an issue or to solve a problem. A major advantage of using dyads—especially in a fairly large group—is that they provide an opportunity for individuals to get to know each other more intimately than they could in a group-as-a-whole. According to Jacobs, Harvill, and Masson (1988), dyads are useful in developing comfort within a group, warming up group members, helping group members process information, helping a group finish a topic, getting certain group members together, increasing member interaction, offering a change in the group's format, and providing time for the group leader to think.

In the early stages of a group, when its members are uncomfortable, dyads can be used as a way of making the experience more personal. Rather than having to talk to eight or so other members, each group member can talk to one other person, which is not as threatening. As a result of their work in dyads, when the group members return to the group, they usually feel less anxiety.

Dyad activities can last anywhere from 2 to 20 minutes. If the time allotted is too short, the members will complain that "We just got started and had to stop." If, on the other hand, the time allotted is too long, the members will become bored and drift away from the original topic.

ELICITING FEELINGS

Certain activities are especially useful in bringing to the surface powerful emotions that are experienced but not articulated by group members. Because the focus of such activities is on the activity itself and not the person, participants are more willing to share their feelings during these activities.

Poetry can be a nonthreatening vehicle for clients to express their feelings (Lessner, 1974). A group worker can use published poems, poems written by individual members, or poems written collectively by all the members of the group. Mazza and Prize (1985) describe the use of both poetry and music in short-term therapy with college students. These authors report that poetry and music each simulate group interaction and is useful in treating the interpersonal aspects of depression. For example, poems such as "If I Should Cast Off This Tattered Coat" by Stephen Crane stimulated group members to talk about their own feelings of sadness and despair. In the same way, popular music with themes of loneliness, depression, and anger served as a catalyst for members to share feelings they were uncomfortable talking about.

To encourage group members to collaborate on their own poem, a group worker can suggest that each individual contribute several lines. Either the leader or one of the members can suggest the predominant theme for the poem. Once the poem is created, the worker can ask each group member to share what the poem means to him or her.

STRUCTURED EXERCISES

Structured exercises are defined as relatively short-term voluntary group experiences in which a group follows some specific set of orders. The precise rationale for each exercise's set of procedures varies, but structured exercises are almost always used for the same purpose—to speed up the group process in some way. In the initial stages of a session, for example, some group workers use a structured exercise to bypass the hesitant, uneasy first steps of a group. Sometimes, a structured exercise is used to help group members quickly, "get in touch with" suppressed emotions, with unknown aspects of themselves, or with their body (Yalom, 1975). Structured exercises include the following:

233
• • • • • • • •

- blind trust walk
- progressive relaxation
- guided fantasy
- family sculpture
- "strength bombardment"
- "moral dilemmas"

Exercises such as these are means, not ends. They have the potential of amplifying material that is present and of encouraging exploration of where the material leads. But for group workers who become overly concerned with the actual activity, these exercises become ends in themselves. When this occurs, the heart of the group process has been lost (Corey, Corey, Callanan, & Russell, 1988).

ACTIVITIES WITHIN AN INSTITUTIONAL SETTING

Institutional settings, by their very nature, create a network of groups: living, work, therapy, education, and recreation groups. In addition, there is the communal group of the total institution. Whether the setting is a mental hospital or a children's institution, the "community" in which the client lives has its own leadership, sources of authority, culture, and methods of communication.

But, this community is like no other. It is a treatment center for disturbed, as well as disturbing, individuals. Without exception, their illnesses and problems have reflected negatively and often destructively on their interpersonal relationships.

Residential treatment takes into account the complication of combining a client's everyday living arrangements and the client's treatment program. It addresses the problems that brought the client to the institution and provides opportunities for the client to learn to cope with life situations emerging out of living with other people on a 24-hour basis. The realities of daily living, thus, become opportunities for the client's growth, socialization, and treatment.

Group workers in organizations such as hospitals are not independent practitioners to the same degree that they would be in a social agency. In a treatment group sponsored by a family-service agency, for example, the group's goals are formulated to match very broad guidelines imposed by the agency. In a hospital, a group's goals may be quite restricted and dictated by each group member's treatment needs and desires. Here, the social worker is always a member of a treatment team and affects, as well as is affected by, other team members, such as the patient's physician, psychologist, adjunctive therapists, and nurses.

Group living constitutes a primary life experience for a client, that temporarily replaces the client's primary family living. The client's floor, unit, cottage, or ward serves as "home base" and an arena for everyday living experience with his or her peers and staff, and—in the context of a larger community—the institution. Group living furnishes the basic ingredients for ego growth and is, according to Maier (1965), the marketplace of ego development.

INFORMAL PATIENT GROUPS

While we normally think of group workers as leaders of formal groups, there are times when we deal with informal groups. For example, 25 or so patients living on a ward have little or no choice as to whom they live with. They do, however, have choices as to whom they spend their leisure time with. They can and do develop small informal groups—based on proximity and on voluntary interpersonal consent.

Informal groups serve various functions. They provide support to clients going through a similar experience. They provide reassurance to clients during periods of increased anxiety related to such events as admission, lack of movement in therapy, traumatic life experiences, or discharge. They provide encouragement when life does not seem to be getting better.

Such groups also provide a false sense of security when clients are feeling insecure. In a psychiatric hospital, for example, six relatively long-term patients spend a great deal of time together, becoming an informal group. When two new patients are admitted to the ward, one overtly psychotic and the other extremely paranoid, the group of six begin to mock and tease the new patients, calling them "sickies" and "retards."

An informal group such as the one described can be highly destructive. The patients' behavior needs to be addressed openly and therapeutically. As social workers, we are in a unique position to deal with such patients, both individually and in the group. Forming a relationship with an informal group of patients is very similar to the process of forming a relationship with an individual patient. Once a relationship with an informal group is in place, we are in a position to request that the individuals open their ranks to allow other people to enter. We can encourage the members of the informal group to discuss rather than act out their feelings. We can also direct them toward projects that will give them an increased sense of self-esteem and gratification.

A PATIENT-RUN GOVERNMENT

Usually, community meetings are attended by all staff who work and all patients who live in a specific area of a residential institution. It is in these meetings that the group comes to terms with problems of living together. The disturbed or disturbing behavior of an aggressive patient, threats of suicide from a depressed patient, unflushed toilets, unappetizing food, and a staff person or patient who is leaving the unit are all potential community problems. Community or ward meetings are crucial in maintaining an open network of communication.

In a psychiatric hospital based on a therapeutic-milieu model, two adolescent girls on one of the living units struck a well-liked nurse, took her keys, and left the hospital. Although everyone on the floor was aware of the incident, there was relatively little open discussion about it among the patients, among the staff, or between patients and staff. Staff/patient relationships became increasingly strained. Patients reported that the atmosphere was so charged with anger that nobody could talk about the issues.

During a community meeting, the group worker raised questions about the atmosphere in the living unit. After some silence, the patients began to express anger toward the girls who had left the hospital. They said they were afraid the staff might retaliate by taking away some of their own privileges and responsibilities. The worker encouraged the patients, as well as the nursing staff, to talk about their feelings. As the meeting progressed, nursing staff members shared their feelings of anger and frustration and their fear that other staff members would get hurt. After that discussion, both the nursing staff and the patients were noticeably less anxious, and floor life returned to normal. A week later, when the two girls were returned to the hospital, a number of the patients made it a point to tell the girls how angry they felt about the girls' aggressive behaviors (Reid, 1968).

Large hospitals may have a patient council made up of representatives from all wards. Patients' representatives are elected from their respective living units and assume responsibility for representing their unit at meetings of the patients' council. The patients' council meetings are also attended by senior representatives from areas such as nursing, food service, social work, and adjunctive therapy.

Harlow (1964), in discussing how the emotional tone of unit meetings relates to the atmosphere of the hospital, observes:

> When the patients turn their attention to petty, trivial complaints, such as boredom with the food or staff failing to knock on their door, usually one of two things is happening. . . . [Either] the patients are avoiding talking about some real issues which they are troubled about that have to do with group living, or they are reacting and sensing some unrest in the staff and their feelings of security are threatened. In the council, the patients' feelings toward authority are highlighted around discussions of policy which affects their

daily living. This occurs during each meeting as the patients seek to establish a working relationship with the other members of the council [p. 7].

In summary, the patients' council provides each patient's representative with opportunities to experience three types of relationships—first, a relationship with other council members; second, a relationship with the hospital staff; and third, a relationship with the patients whom the council member represents.

ACTIVITY GROUPS

Group activities offer psychiatric inpatients many advantages. Among these advantages are the presentation of ego models, opportunities for social involvement and behavior feedback, chances to enhance their self-esteem, opportunities to learn new knowledge and skills, remedial social education, and social sanctions (Towey, Sears, Williams, Kaufman, & Cunningham, 1966).

A group of inpatients in a private psychiatric hospital questioned whether it would be possible to form a public-speaking group. To clarify their ideas further, the patients and a social worker visited a public-speaking club in a local state hospital. There they had the chance to see a similar group in action and to learn from its members how the club worked.

As the public-speaking club began to develop, its members continually looked to the group worker to run the club and to bring in new members. The worker refused, making it clear that he would help them but would not do the work for them. The members spent the first few meetings struggling with the question of whether to stick to the format used by the other club, or to devise a format of their own. Meanwhile, one of the members constructed a speakers' guide for evaluating and selecting topics for speeches. Another made time cards to let the speakers know how much time they had left. Two patients began a campaign to increase membership in the club, putting up signs throughout the hospital.

During meetings, each member had an opportunity to speak and to play an active role, for example, as timekeeper or evaluator. At the beginning of each meeting, the patient who was serving as chairperson suggested a topic, and all members were expected to speak on it for no longer than two minutes. At the end of each talk, participants discussed the content, style, and manner of the presentation.

At first, evaluating one another was difficult, especially for new members. As trust and group cohesion grew, however, members were able to point out inconsistencies in one another's thinking and speaking, and sometimes in their own. Mr. Kirk, a lonely, overweight 36-year-old man who had long denied his illness, joined the speaking group shortly after it was formed. Soon, members began to criticize his speeches, saying he made too many generalizations and jumped from point to point without any logical connection. At first, Mr. Kirk defensively denied the comments, viewing them as hostile attacks. Gradually, however, he began to recognize that in spite of these negative comments, no one was out to hurt him. He realized that observations of the group members reflected their interest in helping him become a better speaker (Reid, 1968).

A SPECTRUM OF GROUPS

237

• • • • • • • •

Workers leading groups in treatment facilities such as psychiatric hospitals have to cope with many problems unique to their setting that make traditional theory and approaches to group work insufficient (Griffin-Shelley, & Trachtenberg, 1985). The most difficult of these problems is the heterogeneity of group members. Psychiatric units are generally made up of patients with a broad range of diagnoses—for example, a mixture of clients with depression, narcissistic character disorders, alcoholism, sexual disorders, borderline personalities, and psychoses. Even within these diagnostic categories, there are variations in patients' ability to function. And the therapeutic level of each group tends to float to the lowest level of patient functioning.

Groups in treatment facilities can be established based on any level of patient functioning, whether low, medium, or high. Generally, low-level and medium-level groups are held in the living unit.

Low-level groups consist of patients who are egocentric, very concrete, and at times nonverbal. Group goals for low-functioning patients include learning to accept structure, improving reality testing, listening, concentrating on one subject for several minutes, ego building, developing life skills, and interrupting psychotic thinking.

Compared to members in low-level groups, members of medium-level groups are more abstract, general, and open to talking about their feelings and past experiences. Medium-level groups center on values clarification, dealing with family relationships, being assertive, and talking about emotions. Medium-level groups are less structured, with more responsibility given to members.

High-level groups are designed for patients who are usually on "full privileges" and can profit from an intensive form of group psychotherapy. These patients are capable of abstract thinking, have verbal skills, and can use problem-solving approaches.

In many hospitals, particularly in state institutions, once patients reach a level at which their behavior and symptoms are no longer disturbing, they return to the community, often before they are ready. For a group worker, this situation can be frustrating for a number of reasons: First, the rapid turnover of patients prevents cohesion and bonding from taking place in most hospital groups. Second, the "healthier" patients are usually moved out of a group before they can contribute to the growth of the group's less healthy members. Thus, a high-level group may be desirable but may not be something the clinician has much opportunity to work with in a hospital setting.

Activities appropriate for low-level and medium-level groups differ (Griffin-Shelley & Trachtenberg, 1985; Griffin-Shelley & Wendel, 1988). In low-level groups, activities include listening to calming music, engaging in movement activities, drawing, learning basic hygiene and grooming skills, cooking, and learning how to cope with the social welfare system. In medium-level groups, activities include writing plays, short stories, or poetry; preparing job applications; selecting, preparing, and eating nutritious foods, budgeting and balancing a checkbook; and hunting for and taking care of an apartment.

GROUP WORK WITH STAFF MEMBERS

Within a residential treatment facility, a clinician's focus may be that of developing each staff unit as a work group, with its members capable of acting together to accomplish shared goals. According to Bunker and Wijnberg (1988), cohesion among staff members is particularly important in human-service organizations because the alternative of fragmentation, isolation, and alienation impairs each worker's individual performance and the staff members' capacity to act in concert. Fragmentation is particularly disruptive and dispiriting. It deprives staff members of opportunities to help one another and limits the supply of emotional support available to each staff member. In short, developing teams of workers and pooling the resources of each work group may minimize the potential for therapeutic and organizational disasters.

Sickness, pain, termination of relationships, death, and grief all provoke severe chronic anxiety in health-care professionals. As a way of coping, the professionals and the institution-at-large have to create an elaborate set of defenses. Barber (1985), in his description of a twice-monthly support group for nursing staff on a cancer ward, notes that presenting their cases to one another helped the staff members deal with problem situations. The staff members, he points out, were able to use the group for both support and for problem solving. Over time, the support-group meetings reportedly resulted in more satisfying and productive interaction not only between staff members but also between staff members and patients and between staff members and the insitution-as-a-whole.

In the early stages of this support group, the worker's role was that of consultant—a person who could explain key concepts, outline role guidelines, and provide support. As the group progressed, the leader's role became one of asking questions, facilitating discussions, and keeping the focus of discussion on relationship issues.

Over time, a cohesive group of this nature can become adept at acknowledging differences in experiences and in perceptions and using these differences constructively. The capacity to provide one another support, to respect differences, to problem solve, and to learn from one another's personal experiences is a mark of a self-aware and competent work group.

IN SUMMARY

This chapter discusses the use of activities in group work. There is a wide range of nonverbal activities that can be used in group. Such activities may focus on the accomplishment of an activity, but should always focus on the process that occurs as people work toward accomplishing the activity. The selection of activities can not be left to chance. Instead, a group worker must be sure to select activities that will help group workers achieve specific treatment objectives. The group worker must avoid misusing activities and thereby masking certain situations and hindering a group's development.

239
· · · · · · · ·

     The quantity and quality of a group worker's activity will depend on the ego strength of the group's members. The lower the socioemotional level of the members, generally the more active the worker needs to be. Skill-training is especially beneficial for both low-functioning and high-functioning members. Two activities that are particularly useful are role-playing and assertiveness training. In residential treatment centers, such as psychiatric hospitals, social workers usually work with patients' governments, activity groups, staff groups, and informal groups of patients. In these settings, it is useful to offer a spectrum of groups in order to respond to the heterogeneity of the patient population.

SUGGESTED READINGS

COREY, G., COREY, M., CALLANAN, P., & RUSSELL, M. (1988). *Group techniques* (rev. ed.). Pacific Grove, Calif.: Brooks/Cole. See Chapters 1 and 2.

MIDDLEMAN, R. (1968). *The non-verbal method in working with groups*. New York: Association Press.

VINTER, R. (1974). Program activities: An analysis of their effects on participant behavior. In P. Glasser, R. Sarri, & R. Vinter, (Eds.), *Individual change through small groups* (pp. 233–243). New York: Free Press.

WHITTAKER, J. (1974). Program activities: Their selection and use in a therapeutic milieu. In P. Glasser, R. Sarri, & R. Vinter (Eds.), *Individual change through small groups* (pp. 244–257). New York: Free Press.

WILSON, G., & RYLAND, G. (1949). *Social group work practice: The creative use of the social process*. Cambridge, Mass.: Riverside Press. See Part II.

YALOM, I. (1983). *Inpatient group psychotherapy*. New York: Basic Books.

THE MIDDLE PHASE OF TREATMENT

During my first year of graduate studies, I was a group worker with eight emotionally disturbed preadolescent boys in a children's village. Each week, I struggled with the task of finding activities that were interesting and that fit the therapeutic goals of the group. Craft projects, swimming, and kickball were all becoming a bit stale.

Mel, my office mate and a second-year graduate student, recommended that I have the group make handmade ice cream. He had successfully used the activity a week earlier with some adolescents he was working with at a Jewish Community Center. Since I had never made ice cream before, I was a bit reluctant. Mel promised it would be easy.

When I mentioned the idea to the boys, they were ecstatic. Quickly, the idea grew from making ice cream to having banana splits covered with strawberries, chocolate sauce, nuts, and whipped cream. This was probably the first program idea that everyone agreed on.

The day of the meeting, I gathered together the ingredients, plus the rock salt, the ice, and three old-fashioned hand-cranked ice-cream makers. Now, in class we had been warned to try out an activity before doing it with a group. Unfortunately, I didn't have the time. "Heck," Mel said, "just wing it. What can go wrong?"

The boys started out with a flourish. First, they had a contest to see who could crank the fastest. Then, they held a contest to see who could crank the longest. The competition and the promise of the banana splits were a marvelous reinforcer. Soon, however, the boys became tired and bored. "Let's eat!" one of them yelled. With that, the lids on the ice-cream makers were unceremoniously torn off.

Much to everyone's surprise, the creamy liquid appeared no different than when we began, with the exception of the salt-covered ice now floating on the surface.

Recognizing that this might be a long process, I suggested some running games, which the boys did halfheartedly. Within ten minutes, they again began to pry open the containers, only to find once again that the white milky substance was still liquid.

Frustration continued to build. Fingers soon were into the chocolate sauce and strawberries, and a banana fight broke out. One boy put his hand into the whipped cream and smeared it over the face of the group's scapegoat.

Disappointed, the members began to drift away. Some went back to the cottage to watch television, while others went to play softball. Three of the boys just roamed the village getting into mischief, eventually breaking four windows. I, on the other hand, was left with three pails of half-made ice cream; partial containers of chocolate sauce, cream, and strawberries; and a playground covered with squashed bananas.

I learned two important lessons from the experience. Rule No. 1: If you aren't certain about an activity, try it out. Rule No. 2: Learn to be uncertain.

• • •

This chapter deals with the middle stage of group treatment. It is during this period that cohesion begins to appear, stabilization occurs, and much of the therapeutic work is done. The chapter answers this question: Once a group has moved beyond the beginning stage of treatment, how does the group worker address the individual needs of the group's members and help the group meet its objectives?

MAINTENANCE ISSUES

The middle stage of a group evolves as a result of each group member's growing sense of trust in the other members, in the worker, and in the group process. There is a definite move from the tentative involvement typical of the beginning stage to a greater feeling of commitment. The members listen to each other and provide support. They share. In short, they develop a greater sense of "we" as opposed to "I" and demonstrate a greater sense of cohesiveness and spirit of cooperation.

For the average group, however, the middle stage is not necessarily smooth. There is usually conflict, discomfort, and anxiety. There are still overt and covert questions about the group and its purpose, as demonstrated by members' comments such as, "Tell us again what we are supposed to be doing" and "I don't know if I trust you enough to tell you what I'm really feeling." There is also subtle testing of the worker to determine his or her reliability and competence.

Productivity within the group generally increases. The members are willing to identify their goals and concerns and to assume responsibility for making changes. They engage in more risk-taking and action-oriented behaviors than before. They are more likely to engage in genuine self-disclosure, often expressing strong emotions. The members are also more likely than before to talk directly to one another rather than to the worker. And they appear more secure and therefore less concerned about the other members' and the worker's expectations.

A common history begins to develop within the group. Whereas, days or weeks ago, the individuals were strangers, transparent threads now link them together. Their disclosure of feelings, thoughts, and experiences has resulted in a growing understanding of each other's world outside the group. Names of spouses, children, and friends are coming to be recognized and tied to places and events.

Although still very much a part of the group, conflict is no longer a threat to the group's very existence as it was in the group's early stages. Instead, group members now see conflict as a normal event. They have begun to use accommodation and integration to manage conflict within the group. The members can get angry and express painful feelings. But they can also hug and laugh together. They feel a sense of urgency in resolving controversy; however, they do not experience so much tension that distortion and defensiveness block their resolution of the controversy.

PRODUCTIVE AND NONPRODUCTIVE GROUPS

Productive and nonproductive groups in the middle stage of treatment are not alike. In a productive group, a healing attitude develops as members begin to experience acceptance for who they are. The members of a productive group interact in more ways and feel less of a need to erect facades than do the members of a nonproductive group.

In contrasting productive and nonproductive groups, Corey and Corey (1987) describe a number of additional differences. In a productive group, there is trust of other members and the worker. There is a willingness to take risks and share meaningful here-and-now reactions. Goals are clear and specific; they are determined by the members and the worker. Leadership functions are shared by the group, and members therefore feel a sense of power. Cohesion is high: group members feel close emotional bonds with each other and the worker. When conflict occurs among members or with the leader, it is acknowledged, discussed, and resolved. Feedback is given freely and accepted without defensiveness.

In a productive group, there is a respect for individual and cultural differences. There is an emphasis on combining feeling and thinking. There is the expression and release of emotions and an interest in discovering the meaning of various emotional experiences. There is a sense of hope; members feel that constructive change is possible. Communication is clear and direct. Group members use out-of-group time to work on problems raised in the group.

A nonproductive group, according to Corey and Corey (1987), is quite different from a productive group. For starters, a nonproductive group is characterized by fuzzy, abstract, and general goals. There is mistrust, as evidenced by an undercurrent of unexpressed hostility. The members feel excluded by or cannot identify with one another. A nonproductive group has a there-and-then focus; any conflicts or negative feelings that arise in the group are ignored, denied, or avoided. The group members feel distant from one another rather than feeling close and expressing empathy. The limited feedback given is rejected defensively. The members feel helpless, trapped, and victimized. Their communication is unclear and indirect.

Confrontation in a nonproductive group, is done in a hostile, attacking way, which causes the confronted member to feel judged and rejected. The members blame other people for their personal difficulties and are not willing to take action to change. The members and/or leader(s) use power and control over each other. Conformity is prized, and individual differences are devalued. The group's dynamics depend heavily on group members' cathartic experiences, but the members make no effort to understand their experiences. The members seldom think about the group when it is not meeting.

COMMUNICATION PATTERNS

By paying attention to group members' language and speech, we therapists come to understand their feelings, thoughts, and attitudes. Our own communication patterns provide a way for us to influence the members' self-awareness and behavior, and provide us with a means of modeling for the members ways to effectively send and receive messages.

SHOULDS, SHOULDN'TS, AND OUGHT TOS

There are group members whose messages to themselves are marked by *shoulds, shouldn'ts,* and *ought tos:* "I **should** get a job," "I **shouldn't** feel the way I do," and "I **ought to** get my life together and stop complaining." Often, these individuals direct the same judgmental words at other people: "You **should**. . . ." You **shouldn't** . . . ." and "You **ought to**. . . ."

Group members need to hear how they use these words and the messages imbedded in their remarks. These words in themselves suggest powerlessness instead of choice. More functional phrases for group members to use include "I choose. . . ." I want. . . ." and "I will. . . ."

OVERGENERALIZING

A false assumption results whenever someone makes an assumption based on the premise that **one** instance is an illustration of **all** instances. Group members often make false assumptions—broad and inaccurate generalizations—as to the *who, where,* and *when* of their lives. For example:

Who

- **"All men** are that way."
- **"Women** are just like that."
- **"Everybody** does the same thing."
- **"Nobody** would ever do something like that."

Where

- **"Everywhere** I go people look at me."
- **"Nowhere** in this hospital can I find someone who cares."

When

- "This **always** happens to me."
- "It will **never** happen."

As therapists, we must encourage individuals to examine their words to determine the congruence between their words and their meaning and also to reexamine their basic assumptions. Are all men a certain way? Is it true that everywhere the member goes, people look at him or her? Will something never happen?

SPEAKING FOR SOMEONE ELSE

Sometimes, one group member tries to speak for another member. For example, one member might interject, "What John is really trying to say is. . . ." or "What John means is. . . ." If this situation recurs, a number of inferences can be made. First, the "talker" (the person who made the original statement) is an incompetent communicator, at least in the "interpreter's" mind. Second, the "interpreter" is anxious about where the interaction is leading and wants to avoid some type of future problem. Third, the "talker's" remarks needed further explanation because they were unclear.

Intervention can be directed at both the "talker" and the "interpreter." The talker needs to deal with any inability he or she has in communicating messages in a way that other people can easily understand. He or she may have such difficulty communicating not only within the group but also with people outside the group—with friends and family members who frequently come to his or her aid. If this is the case, the group member might set for himself or herself the goal of speaking more clearly inside and outside the group, as well as not letting other people speak for him or her. The member might share this goal with the group and ask the other group members to assist him or her in communicating more clearly but without speaking for him or her.

The interpreter needs to deal with his or her need to rescue other people. The group worker might ask the interpreter, "How often do you rescue other people when they are talking?" It is also useful for the group worker to question the interpreter's assumption that he or she really does know what the other person is feeling or thinking.

247

• • • • • • • •

FOCUSING ATTENTION ON THE WORKER

There is a tendency in the beginning stage of group treatment for group members to direct most of their attention toward the group worker instead of toward other group members. Because of the worker's preeminence in the group, this is a natural tendency and to be expected. This preeminence has two major sources: (1) the worker's activity in initiating the group and beginning the group process and (2) the authority vested in the worker by the organization sponsoring the group and by the community (Vinter, 1974).

If the members of a group are unfamiliar with groups or have been in individual counseling, they will assume that the group worker is the major source of therapy. Gradually, the worker needs to direct the group's attention away from himself or herself—so that no one person is central to the group-as-a-whole. If this is not done early in the group's development, the group's members will become dependent on the leader, expecting him or her to assume most of the responsibility for the group.

As a group progresses, we therapists can focus questions directed at us back to the group members. For example, we might refocus a member's question by responding "Frank, that's a good question. How would the rest of you answer what Frank asks?" or "I think some of you can answer that question as well as I can." Or we can give feedback by pointing out communication patterns to the group and simultaneously noting that each person has knowledge and information that can be useful. We might say, "Each of you has already demonstrated that you can answer that question as well as I can. What are your thoughts, John?"

In other words, as a way of promoting interaction, we gradually relinquish the expert role in the group.

By being sensitive to group members' nonverbal cues, a group worker can gently direct questions to the members. As individuals nod and shake their heads, grimace, smile, roll their eyes, cross their arms, pull their chairs back, or wink at one another, for example, we can use this data to link members together. To do this, we might say, "Frank, when you asked that question, I saw several members smile like they had the answer. Let's find out."

SPECIAL PROBLEMS

No two group sessions are the same. One week, group members are energized, excited, insightful, and sensitive to each other's needs. The following week, the members seem flat, energyless, obtuse, closed off, hostile, and noncommunicative. In some group sessions, everyone shares, while in other group sessions, getting members to talk—let alone to share feelings—is next to impossible. There is no way to predict from week to week what will happen. Because of this, a group worker needs to be prepared for the unexpected and willing to be flexible.

Problem situations and barriers occur in the life of every group. By thinking about them in advance, a group worker is in a position to identify various ways of responding. As group therapists, we may have limited power in preventing certain situations from occurring, such as a member's calling us a name or walking out of a session. We do, however, have power over the way we respond.

During group sessions, we need to constantly ask ourselves this question: what is each group member and the group trying to communicate by their actions? Rambling and group silence are two common patterns of communication used by group members. Each pattern in its own way can be frustrating for us. For this reason, it is valuable for us to look behind the pattern to determine its purpose or meaning.

RAMBLING AND IRRELEVANT INFORMATION

Clinical groups often contain one or more members who ramble on about subjects that are of limited importance to the other participants. A rambling member may profess, lecture, and pontificate, thereby providing irrelevant observations that inhibit other group members from working on their personal goals and sapping the strength of the group. The rambler may digress into story-telling and into recounting elongated personal histories about people and situations who are unfamiliar to the other members.

A group worker who secretly feels pressured to keep a group going may experience a sense of relief when the rambler starts to digress, because there will be fewer painful silences with which to contend. And the other participants, not wanting to be rude, and taking their cues from the leader, will obediently listen. As they listen, they will begin to wonder whether they, too, will be expected to go into the same detail. It is not long until the worker and members are bored. The group is now into a pattern that everyone apparently assumes to be helpful yet silently recognizes as having no real value.

A monopolist may use words as a way to control the group. Even when a rambler is revealing what appears to be significant aspects of himself or herself, the rambler may be either consciously or unconsciously trying to control the group's potential impact on him or her (Dinkmeyer and Muro, 1971). As long as the person is speaking, he or she holds the group's attention, limits the group's discussion, and minimizes the probability of being confronted by other members.

A group worker has to be willing to confront a monopolist. Unless this occurs, the monopolist's behavior will continue, with the other members retreating into their own private worlds. It is also important for the worker to establish a group norm as to irrelevant activity—that is, information that does not fit the purpose of the group. To do this, a group worker might respond to a monpolist by saying "Carol, I'm lost. What is your point?" or "How does this fit with what we have been talking about?"

Other group members who are obviously uncomfortable with the extraneous data can be valuable resources to the group worker. For example, the worker might turn to a group member and say, "John, you look bored as Carol is talking. What are you thinking?" or the worker might ask the monpolist, "Stop for a second, Carol, and look around the room. What nonverbal messages are you getting from the other members?"

SILENCE IN THE GROUP

Silence in a therapy group can be a frustrating experience for group workers. It implies that nothing is happening or that the group members are resisting. Over the years, group workers have been advised to "sweat it out"—to let the members react to the silence and come to grips with their personal discomfort. It has been my experience, however, that silence for more than a couple of minutes generates unnecessary anxiety for the worker, as well as for the members.

Often, it is the immature or extremely anxious group members who finally break the silence. They do so because of their agonizing discomfort. But they will resent doing so, feeling exploited by the worker and the other members.

It is a mistake for a group worker to assume that a group's silence necessarily means either a lack of cooperation or a collective conspiracy against the leader. A group's silence can have many different meanings. It can signify a reflective period during which group members are mulling over some experience that has just been discussed in the group. The silence can be linked to embarrassment because of something that has just been revealed. Not knowing what to say, the group members may choose to say nothing.

In the beginning stages of a group, members are often silent out of confusion and a lack of awareness of what is expected of them. Some members may be surprised by the intensely personal mode of interaction, by the expression of feelings, and/or by painful self-disclosures. Other members may fear ridicule and thus say nothing.

In addition, it is not unusual for group members to be silent at the beginning of a session because they are not psychologically warmed up. An activity to get them started, such as a finish-the-sentence round, may open up a discussion, encouraging the members to recall the previous meeting, to describe some of its high points, and to identify any unfinished business may also be an effective way to start a discussion.

Some group members tend to be very quiet. When questioned as to the reason for their silence, they respond that they are always this way or that they learn more from watching and listening to other people than from talking. It is valuable for the leader to encourage these members to discuss their silence in the group, particularly their discomfort in sharing their feelings and thoughts with other people.

The silence of an individual group member may be symptomatic of the member's resistance to the group process. Some participants refuse to participate and demonstrate their power by withholding—and thereby ignoring the established purpose of the group. If a group worker chooses to remain silent, a contest or standoff between such group members and the worker may result, with neither willing to give in. This is especially true with adolescent groups who may feel a need to beat the worker in a game of "who's got the power?"

There is no single way for a group worker to handle a group's silence. The worker can select one person and ask that person to comment on the silence. For example, the worker might say "Sandy, the group is silent right now. What do you think is going on?" We can also direct our remarks to the group-as-a-whole, saying "You have all been quiet. What's going on?" or "There have been a number of long silences. What do they mean?"

In summary, a group's silence can be either productive or nonproductive. A group's silence is productive when the members of the group are processing something that was said or done. A group's silence is nonproductive when members are quiet because they are confused, angry, fearful, or resistant.

● **Techniques: Practical considerations**
  1. Ask yourself: Am I disturbed by the group's silence?
  2. Ask yourself: Do the group members seem to be disturbed by the silence?
  3. Ask yourself: Are the group members really not participating?
  4. Ask yourself: What advantage is there in allowing the group's silence to continue?
  5. Ask yourself: Is the group's silence a productive or nonproductive silence?

TRANSFERENCE REACTIONS IN A GROUP

Strictly speaking, **transference** refers to a person's projection of fantasies and feelings that he or she originally experienced in relation to a primary figure in his or her life onto the person's therapist. We have learned from Freud the special, even volatile, powers that exist in a psychotherapeutic encounter. The psychiatrist, Joseph Breuer, was frightened when he discovered the intensity of the feelings his patients had for him. Freud is said to have begun sitting out of sight of his patients as a way to minimize the influence of his own expressive gestures and reactions on them.

In recent years, transference has come to refer to a person's displacement or projection of his or her feelings, fantasies, and behaviors from one context to another. According to Sands (1983), transference in this more generic sense refers to feelings, fantasies, and behaviors deriving from a person's life experiences that are applied inaccurately to new situations. In its mildest form, a transference is a mere error such as that which occurs when we mistake another person for someone else. In a more extreme manifestation, a transference is a major error such as that which occurs when we perceive and react to a person totally apart from who the person really is.

Leaders using a psychosocial approach tend to evoke fewer transference reactions than those using a more classical psychoanalytic approach. There are a number of reasons for this difference. First, in a psychosocial treatment program, there is great emphasis on the present and only limited discussion of the past, including the client's relationship with his or her parents. Second, there is only limited discussion of dreams and fantasies and only limited free association. Third, the therapist is active, not passive, and deals with the client's unrealistic perceptions right away.

According to London (1969) in a psychoanalytic treatment program, the therapist's personal anonymity helps promote the client's transference reaction because the therapist withholds information that would give the client a realistic basis for evaluating and responding to him or her. Since the client knows little about the analyst's life or what the analyst is really like, the things the client attributes to the analyst and the emotions the client experiences in the analyst's presence must be taken from the client's experience with other people.

Still, transference reactions are commonplace in psychosocial oriented group work and can affect a client's treatment. For example, it is not uncommon for a group member to react angrily toward a group worker for no apparent reason. Usually, when such transactions are examined closely, it becomes clear that the group worker stands for a significant person from the member's past—such as a teacher or a domineering father. Transference occurs whenever emotional reactions that actually belong to a person in the client's past are inaccurately transferred by the client onto the worker. We can use such transference reactions both to conceptualize client dynamics and to help the individual client resolve his or her conflicts within the therapeutic relationship.

TRANSFERENCE AS AN EVERYDAY OCCURRENCE

To some degree, transference is an ordinary experience that characterizes most human relationships: we all systematically misperceive other people based on our previous learning, which we overgeneralize to new situations. According to Jung (1968), "anything can be a matter for projection . . . . All activated contents of the unconscious have the tendency to appear in projection . . . . There are even transferences to animals (p. 158).

In the early stages of a group, its members may feel a need to imbue the group worker with superhuman features (Yalom, 1985). The worker's words are given more weight and wisdom than they possess. Equally astute contributions made by other group members are ignored or distorted. The worker's errors, faux pas, and absences are seen as deliberate techniques that he or she is employing to stimulate or provoke the group for its own good. The group members assume there are great calculated depths to each of the worker's interventions, that he or she predicts and controls all the events of the group.

When the worker confesses puzzlement or ignorance in such a situation, that response, too, is regarded as part of the technique, deliberately intended to have an effect on the group. These projections are inaccurate and distorted in that the group members are seeing the worker as an embodiment of their own fantasies, rather than perceiving who the worker really is.

It is inaccurate to think that all the feelings the group members have toward the group worker are simply signs of transference. A group member could feel affection toward a group worker because he or she genuinely likes the worker and enjoys the worker's sense of humor. Similarly, a group member might be realistically angry at the worker because the worker has been rude or has made an insensitive remark. A group member's affection or anger does not have to be an irrational response triggered by past situations in the member's life.

The **sources** of a group member's transference are not limited to recipients of his or her childhood love, or even to human beings. Anyone, or anything, can be a source of someone's transferred experiences. Likewise, anyone can be the **object** of someone's transferred experiences. The more unknown the other person in a new relationship is, the more likely it is that the client will give him or her qualities that derive from the client's fantasy life. Until such misinterpretations surface and are discussed, the new relationship will contain distortions by the client of the real characteristics of the new person in the client's life (Sands, 1983).

UTILIZING THE TRANSFERENCE REACTIONS

In group work, transference is not limited to client's projections onto the worker. A group member may also endow other group members with qualities the member associates with people from his or her past or present and then may behave unrealistically or inappropriately toward the other group member.

A group worker's style is an important factor in the nature and quality of group members' transference. Authoritarian therapists are likely to stimulate a client's transference to themselves as parent figures, and to other group members as siblings. Therapists who play a less prominent role and who facilitate intense interactions intensely among group members, generally stimulate fewer transference reactions. Nevertheless, the exposed position of any group leader makes him or her a tempting target for group members' transference.

It is important that a group member come to understand the nature of his or her transference, particularly in the member's relationship with his or her therapist. Jan, a 25-year-old graduate student, participated in a short-term growth group I led. During the first six sessions, Jan remained aloof, disclosing very little personal information about herself. When I confronted her with her lack of involvement, she immediately became angry and blamed me for being insensitive. Other members of the group came to her defense, questioning my professionalism. The following is an entry from Jan's journal.

> I do not believe that I really worked until the session where we discussed how angry I had been after the previous session. During the two-week break, I did a lot of thinking and in that session, I was able to put some things together. I realized my flippant response to the leader, when he said my investment was about 40%, was that of a child. He reminded me so much of my father and the ability he [my father] has to reduce me to a child.

As Jan was able to talk about her anger, issues about her father and the quality of their relationship came to the surface. She spoke of her feelings of powerlessness and her reluctance to be angry for fear of being punished.

The comprehension and change a group member can glean from reducing his or her transference in the relationship with his or her therapist is an important step in the member's understanding and changing relationships with his or her parents and other authority figures. By experiencing nurturance, acceptance, support, and freedom to develop autonomy within an empathetic relationship with the worker, the member can gain compensatory experiences. These experiences can substitute for lacks or distortions in the member's relationships that may stem all the way back to his or her early childhood (Levine, 1979).

A group worker needs to be alert to situations in which a group member seems to be transferring emotional reactions from past relationships onto current relationships. One of the most effective ways for a group worker to do this is by investigating how various group members are perceiving and reacting to the worker and to each other in a given situation. The leader might ask a member who seems to be transferring emotional reactions to him or her to express whatever the member is feeling at the moment. In the following questions, the worker is responding to transference directed to himself or herself. But the worker can use similar questions when the object of transference is another group member.

- "What are you feeling toward me right now?"
- "When you find yourself thinking about the group, what kinds of feelings do you have about me?"
- "What do you think I am feeling toward you right now?"
- "What do you think I expect you to do in this situation?"

These questions of a here-and-now nature make the member's transference reaction overt and allow the therapist and the other group members to address the reactions as part of the treatment process. In the same way, exploring other members' reactions, may reveal new examples of transference that need to be dealt with in the group.

A group member's emotional reaction cannot always be thought of as irrational. Many times, an emotional reaction does not fit the present circumstances but does make sense when placed within the context of the person's history—that is, real-life events have legitimately caused the individual to feel the way he or she does. Although it is paradoxical, transference reactions ultimately reveal that the member's feelings always make sense (Teyber, 1988).

MANAGING CONFLICT

A group without conflict is a dead group. Conflict is an inevitable and normal part of groups and is a necessary and integral part of the therapeutic process. Conflict has the potential of enhancing the understanding and the strength of relationships among group members (Northen, 1988). But conflict also has the potential of overwhelming a group to the point of draining its life energy, creating resentment and generating hostility among its members, and psychologically damaging its members.

Few individuals, including practitioners, are comfortable with conflict. We do our best to avoid conflict, hoping that it will go away. Because of the anxiety that conflict generates within us, our tendency is to extinguish or suppress it whenever it surfaces. As therapists, we may be excessively warm and friendly or nonconfrontational and quick to smooth over differences. Or may be apathetic and do nothing, causing greater divisiveness, scapegoating, or acting out. At the other extreme is the worker who is excessively challenging as a way of being in control. Underlying the worker's actions is the belief/assumption/supposition/premise that the best defense is good offense.

Rather than avoiding conflict, the transcending objective for a group worker needs to be that of helping group members grow and profit from conflict. One way for the worker to do this is by "holding the system steady—that is, by ensuring stability and continuity within the group (Henry, 1981). Even though a conflict can cause group members to experience anger, hurt, and hostility, the worker can provide a stable environment in which the members can talk about their feelings, examine the circumstances, and work through the conflict.

According to Cowger (1979), a group worker needs to be willing to address conflict in an open manner and to avoid defining situations in ways that suggest participants are winners and losers.

Confront rather than avoiding conflict. Conflict has to be confronted in an open manner. For most groups, the principle that it is all-right to have conflict needs to be established as a group norm from the group's very beginning. This norm can be discussed in each pregroup interview and made a part of the contract with group members. However, for some groups, the worker may want to wait until a conflictual situation arises before establishing norms for handling conflict. This provides the group the opportunity to develop its own norms for dealing with conflict.

Avoid fostering win/lose situations.   Win/lose situations are based on competition and result in a loss of motivation by the losers, a decrease in group cohesion, and severe maintenance problems for the group. As a win/lose conflict escalates, often accompanied by strong communication, such as an angry tone of voice, sarcasm, yelling, participants in the conflict lose their perspective about the magnitude of the conflict. To prevent a conflict from reaching this point, a group worker (1) might point out the common ground between the protagonists, (2) might partialize the problem, and (3) might have the main protagonists argue each other's position.

Clarify and interpret the process.   During contentious situations, communication lines become tangled. Misinterpretation of verbal and nonverbal cues leads to confusion, anger, anxiety, and hurt feelings. A group worker can begin to manage the problem effectively by pressing as soon as possible for a mutual definition of the conflict. In addition, the worker can review with participants the events that led up to the conflict, especially the verbal and nonverbal behaviors. The worker can help the group members partialize the problem by breaking the problem into more manageable parts, clarify areas of agreement and disagreement. The worker can also have the group members share their observations and perceptions.

Maintain a relationship with the whole group.   A group worker must pay attention to the needs of the whole group during a conflict. By doing this, the worker can help the group members realize that the problem is significant beyond the interaction occurring between the protagonists. The members come to see that a conflict in the group is not just a problem between a couple of individuals; the conflict affects each member of the group directly or indirectly. The more the entire group realizes it has a stake in resolving the conflict, the greater will be the resources available for resolving the conflict. By including other members in the conflict, the leader also elicits more neutral opinions.

Set standards and ground rules.   For a conflict to be dealt with in a constructive way, a group needs to have a structure and agreed-on norms that protect its members from harm, abuse, and embarrassment. These are the boundaries that members must be able to count on and that define the range of behaviors tolerated within the group.

These boundaries are best defined in a matter-of-fact way at the beginning of the group. For many groups, the concept of boundaries will have only limited meaning until a situation arises in which voices are raised and individuals are calling each other names. It is at this time the rules will begin to make sense to the group members.

One norm that a group leader should always establish for a group is that the group members are to remain in the meeting room, in spite of their feelings. If a member is angry at the leader and leaves the room, there is no way to solve the problem. This action also places the worker in the quandary of staying with the group or going after the member. If an angry member is exiting the group, he or she should be encouraged to return as soon as possible to address the issue.

Group norms regarding conflict resolution might include:

- It is all right to be angry.
- There is no hitting or name calling.
- Even though you are angry, stay in the room.

ENCOURAGING CONFLICT

There may be times when a group worker consciously stimulates and even precipitates conflict. Forman (1967), in discussing his work with older adults in a community center, observes that group members often become overly dependent on the host agency for assistance, giving up some of their own responsibility, as well as some of their power.

> the agency for some years had accepted responsibility for handling the group's correspondence. The worker's attempts to encourage group members [to] assume this task met with failure even though there were capable members who could have done so. Finally, the worker created a crisis situation by refusing to allow agency staff to write "thank you" notes after a club program. After much argument, controversy, and discussion, the group assumed this responsibility [p. 83].

The results of the worker-generated crisis were twofold: (1) the group members found that they were capable of working together to handle a group responsibility, and (2) a meaningful group role was established for one group member—the member who agreed to be the group's correspondent.

In another instance, the same worker confronted the club's power structure when that clique subjected to ridicule, verbal abuse, and rejection one member's comments and questions. The worker verbalized the group member's questions to demonstrate that he valued differences of opinion and respected the right of each member to ask questions. The worker also served as a shield for the hostility of the power structure, which encouraged several more group members to take more active roles in group life. As a result, many of the club's members internalized this new, more open pattern of discussion and decision making and started setting their own limits for the power structure.

CONFLICT AND INPATIENT GROUPS

Many psychiatric inpatients have significant problems dealing with anger. They either express anger in destructive ways, or they are so threatened by anger that they stifle it and suffer consequences of internalization such as psychosomatic illness, self-hatred, and depression. According to Yalom (1983), a small inpatient therapy group cannot and should not be asked to deal with patient's overt rage. The clinician must not assume, says Yalom, that since many patients in a group have problems with anger, the clinician should encourage these individuals to "get their anger out" and to deal with it in the therapy group. Instead, the clinician's aim should be rapid resolution of the patient's anger and not conflict evocation. Yalom writes, the inpatient group therapist should not pretend that anger does not exist in a group. Rather, the therapist's task is to find a way as quickly as possible to help each patient deal with his or her anger in a fashion that does not disrupt the safe atmosphere of the group.

ROLES AND PATTERNED BEHAVIOR

Individual group members exhibit patterns of behavior that not only fulfill their own personal needs, but also serve various group functions. In a therapy group, it is seldom easy to differentiate between the specialized functions a group member plays within the group and that person's characteristic patterns of behavior. The fact that groups often typecast their members by using certain of their members' personal behaviors to fill certain group functions confuses the matter further (Rutan & Stone, 1984).

Some group roles facilitate a group's efforts to work on problems by encouraging exploration of members' feelings or important topics. These roles have been assigned a host of specific titles—for example, encourager, gatekeeper, harmonizer, and standard setter (Benne & Sheats, 1948). The function of each of these roles is to in some way strengthen and maintain the group. However, another set of group roles is nonfunctional. Roles such as playboy, blocker, self-confessor, and aggressor are nonfunctional and sometimes harm the group and detract from the work it is trying to do.

It is important to understand that a group requires roles both to help regulate group members' feelings and to further the group's work. A group might depend on one particular group member to perform both these functions or might depend on several individuals to play just one role. For example, in a group situation that spawns intense emotions, two members might regulate the intensity of the feelings—one by joking and one by using another form of diversion.

Each group member enters a group with a specific repertoire of roles that he or she has already used in other life situations with some degree of success. But it is not unusual for a group member to take on a role in a group that has caused the member some difficulty in the past. If the member has trouble playing the role he or she has accepted, the worker has an opportunity to intervene therapeutically and deal with the member's needs and unconscious conflicts, which have become observable in his or her current attempt to play the role.

• • • • • • • •

The following are descriptions of other familiar individual roles commonly found in groups. The list represents only a fraction of the multiplicity of patterns brought about by the interplay of environmental forces, internal group processes, and individual dynamics.

A PLACATER

Placaters talk in an ingratiating way, seldom disagreeing and always trying to please. They talk as though they would never do anything just for themselves. They need the approval of others. Bandler, Grinder, and Satir (1976) describe a placater as a "yes man," who appears syrupy and martyrish.

A client who plays this role is very sensitive to the needs of the other people. Consequently, the client is often used by others and resents it. But the client is afraid to express his or her resentment because of self-doubts. Such a client talks very openly about his or her problems and makes others feel close because he or she seems to have problems in common with most if not all the members (Ohlsen, 1970). Such a client is often helped with all of his or her difficulties except the one with which the client needs help most—being controlled by others. This problem the client may never discuss openly.

AN ASSISTANT THERAPIST

Assistant therapists tend to take over the functions they attribute to the group worker. A client who plays this role asks leading questions of other members, analyzes behavior, and is always ready with an interpretation. According to Kadis, Krasner, Weiner, Winick, and Foulkes (1974), this pattern may result from the client's need to ingratiate himself or herself in an attempt to acquire the worker's support. Or the client may experience intense rivalry with the group worker and attempt to destroy the worker's credibility by displaying himself or herself as even more confident and helpful.

A CLOWN

It is common in small groups to find a member who can be relied upon to offer a quick one-liner, pun, or practical joke. This clown or jester usually has a symbiotic relationship with the group. The group needs him or her to play the role; and the clown needs to play the role.

In certain situations involving stress, anxiety, or threat, the behavior of a clown may help the group avoid a problem or survive a crisis (Heap, 1977). For instance, anxiety is often generated in a new social situation in which the participants are strangers. The group's tension may be relieved by a person who makes a joke about the situation. Responding to the joke enables the participants to displace their tension and discomfort by sharing their first positive experience— laughter. In return, the clown, is rewarded by attracting the attention of the group and beginning to establish his or her position in the group.

A SCAPEGOAT

Scapegoating is basically a defense mechanism manifested by group members who project their own anxiety and/or pathology onto someone else (Coser, 1956; Balgopal & Vassil, 1983). The object of their projection may embody characteristics toward which the other members are especially fearful or especially attracted. Group members may identify and attack a scapegoat simply because they desire to focus attention away from themselves. Or they may identify and attack a scapegoat simply because they find the scapegoat's words or behavior disturbing.

Often, a group member who becomes a scapegoat is distinguished by behaviors deviant from the group norm. The scapegoat may be unaware of his or her nonverbal cues that generate the reactions he or she gets from the group. Sometimes, a scapegoat has difficulty with adaptive learning. Occasionally, however, a scapegoat's only "sin" is being a new member in a group.

AN INTELLECTUALIZER

Thinking their feelings away is a favorite pastime of intellectualizers. An intellectualizer in a group may appear in any of several disguises. The client may constantly "clarify" by asking a vast array of questions meant to help other group members sort out their lives. The client may relate things to the group that are of no general concern to anyone and that have little or no emotional significance attached to them. The client may begin sentences with the phrase "I feel" and finish them with thoughts and ideas rather than feelings. And the client may spend much of the group's time talking about books and theories instead of emotions and personal experiences.

A SILENT AND/OR WITHDRAWN MEMBER

A silent member and a withdrawn member of a group may be one and the same; or they may be very different individuals and have different reasons for not talking (Ohlsen, 1970). Some quiet members of groups are deeply involved in interacting with other people but with a minimum of talking; other group members may serve as their mouthpiece. Usually, these "silent members" openly reveal their problems early in the group so they are not looked upon with suspicion. An inexperienced group worker might often assume that because a group member is generally silent, the member is not involved. However, silent members are usually very involved—although not overtly. Behind their eyes can be a great deal of activity.

Withdrawn members tends to have a more negative self-image than silent members. When called upon, withdrawn members feel put on the spot and have difficulty articulating their feelings. Compared with silent members, withdrawn members tend to be less confident that they can be helped by counseling.

259
• • • • • • • •

A SOCIAL ISOLATE

A social isolate is someone who is present but does not reach out to other people. The person's lack of affiliation with others in the group may result from a limited capacity to get along with other people. The true isolate is ignored. His or her contributions go unnoticed. And his or her opinions are not asked for (Hartford, 1971). A social isolate generally does not become a group's scapegoat; to become a scapegoat, the social isolate would have to begin to receive attention—albeit negative attention—from the group.

A RESCUER

Rescuers in a group are quick to come to the assistance of other group members whenever there are tears or confrontation. Rescuers cannot stand seeing another person in any kind of pain—physical or psychological—even in cases in which the pain is beneficial. Egan (1970), who uses the term *Red crossing,* writes that rescuing frequently occurs in a group when one of its members is being confronted. In such a situation, a rescuer might give approval to the confrontee's behavior—whether or not the confrontee actually approves of his or her own behavior. The rescuer might try to rationalize away the confrontee's guilt or responsibility. The rescuer might also remind members that they, too, have behaved similarly and should not be harsh on their suffering group member.

A rescuer is not the same as a group member who intervenes because he or she believes that a group confrontational process has become irresponsible, negative, and profitless in a particular case.

IDENTIFYING BENEFICIAL ROLES

Not every behavioral pattern or role used by group members is self-destructive or pathological. It is important for a group worker to distinguish between the roles that are useful and adaptive in a group and those that are destructive and constraining. A role that may be functional in light of the development of the group-as-a-whole may be constricting for a particular member, or vice versa. In addition, a particular role can be healthy and functional; however, pushed to an extreme, it can become pathological and dysfunctional.

● Techniques: Practical considerations

1. When assessing an individual's role in a group, consider the meaning of the behavior not only to the person but also to the group-as-a-whole.
2. Be sensitive to your own personal reaction to each group member.
3. Encourage group members to identify patterned behavior within their group and the function the behavior serves.

AN ACTION ORIENTATION

261
········

It is not enough for group members to be productive just inside their group. The success or failure of a group treatment program will be determined by the changes in each group member's life outside the group, particularly in his or her work, play, and ability to love. If the group member experiences no identifiable change—or greater wholeness—outside the group, the group treatment has not been successful.

Often, as clients try to make progress in their life outside their group, they find themselves stuck in a situation—unable to move forward and fearful of moving backward. Such a situation leads to an internal separation within a client. Often, the client's urge to move forward is counter-balanced by fear, self-doubt, self-flagellation, and a sense of self-betrayal. The client recognizes what is life-enhancing—for example, losing weight, no longer drinking, getting a job, giving up drugs— but realizes that this option is fraught with danger and risk. Out of fear and anxiety, the client shrinks from making a decision, thereby remaining in the destructive situation and continuing behaviors that are "safe," comforting, and self-defeating.

As group workers, we constantly challenge our clients to stretch beyond their comfort zone. Sometimes, a client's reluctance to take risks is related to severe emotional illness. More typically, however, it has to do with a client's realization of the work involved in giving up unprofitable pleasures. Such a client is not mentally ill. Rather, he or she is living halfheartedly, shrinking from full involvement in life. This client's life is one of quiet desperation, docility, and conformity in place of intimacy, love, and passion.

Among the basic fears a client may feel in letting go of a self-defeating pattern are these:

- "I will appear dumb and incompetent."
- "I will be weak and vulnerable."
- "I will not be able to cope."
- "I will be unable to control my emotions."
- "I will go crazy and have to be hospitalized."
- "I will lost the limited security I now have."
- "I will be terribly hurt."
- "God will punish me."
- "People will laugh at me."
- "I will lose control and hurt someone."

Clients use "techniques" for keeping their unproductive habits in place and for implementing their self-defeating choices. Some of the techniques they commonly use are these: distorting feedback, manipulating people, labeling themselves and others, intellectualizing, and building walls in relationships. Other techniques include:

- appearing to agree with other people when they really don't
- putting unrealistic expectations on themselves

- misusing drugs
- responding to life in a feelingless manner
- lying
- blaming the past for today's problems
- picking friends who encourage self-defeating actions
- looking dumb and appearing irresponsible

Many clients have a tendency to disown an action by shifting the responsibility for it someplace else. For example, a client may blame his or her experiences for some of his or her current behavior. A client may blame society, his or her parents or friends, or God. A client may even blame a part of himself or herself over which the client feels he or she has little control, as illustrated by a patient who says, "I would be successful if it weren't for my [nerves, bad eyes, deafness, mental illness, depression, bad back, and so forth]." The following are other typical disowning statements clients make:

- "It's a family characteristic. I was born this way."
- "It's a habit. I have always done it."
- "My parents always did it."
- "I was drunk when I did it."
- "My feelings just took over."
- "Something just won't let me change."
- "I was so confused; I couldn't do anything else."

Disowning is a way for a client to keep self-defeating patterns in place. When a client recognizes ways in which he or she disowns, the client has taken the first positive step toward giving up these self-defeating behaviors. Cudney (1975) writes, "If a person could not disown, he would be forced to stand naked to the truth of what he does to hurt himself and it would, in full truth appear ridiculous" (p. 58). Giving up disowning behaviors is an important step in becoming a fully integrated person.

Disowning, helplessness, and powerlessness are all directly related. The more an individual disowns, the more helpless and powerless the person is to do anything proactive that leads to change. To disown means to have little or no control over one's life.

EMPOWERMENT

Meaningful change in a group member's life requires work on his or her part. If the member does not act on his or her own behalf, nothing happens. In physics, the law of inertia states that a body at rest tends to stay at rest, unless something occurs to make it move. Many clients suffer from psychological inertia. For a multitude of reasons, they are "at rest"—they either are unable to or choose not to move.

As long as a client stays in a state of inertia, the client's life can be compared to a self-defeating loop. For example, Angie, a woman battered by her husband, chose to stay with him because she had no place else to go. Her low self-esteem prevented her from applying for a job or returning to school for job training. Fearful that her husband would again physically abuse her, Angie became passive, resulting in even lower self-esteem and a lack of self-confidence.

But, with help, Angie overcame her inertia. At the recommendation of her minister, Angie joined a women's treatment group sponsored by a community mental health agency. In the group, she spoke very little at first; however, with each session Angie said more. She gained confidence and had a growing sense of self-worth. Feeling better about herself, Angie applied for a minimum-wage job at a fast-food chain. Her employer liked her work so much that after a month, he gave her a substantial raise. With the additional money, Angie had her hair styled by a professional and purchased new clothes. Her friends were excited about Angie's transformation and told her how good she looked. Feeling greater self-confidence, Angie became increasingly more assertive with her husband. Angry with Angie's behavior one evening, her husband threatened to hit her. Angie stood up to her husband and made it clear that if he ever struck her again, she would divorce him.

MAKING PROACTIVE CHOICES

A client's movement beyond inertia may occur in very small steps. For Angie, the first step was joining the treatment group and taking part in its sessions. The more she shared, the easier it was to talk about herself and her problems with her husband. For every client, as for Angie, there comes a point in a treatment program, however, when talking about problems is not enough. The member has to begin to make proactive choices about his or her circumstances. In the final analysis, it is up to the individual to decide what it is he or she needs to do for himself or herself.

Making a commitment to proactive choices means the client must begin to apply what he or she has learned and must begin to put his or her plans into action. It means going beyond the "I would like to" and "I want to" phase and moving to the "I'm going to" phase. The moment the client actually makes this commitment is especially frightening because the potential risks are no longer in the distant future but, instead, are close at hand. Angie, for example, was frightened by the specter of two very different kinds of risks. First, Angie was afraid to apply for the fast-food job because she thought she probably would not be hired. And she felt that being turned down would deal one more blow to her already brittle self-image. In Angie's thinking, it might be safer not to apply at all; then, she would not have to experience rejection. Second, Angie was frightened because if she were offered the job, having it would mean being away from home at suppertime, and Angie anticipated that her husband would be enraged if she were not home to make his supper. Despite her fears, Angie made the commitment to get the job and got it. In spite of her success, however, she felt pangs of disloyalty, as though she were betraying her husband.

There is an ancient Chinese expression that a thousand-mile journey begins with the first step. Even though a client makes a decision to do something, the client may experience feelings of near-paralyzing doubt and fear. And, as Haussmann and Halseth (1983) found in their work with a group of depressed women, group meetings in which participants take risks and shared previously kept family and personal secrets are usually followed by sessions characterized by anxiety and withdrawal.

HOMEWORK

Having a group member take on an action assignment, or homework, is especially useful right after he or she makes a breakthrough. The objective of such homework is to help the member think about and work on his or her goals between sessions and try out new behaviors he or she has learned in the group. At the next meeting, each member can discuss with the rest of the group any homework assignments he or she has completed. Doing the homework and relating the results to the group provides each member with opportunities to gain success in a particular aspect of their life and to share their experience with other group members.

A group worker can present homework in more than one way. One of the best ways is to suggest that each group member "take on" a reasonable task based on something he or she has learned in the group session. Another way is for the worker to assign a group member a task based on something the member struggled with in the group.

Homework may take many forms. For example, a group leader may ask a group member to write something, such as a general autobiography, or an autobiography related to a specific issue— for example, relationships with members of the opposite sex. Or a group leader may ask a group member to talk to a particular person or to accomplish some other specific task related to the member's life situation.

UNINTENDED CONSEQUENCES

Participating in a group experience can be emotionally damaging for some people. While the danger of groups has been known for many years, the research by Lieberman, Yalom, and Miles (1973) on encounter groups brought the point home. Defining group casualties as individuals who, eight months after group therapy, were more psychologically distressed and/or employed more maladaptive mechanisms of defense than before their therapy, the authors concluded that a number of participants acquired emotional problems. The authors found that in the 17 encounter groups studied, close to 8 percent of the members were casualties, and another 8 percent experienced some "negative" changes.

The conditions researchers associate with group casualties vary and include the individual characteristics of the members, relationships within the group, and the style of the leader.

MEMBERS' CHARACTERISTICS

Group members who have a history of psychological problems are likely to experience negative outcomes as a result of a group. The degree of pathology that can be tolerated in a group depends on the type of group. For example, the behavior of an unstable member might stand out as deviant in an encounter group. The same behavior might be accepted by the members of a psychotherapy group (Galinsky & Schopler, 1977). Other personal characteristics of a group member that might predict the member's distress include inadequate defense mechanisms, a lack of attraction to the particular group, and an inability to perceive expectations accurately.

As group workers, we cannot eliminate all the psychological risks for the members of a group. We can, however, spot potential problems during the pregroup interview and take action before the initial session. For example, we might put a candidate into another group or schedule the client for individual rather than group treatment. Or we might specify our own responsibilities in the contract and have the member, state explicitly what they are and are not willing to explore and do in the group.

INTERPERSONAL RELATIONSHIPS

Relationships within a group can be painful. There may be scapegoating, destructive confrontations, and harmful socializing among members. There may be a lack of group structure and little or no clarity about group norms. There may be coercive norms that demand participation before members are ready and that encourage attacks on members' defenses related to matters about which the members are sensitive.

If a group's work is to be accomplished and the group's participants are to be protected from destructive pressures, both the group members and the group leader(s) must understand their responsibilities and roles, as well as the rules and guidelines for governing behavior within the group. It is also important that coercive or high-pressure tactics be avoided and individual differences be tolerated in the group (Galinsky & Schopler, 1977).

LEADERSHIP STYLE

Leaders in groups with high casualty rates have been characterized as being charismatic, insufficiently trained, impersonal, and lacking an ability to diagnose problems. The most effective leaders were rated moderate in terms of stimulation and high in terms of caring (Lieberman, Yalom & Miles, 1973). Group leaders should care about what happens to the individuals in their groups, should possess well-developed assessment skills, and should be moderate in their approach. They should also have the training and theoretical background to make the group experience meaningful for group members (Galinsky & Schopler, 1977).

● **Techniques: Practical considerations**

1. Encourage group members to ventilate their feelings— especially any anger and guilt they feel within the group or because of the group.
2. Be sure the guidelines and goals for a group are clear to its members.
3. Pay careful attention to a group composition; in particular, avoid bringing together a group of members who are extremely different from one another.
4. Establish norms in a group that promote support for individual members and allow for the individual differences in group members.
5. If a group member cannot be protected in a particular group, help the individual leave the group.

IN SUMMARY

The middle phase of a group's treatment program is a time of commitment, intimacy, and sharing. There is greater mutual exploration, integration, and cohesion among group members than there was during the group's early phase. Productivity within the group increases, and the members are more committed than before to working toward their identified goals. Conflict is less of a threat, in that the members have developed ways of managing disagreements before the conflict becomes overwhelming.

Encouraging a group member to analyze and reconsider the language patterns the member uses provides a way for a group worker to influence the member's self-awareness and behavior. During the middle phase of group treatment, it is important for a group worker to address group and individual behaviors that detract from the group's purpose. These behaviors include excessive silence as well as monopolizing. The group worker assumes an action orientation, continually empowering the members to stretch beyond their comfort zone.

SUGGESTED READINGS

CUDNEY, M. (1975). *Eliminating self-defeating behaviors*. Kalamazoo, Mich.: Life Giving Enterprises. See Chapters 3–5.

HARTFORD, M. (1971). *Groups in social work*. New York: Columbia University Press. See Chapters 8–10.

HEAP, K. (1977). *Group theory for social workers: An introduction*. New York: Pergamon Press. See Chapters 5 and 6.

LIEBERMAN, M., YALOM, I., & MILES, M. (1973). *Encounter groups: First facts*. New York: Basic Books. See Chapters 7–10.

THE ENDING STAGE OF TREATMENT

*T*he ending of an ongoing group can be as painful for the worker as it is for the members. Several years ago, I led a self-actualization group for clergy. Initially, the group members—all men—were reluctant to share their thoughts and feelings in anything other than a superficial manner. As the group progressed, individuals began to take risks, disclosing feelings of joy, frustration, anger, and pain. Each, in his own way, shared the comedy and tragedy of his life. There were laughter and tears, rage and caring, and agreement and disagreement. There were moments of spirited conflict, as well as moments of gentle tranquility.

The last session was marked by sadness and anxiety. Some of the members pulled back by saying little, while others openly revealed their feelings of loss. There was a collective sense of relief that now Tuesday afternoons would be free and they could pursue other interests or spend time with their families.

One of the ministers spoke of his difficulty with saying good-bye, and his tendency to avoid intimate relationships, knowing they would eventually end. This resonated within the group. Several men told stories of their anguish in moving from churches they had come to love.

I spoke of my own mixed emotions about the group's ending. I had come to enjoy each person and looked forward to the group each week, but like the members, I also needed to move on to other things in my life. Deep within, I knew I would miss the hour and a half spent together, particularly the genuine caring, the feeling of trust, and the luxury of acceptance.

Even though we would occasionally see each other at meetings and functions, it would never be quite the same. I, too, was grieving the end of the group and was having to say good-bye to people I had come to care for.

I wonder, sometimes, if clients have any idea how much they truly enrich our lives. For the clinician, the helping process is an education, an adventure, and a mirror.

• • •

This chapter deals with the final stage of the therapeutic group process and focuses on termination and evaluation. The two questions this chapter addresses are these: (1) how do I successfully terminate a group? and (2) how do I know whether a group has been helpful to its members?

Although this chapter on the final phase of group treatment is the last chapter in the book, there is a distressing paradox. Logistically, termination and evaluation occur at the end of therapy. They have their genesis, however, in the initial stage of the treatment process and cannot be left to the final stage of therapy to be discussed. Movement toward termination actually begins in the pregroup interview and in the initial session of the group. Evaluation is ongoing and a part of the overall therapeutic experience. Termination and evaluation are placed in the last chapter primarily for the convenience of both the author and the reader.

TERMINATION

In group treatment, there is a beginning, a middle, and an end, each phase having its own dynamics and characteristics. Of the three phases, the ending is probably the least understood and often the most difficult for group members and the leader. It is a difficult period because the members are aware that this special experience—and the community of which they have been a part and which they have helped create—will soon dissolve. Endings involve the discomfort of the present and also touch on discomforts of the past.

Termination is a time to say good-bye to people who have become significant during the lifetime of the group. Group members may have shared pain, sadness, anger, and frustration. Rather than diminishing the members' sense of loss, this sharing will make their separation that much more difficult. Just as beginnings are psychologically imbued with feelings of birth, so endings are imbued, in varying proportion, with the feeling of death and of separation (Smalley, 1967).

Yet, endings are welcomed and even hoped for. Termination carries with it a sense of accomplishment, freedom, and moving on to new situations. The ending of a therapy group means no longer having to be at a certain place at a certain time. It means not having to deal with particular individuals who cause stress and discomfort. Still, group members feel ambivalent: they experience a mixture of sadness and relief.

GRIEVING PROCESS

The grieving process experienced by group members at the end of their group can be likened to the grief process experienced by individuals mourning the death of a friend or relative. Because group members and leaders often form close attachments and bonds, a group's termination requires these individuals to work through the grief they feel over the breakup of their close ties. Movement through the grief process involves group members' giving up the group and substituting something else for it (Hess & Hess, 1984).

Near a group's end, its members may deny that the group is actually ending. They may "forget" that a specific date for termination was discussed during the initial session. They may express anger that "now that things are really happening, it's time for the group to end. Perhaps some group members have just begun to recognize the group's value and to see that they are beginning to grow. They may feel guilty that they have not yet accomplished enough. Or they may regret disclosing certain pieces of information.

It is not unusual for the group members to attempt to strike a bargain with the worker for extension of the group. They might plead, "We are just beginning to come together as a group! How can we quit now?" The members may feel depressed because what has occurred in the group will never be replicated. Finally, however, the members will reach the final step in the grieving process—acceptance. They will acknowledge their loss and begin to think positively about what will take place once the group is over.

Just how individual members and the group-as-a-whole handle a group's termination depends on factors such as how long the group has existed and how much bonding has taken place in it. Members participating in a short-term, open-ended group generally have less of a problem with their group's termination than members of a long-term group. Group members who have developed close bonds and intensive, meaningful relationships in their group usually have greater difficulty giving up the group.

VARIATION IN RESPONSE

A group worker must be careful not to assume that all group members will experience or express their grief in a lockstep fashion or that all the members will react to the group's end with the same intensity and at the same time. For example, one or two members may experience a few of these feelings one week and then appear totally accepting the following week. Other members may experience all of these feelings during a single session.

The group's ending process triggers in the minds of its members reactions that they link to leaving behind other places and other people. Any termination has a way of bringing to the surface past losses buried in the members' unconscious. Perhaps these painful losses and good-byes were never adequately grieved or resolved. The members probably each have memories of parents, lovers, or special friends who left and did not return. They probably have feelings of being abandoned by people who had once professed love and caring but who never bothered to write or, perhaps, even to say good-bye. All these losses can come back to the surface when group members are getting ready to say good-bye to their group.

Reasons for Group Termination

Therapy groups can end for many different reasons. First, and ideally, a group ends because the individual group members and the group-as-a-whole have reached their treatment objectives. The members can expect to function satisfactorily and to continue to progress on their own. When a termination of this nature occurs, it is usually because the members have been involved in goal setting in the early stages of the group.

Second, a group may end because of a predetermined time limit set for it by the group worker and/or the group's members. Time-limited groups are established with the expectation of ending at a certain time, such as in ten weeks, after ten sessions, or just before Christmas. In effect, the process of ending in this type of group is a winding down of the therapeutic process that the group's worker and members hope is no longer needed.

Third, a group may end because it cannot achieve a sufficient level of integration or momentum to function adequately. This situation may result from a lack of interest in or commitment to the group's purpose on the part of the group's members. Or this situation may occur because the sponsoring agency does not have interested or qualified staff to lead the group. Or it may happen because members may have dropped out and no new members were available to replace them.

Fourth, a group may end because its mechanisms for coping with internal or external pressures on its members have become maladaptive (Johnson, 1974). In short, the group has reached a point at which it is harmful to its members or other people. Rather than helping, the group has become destructive.

Not all therapy groups die. Participants in open groups deal with beginnings and endings on a regular basis. Old members leave and new members come. Even when only one or two members terminate, the dynamics of an open group are affected by their loss. Any member who terminates from the group's therapeutic process, at the same time disengages from the attachments he or she has made to multiple others in his or her group.

Termination of a Group

Although a group may end on a predetermined date, as in the case of a time-limited group, not all of the members will be ready to stop at that specific time. Even though some of the members may have reached their goals, others will be far from reaching theirs.

The Group's Reaction

As the date for a group's termination approaches, its members experience discomfort, as well as anticipation. Just as they felt anxiety at coming together in the group's earlier stages, they now feel anxiety about the group's separation and the breaking of the bonds they have formed in the group. Garland, Jones, and Kolodny (1973), in discussing group members' reactions to the termination of a group, note a number of "devices" members typically employ to forestall terminating, on one hand, and to accomplish it, on the other.

One device group members may use is **denial.** They may simply "forget" the group is ending. They may be engaged in **clustering.** In other words, they may band closer together and become a more cohesive group. They may engage in **regression,** or a sliding backward, often characterized by members displaying anger toward and greater dependency on the worker. They may even "perform regressive fugue," using behavior reminiscent of each of the group's earlier developmental stages. In that case, the theme "We still need a group" becomes apparent, as the members attempt to convince the leader that the group is still necessary because their problems have not been resolved. The group members may use **recapitulation,** a reenactment or review of past activities and events in the group. Or the members may opt for **evaluation,** or comparing past events or experiences in the group with things that are presently going on there.

Another device group members may use is **flight** from the reality of the group's termination. This flight may be nihilistic or positive in nature. Nihilistic flight takes the form of missing meetings or dropping out of the group before the date of termination. Positive flight is a more constructive "self-weaning" from the group—by, for example, developing new interests or friends outside the group while continuing as a group member.

INDIVIDUAL REACTIONS

Group members react to the end of their therapy group in various ways. They may decide to end their own participation before the announced last session as a means of controlling their anxiety. Rather than the member "being ended" the member does the ending. They may become very dependent and needy, displaying dysfunctional, or unproductive, behaviors that were apparent during the beginning stages of the group. The message embedded within their behavior is "Don't end the group yet. My problems have come back!"

Henry (1981) observes that group members often become excessively compliant and conforming, even coming early for sessions with the hope of conveying to the group worker the importance that they attach to the worker and to the group experience. It is as if they could "buy" the continuation of the group by becoming very "good" members. The member may begin to bring gifts; invite the worker to dinner; request continued social interaction with the worker after the group ends; ask to become friends with the worker; and offer their address with the hope of establishing an ongoing relationship with the worker.

WORKER'S REACTION

A group leader is by no means immune to the effects of groups' members' departures and groups' endings. In the same way that clients are touched by separation, loss, and good-byes, the worker has memories and affects that are stirred. And these can produce potentially powerful countertransference. The therapist may find numerous reasons to interfere with a client's departure, reflecting the therapist's own separation problems. Similarly, the worker may be uncomfortable with the wide range of intense emotions evoked by terminations and therefore may not address group member's resistance, and acting out, which are part of every termination (Rutan & Stone, 1984).

In instances of premature terminations, a worker may suffer the narcissistic wound of not having been successful or being rejected. In an especially difficult group, the worker may fear that if one member leaves, others will soon follow. What is difficult for the worker to deal with in that case is the sense of losing control and the fear of looking bad in the eyes of others.

In the same way that separation triggers feelings in a group's members, it also triggers feelings in the group's leader. The worker's ability to deal with these feelings in the helping interaction depends on an acute awareness of the meaning of separation in the worker's own life. Therefore, the clinician's own experiences with separation and assumptions about clients' feelings emerge as areas that require much reflection on the part of the clinician (Hess & Hess, 1984).

FOCUSING ON TERMINATION

The leader of a time-limited group has to repeatedly call the group members' attention to the group's termination. This is a must at the group's beginning and becomes a dominant theme as the group reaches the midpoint. There is a natural temptation, aided by the members' resistance, for a worker to discount the importance of the approaching ending. The worker walks a fine line between holding the reality of the group's termination before the group members and helping the group continue to work until the last member walks out the door.

The worker helps the members understand their reaction to the termination process. Metaphors of death, divorce, and graduation begin to surface and are explored. Irregularly attending members are helped to understand their behaviors. Members who resonate to the theme of good-bye from their own personal histories of unresolved grief are helped to put their losses into perspective.

The final phase in the life of a group is critical, for this is the time when the group's members consolidate their learning. It is a time to discuss members' accomplishments, as well as areas of continuing concern. This "accounting" is a realistic appraisal of whether, and to what degree, individual and group goals have been achieved.

273

As a group comes to a close, it is useful for the worker to have each group member share a brief summary of how the member perceives himself or herself in the group, major issues he or she has dealt with, achievements, conflicts, turning points, and work left unfinished. It is also useful for the worker to follow-up each member's self-summary with a request that the rest of the group describe what they perceive and feel about the individual. While the giving and receiving of feedback has been a regular part of the group, this final summation is often what all the members carry with them long after the group has ended.

TERMINATION BY A MEMBER

Patterns of endings in groups are as diverse as patterns of beginnings. Some people quit with advance notice; others disappear, after one or two sessions, never showing up again. Some quit prematurely; others leave once they have achieved specific goals. In many instances, clients leave a group because they are worn out from their work in the group yet are still experiencing no appreciable difference in their lives.

If a client terminates early in a group's development, his or her leaving generally has little impact on other group members. If, on the other hand, the group has become a cohesive unit, group members who remain may feel both guilt and envy. Their guilt arises from their belief that they did something to drive the departed member away. Comments characteristic of such guilt are as follows:

- "Did we say something to hurt him?"
- "What could we have done to keep him in the group?"
- "I knew he was unhappy and didn't say anything."
- "I wish I wouldn't have pushed him so hard."

The group members' envy is based on the ambivalence experienced by every member in the group. In spite of each person's commitment and attendance, a part of him or her wishes to avoid belonging to the group. Similarly, a part of each group member does not want to experience the difficult and painful task of growing. Therefore, one client's leaving represents something the rest of the group would also like to do. This feeling is masked by reaction formation in the remaining members, and they increase their dedication to the group. The more mature the group, the greater the potential for the worker to help its members to examine their feelings of guilt, envy, and anger.

MEMBER DISSATISFACTION

Individual group members terminate because they are dissatisfied with their own progress, with their relationships with other group members or with the group leader, or with some combination of these. When a client withdraws without notification, the question for the worker becomes this: how much energy should I put into contacting the client for follow-up, closure, or a possible return to the group?

Even though the worker may be frustrated or angry with the member for not giving notice, it is advisable for the worker to contact the person to determine if he or she has, in fact, terminated and to discover his or her intentions. The worker can then invite the individual back for one final session to share thoughts and feelings with the group. It is not unusual for the individual, upon returning to the group, to talk about his or her frustration, disappointment, or other feelings and then to rejoin the group with an increased sense of commitment.

Often, a member's decision to leave a group is not an isolated event. Instead, the decision is a continuation of a long-standing behavioral pattern—for example, a pattern of leaving the scene when he or she is being challenged or when other group members do not agree with him or her. If this is the case, the clinician needs to help the departing member examine the pattern, looking not only at the present situation but also at what has transpired in the past. Needless to say, the worker must do this with considerable empathy and tact because of the potential threat to the client's self-esteem. On occasion, the whole process is a test unconsciously designed by a client to discover whether the worker or the group really care to have the client stay.

Focusing just on the client in question, according to Rutan and Stone (1984), is usually insufficient to understand fully what is occurring. Rather, the group worker needs to focus on both the client and the group situation. It is useful for the worker to help the client be curious about the decision to leave at a particular point in time. By understanding the decision to leave in the context of the group process, the client can put into perspective not only his or her own actions, but also what is occurring in the group. Doing this provides both the client and the worker a more comprehensive and dynamic understanding of the client's impetus for wishing to leave. Doing this also makes it easier for the client to remain in the group in a face-saving manner.

A group member's premature termination places in bold relief the very real limitations on the influence the group worker or the group-as-a-whole can have on a member's personal decisions. As therapists, we may believe sincerely that someone should definitely not leave a group and may make every effort to communicate this conviction, yet the client may still leave.

In subscribing to the principle of self-determination as social workers, we must keep in mind that we are not experts on what is right for clients. We can assist them in considering possible alternatives and the consequences. We can also share with the clients our own thinking, not as a way of directing their lives, but rather as an additional source of information for them to consider.

A clinician, according to Brenner (1982), never knows what will be the "final" session for a client. Any visit, including the first, may be the last. Therefore, he advises this:

275

Do your best work in each and every meeting, respect clients' rights to come and go as they please, and you will have a lasting influence on many people who come to you for help. Further, they likely will consider seeing you again— or will be reassured by the knowledge that they may if they wish—if life's stresses become too great [p. 103].

COMPLETED TREATMENT

In a successful group-treatment program, the group worker, the terminating member, and the other group members can all see signs that the client is preparing to leave the group because the client is about to meet his or her treatment objectives. They can see evidence of the client's transfer of learning and greater functional risk taking. They hear reports by the client that he or she is functioning better outside the group. They can also see that the group is becoming less important to the client and that the client is developing new resources in his or her life that are sustaining and life-giving. Generally, the client has been in the group for some time and have seen new members enter treatment and improved members terminate their treatment. The client has witnessed a spectrum of terminations before saying their own good-byes.

It is not unusual for a group worker to allow too little time for group members to process and learn from the feelings generated by termination. A client's actual departure date should be far enough in the future to allow for full exploration and elaboration of the event by the client and the group. As a rough guideline, this entire process might take one month for each year that the client has been in the group (Rutan & Stone, 1984).

As is the case near the termination of a group-as-a-whole, an accounting or assessment of how well a departing client has achieved his or her goals is in order. The client should be helped to address what brought him or her to the group in the first place, things he or she has accomplished, as well as things left for the client to do. It is important for the client to share his or her goals beyond the group with the group.

Levine (1979), observing the effect of a client's termination on his or her group, writes that a group member who plays certain roles is more definitely missed than a group member who plays other roles. For example, a group member who has been a stimulator of discussion or an injector of anxiety will be more directly missed. Most dramatic to a group, however, will be the loss of the "group thermostat"—the person who cuts off members' rising anxiety. Without someone there to decrease their level of anxiety, the group members now become more frightened of anxiety-laden subjects.

• Techniques: Practical considerations

1. Remind each group early about the date of its termination.
2. As leaders, we may want to disclose to the members of a terminating group our own feelings about the groups' coming to an end.
3. Have group members speak in concrete terms about their feelings and what they have accomplished.

4. Set aside time for unfinished business.
5. Encourage departing group members to share how they will apply what they have learned in the group to their future problems.

EVALUATION OF OUTCOME

Basic to the helping process in general and to its termination in particular is an assessment of whether or not the treatment program was effective and efficient and whether it achieved its intended goals. More specifically, these questions must be answered: Who was helped most by the group? Who failed to profit from the experience? Who was hurt by it? To what extent were the group members committed to change their behavior?

While few clinicians would argue with the integration of research and group work or the value of a practitioner's using research to systematically evaluate his or her practice, there has been a dearth of information on such evaluation. Of the more traditional textbooks on social group work, relatively few (Glasser, Sarri & Vinter, 1974; Garvin, 1981; Toseland & Rivas, 1984) have attempted to build a bridge between practice and research in work with groups.

The idea of evaluation is a thorny issue for most practitioners, whether they work with individuals, families, or groups. On the one hand, group workers feel pressured to evaluate their practice out of a need for accountability and for an empirically validated practice. On the other hand, the demands of a practice are extensive and require a tremendous amount of time and energy. The bottom line is that few workers systematically evaluate their practice. Therefore, the supposed linkage between research and clinical social work practice is practically nonexistent.

In spite of this reality, there are significant practical benefits that group workers can derive from conducting an evaluation of their group work (Toseland & Rivas 1984):

1. Evaluations can satisfy the workers' curiosity and professional concerns about the effects of specific interventions they perform while working with a group.
2. Information from evaluations can help workers improve their leadership skills.
3. Evaluations can demonstrate the usefulness of a specific group or a specific group work method to an agency, a funding source, or society.
4. Evaluations can help workers assess the progress of group members and the group in accomplishing agreed-upon purposes.
5. Evaluation allows group members and others who may be affected to express their satisfactions and dissatisfactions with the group.
6. Evaluations give workers the opportunity to develop knowledge that can be shared with others who are using group methods for similar purposes and in similar situations [p. 304].

METHODS OF EVALUATION

There are a multitude of approaches to collecting information about group work. These include collecting testimonials, reports, and group histories; making direct observations; reviewing audiotapes or videotapes of group meetings; and using reliable scales and measures.

A fundamental question in selecting a method of evaluation is the degree of objectivity versus subjectivity that the method involves. Corey (1990), characteristic of many group workers, underscores the value of objectively assessing a group. He laments, however, the lack of adequate instruments sensitive enough to discern changes in clients. In spite of the use of a variety of tests and inventories used both before and after a group experience, he says, "none of these measures were adequate in detecting subtle changes in attitudes, beliefs, feelings and behavior. Consequently, I have come to rely on subjective measures that include a variety of self-reports" (p. 138).

TESTIMONIALS

A widely used evaluation measure is a written or an oral self-report in which the group member and, for example, his or her parents and child-care worker are asked to respond to a series of questions about a particular phenomenon. As part of his or her testimonial, each respondent reports his or her observations, telling what he or she thinks. Questions asked of a client during this evaluation might include: "Were you satisfied with the group?" "In what ways have you changed from being in the group?" and "Have your changes been lasting so far?"

The following statements is from the journals of a group member in a self-actualization group:

> I sometimes think as a recovering addict that I'm different from so-called "normal people" in that I'm too emotional. After being in the group, I realized that "I'm ok, you're ok," and even though my past experiences or my socioeconomic level may be different, we all came together where feelings were involved. The group was a real healing time for me.

Another member wrote,

> I feel that I gave a lot to this group, risked to a great extent, and consequently learned a great deal about myself and my style of interaction. I thoroughly enjoyed the experience and feel that its fortuitous convergence with my individual therapy has helped me to understand and accept myself just a bit more.

According to Rogers (1970a), a naturalistic study that focuses on the personal and subjective views of a group's members provides the deepest insights into the significance of their group experience. These self-reports provide insight into the process and the outcomes from the members' personal perspective. According to Rogers, this phenomenological type of study "may well be the most fruitful way of advancing our knowledge in these subtle and unknown fields" (p. 133).

Corey (1990) uses subjective reports in the form of "reaction papers," individual postgroup interviews, follow-up meetings, and questionnaires mailed to group members. Before a group begins, its members are asked to write down their concerns and what they expect from the group. During their group-treatment program, they are encouraged to keep an ongoing journal of their experiences both in the group and outside the group. Shortly before the group ends, Corey has the members write several reaction papers, with each paper recounting a significant occurrence in the group and describing what the member liked best and least about the experience.

Once the group ends, Corey again asks the members to write reaction papers evaluating their experiences. During a postgroup meeting, the members are requested to fill out a brief questionnaire evaluating the techniques used, the group leader, the impact of the group on them, and the degree to which they think they have changed because of their participation in the group.

It would appear that the simplest and most direct means of assessing a client's progress in treatment is to talk to the client directly. However, this approach is fraught with serious pitfalls. Standards for such reporting vary among clients and between clients and their group leader. The reports are subject to various unconscious distortions, as well as to conscious or semiconscious motives.

Out of deference and courtesy toward the group worker, for example, a client may feel duty-bound to express gratitude and satisfaction. If so, the message "Your group made a new person out of me!" or "What happened to me was just too special to describe!" will come through loud and clear. Although such testimonials are manna to the practitioner's ego, they may have little validity.

CONTENT ANALYSIS

From an analysis of a group interaction, a group worker can obtain other group members' reactions to a specific client, as well as a client's reactions to himself and to others. Such a content analysis has been used to study workers' interventions, group members' expectations, and initial group meetings (Duehn & O'Conner, 1972; Gentry, 1974, 1978; and Brown, 1971).

Gentry (1978), in discussing the use of audiotapes in analyzing the content of group sessions, notes two key concepts that need to be determined in advance: (1) the unit for analysis or scoring and (2) the categories for analysis. The unit for analysis or scoring refers to the portion of content that will be the standard measure uniformly used as each session's content is coded. This unit provides the boundaries or criteria for the study of all the session's content. For example, a unit for analysis could be a single verbal action by any group member or the leader, bounded on either side by the speech of anyone else.

The **categories for analysis** refers to the classification scheme by which the units of content are systematically organized for coding and counting. An example of categories for analysis might be the themes or topics discussed in the group session.

PROCESS ANALYSIS

Whereas content analysis focuses on what is being communicated, process analysis focuses on how it is being communicated. Possible areas of analyses include these: how often each person speaks, where each member sits, whom each member walks in with, how fast each person talks, and how often each person talks to every other person in the room. Group processes such as decision making can be located and described. Process analysis has also been used to examine the number and the length of silences per session.

SOCIOMETRY

Sociometry is a technique for measuring the social relationships that link group members. It can be used to determine the patterns of interaction between group members and the degree to which each member is accepted into the group by the other members. Although a simple procedure, it yields a comprehensive picture of a group and thus facilitates in-depth understanding of how the group functions.

To use this evaluation method, a group worker can develop a written questionnaire tailored to a specific group, taking into account the group members' ages, socioemotional levels, and typical activities. The test should be broad enough to include questions related to a wide range of group activities such as work, play, emotional-support, and other activities. The questions should be worded in such a way that members state their preferences regarding other group members. In each question, the individual should be asked to name a limited number of group members— usually three—with whom they would like to spend time.

The following questions are typical of the kind asked on a sociometric test:

Work: List three members with whom you would like to work.
Play: Name three members with whom you would like to go to a basketball game.
Emotional support: Which three members would you go to if you were sad or in pain?
Social activity: Identify three members you would like to have as friends.

This kind of questionnaire can be administered to the entire group at one time or to individual group members at different times. While far from being a precise measure, this kind of test does indicate which group members are the group favorites, which members are infrequently chosen, and which members form pairs— list each other as their first choice. From these lists of preferences, the worker can plot out the subgroupings, the isolates, and the indigenous leaders in the group, as defined by their peers.

While a sociometric measure can be used at any point in a group's development, it has particular value in a group's early stages and again as the group comes to an end. The data the worker collects provides a simple measurement of how members subjectively feel about one another and the degree to which their feelings change over time. The data also can be correlated with such phenomena as members' attendance and participation in the group and the group's productivity.

A more process-oriented form of sociometrics is the "subjective" sociogram. This sociogram depicts the seating arrangements of people in any given group session. It shows who talks to whom and the amount of time each set of individuals talks. The Interaction Process Analysis scale developed by Bales (1950, 1970) is one instrument available for analyzing group interactions related to task and maintenance issues. Because of the difficulty of simultaneously leading the group and using such an instrument, however, a group leader who wants to develop this kind of sociogram must have the assistance of an observer.

Some observations do provide the quality of information that leads to obvious interpretations or conclusions. Much of what comes out of the analysis, however, will be conjecture and should be checked out with the group members or repeated over time, for accuracy (Posthuma, 1989). According to Heap (1977), the interpretation of sociograms, beyond the membership of subgroups and the ratings and direction of attraction and isolation, are only speculative. Without using other kinds of supplementary observations and tests, a group leader cannot deduce the emotional content of the relationships, the qualitative aspects of the relationships, or the causative explanations of the relationships.

MEASUREMENT INSTRUMENTS

For group members with certain socioemotional needs, there are a multitude of self-rating instruments available. Self-rating tests are usually given to group members right after a group begins and then again at the conclusion of the group. Some examples of commonly used self-rating inventories with particular themes are as follows: for aggressive, unassertive, or shy individuals, the Gambrill-Richey Assertion Inventory; for anxiety-related problems, the S-R Inventory of Anxiousness by Endler, Hunt, and Rosenstein (1962).

Another self-rating resource is the CORE Battery, an evaluation kit developed by the Research Committee of the American Group Psychotherapy Association (MacKenzie & Dies, 1982). It includes multiple measures, elicits both objective and subjective viewpoints, and evaluates subjective impressions by comparing them with behavioral observations. The CORE

Battery also combines individualized measurements and assesses various areas of group member's functioning. Such a package, or even parts of it, can simplify an evaluation by the practitioner, striking a reasonable compromise between comprehensiveness and realistic time demands (Anderson, 1986).

An innovative approach is the Clinical Measurement Package developed by Hudson (1982). This set of paper-and-pencil scales are used as a repeated measure in single-system research. Easy to administer and score, these scales address group members' depression, self-esteem, marital discord, sexual discord, parent-child relationships, intrafamilial stress, and peer relationships.

A problem with many of the self-rating instruments used in group research is that they are often not relevant to the group members' experiences within the sessions. Too often, workers using pretest/posttest designs have assumed that as long as they can demonstrate the efficacy of their interventions, what happens during the sessions makes little difference Dies & MacKenzie, 1983). A way to evaluate a group's outcome from the standpoint of the individual group member's unique experiences within the treatment settings is to measure repeatedly during the course of treatment—instead of just at the beginning and at the end. Doing this serves to keep group members task-oriented and provides regular monitoring of each client's progress.

SINGLE-SUBJECT RESEARCH

Single-subject design refers to the repeated collection of information on a single system over time. For our purposes, the "system" can be either an individual or a group. It can also be a family, an organization, a community, or some other collectivity. According to Bloom and Fisher (1982), there are a number of specific steps to follow in using a single-system design:

Specify the problem. A key aspect is specifying the problem that the practitioner and the client agree needs to be changed.

Measure the problem. Whether the problems are thoughts, communication patterns, group activities, or feelings, there has to be measurement.

Repeated measures. The heart of single-system research is collecting repeated information over a period of time.

Baseline. Before intervention is begun, data on the problem is collected. This baseline data is used in the assessment and later as a basis for comparison with data collected while the actual intervention program is being carried out.

Design. Ways of collecting data are established in advance.

Clear definition of intervention. The intervention being used needs to be specified. There is a logical relationship between the intervention program and the problem the worker is trying to change.

Analysis of data. Single-system designs rely heavily on visual analysis of changes in the data [pp.8-9].

TARGET BEHAVIORS

As group workers, we target for change some aspect of the each group member's functioning. That is, we decide what is to be measured before and after our intervention so we can monitor the effects of our intervention. The term targeting implies that any change we want to bring about in the member's functioning is either a goal of treatment or an indicator of progress toward a treatment goal (Nelsen, 1981). We might, for example, target the number of times a child misses school each month and then use that target as an indicator of progress toward a treatment goal we have set for the child.

To conduct single-subject research, we must make sure our treatment goals are stated specifically and precisely. We must include the conditions under which each goal will be reached. For example, we might say, "by the end of his treatment program, Fred will be attending school five days a week, unless he is sick." Or "By the end of her treatment program, Heather will be able to sit through a group session without talking to herself or walking out." Too often, practitioners state goals in long-term, global terms or in such a manner that they cannot be operationally defined.

Similarly, goals are frequently stated in a such a way that they cannot be measured. Because of their vagueness, they have little or no validity. This is illustrated in the following goals:

- "John will feel better about himself."
- "John will develop a better self-image."
- "John will get along better in the group."
- "John will have more friends."

While the goals "John will feel better about himself" and "John will develop a better self-image" are not inappropriate, they need to be made less global and more precise. The practitioner might compile, along with John, a list of behaviors the young man will display when he does feel better about himself—examples might include requesting a date, joining a fraternity, or talking more positively about himself.

INTERMEDIATE GOALS

Practitioners, as well as group members, need some way stations on the road to the members' final goals. These way stations are intermediate goals, or direct, recognizable steps that can be taken toward the achievement of a final goal. In a situation where a child is not attending school, for example, a long-term goal might be the child's full attendance every school day. An intermediate goal might be for the child to get up in time for the school bus and to attend school three days a week.

A type of goal closely linked to intermediate goals are **facilitative goals.** These goals are absolutely necessary for the final goals to be reached.

••••••••

Examples of facilitative goals are for the member to continue in the group, to share his or her feelings in the group, to behave constructively in sessions, and to stay in the room even when he or she is angry.

MONITORING

Group workers need to be aware of what goals group members are achieving and what interventions seem to be helpful. A way group workers can stay abreast of these matters is by ensuring that someone is monitoring or counting individual or group behaviors. This monitoring can be done by the worker, by the group member, or by someone else, and it can be done using a variety of methods.

Group worker as monitor. A group worker can only monitor those behaviors that occur in the group. Still, the group worker is in a unique position to measure those changes. One of the advantages of the therapist's being the monitor is that the monitoring process is then viewed by the group member as a central part of the treatment. Also, immediate feedback about ongoing changes in the group is available to the worker. If, for example, a member's maladaptive behaviors are increasing and the member's adaptive ones are decreasing, the leader knows immediately that what he or she has been doing is ineffective, possibly detrimental, and needs to be altered (Rose, 1973).

Self-monitoring. Similar in nature to monitoring by a group worker but potentially more accurate is *self-monitoring, self-observation,* or *self-recording*. These are terms used to describe clients' records of their own behaviors, thoughts, and feelings. Self-monitoring is a two-step process: (1) a client identifies occurrences of a particular behavior and then (2) systematically records his or her observations of it. Generally, self-monitored records are frequencies of inner behaviors or observable events converted into a rate of the number of times the behavior has occurred. The results are graphed or charted so that both the client and the worker can observe what change has occurred over time (Kopp, 1988).

Diaries or logs. A diary or log is an organized journal of any event or activity occurring outside the group that a member considers relevant to his or her problem. This device serves the purpose of helping the member systematically and objectively chart events in order to avoid any distortions of memory when he or she later presents the information to the group. Client diaries includes a prepared form that has listed across its top the types of information the worker wants collected (Bloom & Fisher, 1982). This list will vary with the nature of the client's problem but generally involves the reporting whether or not some event or behavior occurred that affected the client's problem. It also includes how the individual responded.

Role-playing. Another way group workers can collect data on group members' progress is through the use of role-playing in the group (Rose, 1981). To save the group's time, a group worker can have group members prepare in pairs or triads for later role-playing in front of the group. One member in each subgroup can prepare a role-play of an actual experience that has happened to him or her during the week, instructing one or more subgroup members in the role of the significant others. Eventually, each pair or triad will present the situation to the entire group. Often used in conjunction with group members' diaries, role-playing helps define the situations that have occurred in group members' lives outside the group.

Pretest/Posttest. A simple pretest/posttest design is highly compatible with clinical practice. For example, checklists that are standardized instruments with extensive norms and empirical support—such as the Self-Report Inventory in the CORE Battery—are easy to use. Such a checklist is something members can readily complete and workers can easily score (Anderson, 1986). It can be used in pretesting for an initial assessment and then used in posttesting for a final evaluation.

IN SUMMARY

The ending phase of group treatment can be any type of termination of or from a group—planned or unplanned. Ideally, the termination of a client's treatment occurs when the client no longer needs the group. Planned terminations occur when the leader makes a judgment that there has been sufficient progress or the group ends at an established time. Unplanned terminations occur when clients leave a group prematurely. Generally, the ending of a treatment program—planned or unplanned—generates both positive and negative feelings in the group worker and group members. As any treatment program comes to an end, the worker and members should review what has been accomplished, anticipate future problems insofar as they are able to do so, and say their good-byes. To the extent that it is appropriate, the group worker should encourage group members to mourn their loss of the group.

Evaluating the outcome of a treatment program is another part of the ending process. The group worker should evaluate the results of the treatment process to find out whether or not the group's purpose and each member's goals were realized. There are a number of data-collection tools available for monitoring a group. These include testimonials, content analysis, and sociometry. The single-system research method is a vehicle for measuring the degree of change that has occurred in each group member. Evaluation is made more precise if there is a method for assessing changes in attitudes, relationships, and behaviors periodically during the life of the group. Finally, the group worker's appraisal of the quality of his or her practice and its outcome is an ongoing process.

SUGGESTED READINGS

ANDERSON, J. (1986). Integrating research and practice in social work with groups. *Social work with groups, 9*(3), 111–124.

BLOOM, M., & FISHER, J. (1982). *Evaluating practice: Guidelines for the account-able professional.* Englewood Cliffs, N.J.: Prentice-Hall. See Chapter 11.

DIES, R., and MacKENZIE, K. (Eds.). (1983). *Advances in group psychotherapy: Integrating research and practice.* New York: International Universities Press. See Chapter 1.

JOHNSON, C. (1974). Planning for termination of the group. In P. Glasser, R. Sarri, & R. Vinter (Eds.), *Individual change through small groups* (pp. 258-265). New York: Free Press.

NELSEN, J. (1981). Issues in single-sbuject research for nonbehaviorists. *Social work research & abstracts, 17*(2), 31–37.

ROSE, S. (1981). Assessment in groups. *Social work research & abstracts, 17*(1), 29–37.

YALOM, I. (1985). *The theory and practice of group psychotherapy* (3rd ed.). New York: Basic Books.

EPILOGUE ....

In discussing the process of becoming a writer, the author Flannery O'Connor has observed, "One thing that is always with the writer, no matter how long he has written or how good he is, is the continuous process of learning how to write." This axiom also holds true for social workers' leading of groups. One thing that is always with the practitioner, no matter how long he or she has led groups or how effective he or she is, is the continuous process of learning how to lead.

REFERENCES ....

ABRAMSON, M. (1975). Group treatment of families of burn-injured patients. *Social casework, 56*(4), 235–241.

ADDAMS, J. (1909). *The spirit of youth and the city streets*. New York: Macmillan.

AGUILERA, D., & MESSICK, J. (1982). *Crisis intervention: Theory and methodology* (4th ed.). St. Louis: C. V. Mosby.

ALDRIDGE, G. (1953). Program in a camp for emotionally disturbed boys. *The group, 16*(2), 13.

ANDERSON, J. (1984). *Counseling through group process*. New York: Springer.

ANDERSON, J. (1986). Integrating research and practice in social work with groups. *Social work with groups, 9*(3), 111–124.

ARIES, E. (1973). *Interaction patterns and themes of male, female and mixed groups*. Unpublished doctoral dissertation, Harvard University, Cambridge, Mass.

BACH, G. (1954). *Intensive group psychotherapy*. New York: Ronald Press.

BACH, G., & GOLDBERG, H. (1974). *Creative aggression*. Garden City, N.Y.: Doubleday.

BALDEN-POWELL, R. (1909). *Scouting for boys*. London.

BALES, R. (1950). *Interaction process analysis: A method for the study of small groups*. Reading, Mass.: Addison-Wesley.

BALES, R. (1970). *Personality and interpersonal behavior*. New York: Holt, Rinehart & Winston.

BALGOPAL, P., & VASSIL, T. (1983). *Groups in social work: An ecological perspective*. New York: Macmillan.

BANDLER, R., GRINDER, J., & SATIR, V. (1976). *Changing with families*. Palo Alto, Calif.: Science and Behavior Books.

BARATZ, S., & BARATZ, J. (1970). Early childhood intervention: The social science base of institutional racism. *Harvard educational review, 40*, 29–50.

BARBER, W. (1985). Cancer ward staff group: An intervention designed to prevent disaster. *Small group behavior, 16*(3), 339–353.

BARNETT, H. (1918). *Cannon Barnett, his life, work and friends*. London: John Murry.

BENJAMIN, A. (1981). *The helping interview* (3rd ed.). Boston: Houghton Mifflin.

BENJAMIN, A. (1978). *Behavior in small groups*. Boston: Houghton Mifflin.

BENNE, K., & SHEATS, P. (1948). Functional roles of group members. *Journal of social issues, 4*(2), 41–49.

BENNIS, W., & SHEPARD, H. (1956). A theory of group development. *Human relations, 9*(4).

BERTCHER, H., & MAPLE, F. (1974). Elements and issues in group composition. In P. Glasser, R. Sarri, & R. Vinter (Eds.), *Individual change through small groups* (pp. 186–208). New York: Free Press.

BEUKENKAMP, C. (1952). Some observations made during group therapy. *Psychiatric quarterly supplement, 26,* 22–26.

BINFIELD, C. (1973). *George Williams and the Y.M.C.A.* London: Heinemann.

BLOCH, D. (1978). *"So the witch won't eat me": Fantasy and the child's fear of infanticide.* Boston: Houghton Mifflin.

BLOCH, S., & CROUCH, E. (1985). *Therapeutic factors in group psychotherapy.* Oxford: Oxford University Press.

BLOOM, M., & FISHER, J. (1982). *Evaluating practice: Guidelines for the accountable professional.* Englewood Cliffs, N.J.: Prentice-Hall.

BOGARDUS, E. (1937). Ten standards for group work. *Sociology and social research, 21,* 176.

BOGARDUS, E. (1939). The philosophy of group work. *Sociology and social research, 23*(July/August), 567.

BONNER, H. (1965). *On being mindful of man.* Boston: Houghton Mifflin.

BOYD, N. (1935). Group work experiments in state institutions in Illinois. In *Proceedings of the National Conference of Social Work 1935* (pp. 339–352). Chicago: University of Chicago Press.

BRAATEN, L. (1975). Developmental phases of encounter groups and related intensive groups. *Interpersonal development, 5,* 112–129.

BRENNER, D. (1982). *The effective psychotherapist: Conclusions from practice and research.* New York: Pergamon Press.

BRETON, M. (1985). Reaching and engaging people: Issues and practice principles. *Social work with groups, 8*(3), 7–21.

BROWN, J., & AREVALO, R. (1979), Chicanos and social group work models. *Social work with groups, 2*(4), 331–342.

BROWN, L. (1971). *Social workers' verbal acts and the development of mutual expectations with beginning client groups.* Unpublished doctoral dissertation, Columbia University, New York.

BUCHANAN, D. (1976). Group therapy for kidney transplant patients. *International journal of psychiatry in medicine, 6*(4), 523–531.

BUNKER, D., & WIJNBERG, M. (1988). *Supervision and performance: Managing professional work in human service organizations.* San Francisco: Jossey-Bass.

BURTON, A. (1972). The therapist has a small pain. In A. Burton and Associates (Eds.), *Twelve therapists: How they live and actualize themselves* (p. 194). San Francisco: Jossey-Bass.

CAMERON, N. (1963). *Personality development and psychopathology: A dynamic approach.* Boston: Houghton Mifflin.

CARKHUFF, R., & BERENSON, B. (1967). *Beyond counseling and therapy.* New York: Holt, Rinehart, & Winston.

CARKHUFF, R., KRATOCHVIL, D., & FRIEL, T. (1968). The effects of professional training: Communication and discrimination of facilitative conditions. *Journal of counseling psychology, 15*(1) 102–106.

CARLOCK, C., & MARTIN, P. (1977). Sex composition and the intensive group experience. *Social work, 22*(1), 27–32.

CARTWRIGHT, R., & LERNER, B. (1963). Empathy, need to change and improvement with psychotherapy. *Journal of consulting psychology, 27,* 138–144.

CHEKHOV, A. (1964). Ward 6. In D. Magarshack, (Trans.), *Lady with Lapdog and other stories* (pp. 131–186). London: Penguin. (Original work published 1892)

COELHO, G., HAMBURG, D., & ADAMS, J. (1974). *Coping and adaptation.* New York: Basic Books.

COFER, D., & NIR, Y. (1976). Theme-focused group therapy on a pediatric ward. *International Journal of Psychiatry in Medicine, 6*(4), 541–550.

COLSON, D., ALLEN, J., COYNE, L., DEXTER, N., JEHL, N., MAYER, C., & SPOHN, H. (1986). An anatomy of countertransference: Staff reactions to difficult psychiatric hospital patients. *Hospital and community psychiatry, 37,* 923–928.

COMBS, A., & AVILA, D. (1985). *Helping relationships: Basic concepts for the helping professions.* Boston: Allyn & Bacon.

COMPTON, B. & GALAWAY, B. (1984). *Social work processes* (3rd eds.). Homewood, Ill.: Dorsey Press.

COREY, G. (1990). *Theory and practice of group counseling* (3rd ed.). Pacific Grove, Calif.: Brooks/Cole.

COREY, G., COREY, M., CALLANAN, P., & RUSSELL, M. (1988). *Group techniques* (rev. ed). Pacific Grove, Calif.: Brooks/Cole.

COREY, M., & COREY, G. (1987). *Groups: Process and practice* (3rd ed.). Pacific Grove, Calif.: Brooks/Cole.

CORSINI, R., & ROSENBERG, B. (1955). Mechanism of group therapy: Processes and dynamics. *Journal of abnormal and social psychology, 51,* 406–411.

COSER, L. (1956). *The functions of social conflict.* New York: Free Press.

COURNOYER, B. (1984). Basic communication skills for work with groups. In B. Compton & B. Galaway (Eds.). *Social work processes* (3rd ed.). Homewood, Ill.: Dorsey Press, 294–303.

COWGER, C. (1979). Conflict and conflict management in working with groups. *Social work with groups, 2*(4), 309–320.

COYLE, G. (1960). Group work in psychiatric settings: Its roots and branches. In *Use of groups in the psychiatric setting,* (pp. 12–45). New York: National Association of Social Workers.

COZBY, P. (1973). Self-disclosure: A literature review. *Psychological bulletin, 79,* 73–91.

CROSBY, C. (1978). A group experience for elderly, socially isolated widows. *Social work with groups, 1*(4), 345–354.

CUDNEY, M. (1975). *Eliminating self-defeating behaviors.* Kalamazoo, Mich.: Life Giving Enterprises.

CUMINGS, J., & CUMINGS, E. (1962). *Ego and milieu.* London: Tavistock Publications.

DANISH, S., D'AUGELLI, A., & BROCK, G. (1976). An evaluation of helping skills training: Effects on helper's verbal responses. *Journal of counseling psychology, 23,* 259–266.

DAVIS, L. (1979). Racial composition of groups. *Social work, 24,* 208–213.

DAVIS, L. (1980). Racial balance: A psychological issue. *Social work with groups, 3*(2), 75–85.

DAVIS, L. (1984). Essential components of group work with black Americans. *Social work with groups, 7*(3), 97–109.

DAVIS, M., SHARFSTEIN, S., & OWENS, M. (1974). Separate and together: All black

291
• • • • • • • •

therapist group in the white hospital. *American journal of orthopsychiatry, 44,* 19–25.

DICKERSON, M. (1981). *Social work practice with the mentally retarded.* New York: Free Press.

DIES, R., & MACKENZIE, K. (Eds.). (1983). Advances in group psychotherapy: Integrating research and practice. New York: International Universities Press.

DINKMEYER, D., & MURO, J. (1971). *Group counseling: Theory and practice.* Itasca, Ill.: F. E. Peacock.

DOUDS, J., BERENSON, B., CARKHUFF, R., & PIERCE, R. (1967). In search of an honest experience: Confrontation in counseling and life. In R. Carkhuff & B. Berenson. *Beyond counseling and therapy* (pp. 170–179). New York: Holt, Rinehart & Winston.

DOUGLAS, T. (1976). *Groupwork practice.* New York: International Universities Press.

DUEHN, W., & O'CONNER, R. (1972, November). *A study of client content expectancies as related to interactional process during short-term group counseling.* Paper presented at the First Southwest Regional Meeting of the American Orthopsychiatric Association, Galveston, Tex.

DURKIN, H. (1981). Foundations of autonomous living structures. In H. Durkin (Ed.) *Living groups: Group psychotherapy and general systems theory* (pp. 75–103). New York: Brunner/Mazel.

DYER, W. & VRIEND, J. (1975). *Counseling techniques that work: Application to individual and group counseling.* Washington, D.C.: APGA Press.

EDWARDS, A. (1982). The consequences of error in selecting treatment for blacks. *Social casework, 63*(7), 429–433.

EDWARDS, E. & EDWARDS, M. (1980). American Indians: Working with individuals and groups. *Social casework, 61,* 498–506.

EGAN, G. (1970). *Encounter: Group processes for interpersonal growth.* Pacific Grove, Calif.: Brooks/Cole.

EGAN, G. (1982). *The skilled helper: A model for systematic helping and interpersonal relating.* (2nd ed.). Pacific Grove, Calif.: Brooks/Cole.

EGAN, G. (1990). *The skilled helper: A systematic approach to effective helping* (4th. ed.). Pacific Grove, Calif.:Brooks/Cole.

EISNER, E. (1979). *The educational imagination: On the design and evaluation of school programs.* New York: Macmillan.

ENDLER, N., HUNT, J., & ROSENSTEIN, A. (1962). An S-R Inventory of Anxiousness. *Psychological monographs, 76* (536).

ERIKSON, E. (1959). *Identity and the life cycle.* New York: International Universities Press.

ERICKSON, R. (1987). The question of casualties in inpatient small group psychotherapy. *Small group behavior. 18*(4), 443–457.

ETCHEVERRY, R., SIPORIN, M., & TOSELAND, R. (1986). The uses and abuses of role-playing. In P. Glasser & N. Mayadas (Eds.), *Group workers at work: Theory and practice in the 80's* (pp. 116–130). Totowa, N.J.: Rowman & Littlefield.

ETTIN, M. (1986). Within the group's view: Clarifying dynamics through metaphoric and symbolic imagery. *Small group behavior, 17*(4), 407–426.

FISHER, J. (1978). *Effective casework practice: An eclectic approach.* New York: McGraw-Hill.

FISHER, R. (1949). Contributions of group work in psychiatric hospitals. *The group, 12,* 3–10.

FLAPAN, D., & FENCHEL, G. (1987). *The developing ego and the emerging self in group therapy.* Northvale, N.J.: Aronson.

FORMAN, M. (1967). Conflict, controversy, and confrontation in group work with older adults. *Social work, 12*(1), 80–85.

FOULKES, S., (1964). *Therapeutic group analysis.* London: Allen and Unwin.

FOULKES, S., & ANTHONY, E. (1957). *Group psychotherapy: The psychoanalytic approach.* Baltimore: Penguin.

FRANKL, V. (1962). *Man's search for meaning.* New York: Washington Square Press.

FREIDMAN, W. (1989). *Practical group therapy: A guide for clinicians.* San Francisco: Jossey-Bass.

FREY, C. (1987). Minimarathon group sessions with incest offenders. *Social work, 32*(6), 534–535.

GALINSKY, M. & SCHOPLER, J. (1977). Warning: Groups may be dangerous. *Social work, 22*(2), 89–94.

GALINSKY, M., SCHOPLER, J., SAFIER, E., & GAMBRILL, E. (1978). Assertion training for public welfare clinics. *Social work with groups, 1*(4), 365–379.

GARLAND, J., JONES, H., & KOLODNY, R. (1973). A model for stages of development in social work groups. In S. Bernstein (Ed.), *Explorations in group work* (pp. 17–71). Boston: Milford Press.

GARVIN, C. (1981). *Contemporary group work.* Englewood Cliffs, N.J.: Prentice-Hall.

GENDLIN, E. (1970). A short summary and some long predictions. In J. Hart & T. Tomlinson (Eds.), *New directions in client-centered therapy.* Boston: Houghton Mifflin.

GENTRY, M. (1974). *Initial group meetings—Concepts and findings for social work education and practice.* Paper presented at the Annual Program Meeting of the Council on Social Work Education, Atlanta, Ga.

GENTRY, M. (1978). Tape recording group sessions; A practical research strategy. *Social work with groups, 1*(1), 95–102.

GITTERMAN, A. (1986). Developing a new group service: Strategies and skills. In A. Gitterman and L. Shulman (Eds.), *Mutual aid groups and the life cycle* (pp. 53–71). Itasca, Ill.: F. E. Peacock.

GITTERMAN, A., & SHULMAN, L. (1986). *Mutual aid groups and the life cycle.* Itasca Ill.: F. E. Peacock.

GITTERMAN, A., & SCHAEFFER, A. (1972). The white professional and the black client. *Social casework, 53*(5), 280–291.

GLASSER, P., & MAYADAS, N. (Eds.), (1986). *Group workers at work: Theory and practice in the '80s.* Totowa, N.J.: Rowman & Littlefield.

GLASSER, P., SARRI, R., & VINTER, R. (Eds.). (1974). *Individual change through small groups.* New York: Free Press.

GLASSER, W. (1977). Promoting client strength through positive addiction. *Canadian counsellor, 11,* 173–175.

GLASSMAN, U., & KATES, L. (1983). Authority themes and worker-group transactions: Additional dimensions to the stages of group development. *Social work with groups, 6*(2), 33–52.

GLATZER, H. (1956). The relative effectiveness of clinically homogeneous and heterogeneous psychotherapy groups. *International journal of group psychotherapy, 5,* 258–265.

GOLDSTEIN, E. (1984). *Ego psychology and social work practice.* New York: Free Press.

GORDON, T. (1955). *Group-centered leadership.* Cambridge, Mass.: Riverside Press.

293

• • • • • • • •

GOTTESFELD, M., & PHARIS, M. (1977). *Profiles in social work*. New York: Human Service Press.

GOULDING, R. (1975). The formation and beginning process of transactional analysis groups. In G. Gazda (Ed.), *Basic approaches to group psychotherapy* (pp. 234–264). Springfield Ill.: Charles C. Thomas.

GOUWENS, D. (Ed.). (1964). *Social group work: A new dimension in V.A. social work*. Jefferson Barracks, Mo.: Veterans Administration Hospital.

GREEN, J. (1982). *Cultural awareness in the human services*. Englewoods Cliffs, N.J.: Prentice-Hall.

GREENSON, R. (1967). *The technique and practice of psychoanalysis*. New York: Universities International Press.

GREENSPAN, M. (1983). *A new approach to women and therapy*. New York: McGraw-Hill.

GRIFFIN-SHELLEY, E., & TRACHTENBERG, J. (1985). Group psychotherapy with short-term in-patients. *Small group behavior, 16*(1), 97–104.

GRIFFIN-SHELLEY, E., & WENDEL, S. (1988). Group psychotherapy with long-term inpatients: Application of a model. *Small group behavior, 19*(3), 379–385.

GRINNELL, R. (1985). *Social work research and evaluation* (2nd ed.). Itasca, Ill.: F.E. Peacock.

GROTJAHN, M., KLINE, F., & FRIEDMANN, C. (Eds.) (1983). *Handbook of group therapy*. New York: Van Nostrand Reinhold.

GUMP, P., & SUTTON-SMITH, B. (1955). The "it" role in children's games. In E. Averdon and B. Sutton-Smith (Eds.), *The study of games* (pp. 390–397). New York: Wiley.

HANSEN, J. (1978). *Counseling process and procedures*. New York: Macmillan.

HARLOW, M. (1961). Group work in a psychiatric hospital. In R. Felix (Ed.), *Mental health and social welfare* (pp. 152–174). New York: Columbia University Press.

HARLOW, M. (1964, February). *A system of groups in the hospital community: Dealing with the social functioning of the patient population*. Paper presented to the medical staff of the C.F. Menninger Memorial Hospital, Topeka, Kans.

HARTFORD, M. (1971). *Groups in social work*. New York: Columbia University Press.

HARTMANN, H. (1964). *Essays on ego psychology*. New York: International Universities Press.

HAUSSMANN, M., & HALSETH, J. (1983). Re-examining women's roles: A feminist group approach to decreasing depression in women. *Social work with groups, 6*(3/4), 105–115.

HEAP, K. (1977). *Group theory for social workers: An introduction*. New York: Pergamon Press.

HENRY, M. (1988). Revisiting open groups. *Groupwork, 1*(3), 215–228.

HENRY, S. (1981). *Group skills in social work: A four-dimensional approach*. Itasca, Ill.: F. E. Peacock.

HEPWORTH, D., & LARSEN, J. (1986). *Direct social work practice: Theory and skills* (2nd ed.). Chicago: Dorsey Press.

HESS, H., & HESS, P. (1984). Termination in context. In B. Compton and B. Galaway, (Eds.), *Social work processes* (3rd ed., pp. 559–570). Homewood, Ill.: Dorsey Press.

HINCKLEY, R., & HERMANN, L. (1951). *Group treatment in psychotherapy: A report of experience*. Minneapolis: University of Minnesota Press.

294

HIRAYAMA, H., & VAUGH, H. (1986). Reaching out to alienated, chronically ill black elderly through groups at inner-city primary health care centers. In P. Glasser & N. Mayadas (Eds.), *Group workers at work: Theory and practice in the '80s* (pp. 190–202). Totowa, N.J.: Rowman & Littlefield.

Ho, M. (1976). Social work with Asian Americans. *Social casework, 57*, 195–201.

HOLLIS, F., & WOODS, M. (1981). *Casework: A psychosocial therapy* (3rd ed.). New York: Random House.

HUDSON, W. (1982). *The clinical Measurement Package: A field manual*. Homewood, Ill.: Dorsey Press.

JACOBS, E., HARVILL, R., & MASSON, R. (1988). *Group counseling: Strategies and skills*. Pacific Grove, Calif.: Brooks/Cole.

JAHODA, M. (1958). *Current concepts of positive mental health*. New York: Basic Books.

JOHNSON, C. (1974). Planning for termination of the group. In P. Glasser, R. Sarri, & R. Vinter (Eds.), *Individual change through small groups* (pp. 258–265). New York: Free Press.

JOHNSON, W. (1951). Being understanding and understood: or how to find a wandering horse. *Etc. 7*(3) 178–179.

JOURARD, S. (1968). *Disclosing man to himself*. New York: Van Nostrand.

JOURARD, S. (1971). *The transparent self*. New York: Van Nostrand.

JUNG, C. (1968). *Analytic psychology: Its theory and practice*. New York: Random House.

KADIS, A., KRASNER, J., WEINER, M., WINICK, C., & FOULKES, S. (1974). *Practicum of group psychotherapy* (2nd ed.). Hagerstown, Md.: Harper & Row.

KADUSHIN, A. (1972). *The social work interview*. New York: Columbia University Press.

KAPLAN, K. (1988). *Directive group therapy: Innovative mental health treatment*. Thorofare, N.J.: Slack.

KAVANAUGH, J. (1985). *Search: A guide for those who dare to ask of life everything good and beautiful*. New York: Harper & Row.

KELLERMAN, H. (1979). *Group psychotherapy and personality*. New York: Grune & Stratton.

KIRESUK, T., & LUND, S. (1975). Process and outcome measurement using goal attainment scaling. In J. Zusman & C. Wuster (Eds.), *Program evaluation: Alcohol, drug abuse, and mental health services* (pp. 28–30). Lexington, Mass: Lexington Books.

KLEIN, A. (1972). *Effective groupwork: An introduction to principle and method*. New York: Association Press.

KONOPKA, G. (1983). *Social group work: A helping process* (3rd ed.). Englewood Cliffs, N.J.: Prentice-Hall.

KONOPKA, G. (1978). The significance of social group work based on ethical values. *Social work with groups, 1*(2), 123–131.

KONOPKA, G. (1983). *Social group work: A helping process* (3rd ed.). Englewood Cliffs, N.J.: Prentice-Hall.

KOPP, J. (1988). Self-monitoring: A literature review of research and practice. *Social work research & abstracts, 24*(4), 8–15.

KOPP, S. (1972). *If you meet the buddha on the road, kill him*. New York: Bantam Books.

KOTTLER, J. (1983). *Pragmatic group leadership*. Pacific Grove, Calif.: Brooks/Cole.

295

KÜBLER-ROSS, E. (1969). *On death and dying*. New York: Macmillan.

KÜBLER-ROSS, E., & ANDERSON, J. (1968). Psychotherapy with the least expected: Modified group therapy with blind clients. *Rehabilitation literature, 29*(3), 73–76.

KURLAND, R. (1978). Planning: The neglected component of group development. *Social work with groups, 1*(2), 173–178.

LaFRANCE, M., & MAYO, C. (1976). Racial differences in gaze behavior during conversation. *Journal of personality and social psychology, 33*(5), 547–552.

LANG, N. (1972). A broad-range model of practice in the social work group. *Social service review, 46*, 76–89.

LANG, R. (1973). *The technique of psychoanalytic psychotherapy*. New York: Aronson, p. 421.

LANGER, E. (1989). *Mindfulness*. Reading, Mass: Addison-Wesley.

LAWTON, G. (1958). Neurotic interaction between counselor and counselee. *Journal of counseling psychology, 5*(3), 28–33.

LEE, J. (1915). *Play in education*. New York: MacMillan.

LESSNER, N. (1974). The poem as catalyst in group counseling. *Personnel and guidance journal, 53*(2), 33–38.

LEVINE, B. (1965). Principles for developing an ego-supportive group treatment service. *Social services review, 39*, 422–32.

LEVINE, B. (1979). *Group psychotherapy*. Englewood Cliffs: N.J. Prentice-Hall.

LEVINE, B. (1980). Co-leadership approaches to learning groupwork. *Social work with groups 3*(4), 35–38.

LEWIS, H., & STREITFELD, H. (1972). *Growth games*. New York: Bantam Books.

LIEBERMAN, M. (1981). Group methods. In F. Kanfer & A. Goldstein (Eds.), *Helping people change* (pp. 61–83). New York: Pergamon Press.

LIEBERMAN, M., LAKIN, M., and WHITAKER, D. (1968). The group as a unique context for therapy. *Psychotherapy: Theory research and practice* (Winter, 1968) 5(1), 29–35.

LIEBERMAN, M., YALOM, I., & MILES, M. (1973). *Encounter groups: First facts*. New York: Basic Books.

LOCKE, E., & LATHAM, G. (1984). *Goal setting: A motivational technique that works*. Englewood Cliffs, N.J.: Prentice-Hall.

LONDON, P. (1969). *Behavior control*. New York: Harper & Row.

LONERGAN, E. (1982). *Group intervention: How to begin and maintain groups in medical and psychiatric settings*. New York: Aronson.

LUBELL, D. (1986). Living with a lifeline: Peritoneal dialysis patients. In A. Gitterman & L. Shulman (Eds.), *Mutual aid groups and the life cycle* (pp. 283–296). Itasca Ill.: F. E. Peacock.

LUCHINS, A. (1964). *Group therapy: A guide*. New York: Random House.

LUM, D. (1986). *Social work practice and people of color: A process-stage approach*. Pacific Grove, Calif.: Brooks/Cole.

MacKENZIE, K., & DIES, R. (1982). *The CORE Battery: Clinical outcome results*. New York: American Group Psychotherapy Association.

MACKEY, R. (1985). *Ego psychology and clinical practice*. New York: Gardner Press.

MAEDER, T. (1989, December). Wounded healers. *The Atlantic monthly*, pp. 37–47.

MAIER, H. (Ed.). (1965). *Group work as part of residential treatment*. New York: National Association of Social Workers.

MALONEY, S. (1963). *Development of group work education in social work schools in the U.S.* Unpublished doctoral dissertation, Case Western Reserve University, Cleveland, Ohio.

MALTSBERGER, J., & BUIE, D. (1974). Countertransference hate in the treatment of suicidal patients. *Archives of general psychiatry, 30*(5), 625–633.

MALUCCIO, A. (1974). Action as a tool in casework practice. *Social casework, 55*(1), 30–35.

MARSHAK, L. (1982). Group therapy with adolescents. In M. Seligman (Ed.), *Group psychotherapy and counseling with special populations* (pp. 185–214). Baltimore: University Park Press.

MARTIN, P., & SHANAHAN, K. (1983). Transcending the effects of sex composition in small groups. *Social work with groups, 6*(3/4), 19–32.

MASLOW, A. (1954). *Motivation and personality.* New York: Harper Brothers.

MASLOW, A. (1962). *Notes on unstructured groups at Lake Arrow Head.* Unpublished mimeograph.

MASLOW, A. (1968). *Toward a psychology of being* (2nd. ed.). Princeton, N.J.: Van Nostrand.

MAZZA, N., & PRICE, B. (1985). When time counts: Poetry and music in short-term group treatment. *Social work with groups, 8*(2), 534–66.

McCARLEY, T. (1975). The psychotherapist's search for self renewal. *American journal of psychiatry, 132*(3), 221–224.

McCLELLAN, M. (1972). Crisis groups in special care areas. *Nursing clinics of North America, 7*(2), 363–371.

McCLURE, B. (1987). Metaphoric illumination in groups. *Small group behavior, 18*(2), 179–187.

McNEELY, R., & BADAMI, M. (1984). Interracial communication in school social work. *Journal of social work, 29*(1) (January–February).

MECHANIC, D. (1974). Social structure and personal adaptation: Some neglected dimensions. In G. Coelho, D. Hamburg, & J. Adams (Eds.), *Coping and adaptation* (pp. 32–44). New York: Basic Books.

MENNINGER, K., & HOLTZMAN, P. (1959). *Theory of psychoanalytic technique.* New York: Basic Books.

MIDDLEMAN, R. (1968). *The non-verbal method in working with groups.* New York: Association Press.

MIDDLEMAN, R. (1980). The use of program: Review and update. *Social with groups, 3*(3), 5–21.

MOURSUND, J. (1985). *The process of counseling and therapy.* Englewood Cliffs, N.J.: Prentice-Hall.

MULLAN, H., & ROSENBAUM, M. (1978). *Group psychotherapy: Theory and practice.* New York: Free Press.

MURO, J., & FREEMAN, S. (1968). *Readings in group counseling.* Scranton, Pa.: International Textbook.

MURPHY, L. (1962). *The widening world of childhood.* New York: Basic Books.

MURPHY, L. (1974). Coping, vulnerability, and resilience in childhood. In G. Coelho, D. Hamburg, and J. Adams (Eds.), *Coping and adaptation* (pp. 69–100). New York: Basic Books.

NADELSON, T. (1977). Borderline rage and the therapist's response. *American journal of psychiatry, 134*(7), 748–751.

NAPIER, R., & GERSHENFELD, M. (1989). *Making groups work: A guide for group leaders.* (4th ed.). Boston: Houghton Mifflin.

NATIONAL ASSOCIATION OF SOCIAL WORKERS. (1984). *NASW standards for the practice of clinical social work.* Boston: Author.

297

298

NELSEN, J. (1981). Issues in single-subject research for nonbehaviorists. *Social work research & abstracts, 17*(2), 31–37.

NELSEN, J. (1984). Intermediate treatment goals as variables in single-case research. Social work research & abstracts. *20*(3), 3–10.

NICHOLAS, M. (1984). *Change in the context of group therapy.* New York: Brunner/ Mazel.

NORTHEN, H. (1988). *Social work with groups* (3rd ed.). New York: Columbia University Press.

NOWINSKI, J. (1990). *Substance abuse in adolescents and young adults.* New York: Norton.

O'BRIAN, C. (1977). Group therapy of schizophrenia. *Current psychiatric therapies, 17,* 149–154.

OHLSEN, M. (1970). *Group counseling.* New York: Holt, Rinehart & Winston.

ORADEI, D., & WAITE, N. (1974). Group psychotherapy with stroke patients during the immediate recovery phase. *American journal of orthopsychiatry, 44*(33), 386–395.

PAPELL, C., & ROTHMAN, B. (1966). Social group work models: Possession and heritage. *Journal of education for social work, 2,* 66–77.

PAPELL, C., AND ROTHMAN, B. (1980). Relating the mainstream model of social work with groups to group psychotherapy and the structured group approach. *Social work with groups, 3*(2), 6.

PARKER, S. (1958). Leadership patterns in a psychiatric ward. Human Relations. 11, 287–301.

PARLOFF, M. (1969). Discussion of accelerated interaction: A time limited approach based on the brief intensive group. *International journal of group psychotherapy, 28,* 220–235.

PERLMAN, H. (1975). In quest of coping. *Social casework, 56*(4), 213–225.

PERLMAN, H. (1979). *Relationship: The heart of helping people.* Chicago: University of Chicago Press.

PERNELL, R. (1986). Old themes for a new world. In P. Glasser & N. Mayadas (Eds.), *Group workers at work: Theory and practice in the '80s* (pp.11–21). Totowa, N.J.: Rowman & Littlefield.

PFEIFFER, J., & JONES, J. (1975). *A handbook of structured experiences for human relations training.* (Vols. 1–5). La Jolla, Calif.: University Associates.

PIERRAKOS, J. (1978). Core-energetic process in group therapy. In H. Mullan & M. Rosenbaum (Eds.), *Group psychotherapy: Theory and practice* (p.256). New York: Free Press.

PINCUS, A. & MINAHAN, A. (1973). *Social work practice: Model and method.* Itasca, Ill.: F. E. Peacock, p. 151.

POLANSKY, N. (1982). *Integrated ego psychology.* New York: Aldine de Gruyter.

POSTHUMA, B. (1989). *Small groups in therapy settings: Process and leadership.* Boston: College-Hill Press.

POWER, P., & ROGERS, S. (1979). Group counseling for multiple sclerosis patients: A preferred mode of treatment. In R. Lasky & A. Dell Orto (Eds.), *Group counseling and physical disability: A rehabilitation and health care perspective* (pp. 115–127). North Scituate, Mass.: Duxbury Press.

PRIDEAUX, T. *We Meet Again* (poem).

RAPPAPORT, R. (1982). Group therapy in prison. In M. Seligman (Ed.), *Group psychotherapy and counseling with special populations* (pp. 215–228). Baltimore: University Park Press.

REDL, F., & WINEMAN, D. (1951). *Children who hate*. Glencoe, Ill.: Free Press.

REDL, F., & WINEMAN, D. (1952). *Controls from within*. Glencoe, Ill.: Free Press.

REDL, F., & WINEMAN, D. (1957). *The aggressive child*. Glencoe, Ill.: Free Press.

REID, K. (1968). Social group work enhances milieu therapy. *Hospital and community psychiatry, 9*(1) (January), 26–29.

REID, K. (1977a). Nonrational dynamics of the client-worker interaction. *Social casework, 58*(10), 600–606.

REID, K. (1977b). Worker authenticity in group work. *Clinical social work journal, 5*(1), 3–16.

REID, K. (1980). Some common problems in working with adolescents. In R. Jones and C. Pritchard (Eds.), *Social work with adolescents* (pp. 208–219). London: Routledge & Kegan Paul.

REID, K. (1981). *From character building to social treatment: The history of the use of groups in social work*. Westport, Conn.: Greenwood Press.

REID, K. (1986). The use of confrontation in group treatment: Attack or challenge. *Clinical social work journal, 14*(3),234–237.

REID, K. (1988). "But I don't want to lead a group!" Some common problems of social workers leading groups. *Groupwork, 1*(2), 124–134.

REIK, T. (1956). *The search within: The inner experiences of a psychoanalyst*. New York: Farrar, Strauss, and Cudahy.

RICHMOND, M. (1930). Some steps in social treatment. *The long view*. New York: Russell Sage Foundation.

ROBERTS, R., & NORTHEN, H. (Eds.). (1976). *Theories of social work with groups*. New York: Columbia University Press.

ROGERS, C. (1961). *On becoming a person*. Boston: Houghton Mifflin.

ROGERS, C. (1962). The interpersonal relationship: The core of guidance. *Harvard educational review, 32*(4) (Fall), 416–429.

ROGERS, C. (1963). The concept of the fully functioning person. *Psychotherapy: Theory, research and practice, 1* (1), 17–26.

ROGERS, C. (1970a). *Carl Rogers on encounter groups*. New York: Harper & Row.

ROGERS, C. (1970b). Looking back and ahead: A conversation with Carl Rogers. An interview by Joseph Hart. In J. Hart & T. Tomlinson (Eds.), *New directions in client-centered therapy* (pp. 502–534). Boston: Houghton Mifflin.

ROSE, S. (1972). *Treating children in groups*. San Francisco: Jossey-Bass.

ROSE, S. (1977). *Group therapy: A behavioral approach*. Englewood Cliffs, N.J.: Prentice-Hall.

ROSE, S. (1981). Assessment in groups. *Social work research and abstracts, 17*(1), 29–37.

ROSENBAUM, M. (Ed.). (1983). *Handbook of short-term therapy groups*. New York: McGraw-Hill.

ROSENTHAL, Y., & BANDURA, A. (1978). Psychological modeling: Theory and practice. In S. Garfield & A. Bergin (Eds.), *Handbook of psychotherapy and behavior changes*. New York: Wiley.

RUBIN, T. (1970). *The angry book*. New York: Collier Books.

RUTAN, J., & STONE, W. (1984). *Psychodynamic group psychotherapy*. Lexington, Mass.: Collamore Press.

SAGER, C., BRAYWOOD, T., & WAXENBERG, B. (1970). *Black ghetto family in therapy: A laboratory experience*. New York: Grove Press.

SANDS, R. (1983). Transference revisted. *Arete, 8*(2), 18–29.

SARETSKY, T. (1977). *Active techniques and group psychotherapy*. New York: Aronson.

299

• • • • • • • •

300

● ● ● ● ● ● ● ●

SARRI, R., & GALINSKY, M. (1967). A conceputual framework for group development. In R. Vinter (Ed.), *Readings in group work practice* (pp. 72–94). Ann Arbor, Mich.: Campus Publisher.

SCHAFER, R. (1983). *The analytic attitude*. New York: Basic Books.

SCHEIN, J. (1982). Group techniques applied to deaf and hearing-impaired persons. In M. Seligman (Ed.), *Group psychotherapy and counseling with special populations* (pp. 143–162). Baltimore: University Park Press.

SCHUTZ, W. (1967). *Joy: Expanding human awareness*. New York: Grove Press.

SCHWARTZ, W. (1961). The social worker in the group. In *New perspectives on services to groups* (p. 7). National Association of Social Workers. New York.

SCHWARTZ, W. (1964). Analysis of papers presented on working definitions of group work practice, 1964. In M. Hartford (Ed.), *Working papers toward a frame of reference for social group work, 1959–1963* (pp. 56–61). New York: National Association of Social Workers.

SCHWARTZ, W., & ZALBA, S. (Eds.). (19971). *The practice of group work*. New York: Columbia University Press.

SCHWARTZ, W. (1976). Between client and system: The mediating function. In R. Roberts & H. Northen (Eds.), *Theories of social work with groups* (pp. 169–197). New York: Columbia University Press.

SELIGMAN, M. (1975). *Helplessness*. San Francisco: W. H. Freeman.

SELIGMAN, M. (Ed.). (1982). *Group psychotherapy and counseling with special populations*. Baltimore: University Park Press.

SHAPIRO, J. (1978). *Methods of group psychotherapy and encounter: A tradition of innovation*. Itasca, Ill.: F. E. Peacock.

SHILKOFF, D. (1983). The use of male-female co-leadership in an early adolescent girls' group. *Social work with groups, 6*(2), Summer, 67–80.

SHULMAN, L. (1984). *The skills of helping individuals and groups*. (2nd ed.). Itasca, Ill.: F. E. Peacock.

SIMONSON, N. (1976). The impact of therapist disclosure on patient disclosure. *Journal of transpersonal psychology, 23*, 3–6.

SLIVKIN, S. (1982). The group framework in the treatment of mentally retarded persons. In M. Seligman (Ed.), *Group psychotherapy and counseling with special populations* (pp. 228–243). Baltimore: University Park Press.

SMALLEY, R. (1967). *Theory for social work practice*. New York: Columbia University Press.

SOLOMON, B., (1976). *Black empowerment*. New York: Columbia University Press.

STANFORD, G. (1972). Openness as manipulation. *Social change*. National Training Laboratories for Applied Science, (12).

STEWART, P. (1964). Supreme Court Ruling: Concurring opinion in 6 to 3 ruling that overturned ban on pornonography. *Simpson's Contemporary Quotations,* (1988), p. 7.

STOLLER, F. (1969). A stage for trust. In A. Burton (Ed.), *Encounter: The theory and practice of encounter groups,* (p. 93). San Francisco: Jossey-Bass.

STREAN, H. (1978). *Clinical social work: Theory and practice*. New York: Free Press.

SUSSMAN, A. (1974). Group therapy with severely handicapped. *Journal of rehabilitation of the deaf, 8*, 122–126.

TEYBER, E. (1988). *Interpersonal process in psychotherapy: A guide for clinical training*. Pacific Grove, Calif.: Brooks Cole.

TILLEY, B. (1984). *Short-term counseling: A psychoanalytic approach*. New York: International Universities Press.

TOCQUEVILLE, A. (1947). *Democracy in America*. H. Reeve (Trans.). H. Commanger (Ed.). New York: Oxford University Press. (Original work published 1899).

TOSELAND, R., & RIVAS, R. (1984). *An introduction to group work practice*. New York: Macmillan.

TOWEY, M., SEARS, W., WILLIAMS, J., KAUFMAN, N., & CUNNINGHAM, M. (1966). Group activities with psychiatric inpatients. *Social work, 11*(January), 50–56.

TOWLE, C. (1954). *The learner in education for the professions*. Chicago: University of Chicago Press.

TROTZER, J. (1977). *The counselor and the group: Integrating training, theory, and practice*. Pacific Grove, Calif.: Brooks/Cole.

TRUAX, C., & CARKHUFF, R. (1964). Concreteness: A neglected variable in research in psychotherapy. *Journal of clinical psychology, 20, 264–267*.

TRUAX, C., & CARKHUFF, R. (1967). *Toward effective counseling and psychotherapy: Training and practice*. Chicago: Aldine-Atherton.

TUCKMAN, B. (1965). Developmental sequence in small groups. *Psychological bulletin, 1965, 63, 384–399*.

TURNER, F. (1978). *Psychosocial therapy*. New York: Free Press.

VAILLANT, G. (1977). *Adaptation to life*. Boston: Little, Brown.

VINTER, R. (Ed.). (1967). *Readings in group work practice*. Ann Arbor, Mich.: Campus Publishers.

VINTER, R. (1974). The essential components of social group work practice. In P. Glasser, R. Sarri, & R. Vinter (Eds.), *Individual change through small groups* (pp. 9–33). New York: Free Press.

VINTER, R. (1974). Program activities: An analysis of their effects on participant behavior. In P. Glasser, R. Sarri, & R. Vinter (Eds.), *Individual change through small groups* (pp. 233–243). New York: Free Press.

WARNER, I. (1975). *Principles of psychotherapy*. New York: Wiley.

WEICK, A., RAPP, C., SULLIVAN, P., & KISTHARDT, W. (1989). A strength perspective for social work practice. *Social work, 34*(4), 350–354.

WEINBERG, G. (1984). *The heart of psychotherapy*. New York: St. Martin's Press.

WEINER, I. (1975). *Principles of psychotherapy*. New York: Wiley.

WEINER, M. (1986). *Practical psychotherapy*. New York: Brunner/Mazel.

WESTERN RESERVE UNIVERSITY, SCHOOL OF APPLIED SOCIAL SCIENCES. (1923). A training course in group service work (announcement).

WHITE, R. (1974). Strategies of adaptation: An attempt at systematic description. In G. Coelho, D. Hamburg, and J. Adams (Eds.), *Coping and adaptation* (pp. 47–68). New York: Basic Books.

WHITTAKER, J. (1974). Program activities: Their selection and use in a therapeutic milieu. In P. Glasser, R. Sarri, & R. Vinter (Eds.), *Individual change through small groups*. New York: Free Press.

WILLIAMS, M. (1966). Limitations, fantasies, and security operations of beginning group psychotherapists. *International journal of psychotherapy, 16*(2), 150–162.

WILSON, G. (1941). *Group work and case work: Their relationship and practice*. New York: Family Welfare Association.

302

••••••••

WILSON, G., & RYLAND, G. (1949). *Social group work practice: The creative use of social process.* Cambridge, Mass.: Riverside Press.

WUBBOLDING, R. (1988). *Using reality therapy.* New York: Harper & Row.

YALOM, I. (1985). *The theory and practice of group psychotherapy.* New York: Basic Books.

YALOM, I. (1983). *Inpatient group psychotherapy.* New York: Basic Books.

YOUCHA, I. (1976). Short-term in-patient group: Formation and beginnings. In H. Rabin & M. Rosenbaum (Eds.). *How to begin a psychotherapy group* (pp. 119–137). New York: Gordon and Breach.

AUTHOR INDEX ········

304
• • • • • • • •

305

• • • • • • • •

SUBJECT INDEX ....

TO THE OWNER OF THIS BOOK:

I hope that you have found *Social Work Practice with Groups* useful. So that this book can be improved in a future edition, would you take the time to complete this sheet and return it? Thank you.

School and address: _____

Department: _____

Instructor's name: _____

1. What I like most about this book is: _____

_____

_____

2. What I like least about this book is: _____

_____

_____

3. My general reaction to this book is: _____

_____

4. The name of the course in which I used this book is: _____

_____

5. Were all of the chapters of the book assigned for you to read? _____

If not, which ones weren't? _____

_____

6. On a separate sheet of paper, please write specific suggestions for improving this book and anything else you'd care to share about your experience in using the book.

Optional:

Your name: _____ Date: _____

May Brooks/Cole quote you, either in promotion for *Social Work Practice with Groups,* or in future publishing ventures?

Yes: _____ No: _____

Sincerely,
Kenneth E. Reid